Praise for *Relational C*

"An exceedingly important contribution
Altman et al. widen the lens through which relationships of children can be
viewed. Their book provides a comprehensive picture, with detail and complexity of the relational world of the child and how we as therapists can enter
this world and help create change within it." —*Psychoanalytic Social Work*

"The relational and the developmental point of view have never been brought
together in an adequate way. This up-to-date scholarly, yet practical, integration opens a new vista within relational psychoanalysis and pioneers a fresh
approach in the psychoanalytic treatment of children and adolescents. It is a
work of great and lasting value to the field."
—Peter Fonagy, author of *Attachment Theory and Psychoanalysis*
and coauthor of *Affect Regulation, Mentalization,*
and the Development of the Self

"Taking on the task of integrating the important insights from traditional child
analytic theory, the innovations of adult relational psychoanalysis, and recent
research on the infant and child, the authors have written a requisite text for
all child therapists. From an interpersonal, relational perspective they have presented a very clear, extensive rethinking of our notions of developmental process,
psychopathology, work with parents, play and, finally, therapeutic action itself.
Exemplifying the very process they are describing, the authors remain open,
nondidactic, and ever aware of the multiplicity of factors confronting the child
therapist. Full of rich and lively clinical details that bring us directly into the
consulting room, this book demystifies the nature of child treatment."
—Pearl-Ellen Gordon, coeditor of *The Mind Object:*
Precocity and the Pathology of Self-Sufficiency

"This is truly an outstanding body of scholarly work that bridges a long-endured
historical void in the field of child psychotherapy and theory. It provides an
extremely important contribution to the field by effecting an integration of
what has until now been most often represented as incompatible models of
development and technique in the field. [The authors] refuse a rigid adherence
to one conceptual model or mindset, instead making it their objective to address the unique treatment needs of the child. Therefore, this volume is a must
read for both the novice and the seasoned clinician. This book has as much
to offer the practitioner working in community mental health agencies, particularly those in the inner city and in clinics with culturally diverse populations, as it does to therapists in private practice."
—Kirkland C. Vaughans, editor-in-chief of
the *Journal of Infant, Child, and Adolescent Psychotherapy*

Relational Child Psychotherapy

Relational Child Psychotherapy

Neil Altman, Richard Briggs, Jay Frankel, Daniel Gensler, and Pasqual Pantone

OTHER

Other Press
New York

Copyright © 2002 Neil Altman, Richard Briggs, Jay Frankel,
Daniel Gensler, and Pasqual Pantone

First softcover printing 2010
ISBN 978-1-59051-422-1

Production Editor: Robert D. Hack

This book was set in 11pt Goudy by Alpha Graphics of Pittsfield, New Hampshire.

10 9 8 7 6 5 4 3 2 1

The Library of Congress has cataloged the hardcover edition as follows:

Relational child psychotherapy / Neil Altman . . . [et al.].
     p. cm.
     Includes bibliographical references and index.
     ISBN 1-59051-000-3
     1. Child psychotherapy. 2. Psychotherapist and patient. 3. Parent and
child. I. Altman, Neil, 1946-

     RJ504 .R45 2002
     618.92'8914—dc21

                                                              2002021131

Contributors

Neil Altman is Associate Clinical Professor in the Postdoctoral Program in Psychotherapy and Psychoanalysis at New York University, and co-Editor of *Psychoanalytic Dialogues: A Journal of Relational Perspectives*. He teaches and supervises at the Training Program in Child Psychotherapy and Psychoanalysis at the National Institute for the Psychotherapies, and supervises in the Child Psychotherapy and Psychoanalysis Training Program at the William Alanson White Institute. Dr. Altman is the author of *The Analyst in the Inner City: Race, Class, and Culture through a Psychoanalytic Lens* (Analytic Press, 1995) and numerous professional articles.

Richard Briggs is Faculty and Supervisor, William Alanson White Institute, former co-Director, Center for the Study of Psychological Trauma, White Institute. Dr. Briggs was the Chief Psychologist of the Greater Bridgeport Child Guidance Center for a number of years and also directed a day treatment program at the Albert Einstein College of Medicine. He is in private practice in New York City and in Wilton, Connecticut.

Jay Frankel is an Associate Editor of *Psychoanalytic Dialogues*; Faculty, Supervisor, and former co-Director at the Manhattan Institute for Psychoanalysis; Supervisor at the New York University Postdoctoral Program in Psychotherapy and Psychoanalysis and at the Institute for Contemporary Psychotherapy; and Supervisor in the Child and Adolescent Psychotherapy Training Programs at the William Alanson White Institute and the National Institute for the Psychotherapies.

Daniel Gensler holds various positions at the William Alanson White Institute in New York City, including Director of the Child Adolescent Clinical Services, Assistant Director of the Adult Services, Steering Committee member of the Trauma Response Service, Supervising Analyst and Instructor. He also supervises psychology students at Adelphi University, Garden City, New York. He is the author of three contributions to *Contemporary Psychoanalysis* on adult learning disabilities, children's dreams, and therapists' responses to the attacks on September 11.

Pasqual Pantone is Supervising Analyst, Faculty, Division of Psychoanalysis, William Alanson White Institute; co-Founder, former co-Director, Faculty and Supervisor, Child and Adolescent Psychotherapy Training Program, William Alanson White Institute; Faculty and Supervisor: Institute for Contemporary Psychoanalysis, New York; Manhattan Institute for Psychoanalysis; Northwest Center for Psychoanalysis, Seattle and Portland.

Contents

Acknowledgments

This is the part of the book we have all looked forward to writing, for two reasons. First, it's an opportunity to express our gratitude and reconnect with those colleagues, friends, and family who helped us in important ways in the writing of this book; and second, it means we're done.

This project arose out of an ongoing group whose purpose is to study child therapy in the context of our interpersonal and relational psychoanalytic backgrounds. The group began in 1991 and spent years looking for a task—six characters, and then five, in search of a script (Susan Warshaw was also a member for several years). We discussed cases, wrote and presented papers, and considered founding a child therapy training program. Ultimately, we realized that writing a book was what we had already started doing.

So our first acknowledgment is to each other, our co-authors. Each of us has gotten from all of the others extensive feedback, advice, direction, ideas, editing, help, supervision, support, and encouragement. We have become a good working group, and we have fun working together.

We also want to thank the children and parents we have worked with, some of whom, in disguise, show up in these pages. They have been our most important teachers. Winnicott was most eloquent on this point in his dedication to *Playing and Reality* (1971a). That entire dedication reads: "To my patients who have paid to teach me."

We would also like to thank Lewis Aron—one of the founders of our group, though he did not continue with us—for his very helpful reactions and ideas about an earlier draft of the manuscript.

We are grateful to Michael Moskowitz for his enthusiasm, encouragement, and flexibility, and of course for publishing our book.

Each of us also has a number of other people he wants to thank.

Neil Altman thanks his wife, Roberta, and his daughters, Lisa and Amanda, for their patience and inspiration.

Richard Briggs acknowledges Ed Levenson and Steve Mitchell, who in different ways both have been a stimulus to his thinking; Joan Poll for endless conversations about child treatment; Betsy Wolfe, for her insight, honesty, and loving support; and his children, Alexandra and Bryant, with gratitude for helping him to recognize the very real limits of his knowledge and skill when it comes to kids.

Jay Frankel's thanks go first to his wife, Ellen Arfin, who gave up a lot of time to his working on this book, time that ought to have gone to her and their family. She was supportive and patient and was also a good colleague, providing thoughtful, helpful comments and reactions to various versions of these chapters. He also wants to thank his sons, David and Alexander, now both young men. It was their coming into the world that revived his interest in working with children. Being their father was the most important part of his education about children. He also thanks Susan Fabrick, who provided a lot of the material that shows up in the section on "resilience" in Chapter 6, and also shared her thoughtful reactions to various ideas in the book.

Daniel Gensler thanks his son Joshua for help with collating manuscripts from five different word processors, as well as his wife, Bonnie Steinberg, and his son Micah for their support and forbearance regarding the time he spent at the computer.

Pasqual Pantone wants to thank his wife, Neal, and his daughters, Katherine and Elizabeth, for their love and understanding.

Preface

In 1983, Jay Greenberg and Stephen Mitchell published their seminal book *Object Relations in Psychoanalytic Theory*. In this book they divided psychoanalytic theories into two groups, based upon consistencies in the central beliefs of each group. One group of theories was labeled "drive structural" theories and included what are often referred to as the Freudians. The other group of theories was called "relational structural" theories. By devising this new grouping of theories, Greenberg and Mitchell gathered under one heading several independently developed theories that had in common an interest in object relations and/or interpersonal relations. This group of theories also had in common the rejection of libido as the central force in personality formation. Under the single roof of the term "relational," several schools of psychoanalytic theory could now communicate with each other and be compared and contrasted. Most importantly, a new level of dialogue was promoted. As a consequence of the work of Greenberg and Mitchell and many others, the psychoanalytic world witnessed an explosion of relational literature that made its own creative contributions and enlivened longstanding debates. These relational contributions focused particularly on the early dyadic (instead of triangular) roots of personality formation, and on the interaction of the patient and the analyst in the analytic situation.

This exciting and lively era continues into the present day, when creative psychoanalytic thinking and innovations are thriving. For example, the current synthesis of attachment theories, infant research, and object relations theories has produced a compelling research-based theory of development that has served not only to inform psychoanalytic work itself but also to allow practical applications in early intervention programs. Similarly, interpersonal contributions are being studied in the context of a renewed interest in countertransference in nearly every school of psychoanalysis. This renewed interest has elevated the practice of adult psychoanalysis to new levels of interactive meaningfulness and creativity.

For those of us who are relationally oriented and who also work with child patients, however, these exciting innovations seemed at times to be passing us by. With few exceptions the child psychoanalytic world was, until recently, still heavily influenced by the ego psychological context of its origins, seemingly unaffected by the relational turn in the literature at large. Modern never became postmodern in the child literature. Journal articles, books, and training programs still seemed to be more loyal to their roots than to be searching for their connection to the movements of the present. Eventually, however, groups of relationally oriented analysts began to talk, to write, and to organize themselves toward integrating some of the innovations of the adult relational psychoanalysis into child literature and practice.

The authors of this book are an example of one such group that was formed to consider these possibilities. What were we already doing with our child patients that could better be conceptualized in relational terms? What more was there to examine and implement? Lewis Aron, who in the early 1990s was active both in the Child and Adolescent Psychiatry Training Program at Roosevelt Hospital, New York City, and in the relational group at the New York University Postdoctoral Program in Psychoanalysis, convened a group of child therapists affiliated with these two institutions. We are all grateful to him for organizing these first meetings, as well as to some of the earlier members whose contributions influenced our present thinking: Susan Coates, Barbara

Thatcher, and Susan Warshaw. At the same time, the Child Adolescent Interest Group at the William Alanson White Institute (the group that preceded White's current Child Adolescent Psychotherapy Training Program) was working on the question of why interpersonal theory lacked a child treatment theory, and what to do about it. Several of us who joined the group that Aron organized had already been participating in the interest group at White for several years.

In regular meetings we discovered that we all had in common a wish that our psychoanalytic work with children be more relationally oriented. The group went through many transformations in its purpose, including the contemplation of a child relational-training program to be housed in a New York City psychoanalytic institute. Our meetings eventually emerged into exciting discussions of how we were working with our child patients and their parents, reading interesting articles and books on the topic, and discussing one another's ideas. Soon papers emerged on various subjects, and we presented them in panels at meetings of the Division of Psychoanalysis (Division 39) of the American Psychological Association on two separate occasions. The idea of putting together a book was a natural offshoot of our original purpose of creating a context for generating a conception of child relational psychoanalytic theory and treatment.

We have been gratified to find an audience for our work among the many child therapists who were looking for alternative ways of conceptualizing and explaining the process of child psychoanalysis and child psychoanalytic psychotherapy. Our colleagues range from very experienced psychoanalysts who were developing their own relational approach to child treatment, to newly minted child therapists who were leaning in the relational direction. We also have communicated with classically trained analysts who wanted to know more about what relational psychoanalysis has to offer for their work with patients. Thus this book was written with many types of readers in mind. Some sections are designed for the advanced clinician and others are directed more toward beginners. We hope that this book will help child clinicians, whatever their level of experience, to think through the complex issues that we face daily in our work.

We intend this book to be a comprehensive introduction to the experience of working in psychotherapy with children and parents. As a consequence, it has three sections. After an introductory chapter, we review the theories of development that underlie our work. Then we present a theory of psychopathology in childhood that is rooted in a relational understanding of children and parents. With these two parts to ground the work, we then offer a number of chapters—in Parts 3–5—on the process of psychotherapy itself, from treatment planning to play, from transference to countertransference, from working with the parents and school to working with the larger context in which the child lives. Readers who want to immerse themselves in a complete discussion of child psychotherapy should start at the beginning and read straight through. Yet there may be readers who prefer to use the table of contents to choose the topics that interest them, and we have written each chapter to stand on its own for those readers who would rather use the book in this way.

The focus of this book is on working with children up to the age of 12 or up to the beginnings of puberty. Although there are sections (for example, on cultural differences) that apply to adolescents and their parents, we have not considered in depth the role of parents in work with adolescents, or the specific developmental and diagnostic issues involved. There are important differences in the handling of confidentiality and contact with the school. We wanted to make a contribution to child psychotherapy, and decided to concentrate on that area.

Although we as authors share a common goal in the presentation of our view of a child relational psychoanalysis, we are not of one mind on every topic. Thus, this book cannot be said to have one voice. We have debated whether we needed to sand over the bumps in our final product in order to present a smoother surface. However, in keeping with the very essentials of relational theory itself, we had to recognize the inevitability of plural and diverse opinions—which also, of course, reflects the actual process of five relationally oriented clinicians writing a single book. We invite the reader to read our book with this same inevitable range of possibilities in mind. Many of you will recognize how relational your own child psychotherapy has become, without ever having seen it explicitly described in a book such as this one. Some ideas will be compatible with your thinking and will support your own ideas and clinical work, but others will speak with different voices than the ones to which you are accustomed. We hope that these ideas will cause you to stop and reflect on how you have seen the process of child psychoanalysis and child psychoanalytic psychotherapy, and to renew your clinical practice in useful ways.

1

Introduction

Child psychotherapists practicing today are faced with the challenge of developing a coherent theory and technique while drawing on a number of very diverse traditions. Child psychotherapy has wide-ranging roots in traditions as disparate as psychoanalysis, behavior therapy, and family systems theory. The child analytic tradition, to which we will turn in a moment, is itself complex, with somewhat different paths taken by Anna Freud (1946), Melanie Klein (1932, 1961), Donald Winnicott (1977), and others. From child analysts, contemporary child therapists have available to them a focus on transference and countertransference, the child's conscious and unconscious inner world and fantasy life, and a technique relying centrally on play, with interpretive commentary by the therapist.

Complementary to the psychoanalytic tradition is the focus in behavior therapy on behavior change and symptomatic improvement that often has some urgency when a child is the patient. The cognitive emphasis that has more recently characterized the behavioral tradition allows for a rapprochement with the psychoanalytic focus on inner processing of experience.

From family systems theory (e.g., Haley and Hoffman 1967, Minuchin 1974, Whitaker and Bumberry 1988), child therapists have learned to see the child as an "identified patient" whose symptoms are the manifestations of a dysfunctional family process. Influenced by family therapists, child therapists have broken free from the classical psychoanalytic reluctance to be involved with parents. Child therapists nowadays typically try to influence the family system, as well as help with parenting difficulties, even as they work with the child as patient. This flexibility and complexity of approach has been further reinforced by the experiences many child therapists have had in public clinics, such as community mental health centers, in which therapists are regularly called upon to intervene on multiple levels with families.

Finally, child therapy is heir to the tradition of client-centered therapy, as applied to children by Virginia Axline (1969) and Clark Moustakas (1997). This approach has in common with the psychoanalytic approach of Donald Winnicott a view of play as inherently therapeutic, with the therapist seen as a nonintrusive facilitator of the child's self-discovery.

This diversity presents child therapists with a rich heritage, but, as we noted, it also presents a formidable complexity to integrate in their therapeutic work. We offer this book as an effort to develop such an integration from our own psychoanalytic point of view as influenced by the full range of traditions. We intend to make available to the reader the contributions that psychoanalysts have made to clinical problems faced by all child therapists, such as transference and countertransference phenomena, to take only one example. We will outline current developments in psychoanalytic theory and technique that we think have great relevance for child work, particularly the ways in which analysts have come to think about the therapeutic potential in the interaction between patient and analyst. Finally, we will discuss and demonstrate how we have integrated into our analytic approach the influence of the various nonanalytic traditions. As one example, we will develop a psychoanalytic-systemic model that provides a framework for thinking about work with parents and other family members, bringing family systems concepts together with psychoanalytic concepts like projective identification.

THE ANALYTIC TRADITION:
THE ANNA FREUD–MELANIE KLEIN SPLIT

Child psychotherapy and psychoanalysis was born into a conflicted family. In the 1940s, within the psychoanalytic family, the patriarch Sigmund Freud's legacy was in dispute. On one side, Anna Freud (1946), his biological daughter, had picked up the ego psychological banner. She devoted herself to an exhaustive classification and systematization of the various ego functions, such as defense mechanisms, and a technique that took account of the state of the patient's ego. On the other side, Melanie Klein (1932, 1961) made her own claim as the legitimate upholder of the Freudian vision by focusing on unconscious dynamics and the interpretation thereof. Both women were child analysts, and in relation to that work, their different paths diverged sharply and clearly.

In child work, Anna Freud focused on the child's relative ego immaturity. She believed that interpretive work in relation to unconscious material would be useless, even disruptive, unless the child's defenses and tolerance for anxiety were strong enough. From this point of view, Anna Freud focused on an extended period of building a positive relationship with her child patients, educating them in a way that helped develop ego strength, before introducing anxiety-arousing interpretations of unconscious material. Anna Freud also believed that since children were still attached to their primary objects, their parents, a transference neurosis, with the analyst as object, would not develop as it did with adult patients. Interpretation of unconscious material, then, could not center on transference as it often did with adult patients. Child analysis, for Anna Freud and her followers, would be a very different experience from adult analysis, much more ego supportive and educative, less focused on transference.

Melanie Klein differed sharply with Anna Freud on both these counts. Transference, for Klein, was tantamount to unconscious fantasy, rather than an impulse-defense constellation transferred over from primary, parental relationships. Transference, then, was omnipresent, with children as well as with adults. Klein's approach emphasized immediate interpretation of unconscious fantasy in relation to the analyst, even in the very first session. To take an ego-supportive, educative role, as Anna Freud advocated, would amount to defensive avoidance, on the analyst's part, of the unconscious fantasies organizing the child's perception of the analyst.

Sigmund Freud's opus was so extensive, and his thought evolved and changed so much over time, that one can find support for both these polarized positions in his work. The situation is rather like that of competing religious groups, all of which can find support for their antagonistic positions in the Bible. From one point of view, the Anna Freud–Melanie Klein split could be viewed as similar to sibling rivalry, which highlights and accentuates conflicts that are latent in the parental generation. From another point of view, Anna Freud and Melanie Klein were like warring parents whose child, child analysis itself, developed under the influence of competing loyalties. One of the central arguments of this book is that the polarization which thus evolved has stunted the development of child analysis and child therapy. Freudian child analysts have been slow to take in the rich and exciting development of ideas about transference flowing from British object relations theory. Kleinian child analysts have been slow to recognize iatrogenic problems resulting from their uncompromising insistence on immediate, deep interpretation. The terms of the discussion in child analysis have been set by the need to establish allegiances and a sense of identity in one camp or the other. As a result, there has been a fossilizing effect, an inertia operating against the creativity that can follow upon breaking out of rigid patterns.

WINNICOTT AND BION

With time, a gradual and patchwork rapprochement has been developing between the Kleinians and the Freudians following the initial sharp schism, mediated by Winnicott (1960/1965, 1975) and Bion (1967). D. W. Winnicott emerged, after the "Controversial Discussions" between the Freudians and Kleinians of the early 1940s, as an integrative and synthesizing force. Winnicott's concerns had to do primarily with elaborating and enhancing the role of the interpersonal world, the world of external reality, in psychoanalytic theory. Winnicott brought together the intrapsychic and the interpersonal with his concepts of transitional space and transitional objects. Transitional objects are both created (in psychic reality) and found (in external reality). The quintessential example is the childhood "blankie" that is universally (in our culture) recognized as both the most precious thing in the world (as the child's creation, within the child's subjective reality) and a smelly, dirty old piece of cloth (in external reality). Play is the very essence of a phenomenon occurring in transitional space. Two people playing are each contributing his or her psychic reality, while simultaneously dealing with the other person, and his or her contributions to the shared play, as existing in external reality. For Winnicott, this balance, or tension, between living in one's personal and subjective reality, and the recognition of external reality, was all-important. If the balance were skewed in favor of the external world, the person has to sacrifice his subjective reality, resulting in a way of life that is "false," based as it is on compliance with a nonpersonal reality, for example, a reality imposed by other people. On the other hand, if the balance were skewed in favor of the internal world of subjective reality, the person becomes condemned to endless efforts to make other people comply with his fantasies of omnipotence. Winnicott's (1971a) concept of psychoanalysis as taking place in an overlap of two areas of play brought together psychic reality and objective reality in his conception of the analytic situation, and simultaneously allowed for an integration of Freudian and Kleinian concerns. A playful ambiance in psychoanalysis is inconsistent with intrusiveness on the analyst's part; an intrusive interpretation forces the analyst's reality on the patient, requiring the patient's "false self" (Winnicott 1960/1965) compliance. In this way, Winnicott addresses Freudian concerns about the patient's readiness to hear interpretations. On the other hand, play itself is a royal road to unconscious material in children, corresponding to free association in adult analysis; thus, Winnicott takes account of the Kleinian interest in unconscious fantasy. Between them, the Freudians and the Kleinians had split off the ego from the unconscious: the Freudians by subordinating the interpretation of unconscious fantasy to the strengthening of the child's ego, the Kleinians by ignoring the state of the child's ego in efforts to speak directly to the unconscious. Winnicott's concept of play heals this split, allowing for a nonintrusive approach to all levels of the child's psyche, via participation in the child's play and interpretive commentary from a position situated between the child's and the analyst's reality.

In the Kleinian camp, meanwhile, Bion (1967) came along with his idea of "containing." Classically, Kleinians had focused on interpreting patients' projections, that is their attribution to the analyst of feelings and impulses—aggression, for example—that actually belong to the patient. Interpretation, in this context, returns the projection to the patient in the sense that the analyst tells the patient that the feeling in question is the patient's, not the analyst's. Bion pointed out that the analyst, rather than so quickly returning the projection, can "contain" the feeling, get to know it, think about it, in a way that will allow the analyst to return it to the patient in a more manageable form. For example, a frightened patient might attribute extreme malevolence to the analyst. The analyst, rather than immediately interpreting the patient's aggression, might dwell on his own inevitable feelings of fear and anger in such a situation. Having thus familiarized himself with the patient's psychological world, the analyst's comments are likely to be more empathic and thus more facilitative of the patient's acceptance and integration of the feelings in question.

The concept of containing brings a noninterpretive, participatory analytic function into the Kleinian repertoire.[1] The analytic situation is thus "interpersonalized" in a way that allows for some degree of rapprochement with Winnicott's emphasis on the influence of the outside world, and with Anna Freud's emphasis on the analyst as facilitator of the child's development. In this book, we will attempt to further this Kleinian–Freudian–Winnicottian rapprochement with our examination of the ways in which unconscious fantasy and interpersonal reality are linked, both between parent and child, and between analyst and patient.

DEVELOPMENTS IN THE UNITED STATES

Whereas all three of these founding spirits of British psychoanalysis were child analysts, in the United States child analysis has been a stepchild. Through the 1940s and 1950s, the creativity in American psychoanalysis was directed into an elaboration of ego psychology, under

---

1. Racker (1968) went further in portraying the analyst as a participant with his idea that the analyst identifies with the patient's projections. The analyst is thus seen not simply as an empty container for the patient's projections, but as making the projected feelings his own, contributing his own psychology in the process.

the influence of the medical model that became dominant here. David Rapaport (1967), Merton Gill (1982), and Roy Schafer (1992) were prominent in this development. Otto Kernberg (1985) added a Kleinian and Fairbairnian influence. Interpersonal psychoanalysis, from Harry Stack Sullivan (1953) onward, developed in isolation, dismissed as nonpsychoanalytic by the American establishment. Rapaport, Gill, Schafer, Kernberg, Sullivan: none of these leaders in American psychoanalysis were child analysts or interested in the implications of their work for child analysis. Recently, there has been considerable creative movement in American psychoanalysis as the "relational" point of view has developed around an integration of British object relations theory and American interpersonalism. Adult psychoanalysis has been enriched by this effort to wed the interpersonal focus on the dyadic field, a two-person psychology, to the vision of the intrapsychic world as structured by internalized object relationships, as it has emerged in England. The leaders in this development, Mitchell (1993), Greenberg (Greenberg and Mitchell 1983), and Aron (1996), among many others, have all focused their attention on adult work. The implications of these newer points of view for child work are begging to be drawn. The purpose of this book is to begin this project.

THE AMERICAN RELATIONAL PERSPECTIVE

Let us first review in a bit more detail the basics of the relational point of view as it has developed in adult psychoanalysis. Although there are various subperspectives, there are some common features that can be outlined (see Aron 1996, for a more complete discussion). The relational point of view was originally described in counterpoint to Freudian drive theory. The basic relational idea is that the mind is organized by object relationships rather than by endogenous drives and defenses against those drives, as maintained by drive theory (Greenberg and Mitchell 1983). Sexuality and aggression, as feelings and experiences, are seen as elements of interpersonal relationships, and as organized by the specific character of a particular relationship at a particular time; relationships are not seen as primarily derivative of these drives. A focus on relationship leads to a "two-person" psychology; that is, the analytic field to be studied consists of two people, two minds, in interaction with each other, as opposed to the field of observation conceived of, in "one-person" fashion, as the mind of the patient in isolation. A one-person psychology, in other words, takes the intrapsychic world as its field of observation.

To characterize any psychoanalytic theory as a "one-person" or a "two-person" theory involves some degree of caricature. Yet there are real and significant differences in emphasis. All psychoanalytic theories take account of both one-person, or intrapsychic, elements, and two-person, or interpersonal, elements. The difference between theories has to do with the priority given to one or another of these dimensions in relation to the other, theoretically and clinically. In adult psychoanalysis Freudians and Kleinians, for example, tend to emphasize the pathogenic role of the patient's preexisting unconscious fantasies. As a result, their technical approach prescribes a reserved, relatively anonymous position for the analyst that is presumed to highlight the intrapsychic world of the patient in isolation. The analyst is then perceived as the "object" of sexual and aggressive drives within these unconscious fantasies. The analyst as object is present in the analytic situation for the classical Freudians and Kleinians, but this role is basically organized within the mind of the patient.

Interpersonalists (e.g., Levenson 1992), by contrast, tend to emphasize the pathogenic role of actual interpersonal experience. Accordingly, interpersonalists see the analyst as inevitably a participant in the analytic situation, as well as an observer and commentator. The patient's intrapsychic and unconscious world is seen as largely composed of disavowed perceptions of other people, and of expectations of other people carried forward from earlier experiences. The emphasis thus shifts away from the organizing influence of endogenous drives and "hard-wired" fantasies, and toward the shaping impact of interpersonal interactions, past and present.

All these theories, then, have a place for the intrapsychic and the interpersonal. They differ, however, in how they conceive of the relationship between the two realms.

Recently, in some respects, the various schools of thought have moved to take account of the other positions. For example, Freudians and Kleinians have moved to take relatively more account of the interpersonal dimensions of the analytic relationship. Jacobs (1991), a

Freudian analyst, has given more emphasis to the analyst's participation by viewing countertransference as normally quite pervasive. Kleinians, likewise (Alvarez 1992, Joseph 1989, Racker 1968), have come to see the analyst as a participant under the influence of the patient's projections.

What we are describing as a "relational" theory involves efforts to conceive of the two-person field as comprised of not only an overt interaction but also the internal world and inner experiences, conscious and unconscious, of both participants. It is in this way that the relational perspective integrates one- and two-person psychologies. The focus on the experiential worlds of two people in interaction leads to this point of view being characterized, with variations on the theme, as "intersubjective" (Benjamin 1988, Stolorow and Atwood 1992). Relational analysts look to the analytic interaction itself, the interweaving of transference and countertransference, as the site of the action in psychoanalysis. For purposes of exposition, one can speak of the internal worlds of two people who then engage in an overt interaction (see Daniel Stern [1995] for an elaboration of such a model). This way of looking at the analytic interaction, however, artificially divides the internal from the external world. To speak of the patient for the moment, it is more adequate to say that the manifestation of the patient's internal world is always under the influence of the analyst's presence and behavior. The analyst's behavior, however, is also under the influence of the patient's presence and behavior. Each person evokes certain reactions in the other, selectively attunes to certain aspects of the other, and so on. So, ultimately, we have an intermingling of two subjective worlds, and of internal and external realms, in a way that makes it impossible to draw sharp lines of distinction between who's who, and what was preexisting in the patient's internal object world and what was evoked by the analyst. Relational analysts work and act in this complex and ambiguous interpersonal and intersubjective field. Mutual influence is taken for granted between patient and analyst, but the relationship is seen as asymmetrical, with the analyst having primary responsibility for fostering an analytic inquiry into the interaction (Aron 1996). As patient and analyst together engage in a dialectical process of action and reflection with each other, rigid and constricting patterns in their intrapsychic/interpersonal worlds are loosened up, and possibilities for change emerge.

THE IMPLICATIONS OF A RELATIONAL
APPROACH FOR CHILD WORK

When we consider the child patient–therapist dyad, a relational approach to child work, as compared to a traditional psychoanalytic approach, shifts the focus of the work in three major ways: there is more emphasis on the transference–countertransference interaction, the analyst is seen as potentially a "new" object for the child, and the parents are seen more centrally as participants in the relational field and in the treatment. Turning first to the transference–countertransference interaction, our approach differs sharply from the Freudian/ego psychological model, which defines transference in such a way that it is thought not to be of central significance in child work. The Kleinians, as we have seen, do emphasize transference; their model of transference, however, defined as a projection of the child's internal world of objects and object relations, is not interactive. In our model, in line with our view of the analyst as a participant as well as an observer (Sullivan 1953), transference and countertransference are in continual interaction. Our focus is on the internal worlds of patient and analyst, as well as the interaction between these internal worlds, and the overt interaction that evolves.

To the extent that the focus is on the child's internal world in isolation, the analyst is, basically, an "old" object for the child. That is, the analyst's role is to be available as a target or screen for the child's projection of internal object images. The analyst might be thought of as having a relatively marginal "new" object role. For example, in the Freudian/ego psychological and Winnicottian models, as mentioned above, the analyst is a new object in the sense of a facilitator of development. In the Kleinian model, the analyst's function is essentially to become the container for "old" object images, which then become the target of interpretations. The interpreting analyst is, nonetheless, a new object, as a provider of "good milk" in the form of interpretations. But, when we shift our focus to take account of the analyst as a person for the child in the external world, it becomes possible to think of the analyst as a "new" object for the child in new ways, that is, as a person who may have a transformative impact on the child's internal object representations. From a relational point of view, the analyst can be seen as potentially taking on any and all of the "new object" roles and functions just mentioned, depending on the analyst's judgment about what will be helpful to the child, what will further the analytic process, and—in line with the analyst's personal inclinations—his preconscious and unconscious responses to the child. In addition, however, following Greenberg (1986) and Mitchell (1993) we see much of the potential for therapeutic change in analysis as residing in the dialectic between the analyst's old object and new object participation. That is, in order to become significant to the child, the analyst must be seen in a way that activates the child's preexisting, intense, and sometimes problematic hopes and fears. At the same time, for therapeutic change to occur, one must be able to conceive that something new and unexpected could occur in the interaction with the therapist that could upset the child's expectations and lead to change in her internal object representations.

Turning finally to parental involvement, we differ from all three of the traditional child analytic models in that we do not restrict our attention to the patient–therapist dyad. Recognizing that parents, and often a wider network of caregivers and siblings, are crucial participants in the relational field, we seek a field-theoretical relational model that goes beyond the dyad. To the extent that the traditional models are one-person models, the analytic situation could appropriately be thought of as consisting solely of the child and the analyst, defined narrowly as facilitator or interpreter. Accordingly, work with parents was seen, by Freudians and Kleinians alike, as necessary only to secure their financial and moral support of the analytic process, and perhaps to obtain information about the child's extra-analytic life. Freudians and Winnicottians might also work with parents to enhance their functioning as facilitators of their child's development, the so-called "child guidance" function. If it was thought that parents were unable to foster their children's development adequately, if they were having a nonfacilitative or destructive effect on their children, they would be sent for their own analyses with other analysts.

In our view, by contrast, parents and other caretakers are intrinsic parts of the analytic relational field. In neo-Kleinian terms, we see the field in which projective and introjective processes take place as importantly including the parents. Parental transferences to the child and to the analyst are formative influences on the outcome of the child's development and the analysis. In the first instance, if the child's first environment is the parental unconscious (McDougall 1978), the entire analytic process can be seen as taking place to some extent within that environment. If the child's self-image draws importantly on whom the parents see when they look at the child, there would seem to be crucial therapeutic leverage in work with those images of the child in the parents' minds. Doing this work in the context of the child's analysis offers the opportunity to work "in vivo" with these processes, in direct and vivid fashion. Parental transferences to the analyst, further, are not only important facilitating and impeding influences on the work, but also offer access to important self- and object-images in all participants. Most generally, we view the parent–child–analyst field as one in which splitting processes will result in complex patterns of projection and introjection. To take a typical example: The parents (one or both) may experience a child, Johnnie, as lazy or malicious, reflecting a disowned aspect of the parents' psyche(s). The therapist, by contrast, may experience Johnnie as depressed or overburdened. One parent may be critical of the child, while the other parent takes a protective attitude toward Johnnie. Johnnie, of course, takes in the images of himself that he sees in the minds of his parents and acts in such a way as to reinforce them. Thus, vicious circles get set up. In a case such as we are describing, when the parents see the boy in divergent ways, the boy may also develop a complex, split self-image (e.g., hostile and oppositional with one parent, dependent with the other).

The critical parent may want Johnnie to change in particular ways (e.g., become more disciplined or compliant), while the therapist and perhaps the other parent may feel Johnnie needs empathy and understanding. The parent(s) may have identified one of their children, Joan, the target of idealizing projections, as good, or high achieving, even perfect. Johnnie, the target of more negative projections, gets pegged as defiant or deficient. The critical parent may be used by Johnnie, unconsciously, as an externalization of his own harsh superego (this supergego, of course, may also represent an internalization of the interaction with that critical parent). The therapist may develop a rescue fantasy about Johnnie (perhaps partly as a defense against Johnnie's potential projection of the harsh superego onto the therapist), while the parent(s) experience the therapist as critical and even persecutory toward them. This is just one example of the complex patterns of splitting, projection, and introjection that routinely develop. It seems to us that conceiving of the work as occurring in this entire interpersonal field gives the therapist maximum flexibility to intervene at various points in an effort to heal the various splits. As a "container" for the various projections as they emerge, the therapist is in a position to develop a more integrated view of each family member. That is, by not taking for granted the stereotypes about each person that may have become entrenched, the therapist challenges the splitting process and encourages a more integrated and complex view of each individual. An important aspect of this work is the therapist's work in the countertransference regarding her feelings about each family member. For example, in working with a critical parent, the therapist may well have to cope with feelings toward a critical parent of her own and/or critical feelings toward her own child(ren). In the process, the therapist can simultaneously build a connection with a potentially marginalized parent, and a potentially disavowed part of herself.

Daniel Stern (1995) has offered a "field-theoretical" view of the child treatment process on which we have drawn heavily. Stern, speaking specifically of infant–parent work, conceives of the field as comprised of the mother's representational world, the child's representational world, and the overt interaction between mother and child. Stern mentions the therapist's representational world, without much elaboration, as also part of the field. In the overt interaction, images of the child, as they emerge within the mother's representational world, get communicated to the child and contribute to structuring the child's self-image. Stern believes that therapeutic change can occur as a result of intervention at any point in this field. Change in any part of the field can lead to change elsewhere and everywhere. Thus, the therapist has the widest latitude to make decisions about where intervention is most feasible. When a child is symptomatic, for example, the therapist may decide to work individually with the mother, trying to influence her representation of the child; or he may work with mother and child together to influence the overt interaction.

We would extend Stern's model in a number of ways. We aim to extend his model into later childhood, giving individual work with the child a larger role than is possible in infancy. Whereas work with the parents may be a necessity in infancy for Stern, we view it as desirable at all ages. We develop the role of the representational world of the therapist to a greater extent, viewing countertransference, and the therapist's work in the countertransference, as a crucial aspect of the field. In this way, to a greater extent than Stern, we emphasize interactivity, the mutually influential nature of the therapist–patient relationship. We include the father, siblings, teachers, tutors, and others to a greater extent than does Stern.

Our model of the child treatment process is a field model, like the family systems model, but differs from that theory in crucial respects. In family systems theory, the unit of analysis is the family system. Interventions with individuals are conceptualized in terms of the resulting effects on the system as a whole. The focus is entirely on overt behavior of individuals as constituting the systemic process. We recognize the presence of systemic processes, but we emphasize and seek to work with the representational worlds of the various individuals involved, including ourselves as therapist. We view the representational worlds of the various individuals in a family as to some degree independent and self-sustaining, but also as derived from and interacting with the representational worlds of the other individuals. Family systems models tend to regard the system as an objectively understandable entity, in which the place of each individual is determined by his or her place in the system.

For example, in one family, father may be seen as the distancer, mother as the pursuer, and the eldest son as the parentified child who fills the gap left by the father. We believe that such systemic patterns have enormous shaping power on each individual. They also serve as channels for the externalization of the representational worlds of each family member. That is, in this example, the husband may see his wife in terms of his own intrusive mother, while the wife sees her husband in terms of her unavailable father.

In our model, we also recognize and emphasize that the family and the individuals within it may look different to its various members not only as a function of the person's place in the system, but also as a function of the perceiver's unique representational world. Further, each member, including the child, exerts an influence on the other members based on his or her perception of them. The child in the system just described may identify quite readily with the parentified role, seeing oedipal opportunities therein, for example, or may flee what feels like a smothering over-involvement with the mother.

In our view, the child therapist has the daunting task of taking account of the family as a system, the experiential worlds of the various members, and his or her own experience and participation. We believe that we have no choice, that any of these levels is ignored to the peril of the therapeutic enterprise. Lest the reader immediately feel overwhelmed and despair of being able to function given the complexity we are describing, we hasten to point out that most child therapists juggle these various balls intuitively and quite effectively much of the time. It is rather like riding a bicycle, in which the task, if described in detail, would sound impossible. Unlike the act of riding a bicycle, however, thinking about what one is doing as a child therapist does not necessarily lead to paralysis and dysfunction. We think the extant models tend unnecessarily to oversimplify the task by excluding the family system, in the case of the Freudians or the Kleinians, by excluding the various representational worlds, in the case of the family systems theorists, or by minimizing and marginalizing the transference–countertransference interaction, in the case of the Freudians and systems theorists. Our complex view of the therapeutic field does present the therapist with complex decisions as to where and how to intervene. Our goal in this book is to provide the working clinician with a model to enhance her or his experience of the various levels of the clinical interaction, and to enrich the thoughtfulness with which he or she can reflect upon the various options available for intervention.

PART ONE

Child and Parent Development
from a Relational Viewpoint

Before moving to the clinical applications of our point of view in child treatment, we fill out our theoretical perspective, turning first to recent work in developmental theory from a relational point of view. Traditional developmental theory is based on a concept of the developing individual, separable from the context, interpersonal and otherwise, within which she or he develops. In a field theory such as characterizes our relational point of view, the individual and the environment are inseparably linked, part and parcel of each other. Obviously, then, theories of development of the isolated individual must be rethought.

In this chapter, we track the history of psychoanalytically informed developmental theory from Freud through Mahler and Winnicott to Bowlby and contemporary attachment theorists and researchers. These latter workers, with concepts of internalized relational patterns, provide the kind of link between the interpersonal and the intrapsychic that characterizes the relational point of view. We then move on to a consideration of development through the oedipal period and the middle years of childhood, and through the years of parenthood as well.

2

Infancy and Preschool Years

Psychoanalysis has always been a developmental psychology. Even when Freud abandoned the seduction theory in favor of a psychosexual-stage theory, he was going from one explanation of childhood's impact on adult life to another. Freud moved from the realm of the residual painful effects of actual trauma between children and adults, to the territory of the lifelong influence of childhood intrapsychic psychodynamics. Thus both areas that he had considered at various times to be the sources of adult psychopathology—actual trauma and various types of fixated childhood intrapsychic dynamics—involved an inherent developmental perspective. Freud discovered in both theories that the major or even minor troublesome episodes that happen to children and their parents may act with the passage of time to interrupt the smooth transition from growing child to healthy adult.

This reliance on a developmental approach that began with Freud has raised questions that psychoanalysis has struggled with for over one hundred years, such as: What is the course of normal development? And, What is the impact of the disruptions in normal development on the personality of the child? Basically two types of solutions were devised by psychoanalytic theorists to come to terms with these questions: (1) psychoanalytic theories of development, or postulating from "couch to crib" as Bowlby called it (Bretherton 1995); and (2) developmental research models, or postulating from crib to actual child and adult life, if you will.

PSYCHOANALYTIC THEORIES OF DEVELOPMENT

As listed above, the first solution was for psychoanalysts to construct theories of child development that were garnered from the retrospective reports of adult and even child patients in psychoanalysis, and thereby through sheer repetition to detect key universal developmental issues. As these patients recounted their childhoods, these analysts and theorists were listening for consistencies of experience and/or validation of their own hypotheses. This retrospective reconstruction solution to the question of development has produced the enormously influential theories of Sigmund Freud, Anna Freud, Melanie Klein, Donald Winnicott, Harry Stack Sullivan, Erik Erikson, and Michael Balint, to name only a prominent few.

The test of time has demonstrated that all of the theories springing from retrospective reconstruction have had some lasting merit based chiefly upon the clinical utility of several of the concepts included within each theory. Time has also proven that each theory depended far too exclusively upon the idiosyncratic perspective of the individual theorist to be considered comprehensive in the postmodern era. Each is not without value, and conversely each is not without limitation of vision.

BEGINNING WITH THE FREUDS

Sigmund Freud, for instance, clearly saw the importance of the sexual development of the child, but at the expense of other important areas of human growth. Anna Freud also, with her focus on ego development, added to her father's theory, but she left many other aspects of healthy development unattended. Freud believed that humans were profoundly motivated by their biologically programmed sexual (libidinal) and aggressive drives. Maturity, for Freud, was determined by the shifting cathexis, that is the shifting energic focus, from one erogenous zone to another along a biologically and universally predetermined course.

Infants were presumed to be in an oral stage, according to Freud, based initially upon their concentration on nursing and feeding and their reliance within the first two years on oral exploration as a chief way of knowing their world. Primary process or the proclivity for magical and fantastic thinking, typical of this stage, draws mainly from the pleasure principle and ignores the constraints of reality. Id reigns supreme. The infant pursues pleasure without factoring in realistic considerations. Primary narcissism also predominates, in which the infant is cathected to himself with the whole of his libidinal energy until other objects, such as the mother, become relevant and secondary narcissism sets in (references to mother in this section are to be considered as a rough shorthand for the adult or adults who are carrying out the primary care of the infant). Secondary process thinking arises when the child operates more in keeping with the reality principle. By that time the child can demonstrate a rudimentary ego to regulate impulse and wish, and the ability to balance impulse and wish with the particulars of the environment.

The anal stage succeeds the oral one in the Freudian developmental stages, as the significant focus of parent and child involvement shifts to issues of control and acculturation into the adult world. Through toilet training, the toddler learns to regulate his own body under the partisan eye of the parent who is very much encouraging this step. The capability to say "no" and to challenge the parents, that is, oppositionalism, provides the toddler with some early experiences of independence and autonomy. When the demands of toileting and other behaviors seem to be too much for the toddler for either substantial or arbitrary reasons, "no" provides relief. Parents' handling of oppositionalism and toileting strongly influences the toddler's eventual attitudes toward independence, cleanliness, order, and the body. What initially were means of pleasing parents evolve into lifelong character traits. According to Freud, these traits fit somewhere on the continuum between anal retentive and anal expulsive styles, in other words, withholding and impulsivity. Later Erikson expanded this conception to include retentive-controlling or impulsive ways of relating in various cultural contexts.

Once again, Erikson reworks the key issue of this stage in a relational direction by calling the chief developmental task "autonomy versus shame and doubt." The toddler learns during this stage whether he can function well as an independent individual in his family, or whether his interactions will be characterized by his shame of himself and his doubts of his capabilities to join the world effectively.

IT STARTS EVEN EARLIER— THE INNOVATIONS OF MELANIE KLEIN

A significant and radically different contribution to the comprehension of infancy from a psychoanalytic point of view came from Melanie Klein, who focused exclusively upon the first year of life in her developmental theory. In fact, Klein was the first to postulate that the central psychodynamics of an individual's life all have their roots in the first year. Freudian theory, as we will see in the next section, gave prominence to the third and fourth years of life as containing the central developmental issue, the oedipal complex.

Klein expanded upon Abraham's splitting of the Freudian oral stage into two phases. Abraham called the first stage the oral incorporative stage in order to underline the infant's consuming focus upon the caregiver. The second half of the oral stage was called the oral sadistic stage by Abraham and begins when the infant commences teething. At that time the infant can literally (and eventually figuratively) incorporate biting aggression into the growing repertoire of his behavior.

Klein also split the first year of life into two parts that she called positions, not stages. Klein wanted to emphasize that growth was not a linear process of one stage supplanting another, but of coexisting phases that come to the fore when necessary and recede when other behaviors are indicated. The first phase is called the paranoid-schizoid position. According to Klein, during the first four to six months of life, the infant lives in a black and white world where love and hate, satiation and hunger, intimacy and abandonment, fluctuate as momentary aspects of the mother–infant experience. Positive experiences of having one's physical needs satisfied by the mother aid the infant in constructing a "good" or positive sense of himself and a "good" or positive sense of others in the world. Klein characterized this as an image of an internalized good breast. Negative experiences such as hunger and being misread by the mother contribute to a "bad" or negative sense of self and the internalization of a bad feeling in which one feels persecuted by others. This is symbolized, in Klein's attempt to project herself into the infant's mind, as a bad breast.

Thus there exist simultaneously in the infant's mind separate, good and bad images of the infant's self and object relationships, which remain distinct while the infant is in the paranoid-schizoid position. These unintegrated images of the mother, for instance, can be thought of as comprising at least two separate parts, a good part and a bad one. The infant, according to Klein, lives in a world of part objects, that is, breasts unconnected to the mother's face in the infant's mind, or a loving mother unconnected to an angry one, during the first few months of life, instead of perceiving an integrated whole mother. In this way, Klein felt that the infant maintained the splitting of the good from the bad as a means of protecting the part object that is good from the part object that is bad.

Another pertinent psychodynamic during the paranoid-schizoid phase is the intense rage and envy that the infant is capable of, regarding his wishes to have what he perceives as the good that the other has to offer him. This envy has a ruthless, greedy quality in which the infant is caught in a seeming life or death struggle to get the supplies that he so intensely feels he needs. If the mother can relate to this intensity as a measure of the infant's panic instead of to the greediness, she will help the infant to be less fearful both of his desires and of the feeling that he will not be adequately understood. This type of experience, when repeated often, leads to a preponderance of good feelings toward the mother, and facilitates the development of an integrated sense of the mother as being both good and bad. The infant can hold onto a good feeling about the mother even when he is in distress, because he has had a lot of positive memories to sustain him. Splitting will diminish.

If, on the other hand, the mother too often responds to the greediness aspect of the envy and becomes angry or unable otherwise to comfort the infant, such rageful feelings in the infant and the mother will become exacerbated. This situation activates the central dilemma of the first six months of life for a Kleinian, where fears reach paranoid proportions as the infant conceives of the world as being harmful to him. Then the only safe course is considered to be maintaining the splitting of the good from the bad as a means of protecting the self. This infant is functioning primarily from a paranoid-schizoid position, as opposed to moving into a predominately depressive position around the sixth month of life.

The hallmark of the depressive position is the acceptance of the whole person as the composition of his parts—termed the whole object. That is, the infant now has the capacity to see the mother as sometimes good and sometimes bad, at times present and at other times absent, "in synch" with the infant when needed and "out of synch" sometimes too, and so forth. The title of this position, the depressive position, comes from the affect associated with the infant's wishes for the mother when she is not available, since the infant now has longings to maintain the positive contact with the mother. Alternatively, the infant is now capable of experiencing guilt, as he copes with his fears that the bad experiences he participates in will swamp the good experiences and lead to a loss of love from the mother. The infant feels guilty about the effect of his own destructiveness.

PROJECTIVE IDENTIFICATION

Projective identification is a key concept of Klein's that has been adopted and elaborated by her followers, particularly Bion (1959, 1962), Joseph (1985, 1987), and Ogden (1979, 1982). It has become an influential aspect of modern psychoanalytic thinking. We will take the opportunity to review this important theoretical and clinical concept here in the section on infancy since the utilization of projective identification is purported to have its origins in the earliest days of life.

While the infant is in the paranoid-schizoid position in the first few months of infancy, he needs to regulate the flow of the intensely negative experiences, such as persecutory anxiety, aggressive impulses, destructive wishes, or self-hatred, which flood the infant from time to time. Klein (1946) wrote, "Much of the hatred against parts of the self is now directed toward the mother. This leads to a particular form of identification which establishes the prototype of an aggressive object-relation. I suggest for these processes the term 'projective identification'" (p. 12).

When projection is utilized to deny the infant's impulse to harm or to control the mother, he feels those feelings as if coming from her, and so he feels her to be a persecutor. In psychotic disorders this identification of an object with the hated parts of the self contributes to the intensity of the hatred directed against other people.

While Klein was dealing mainly with projective identification as the expulsion of negative experiences by an infant or as a characteristic of someone who suffers from a psychotic illness, a number of her followers have expanded the concept in a way that stresses the nonverbal, interpersonal, communicative aspects of the concept for everyday people in everyday life. Ogden (1982), one of the clearer writers on this rather confusing topic, stated, "Through projective identification the projector has the primarily unconscious fantasy of ridding himself of unwanted aspects of the self; depositing those unwanted parts in another person; and finally, recovering a modified version of what was extruded" (p. 11).

The originally projected aspect of self is "modified," as Ogden called it, in the third and final aspect of this process. Bion (1962) referred to this function of the recipient as being a "container" of the projected impulses since the recipient, to whom he also referred as the "sensitive receptor," is likely to be in a better position to contain the impulses that are so disturbing to the infant. Ogden (1982) described it as follows:

> If the recipient can deal with the feelings projected into him in a way that differs from the projector's method, a new set of feelings is generated. This can be viewed as a processed version of the original projected feelings and might involve the sense that the projected feelings, thoughts, and representations can be lived with, without damaging other aspects of the self or of one's valued external or internal objects. [p. 16]

This concept of projective identification can also be used to explain how the mother "reads" the infant in her attempts to provide "good" experiences in concordance with the infant's expectations. Since he is without verbal language, the infant communicates to the mother by transmitting how he feels through his array of preverbal messages until the mother comprehends and acts on her understanding of the messages. In a positive scenario, the mother realizes that the infant's distress is disturbing, both to the infant and herself, but manageable. The better adept the mother is at comprehending the infant's state with the help of her awareness of her own inner state, the more appropriate will be her response, and the more positive will be the interaction, satisfying both mother and infant.

For example, an infant screams distress in a manner that alerts and concerns the mother and causes her to consider what action to take. She wonders if the infant is hungry. She says to the baby in a soothing voice, "Are you hungry?" The mother takes in the distress and translates it into a less disturbing feeling. The infant's fear that he is starving is processed by the mother into the reciprocal feeling that his hunger can be satisfied momentarily. The mother prepares to feed the baby and the baby, after he is just a few weeks old and if he can sufficiently allay his distress, recognizes her behavior and intentions. The baby eagerly, and perhaps in spite of his continued distress, anticipates the desired result of his preverbal communication to be fed. When the mother feeds the baby, the circle is completed and the mother and the infant are in harmony with one another around the successful completion of the "I'm hungry"—"Don't worry, I'll take care of it" sequence. This is a case of successful projective identification, and an empathic connection results (Demos 1999). The infant sends a feeling state out to his mother in an attempt to rid himself of his negative state. She picks it up and processes it, and subsequently she performs some appropriate action. The infant learns that expressing his needs is the route to satisfaction, and the infant eventually begins to appreciate the mother as intrinsic to these positive feelings. The mother gains confidence that she can "read" her baby well enough to approach his communications to her with less and less anxiety. Thus a basically positive representation (Emde 1981) of the infant, the mother, and their relationship as feeding partners begins to form bit by bit in the minds of both the infant and the mother. Fonagy and colleagues (1995) describe a similar process with the term *mentalization*.

If the mother cannot "read" these communications to her from the preverbal infant, frustration and negative interactions will ensue. The pair may come to expect that moments of communication from the infant will be unpleasant ones. For instance, what if in the above example the mother mistakes the infant's hunger messages as "I'm cold" messages.

We must wonder, first of all, why she misreads her infant's cues. The mother's own prior experiences with distress and negative emotions are brought to bear on such situations. Yet no matter how tenderly she attempts to warm him up, she will not convey to the infant that he has been understood. The communication process has broken down. The mother has not been perceptive of her infant's feeling state. For whatever reasons, her inner state at that time was not sufficiently synchronized with the infant's needs as she absorbed his emotional messages. This, of course, is not an uncommon occurrence since there is no such thing as a perfectly harmonious pair. If this happens often, however, the infant (and mother) will become frustrated around his hunger feelings. The mother projects her notion into the child instead of seeking an accurate reading of the child (Seligman 1999, Silverman and Lieberman 1999). The infant might eventually become frustrated about his ability to survive in a world where being misunderstood, and therefore persecuted in Klein's way of thinking, is the expectable environment. Concurrently, the mother will also have trouble fueling her representation of herself as a "good enough mother" (Winnicott 1956) and may begin to see caring for the infant in primarily negative terms.

> A mother of a 10-year-old boy with aggressive acting-out problems once said in an initial session of child psychotherapy: "My daughter was a dream, but Joe has been a handful since he was born. We either do things his way or we have a screaming argument over even the littlest things. It's been that way since they handed him to me at the hospital. With my daughter I do nothing wrong; with him I do nothing right."

For a mother to present this material in such a straightforward manner leads the clinician from the relational perspective to question the earliest aspects of the mother–child relationship and how these early incidents grew into a fixed pattern of relatedness between this mother and her son. It will come as no surprise that this boy structured most of his time in psychotherapy around aggressive and competitive interactions with the therapist.

Recently infant research that had focused on the mother–infant dyad has documented the nonverbal communicative aspects of these relationships from the earliest days of life (Beebe and Lachmann 1988, Demos 1992, Fonagy et al. 1995, Stern 1985). Their findings have lent experimental evidence and support to some of the theoretical components of projective identification, particularly the intense emotional communicative processes between infants and their caregivers (Seligman 1999). Their findings have also lent support to psychoanalytic theories of interpersonal intimacy between two people (that is to say, not only mothers and infants), including the relationship between patient and therapist. Ogden (1979, 1982), particularly, has been thorough in his explication of how such intense nonverbal communication operates continually between patient and therapist.

One of the aims of this book is to demonstrate how attention to the nonverbal communicative aspects (whether labeled as examples of projective identification or not) between child patient and child therapist in psychotherapy is of enormous clinical and therapeutic value. While the adult literature on this topic is burgeoning, the child psychotherapy literature pays short shrift to this crucial aspect of therapeutic work with children, despite important exceptions (for example, the journal *Psychoanalytic Dialogues* devoted an entire issue to this topic in 1999).

THE PARTICIPATION OF THE MOTHER — DONALD WINNICOTT

Very few theorists generate the praise and deliver the inspiration that is attributed to Donald Winnicott. In fact, Melanie Klein was so impressed with Donald Winnicott when she was supervising him that she referred her younger son to him for psychoanalysis. Winnicott, in spite of all he learned from Klein and in spite of his respect for her thinking, had ideas of his own about development, ideas he garnered in his years as a pediatrician before he became a psychoanalyst. One of his main contributions was to emphasize the role of the mother. Although the previous section might lead one to believe that Klein gave the mother a prominent role, in fact Klein hardly mentioned the mother. Klein was more concerned with the infant's fantasy life of internal objects than she was interested in the actual flesh-and-blood mother. It was Winnicott who said that how the mother cares for the baby will greatly affect the infant's development. Now to us in the twenty-first century, such an idea is a given, but in Winnicott's time, as unbelievable as it may seem, no one had so unequivocally declared the importance of the mother's influence in psychoanalytic circles. In fact, Winnicott went so far as to say that "there is no such thing as an infant," by which he meant that there is no such thing as considering the infant without considering him in the context of his connection to his mother.

Winnicott (1956) postulated that the mother concentrates so totally on her baby in the first few weeks of life that he described it as a state of "primary maternal preoccupation." The mother is seen to be nearly out of touch with reality as she attends foremost to the baby, without regard for all of the previously typical aspects of her daily life. For instance, distinctions such as night and day or prior rigidly held daily schedules are cast aside as the mother devotes herself entirely to the needs of her infant whatever the time, whatever the place. Winnicott warns fathers not to be alarmed by this turn of events because such preoccupation is a normal and temporary phase for the new mother. Winnicott goes on to contend that the mother's ability to devote so much of her concern to the infant securely "holds" the baby psychologically and creates a safe environment for the infant, in much the same way that actual physical holding creates a secure closeness for the baby when being carried. The security generated by these experiences of being "held" by the mother enables the infant to venture forth into the world at the appropriate time.

In Winnicott's view, the infant is not sent away "cold turkey" from the mother and into the world. He postulated the creation of transitional objects (both internal and external) and transitional spaces that help the baby be with the mother even though she is not present. That is, the infant imbues people, places, and things with the security-enhancing function of the mother in order to take her with him in her absence. Winnicott reveled in these paradoxes of human experience, and the present-absent mother embodied in the transitional object is a good example of the paradoxical playfulness of his theory (refer to Ogden 1985, for more examples of these Winnicottian paradoxes).

In an impossibly safe world in which the infant could always and easily draw upon his internalized holding environment in order to have only positive experiences, something called the "true self" (Winnicott

1960) would evolve unimpeded. The true self is one's unique individuality that would exist if others had not impinged on the infant in some usually subtle, but sometimes very dramatic, ways. Since, however, no mother or environment can or should be perfect, a "false self" develops to protect the undefended vulnerability of the true self and to enable one to function in a world where perfect harmony cannot be expected. The false self is protective, compliant, resistant, and defended to the degree that is necessary for the infant to cope and survive in his particular world. Therefore, psychoanalytic treatment, from a Winnicottian point of view, deconstructs the false self to determine if the threat of perceived danger to the true self necessitates the degree to which the false self will go to defend it.

THE INTERPERSONAL WORLD — HARRY STACK SULLIVAN

Simultaneously with, but independently from, Klein and Winnicott, Sullivan in the United States constructed a theory of development that relied upon interpersonal relatedness as the key. Sullivan wished to depart from the tradition of the libidinally oriented theorists who he felt stressed the biological at the expense of the interactional. Thus to Sullivan, development is a series of successive interpersonal steps in which the child moves gradually from engagements with the mothering one toward more intimate ties with peers and the broader culture. The most detailed and complete presentation of Sullivan's ideas on development is contained in *The Interpersonal Theory of Psychiatry* (1953). This book was compiled posthumously from his lecture notes spanning the years 1944–1947, when Sullivan was teaching at the William Alanson White Institute in New York City.

The infant in Sullivan's theory arrives at birth with biological needs such as hunger, the need for body-heat regulation, and so forth, needs that must be satisfied by others in order for the baby to survive. The expression of these needs in the first weeks of life by fussiness or crying signals the infant's tension to the other, who translates her own resultant tensions involving the care of her baby into the wish to provide tenderness. The initial anxiety is transformed into empathy. This need of the mother to give tenderness to her infant completes an interpersonal circle of intimate relatedness that Sullivan sees as the central dynamism of the beginning stage of life (Sullivan 1953). He did not want to boil down the first year to the mere satisfaction of the infant's oral needs but instead to give priority to the beginnings of interpersonal security in these early interactions. Sullivan saw this growing security as key to the infant's very survival, both physically and psychologically.

In a similar vein, Erikson, also in the United States (and a former colleague of Anna Freud's in Vienna before he came to the East Coast), in his brilliant and socially based reconfiguration of the developmental stages, called this first stage of growth "trust versus mistrust." Here the focus, as with Sullivan, lies upon the infant's formation of a trusting relationship with the mother. Thus the developmental nexus of the first two years of life is located in a relational context instead of attributing it chiefly to physiological needs.

In Sullivan's theory of interpersonal growth, the internal world of the infant becomes constructed over time by the internalized images of actual interactions with another. The internal world in this theory is not composed of fantastic creations, à la Freud, nor are internal objects prewired and established prenatally, à la Melanie Klein. Instead Sullivan believed that an accumulation of these "self-with-other experiences" contributed to the various "personifications" of the other that the infant internalizes from actual events. A type of these organized personifications was labeled the "good mother" by Sullivan. This is the infant's compilation of emotionally positive and tension-reducing experiences with the mother. The "bad mother" personification, on the other hand, is the result of the infant's anxiety-inducing experiences with the mother, where neither tenderness is provided nor tensions reduced (Sullivan 1953). Eventually the infant integrates these personifications into a single mother with both good and bad characteristics.

Prior to this development, Sullivan, like Klein, ventured further into the territory of part objects, where the neonate perceives part of the caregiver's body without connecting it to the rest of the body as a single entity. Specifically, Sullivan talked about the "good nipple," the "bad nipple," and the "wrong nipple" (Shafran 1995, p. 242). Both in form and definition, these entities precisely resemble Klein's notions of the "good breast" and the "bad breast." Sullivan, however, never cited

Klein and we wonder if he were not influenced by her conceptualizations despite the absence of attribution.

In a parallel manner to the formation of the personifications of the mother, the infant constructs personifications of himself in relation to his caregiver, which are described by Sullivan (1953) as "good me," "bad me," and "not me." Through "reflected appraisals" the infant gathers an image of himself as seen in the reactions of others to him and his various behaviors. The "good me" personification arises as the consequence of satisfying and tender experiences that the infant has with his caregivers. These experiences form the basis of the self-personifications that evolve into what Sullivan calls the "self system." Anxious experiences with others, on the other hand, result in maintaining interpersonal and bodily tension and gradually form the basis of the "not me." Eventually the self system screens out not-me experiences from the growing personality through "selective inattention" and seeks to reinforce positive interactions and minimize the anxiety associated with the negative ones. The not-me is the product of experiences with caregivers where parts of the body and certain experiences create such a high level of anxiety in the caregiver that the caregiver forbids the infant from having awareness altogether. As an example, Sullivan noted how many parents' discomfort with sexuality is translated unconsciously by them to their infants through forbidding gestures and mystifying information (Levenson 1983).

SUMMARY

Before moving to the research-based models of development, one can already see the historical progression toward theories of development that focused more intently on the mother–infant pair than the original Freudian position. This idea of the primacy of the mother–infant dyad not only became a cornerstone of relational developmental theory but also profoundly influenced the conceptualization of the therapist's role in the transference. Freud's patriocentric theory was replaced by a matriocentric position for the therapist, and the oedipal constellation seemed less important clinically in many cases than the ramifications of the mother–infant dyad. Thus, preoedipal life gained an inextricably central place in developmental theory and clinical considerations, even before research began to validate its importance.

DEVELOPMENTAL RESEARCH MODELS

The second solution to the problem of understanding the developmental puzzles of human psychic growth in psychoanalysis is the research approach. Renee Spitz (1946) noticed in the infant nursery of a British hospital that the high infant mortality rate was related to the amount of care, attention, and physical contact that the babies received from the nursing staff. Spitz's work demonstrated that studying actual infants as a means to formulate theories of development could render material as valuable, or even more valuable, than theories conceived totally from the reconstructed developmental reports of adults' retrospective focus in psychoanalytic sessions.

THE ATTACHMENT BETWEEN INFANT AND MOTHER — BOWLBY AND AINSWORTH

Bowlby, like Winnicott, a supervisee of Melanie Klein, used Klein's theory as a springboard to develop his own. With both Winnicott and Bowlby, a theory was devised that considered the mother as significantly more important than did Klein.

John Bowlby was skeptical as to whether infants manifested the characteristics that Klein ascribed to them. After completing his training as a psychoanalyst, Bowlby dedicated his life's work to exploring infancy and our relational ties to one another—our attachments and losses. Aside from his psychoanalytic background, Bowlby had always been excited by the discoveries of Darwin on evolution (in fact, one of his last works was a biography of Darwin). Bowlby's lifelong interest in evolution was reawakened in the 1950s after reading Konrad Lorenz's study of imprinting in birds, and it caused Bowlby to consider the implications for humans of ethological imprinting. These diverse influences led Bowlby to speculate about evolutionary adaptations in infants' attachments to their caregivers. Picking up on Spitz's early scientific observations of infants, Bowlby, also in England, designed research protocols (eventually with his American colleague Ainsworth) to explore attachment in the first year of life. Bowlby's and Ainsworth's studies (both together and separately) of attachment between infant and mother are now the backbone of research-based developmental theory.

Attachment research proposes that we are neurologically wired from birth to attach to our caregivers by seeking proximity, interaction, and security in our relationships with them (Ainsworth et al. 1978, Bowlby 1969, Bretherton 1995). Thus attachment rather than libidinal energy is what bonds people. Bowlby linked human attachment processes to the attachment behaviors of all primates. Cited were such behaviors as sucking, wishing to be held, visual tracking, the social smile, and crying as signaling to the mother. He also concluded that to achieve optimal psychological stability through the infant's use of these biologically based, attachment-seeking behaviors, the infant needs to find himself in a close, reliable, and nurturing relationship with his mother. (See Suomi [1995] for reports both supportive and fascinating about primate attachment research.)

If the infant and the mother are attached to one another, this does not signal an end to the infant's problems, because now the infant is capable of reacting with separation anxiety to the absences of the mother. Robertson, a member of Bowlby's research team, was the first to delineate the three now well-known stages of separation reaction: "protest related to separation anxiety, despair related to grief and mourning, and denial or detachment related to defense mechanisms, especially repression" (Bretherton 1995, p. 55). Separation anxiety is the consequence, according to Bowlby (1973), of the infant's seeking attachment gratification in the absence of the mother. While this occurs daily in normal life without severe consequence, a more dire impact results from consistent inattention to the infant's attachment needs or to prolonged separations.

Ainsworth and her colleagues have studied how normal and pathogenic attachment patterns differ from one another in many multicultural studies. They have found that most infant–mother pairs can be divided into at least three patterns of attachment: secure, insecure-avoidant, and insecure-resistant/ambivalent (Ainsworth et al. 1978, Ainsworth and Bowlby 1991). Subsequently Main (Main et al. 1985, Main 1995) a former student of Ainsworth, added a fourth type of attachment, which she called disorganized/disoriented.

Ainsworth and her colleagues used naturalistic observation in the infants' homes, but eventually came to rely upon the "Strange Situation" research protocol to assess attachment levels. This is a tightly scripted research protocol of twenty minutes in duration, during which infants and their mothers are observed in a consistent laboratory play-room setting through a one-way mirror. The infants are scored by trained raters as they are observed reacting to several and various intervals of interaction, absence, and reunion with their mother, episodes that are periodically intensified by the presence of a stranger and invitations to interact made by that stranger. Behaviors are rated in the context in which they are observed in interaction in the mother–infant dyads. For example, crying in the infant does not indicate any one pattern. Rather, it is typical both of some securely attached pairs and some insecure or resistant/ambivalent pairs, depending upon the context of its expression. If the mother reads it appropriately as a signal for reassurance and the infant is soothed and reassured ("There, there, now. You got scared. It's okay to play with the lady. Why not show her how you build with the blocks?"), it is more likely to be judged as consistent with ratings of the secure classification. If the crying not only signals anxiety but prolongs anxious and confused relating ("What are you crying for? No one is going to hurt you. I knew he wouldn't be able to do this without crying his lungs out.") between the mother and infant, it is more consistent with resistant/ambivalent interactions and attachment patterns.

Securely attached infants, as assessed by these research findings, were found to have mothers who respond sensitively, tenderly, and quickly to the signals of their infants. The infants, in turn, were found to manifest low levels of anxiety and anger. There is an easy alternation between attachment behaviors and independent activities on the part of the infants and the mothers.

Insecure-avoidant infants were found in the Strange Situation paradigm to avoid recognition of the mother upon her return after the separation. The infant does not make eye contact with the mother or approach her. The infant's concentration remains on the things in the playroom. The mothers were found to ignore or misread the cues for attachment behavior from their infants. The infant's avoidance is seen as a means of preserving self-control in a situation where great distress and/or anger could result.

The third classification, the insecure-ambivalent/preoccupied group of infants, react with highly expressive displays of distress upon separation. These reactions often do not subside with the return of the mother, as the infant's ambivalence is demonstrated in the confusion he experiences upon reunion. The infant seems neither consoled nor pleased to be reunited with the mother. Although the mothers of these infants were capable of warmth, they typically were unable to read their infant's concerns and thus were not a reliable source of security. These infants' strategies, however, in contrast to their "avoidant" peers, seemed to involve a preoccupation with reaching some level of elusive security with their mothers.

A fourth group has been called disorganized/disoriented by Main (1995) and her colleagues. These infants had no consistent strategy other than to be completely disoriented by the stress of attempting some attachment sequences with their mothers, resulting in the sense that they were impeded in developing some core sense of self in relation to others. Rather than play or interaction, self-soothing and isolating behaviors such as rocking were sometimes evident. Some of these infants even performed self-destructive behaviors such as hair pulling and head banging. Not surprisingly, the incidence of abuse and maltreatment by the parents is the highest in this group. In Chapter 7, we will return to some of the possibly pathological consequences in later childhood of early, insecure attachments.

Recently the focus in attachment research has been to examine the parents' parenting style, as reflected in their descriptions of their own childhoods on the Adult Attachment Interview developed by Main and her colleagues (Fonagy et al. 1995, Main 1995). This scale assesses the parent's "state of mind with respect to attachment." The culmination of this research has resulted in four classifications that parallel the classification of infants' attachment status. The first is the "secure-autonomous" group of parents, who were found to respect attachment from their own childhoods and who facilitate secure attachments in their own children. "Dismissing of attachment" parents constituted the second group; these parents were likely to give unsubstantiated high praise of their own parents, indicative of a defensive process such as repression or dissociation. They were found to be the parents of the avoidant group of infants, who also were attempting to avoid emotional interactions with their parents." A third group of parents were labeled "preoccupied by past relationships," as they were rated to be overly involved with their own childhood experiences, albeit unconsciously in many cases. Their infants were largely in the preoccupied/ ambivalent category, as the parents were found to be unconnected to their infants and resistant to their individuation, in keeping with their own psychological profiles. The final classification of parents was the unresolved/disorganized category. During the interviews, these parents demonstrated distressed reactions to the discussions of traumatic events from their childhoods. They became more disorganized in the interview, compared to parents in the other groups, when discussing troubling issues such as traumatic childhood separations or losses. Parents who had been abused as children, and who were still quite unresolved about their trauma to the point of abusing their own children, are an example of a subtype within this grouping.

SEPARATION-INDIVIDUATION — MAHLER

While Bowlby was beginning his research in England, Margaret Mahler (Mahler et al. 1970, 1975) was in the United States pursuing a phenomenon related somewhat to attachment which she called separation-individuation. Bowlby was rebelling against the psychoanalytic tradition in which he was trained, while Mahler was loyal to the Freudian tradition of ego psychology with which she was affiliated (Mahler had lived in Vienna and had contact with the Freuds there). Her research was designed both to validate her beliefs and to introduce some new concepts about how infants separate from parents and eventually individuate. In a specially designed nursery, she and her colleagues observed volunteer mothers and infants over a period of several years. Her longitudinal study offered enormous impetus to speculation about the "psychological birth of the human infant," as she called it, and her concepts have solidly found their way into clinical work with children and adults.

Several phases of separation-individuation were delineated. In the first two months of life, the infant was seen as going through a normal autistic phase. The infant was believed to be operating within a stimulus barrier which allowed the infant only a peripheral awareness of the ministrations of his mother and others on his behalf. The stimulus barrier was actually Freud's concept of the first few months of life. It significantly differed from opinions that were current by the time Mahler did her research, opinions in Klein's theory, Sullivan's theory, and Bowlby's research. Nonetheless, Freud's concept continued to receive theoretical support within ego psychology circles. The autistic phase was followed by a symbiotic phase from the second month until the fourth or fifth month, in which the infant became so involved in his relationship with his mother that their boundaries were temporarily dissolved to create a state of undifferentiation.

Although Mahler earned the widespread respect of her colleagues, she virtually ignored the trend toward conceiving of the infant as wired for a differentiated connectedness with his mother from the first moment. In fact, this phenomenom of initial relatedness was not observed by Mahler and her associates, as it would be in the future by many infant researchers, particularly Stern. This seeming blind allegiance to Freudian concepts, apparently ignoring some of the available evidence indicating interpersonal processes, has dogged Mahler's theory. Modifications have been made to Mahler's theory in order to consider these relational ideas, especially by Fred Pine but also by Mahler herself. Pine argued that instead of considering Mahler's literal meaning of symbiosis, we should consider that "moments of symbiosis" exist, in infancy and throughout life, in which there is a blurring of boundaries at moments when a merger with a significant other is felt to be a source of weathering through a markedly difficult situation (Pine 1990). Stern (1985) has argued that the concept is more confusing than helpful, but Pine believes that as clinicians we observe such symbiotic moments often in our work and that there is a place for considering symbiosis in our clinical theory.

At 4 or 5 months, Mahler saw the infant entering the period of separation-individuation proper. (The phases before this period were the prelude to this flowering of the infant's individuation.) The first subphase of separation-individuation was called differentiation; it occurs from 4 to 5 months until 7 months. The infant undergoes "hatching" at this time, during which he leaves his so-called enveloped state and focuses his interest in the world at large. The tie to the mother is also witnessed by his "checking back pattern" of looking for her when the infant feels a separation away from her. If the absence of the mother is felt to be disturbing to the infant, he will demonstrate a fearful reaction to strangers, instead of his phase-appropriate exploration and inquisitiveness.

The second subphase of separation-individuation is divided into the early practicing phase and the practicing phase proper. In the former, from the seventh to the tenth month, locomotion away from the mother provides experiences of exciting self-propelled autonomy. The infant returns to his mother for emotional "refueling" when such autonomy becomes fearful and some reassurance is needed. The practicing phase proper is ushered in by upright locomotion and thereby initiates what Mahler called the toddler's love affair with the world. In contrast, at times of distress the child enters a state of "low keyedness" when separations are anxiously felt.

From 18 months until the age of 3 years, the infant is in the third subphase of separation-individuation called rapprochement. Here the toddler enjoys his independent life when he is capable of an optimal emotional link to his mother either in her presence or by carrying her image with him. When such security fails the toddler, he seeks his mother for a tangible connection. Games such as peek-a-boo are thrilling to the toddler, because he can practice reassuring himself that absent others reliably return. By 3 years the child has reached a state of individuality in this theory, and hence has sufficient capacity to use imagination to carry a symbolic mother with him (i.e., object constancy) as he becomes a participant in the extrafamilial environment.

THE INFANT'S INTERPERSONAL WORLD — STERN

Although it is difficult to say precisely when, in the body of psychoanalytic theory, a modern revision replaces the former theory—or, in this case, when a postmodern era replaces the modern one—certainly the work of infant researchers Ainsworth and Stern is within an era totally different conceptually from the one preceding it. The earlier developmental theories of infancy, such as those of Freud, Klein, Winnicott, and Sullivan, among others, were different because they were (1) purely theoretical entities based upon retrospective reports of adult patients in psychoanalysis; (2) random observations of a few children or biased samples (in Klein's case, some of her earliest patients were her own children; Freud's Little Hans was probably the son of one of his female patients; Mahler's sample was volunteer, white, full-time mothers and their babies); and (3) treasured dynamics within the theorist's own childhood (i.e., Freud's oedipal complex; Winnicott's primary maternal preoccupation). In contrast, both Ainsworth and Stern anchored their theoretical contributions upon an understanding of the development of the infant based upon empirical research. That is, actual observation of normatively and clinically controlled samples of infants and their mothers would dictate the terms of their theories. Like Bowlby, Stern was reacting against the trend in psychoanalytic theory to speculate about infant development based upon adult clinical work; he was also reacting against what he saw as biased premises and inadequate experimental samples, such as Mahler's subjects.

Stern trained his sights on the interpersonal connectedness of infants. He devised a research-backed stage theory of the development of self in the infant based primarily upon a compilation of infant research and observation, and included a focus on his own contributions to the infant research literature. Instead of accepting the autistic infant of Mahler, Stern verified earlier speculation that in the first few months of life the infant is in a state of alert inactivity. Stern (1985) relabeled this period as the "sense of an emergent self." He formulated, based upon research, that neonates (1) "seek sensory stimulation"; (2) "have distinct biases or preferences which are innate"; (3) "have a tendency to form and test hypotheses about what is occurring in the world"; (4) "have affective and cognitive processes which cannot be readily separated" (pp. 41–42). These principles were culled after examining the literature and testing actual infants. Stern cited wonderfully compelling examples of infants doing such recognizably interpersonal behaviors as sticking out their tongues at 3 weeks of age after observing an adult do it repetitively. More remarkably in light of the theory at the time, he also cited how infants in the first weeks of life turn their heads toward the voice of their mother or even the father instead of a stranger. It is impossible to think of an enveloped neonate after reviewing his research. And it is impossible not to question theory that exclusively trusted the retrospective reports of adult patients.

But how did Stern account for the prewired alertness of the neonate? To explain, Stern offered his concept of the infant's amodal perception that he defined as the "innate general capacity to take information received in one sensory modality and somehow translate it into another sensory modality" (p. 51). Thus in an experiment at 3 weeks of age, a blindfolded infant sucking on a nubby pacifier will, when the blindfold is removed, gaze at a photograph of a nubby pacifier more than another photograph when given a choice. More commonly, a mother nodding her head in rhythm to a baby's repetitive sound will be appreciated by her infant who is capable of sensing the amodal and personal connection between himself and his mother at a moment of such synchronized behavior. Similarly, Stern contends that it is not so much the type of emotion that is expressed by the mother that creates a sense of connectedness to the infant but the "vitality" of the affect. That is, the intensity of the emotion rather than the emotion itself is the crucial factor (p. 55). He gives as an example the manner in which a mother picks up her infant, which is more important in many cases than the close feeling that the mother has toward the infant when she decides to pick him up.

From 2 to 6 months, Stern viewed the infant's continuing development of a sense of self as entering into a phase of a "sense of a core self." This happens because the infant has many similar experiences of a type that coalesce to form "self invariants" that contribute to the growing feeling of a core self. The mother and other caregivers support the development of these invariant experiences by responding in a similar fashion to these behaviors of the infant, thus highlighting the commonality of the interactional sequence. Beebe (Beebe and Lachmann 1997), in her research of mother–infant interaction, has described a pattern in these pairs of mutual influence whereby subtle, split-second responses from one to the other signal a reinforcement or shift in the sequence, which the other over time learns to respond to, also in split-second fashion, in order to remain in and to continue some mutually pleasurable interaction. These areas of self invariance are listed by Stern (1985) as self-agency, self-coherence, self-affectivity, self-history or memory, and finally being with a self-regulating other.

These varied invariant experiences become organized as "representations of interactions that have been generalized," or RIGs. Thus common events become condensed into a typical RIG that is stored in memory and is elicited as a blueprint for the event. If the event goes according to plan, it will add to the composite representation. If, however, the event is different in some way, it becomes important because "memory is failure-driven in that the specific episode is only relevant and memorable as a piece of lived experience to the extent that it violates the expectations of the generalized episode" (1985, p. 96). This profound statement accounts for our human tendency to concentrate on these "failed" interactions when the ordinary pleasant interaction with a parent is traumatically replaced on one occasion with a troubling experience that then becomes easier to remember than any one positive example of the same interactional sequence. For instance, the way that the father on one occasion refuses an invitation by the infant to engage in rough and tumble play becomes more memorable than any one episode of the father's engagement. Similarly, Beebe (Beebe and Lachmann 1992) describes the disruption-repair sequences of the mother–infant dyad, in which failure to maintain or initiate contact sets in motion a process of reparation.

When these RIGs become patterned as part of the infant's self-regulation with others in such a way that they can provide a sense of interacting with others even in the absence of the others, they are called "evoked companions" by Stern. This is Stern's contribution to an understanding of the infant's capacity to symbolize the mother internally when the external or actual mother is unavailable. As such, it is not an exact facsimile of the mother, but a representation of a composite portrait of being with the mother in some situation. Hence Stern claims his evoked companion is qualitatively different than other similar concepts (such as Bowlby's working model of the mother, Kohut's selfobject, and even Winnicott's transitional objects) because it is an interactional memory and not a static, internal affect-laden image. The similarities, however, are more impressive than the differences. All of these models attempt to describe how the infant can evoke the feeling of the presence of the mother in her absence as a means of promoting security.

The "sense of a subjective self" is Stern's description of the period from seven months to two years. During this time the infant becomes aware that he has an inner subjective sense of his episodes with others and that others are interested in knowing about them. Intersubjectivity in this model, then, is the situation where two people discover that their subjective states are sharable and mutually interesting and therefore that some community exists. Of course, this is the fuel of a good infant–mother relationship, but the speculation proceeds that this is the state of affairs in many human relationships, particularly close ones. "Affect attunement" is that situation where the state between the two participants is characterized by a mutual empathic connectedness. Again Beebe and Lachmann's (1992) research on mutual influences in the mother–infant dyad indicates that such attunement is characteristic of positive mother–infant relationships and serves a model of human attunement in other relationships such as therapist–patient.

With the advent of communicable language, the infant in Stern's model moves to the period of a "sense of a verbal self." From 2 to 3 years of age, the symbolic capabilities of the toddler flourish and add to the existing repertoire a symbolic forum for working out one's self understanding. Finally by the third or fourth year the "narrative sense of self" emerges and provides the basic structure for the individual to comprehend his sense of self for the rest of his life.

SUMMARY

Before we leave this section we would like to emphasize the importance of infancy as not just a developmentally significant time of life, but also clinically crucial in understanding the child patients with whom we work. We align ourselves with the relational orientation within psychoanalysis, which avers that relational patterns learned throughout life but particularly in infancy (since the very survival of the infant is at stake, a point made by Bowlby [1969]) become the bedrock of our personality (Mitchell 1988, 1997). These patterns are enacted (Bromberg 1994, 1996) over and over due to the familiarity and the security (Sullivan 1953) they provide, in spite of the fact that they often elicit unintended, undesirable, or psychopathogenic consequences. Demos (1999) states, "(a) transmission of trauma can be observed in the patterns of transactions that actually occur between parents and their children and (b) . . . these real experiences then shape and influence the children's intrapsychic phantasies and representations of relationships" (p. 219). The infant (and eventually the child) is not alone in creating and perpetuating these relational patterns. This speaks to our belief that parents' transmission of their own unfinished psychological issues adds an important avenue of exploration and clinical focus, both during the assessment of a child and during the disposition of his eventual treatment (Altman 1992, Aron 1996, Beebe and Lachmann 1992, Demos 1992, Fonagy et al. 1995, Main 1995, Seligman 1999, Silverman and Lieberman 1999, Stern 1985, Warshaw 1992).

THE OEDIPAL PERIOD AND THE DEVELOPMENT
OF GENDER ROLE IDENTIFICATIONS

The crown jewel of all developmental conceptualizations is the Freudian oedipal complex. And like the actual Crown Jewels themselves, it is viewed as everything from a precious, eternal treasure to a dated relic. Although Sigmund Freud formulated stages and developmental tasks from birth to adolescence, the oedipal complex is the centerpiece (both literally and figuratively) of Freudian developmental theory and some might say Freudian clinical practice as well. Freud has said that the two hallmarks of adult life are love and work. Both of these life pursuits take shape in the phallic stage, which has as its primary developmental task the successful resolution of the oedipal conflict.

The phallic stage spans the years from the completion of toilet training to the successful entry into elementary school—roughly the ages 3 to 6. This stage is important to the relational theorist also because it is essentially when the child is capable of beginning to understand his relationships to each parent from the added perspectives of gender identities and roles as well as familial and cultural values. For example, many children are exposed to messages during this period that suggest appropriate behavior for boys and girls based on the assumption that they are to become adult men and women someday in their specific culture. Some of these messages are not gender specific, such as "try your hardest in school." But many are gender stereotypic, such as messages dealing with toy selection, which often inherently convey whether such toys are intended to promote activity and aggressiveness or nurturance and family role-playing (e.g., superheroes vs. baby dolls). Freud was very interested in these gender differentiations and was the first to produce a psychoanalytic perspective on them.

To Freud, there were specific and culturally universal paths to the successful identification with the same-sex parent with respect to gender role, sexual identity, and superego development. The well-known sequence for boys was that they would see their father, during these years, as a rival for their mother's affections. Since children of three are rather concrete cognitively, Freud postulated that they wished the father to be gone permanently or dead as a possible solution to the conflict they experienced by his presence. The thought, however, of wishing or even participating in one's father's death raises the issue of retaliation by the father and causes too great a level of anxiety for the boy to bear. Freud postulated that the boy feared that if he continued pursuing the mother, the father would become so enraged that he would castrate his son in order to prevent him from carrying out the plan to have the mother all to himself. As a solution, the boy decides to be pleasing to his father by emulating him and by identifying with his male role, as practiced by the father. The sublimation of the aggression toward the father helps the boy to have the energy necessary for pursuing his interests—usually under the approval and guidance of his parents—such as school, sports, arts, and so forth. Also, by identifying with his father the boy begins the development of his superego, judging right from wrong based on views inculcated from his parents.

For girls Freud was less clear, but a Freudian theory of female oedipal development has been pieced together from Freud's writings and the elaborations of others. It is sometimes called the Electra complex, although not by Freud himself. Girls wishing to have their fathers for themselves see the mother as a potential rival for his affections. They too contemplate the banishment or death of the mother, but as with their male counterparts, the anxiety inherent in such thoughts is too great to bear. The mother was not seen by Freud as not so fierce a retaliator as the father, and thus the fear of being hurt by the mother was not as great an issue. There is no castration anxiety for the girl. Instead, Freud thought that girls would see themselves and their mothers as damaged because females lack a penis. Since the girl could not have a penis, she could at least have a baby and earn the father's affection that way. This stage is the source of penis envy, again according to Freud, since in the growing awareness of gender differences, Freud felt that girls would see themselves as lacking a penis and wish for one. Freud felt that the girl's solution to her oedipal conflict is to identify with the mother and to sublimate the wish to have a baby with the father by acting out maternal roles in her play.

This, of course, is an example of the Victorian and Freud's own genderism that emphasized that the female lacked some characteristics of the male, instead of focusing on the valuable characteristics females have in their own right. Since Freud did not have a feminist perspective, he theorized that female development, because it did not have castration anxiety as a component, was less effective in mustering up the anxiety that would insure the more complete superego development that occurred for boys since boys had, according to Freud, more to lose literally if they transgressed from parental standards. Freud, either by cultural training or personal predilections, seems to have had little appreciation of the equality of the genders.

Does the Freudian oedipal theory actually capture the way boys and girls develop? For some it does, but it certainly is not the universal pattern that Freud believed it was. This early view of the developmental tasks of the 3- to 6-year-old child posits an impossible situation in the oedipal conflict. The boy, for instance, must deal with the wishes to both have a father and to kill the same father, since he sees him as a rival. Similarly, the boy wants to have a mother to care for him but he also wants to marry her and have her for a wife. It is impossible to have both simultaneously, and yet the wish for both does not fade easily. The girl in an oedipal conflict faces a similar paradoxical situation, as her wishes to have a mother and a father to care for her come into direct opposition with her wishes to replace her mother and have her father's baby as his wife. This seemingly impossible quandary was tackled by Melanie Klein in her delineation of the resolution of the depressive position. She described a child's need to integrate both loving and hateful feelings toward the loved person in order to foster an attachment deep enough to survive the ambivalence inherent in all relationships. Klein's reformulations broaden developmental issues beyond the heavy sexual and gender emphasis that Freudian theory depended upon.

For Klein, this adaptation to the problems created by both loving and hating the loved one is the conflict that complicates intimate relationships and is a lifelong developmental issue. This theme has been developed further by other object relational, interpersonal, and relational theorists as a key issue in loving relationships. Such reformulations of development have their roots in the first days of life and continue these issues through the years of three to six and beyond. Development is seen less as stage specific and more as a lifespan process. The task for the relational theorist has been to formulate theories about intimate relationships and gender development that are based less on Freud's oedipal model and its inherent dependence on libidinal energy, and more upon research and a closer read of human development. Awareness of gender role and gender behavior is an additional factor that the preschooler has to deal with during these years, adding to the already complex task of integrating and living with love and hate.

Aron (1993, 1995, 1996), in his update of the oedipal stage from a relational perspective, focuses both on (1) the shift from a three-person system to a two-person system of object relations and (2) the development of subjectivity. One-on-one relations with each parent are sometimes replaced with the triangular possibility of being the odd man out when the parents relate to each other and in essence exclude the child. The child is an equal partner in a relationship at one moment and an outside observer at the next—"self-as-subject" versus "self-as-object." The child becomes exposed in a meaningful way to the parents' subjectivity, that is, the parents' subjective opinions of the child. The child realizes that he sometimes is the subject of his parents' perceptions. These subjective representations are taken in by the child as descriptions of who he is in the parents' eyes. In turn, the child lives in his own subjective world where he develops his own views of the parents as objects of his accumulated observations, which influence his participation with his parents in the actual interactions. Thus an intersubjective world (Benjamin 1988) is created in the oedipal triangle, according to Aron, which becomes the prototype of object relations for adult life. "They need to establish a sense of self as a center for action and thought, and they need to view this self in the context of other selves as an object among other objects" (Aron 1996, p. 73).

In a series of contributions, Jessica Benjamin (1991, 1995, 1998) has reorganized our understanding of the oedipal period from a feminist and relational point of view. At first, identification and attachment come hand in hand. Very young boys and girls are intensely identified with and attached to the primary parent, usually the mother. Mothers are experienced negatively as well as positively. Positive images of mother involve a presence who comforts, cares about, contains, and represents the child's emotional states verbally. Negative feelings concern the mother's power of tantalizing, depriving, rejecting, punishing, or leaving. These experiences are threatening in light of young children's own relative passivity and helplessness.

Concurrently children become aware of another adult, such as the father, mother's partner or lover, or a grandparent. The child starts to make discriminations between the primary relationship with mother and this new relationship. These emotional and cognitive distinctions foster separation-individuation. However, the attachment to the other person is used to replace the attachment to the mother only insofar as the relation to the mother is experienced as intrusive or engulfing. Otherwise, if the second person is at all positive, a boy or girl retains positive identifications and wishes with both figures.

At the same time, gender identity is developing. With the growth of cognitive capacities, infants and toddlers represent their own bodies and their parents' bodies symbolically. In turn, parents react differently to boys and girls. Parents handle, address, and direct their sons and daughters in different ways. Toddlers absorb these differences and use them as they learn to represent themselves as male or female (Silverman 1981). Very young children also learn to distinguish male from female according to the evidence used in families for such categories, such as gender-specific clothing or activities. Girls and mothers, and boys and fathers, are grouped together based on such repeated communications and experiences. Core gender identity, the understanding that one is a boy or a girl, gets consolidated in these ways during the period of separation-individuation. It usually precedes learning about the anatomical differences between the sexes (de Marneffe 1997). As it develops, it comes to include a variety of gender-role assignments.

As very young children's images of their parents become more specific and charged with emotion, gender-role identifications change. Flexible notions of masculinity and femininity (based on the "pre-oedipal overinclusiveness" described by Fast [1990]) can become more rigid. Boys and girls react differently. In response to the negative experiences with mothers described above, some boys partially repudiate their identification with and attachment to their mothers. They split off the image of themselves as passive, dependent and helpless, or as overstimulated but frustrated. With familial or societal encouragement, these images of self get disowned and projected onto the boy's developing image of femininity, of what it is to be a girl or woman. Especially if a mother has been experienced as overwhelming, a boy might displace his image of the mother's capacity for activity, her envied power, onto the image of the masculine, represented by the father, with whom the boy then identifies (Benjamin 1998).

This is where the notions of castration anxiety and penis envy come in. These concepts have been criticized from many sides: for their claims to universal truth, for their one-sided emphasis on the envy and valuation of a male attribute, for their underemphasis of boys' envy of girls, for their over-inclusive use of the penis as a symbol, for their inattention to the effect of hostile and traumatic threats made by parents and other caretakers, and for their reduction of power issues to concrete sexual symbols. Roiphe and Galenson (1981) have used observational data in nursery settings to argue the case for the reality of penis envy and castration anxiety, not only as reconstructed ideas in adult psychoanalyses but as clinically visible phenomena in preschool-age children. However, their work has been criticized by de Marneffe (1997) as skewed by their sample, which was said to include families with uninvolved fathers.

In any event, boys start to compare the fact that they have penises with other facts they come to recognize, that girls have vulvas rather than penises, that women grow breasts, get pregnant, give birth to babies, and nurse babies at their breasts. As the cognitive categories of present and absent are created, a boy wonders about his own body. Could he lose his penis and look like a girl? Could he have babies and nurse them? Longing, envy, and fear mix with interest and awe.

For a boy who has learned to value his own body and the bodies of others, these questions do not become emotional problems. But when there is a substantial degree of anxiety, these issues are troubling. One solution is to disavow the envy and devalue the mother as a person without a penis. Thereafter, according to Benjamin, such boys hold images of masculinity that represent wholeness, separateness, assertion, power, autonomy, or the ownership of desires. Their images of femininity are limited to people who are incomplete, who need excessive dependence or connection, who are seen as passive or inferior or the object of desires. The notion of the feminine has now been reserved for people from whose longings for connection and passivity these boys have consciously distanced themselves. Girls and women are seen thereafter as essentially different. These boys see themselves as either not having feminine features, or as having such features inappropriately. This description is the extreme; most boys vary in the degree to which they have rigidly identified themselves with such masculine images.

Very young girls take a different course as they develop an image of themselves as feminine. Like boys, girls in separation-individuation start off identifying with the primary parent, usually the mother, who is seen as active and powerful. They face the same fears as boys do regarding the mother's power of tantalizing, depriving, rejecting, punishing, or leaving them. As with boys, these experiences can be threatening for girls, in light of their own relative passivity and helplessness. In the rapprochement period of separation-individuation, girls resolve some of the difficulties by turning toward the parent who seems to come and go more in the world (Chodorow 1994). If that parent is the father, then the toddler's experience of a love affair with mobility and exploration gets attached to the father and to the interesting new world he inhabits and represents.

When the father is loved but absent, or when he rejects his daughter's wish to identify with him, a little girl might start to focus on differences, including genital differences, between herself and the father whom she longs for and whom she longs to be similar to. If penis envy develops in this context, as a sign of one of these differences, it carries with it the longing for the father and the frustrated wish to identify with him (Benjamin 1998). On the other hand, when such a girl has a mother who facilitates her separation-individuation, who comes and goes herself, and who supports (by her own example and by direct encouragement) her daughter's desires for involvement and mastery, it is easier for the girl to focus on the father without such an urgent need for his recognition. As a consequence of such a relation with the mother, even when such a father rejects his daughter's wish to identify with him, there is less need for the girl to inspect herself and him to see what it is about her that would keep her from being like him. Under these circumstances, independence, initiative, and mastery are not so rigidly assigned exclusively to the masculine role. The girl can identify with both dependent and independent functioning in both parents, and the fact of having male or female body parts is less linked to rigidly held roles of what boys and girls can and cannot do.

Preoedipal boys and girls retain substantial portions of cross-sex identifications and same-sex attachments. Over time the various pressures to conform to the culture's gender role and gender-identity stereotypes may drive nonconforming identifications and attachments out of conscious awareness, but such pressures are not universal. Imagine a traditional family where the father is the one who enjoys sports and the mother does not, and the mother takes care of the baby and the father does not. If the father is equally enthusiastic for his daughter and his son when attending their sports events, or if the mother expects and teaches her son as well as her daughter to take care of the baby, then the gender expectations that their children develop are inclusive and not rigid. Such children are able to retain more flexible definitions of masculinity and femininity.

During the oedipal years of 3 to 6, children apply another cognitive development to the understanding of their experience, namely the capacity to understand triangular relations. By the age of three or four, children realize that the relations in which they are involved have consequences beyond their immediate situation, affecting a social network in which they participate. A boy or girl will realize or fantasize that pursuing a wish with one parent may lead another person (a sibling, a parent) to have feelings about the child for having that wish (Greenberg 1991).

For example, Freud described the triangular situation of the boy's oedipal complex. In this description, a boy comes to fear that his longing for an exclusive, even incestuous relation with his mother, and his hostile envy of his father's preferred position with his mother, would evoke his father's retaliation via castration or a symbolic equivalent. According to Freud, this fear arises especially after a boy sees that girls do not have penises, a sight that he interprets as confirming the possibility of castration. The outcome for the boy is to give up the competition for the mother in fear, to cede the field to the father and to identify with him rather to continue to experience him as a threatening rival.

Later writers have considered this description incomplete. Greenberg (1991), for example, focused on other feelings involved in the oedipal triangle for boys. Oedipal boys do not feel simply jealous, rivalrous, hostile, and afraid with their fathers. They also love them and are concerned and guilty about the effect of their hostility on them. Many boys want to stay loyal to their fathers despite oedipal rivalry.

For girls, Horney added a corrective to the Freudian motive regarding the longing for a father (Rubins 1978). Girls turn toward their fathers not just to supply a missing penis or a baby, as in Freud's original view, but as a new person to desire and love. As with boys, there can follow genuine feelings of rivalry toward the mother, to want to have her place with the father and to want to be the one to have babies with him. The daughter also gets concerned regarding the effects of this rivalry, on herself and on her mother. Melanie Klein (1975) described girls who are anxious over their mothers' possible anger and retaliation. She believed that such girls then interpret their lack of a penis as a sign that they have already been punished in retaliation for their rivalrous feelings. These considerations lead some girls to forgo the urgent longing for the father and his baby. Dropping the competition with mother, these girls turn to an identification as feminine that includes diminished entitlement to sexual longing, but allows a future as a woman who can have babies like her mother. Other components of their gender-role identification are influenced by both parents' approved images of femininity.

When children are discouraged from including active, powerful, and lusty images in their images of femininity, and when they are not taught that the genitals and bodies of both sexes are equally substantial and valuable, they tend rigidly to identify male with the culture's images of masculinity, and female with cultural images of femininity. Criticizing this trend, modern feminist and relational points of view see masculinity and femininity not as an identity but a multiplicity (Benjamin 1998). Rather than masculine and feminine imagery being normatively correlated with male and female, girls are seen as having the potential for independence, activity, and desire, and boys are seen as having the potential for passivity, connection, and responsiveness. Each sex also envies what the other sex has. This engenders anxiety for both sexes, especially during the oedipal period. Parents respond to their children's envy and interest with their own combination of acceptance and disapproval. In this view, there will always be a tension between the simple categories of male and female, on the one hand, and the more complex multiplicity of masculine and feminine aspects of boys' and girls' identities, on the other hand. Theory can then be freed from normative thinking, and brought more in line with clinical realities of boys' and girls' actual experience. From this perspective, marrying and having children becomes one of a variety of normative ways of becoming male or female, freeing alternative ways of being an adult (such as gay, lesbian, single, or childless adults) from a theoretical pall.

A successful outcome of the oedipal period is to be able to live with ambivalence toward parents, siblings, and eventually friends. This means that a child can envy them while still loving them, can wish them out of the way while still wanting them around. Another successful outcome is to become familiar with one's own inner psychic reality, to experience some ownership and sense of belonging regarding one's needs, feelings, wishes, and interpersonal experiences, and so to be able to live with them, rather than to experience them as unfamiliar and uncomfortable, requiring urgent action to tolerate.

3

Grade School Years and Parental Development

As we noted in Chapter 1, models of development and therapy have different emphases, especially the models we characterize as one-person and two-person models. As children grow through the grade school years and spend their days in classrooms with other children, it becomes harder and harder to model this experience with notions of development that understand growth primarily as something arising from internal forces and occuring primarily within the mind of the child. In this chapter, as we use models to describe the growth of children over the course of elementary school, we find the two-person models of relationship especially useful.

Early models of child development assumed that development needed a motor. The classic psychoanalytic model postulated sexual drives that spurred development. It focused on inner psychosexual development because of the centrality that the theory gave to sexual drives as prime motivators. In this model, other people were important as sources of (or barriers to) instinctual satisfaction. The psyche developed a separate structure, the ego, in order to handle the outside world so as to satisfy the instincts. Ego psychology was then developed (Anna Freud 1936) to account for relations with others by making "object relations" (relations with actual people, internal images of these relations, or internal images of partial aspects of these relations) one of the many functions of the ego.

Concurrently, Jean Piaget (1937) was building a model of cognitive development that assumed that a drive for adaptation spurred development. In this model, cognitive development occurred as the outcome of mental processes such as accommodating schemata to new experiences, and assimilating new experiences to existing schemata. In the Piagetian model, as in the psychoanalytic model, there was an invariant hierarchy of increasingly complex stages of development, each including previous stages.

Both models looked at children's development as an objective process in an objective psychic structure. They are described in more detail later in this chapter. In both models the engine for change was internal and change occurred internally, even though the need for the change derived from interaction with the environment. We see these models as "one-person" models because of the conception that the change engine and the change process were occurring inside the individual.

We contrast these models with "two-person" models that, as noted above, assume that development occurs in a social context. While acknowledging the importance of the body's needs for satisfaction and the mind's tendency to adapt to new experiences, two-person models understand these processes as occurring primarily in the context of interpersonal motives and situations. One consequence of this point of view is that development, moving forward according to the variety of social situations in which children live, proceeds in a less lockstep, more various way than in the hierarchy of stages described in the one-person models.

Within psychoanalysis, the one-person model started to change with the advent of the psychoanalytic school of object relations (Fairbairn 1952, Sandler and Rosenblatt 1962; see also Greenberg and Mitchell 1983). In an object relations point of view, foreground and background were reversed. Object relations and their internalized representations were seen as the primary context for development. The object relations theorists were the first psychoanalysts in Europe to propose that people were basically object-seeking rather than instinct-gratifying. Nonetheless, their focus was still on the development of internal representations of others. In the United States, Sullivan (1953) was developing a fully interpersonal theory of psychiatry, a developmental and clinical theory based on actual interaction over the course of infancy, childhood, and adolescence.

The developmental viewpoint we are presenting combines the interpersonal focus on actual relationships with the object relations description of an internalized world of relations (Pantone 1995). Bodily needs and mental processes are seen as the source of important inner experience whose meaning is largely derived from the child's relational world. In this context, change and growth can be understood as occurring both intrapsychically and interpersonally. Even in the earlier models, development was seen as occurring through interaction with others and with the environment. Some of the concepts of the early models can be retained, but the primary context is now seen as the child's growing relation with the world, especially the human world, as well as its internalized representations.

We expect to find that growth is holistic, with links that correlate the development of emotion, cognition, and social relations. In this expectation we agree with academic research developmentalists such as Sroufe (1995). We are aiming for a unified description of growth that includes individual differences as well as normative change. As children interact with others, the meaning of their behavior, its context and function, all become increasingly complex. New developments rely on prior functioning. Earlier structures influence later developments, but they do not predetermine what will emerge. The relation with the external world and with significant others has a continuing importance throughout development, for healthy change as well as for pathological developments. When development is seen as emerging in the context of ongoing relationships, there is an optimism for positive change (as well as a concern for the impact of trauma) at all stages of life.

We approach developmental models without assuming that linear progress in a model implies health. We think of mental health as requiring the flexibility to let an action or a feeling be experienced on several developmental levels at once, according to the current interpersonal need. Similarly, we find that mental health requires the ability to traverse developmental stages back and forth according to the anxieties and opportunities of the moment. We go into more detail regarding assumptions about mental health and psychopathology in Chapter 6.

INDIVIDUAL DIFFERENCES

Developmental norms show common patterns over childhood in the growth of peer relations, in cognitive and psychosexual responses, in the sense of self, and in moral sensibilities. There are also common patterns of growth for parents over these years. Yet individually, children move along paths specific to themselves, interacting with the others in their lives. Individuality shapes these interactions, and interactions with others in turn gives meaning to individual experience. Relationship and individual experience are intertwined.

Children vary, and they develop variously, in their bodies, within their families, between families, in relation to peers and other adults, as students, in their sociocultural environment, and regarding chance incidents that occur to them. In most of these domains, interaction with others gives meaning to the individual experience. Developmental norms have been seen as useful for orienting therapists to areas of psychological growth that are problematic or underlie the presenting problems. They can also be useful for setting goals and for gauging progress over the course of therapy. However, they only describe general patterns of reaction. The specific details, the subjective meaning to a particular child, the personal significance of events, all develop within the child's own relational matrix. No single developmental scheme has priority of place, and each developmental matrix is most useful once we describe the particular relational context within which the level of development is being assessed.

Children are individuals in their bodies. They are able-bodied or disabled, healthy or chronically ill. They are tall or short, fat or thin, wiry or with low motor tone, graceful or clumsy. They are male or female. They are likely to become homosexual or heterosexual. Whether or not they are born with temperamental differences, such differences become apparent early on and function as if they were constitutional. Other traits are also recognized as influenced substantially by genetics. These include differences in the overall rate of maturation as well as differences in the rates of maturation of different lines of development. There are also inborn differences in degree of curiosity, shyness versus readiness for social engagement, introversion, adaptability, and propensity to a variety of developmental and psychopathological disorders (Neubauer and Neubauer 1990).

Children are individuals in their families. They are born into their families, they are adopted, or they are put out for placement. Parent–child match and mismatch have tremendous influence. Birth order and siblings affect children in profound ways. A child will be an only child, a first child, second, middle, or last-born child. The family of a first-born child presents a different social mix than the family of her younger sister. A younger sister grows up with an older sibling and with older, more experienced parents. The kinds of language stimulation, the unconscious demands for role performance, the parents' patience or impatience vary for each new child in the family. These factors also vary, although to a lesser extent, for each individual child over the course of family life.

Children are individuals in that they come from different families. Parents' models of interaction and their representational worlds (Sandler and Rosenblatt 1962) set much of the worldview and expectation for their children's images of relationships. A family's (and especially the parents') management of anxiety has profound effects on children's development, defenses, security operations, communication style, and sense of self. Children are influenced by their parents' mix of flexibility and rigidity, breadth or narrowness of focus, love or intolerance, self-centeredness or responsiveness. As noted in the last chapter, children are deeply influenced by their parents' attachment styles. These vary from family to family. So do the ways in which parental stimulation and attunement can be helpful or unhelpful. Neglect, physical and sexual abuse, substance abuse by parents or older siblings, depression or other mental illness in the family, all influence a child's growth.

Children are individuals in relation to peers and adults outside of the family. With authority figures, some children rebel and some comply. Some are adept at seeking nurturance and being winsome with adults, and others are poor at this and find themselves neglected. With their peers, children are leaders, followers, bullies, protectors, instigators, mediators, nurturers, provocateurs, included or excluded. Some use pretense and excuse; some are boldly (or awkwardly) direct.

Children vary in their primary out-of-home environment, namely in school. They are smart or dull in the areas valued by the school. They are capable in no area that the school values, in one area, or in many. They are confident or insecure as learners. They value school learning or they have no patience for it. They can focus or they are dreamy; they attend or they do not.

Children vary individually in terms of the sociocultural circumstances of their lives. Poverty or wealth, medical care, physical environment, nutrition, socioeconomic status, immigration, level of community peace or violence, and the nature and quality of school and classrooms—all vary enormously in shaping children's lives. Families vary in race, religion, culture, and in the opportunities and limits of growing up in these groups. Families also differ in the degree of their marginality or embeddedness in relation to the key group identities in their community and neighborhood. Children's individual identity, aspiration, and opportunities are influenced heavily by these factors.

Children also vary by the chance incidents that occur to them. These incidents mean different things to children at different stages of development. Consider the possible impacts on a child of three and on a child of thirteen of any of the following incidents: a community disaster, a death in the family, parents' divorce or remarriage, illness, accident or hospitalization, moves, periods of parental unemployment, the arrival of a new baby in the family, parents' military service, or the departure of an older sibling. The effect of incidents or trauma such as these arise out of the meaning they have for a child, meaning that varies according to a child's prior experience and current social-support system.

We now review some of the common dimensions for understanding children as they grow through the grade school years. These include developmental frameworks for understanding children's peer relations, cognitive and psychosexual responses, and the sense of self and of morality. Then we will discuss the parallel development of parents as their children grow through these years. However, assumptions of relative maturity and immaturity cannot be made simply by "placing" a child's functioning along these lines. Judgments of successful adaptation and response depend heavily on the meaning of a child's responses in light of the particular stresses and challenges she has faced in all the areas of individual experience described above, in the context of her most important relationships. We will expand this theme later, in the chapter on psychopathology.

DEVELOPMENT OF PEER RELATIONS

We do not agree with Judith Harris (1998) that parenting has little influence on children, compared to peer relations. However, it is clear that relationships with other children of roughly the same age are highly influential in development. Over the years of middle childhood, earlier forms of play become more social. Play develops from solitary play, to looking at other children in play, to parallel play, to associative play and (by the years of middle childhood) to cooperative play. Issues of sharing and turn-taking continue to develop. A sense of reciprocity becomes internalized, which is critical to the growing sense of morality in peer relations. This is the period for learning to play by rules, to recognize the play partner's rights and feelings, to distinguish pretend roles from real roles, and to negotiate the mutual use of imagination in developing a play theme.

As oedipal rebellion resolves, rules become internalized as a familiar set of assumptions, part of the background of life. Children can rebel against them, become skillful with them, or try to win by them. Motives to achieve arise in the context of rules. Play becomes structured and formal games become common. Children agree to win or lose games by the same rules. When these rules are flexible, their negotiation becomes a forum for learning about competition, compromise, and cooperation. Children learn to exert influence on their own behalf while they also act considerately. They learn to claim their own interest while acknowledging the other child's bids for influence. Certain areas of psychopathology occur when children are extreme in their handling of rules. For example, an excessively rule-bound child loses touch with his or her own wishes and impulses and can become obsessive or compulsive (perhaps joined by an inborn propensity in this direction); a child who ignores rules becomes egocentric, immature, or conduct disordered.

Friendship develops. Ordinarily, children learn how to be friends through playing. Morality in peer relations starts to include empathy, caring, giving aid, and fairness. Younger children learn to avoid overt conflict with their close friends by creating a climate of agreement, always seeking similarity. As egocentrism declines in later childhood, there is more tolerance of differences and disagreements between friends. Concurrently, the feeling of friendship shifts from admiring and liking one another to a deeper sense of intimacy and trust in preadolescence (usually with a friend of the same sex).

THE WORK OF HARRY STACK SULLIVAN

Sullivan (1953) offered a theory of development based on interaction. In his time, this was a radical innovation. His point of view was very different from the reigning developmental models, such as the Freudian process of an inner unfolding driven by objective forces such as libido (Freud 1905) or the Piagetian process of mental structure built up through cognitive adaptation (Piaget 1937). In these one-person models, either relationships had to be managed to serve drive discharge, or they were the source of material for mental assimilation and accommodation. In Sullivan's two-person model, relationships were put into the foreground—the relational needs for interpersonal security and relief from anxiety; for intimacy and relief from loneliness; and for people with whom to get basic needs satisfied. Sullivan's theory conveyed his belief in the profound ability of new relationships to influence prior patterns of living, allowing reworking of earlier "warps" in personality but also allowing previously healthy children to fall under the influence of "malevolent transformations."

Sullivan examined how children learn to socialize with peers in the context of the development of what he called the self-system, namely, a person's ability to maintain self-esteem and minimize anxiety. Early in childhood, boys and girls figure out how to get their way even when authority opposes it. To avoid the anxiety of punishment, they learn to conceal, to deceive, and to make excuses and rationalizations. They learn to act, at first dramatically and then more smoothly, like the authority, in relation to peers and to imaginary partners. They start to conceal their anger and experience resentment instead.

When open anger is consistently likely to elicit punishment and anxiety, children might become passive-aggressive. Alternately, they might become bullies. Then such children take out their feelings of resentment on fellow peers via angry dramatizations of themselves as the authority. When children repeatedly discover that asking for tenderness leads to being teased or hurt or anxious, they start to act as if they live among enemies. As a result they become belligerent and mistrusting, an unfortunate development that Sullivan called a malevolent transformation.

If children do not have play partners, they become lonely and make up imaginary companions. However, as they move into the school years, they learn to make the critical distinction between fantasy and reality so as not to be laughed at or punished regarding their attachment to imaginary friends. The attachment to imaginary companions then diminishes, to be replaced by the need for peers to play with. In the elementary school years, which Sullivan called the juvenile years, children need the acceptance of peers for play and other socializing, without needing the kind of intimacy that develops in preadolescence.

The grade school years are a time for learning to subordinate one's wishes in order to cope with bullies and with adult authorities, and to accommodate the varieties of lifestyle the child comes across. Sullivan noted how cruel some children can be in their insensitivity to other's feelings, to the importance of other people and to everyone else's need for personal worth. In reaction to peers' crudely direct criticisms, children are highly motivated to learn when subordination and accommodation are useful in avoiding teasing and anxiety.

Children also learn what can be done with impunity. Occasions for competition, compromise, and conformity are everywhere. These occasions afford the child the chance to learn how to protect self-esteem through realizing what is approved and through learning ways of relating that feel secure. During these years children learn more of the skills of selective inattention. Children inattend to those wishes, feelings, interests, and concerns whose expression elicits responses from others that make the child unbearably anxious.

This is also the time for inclusion, exclusion, and ostracism. Peers' judgment of a child's reputation is occasion for painful or satisfying experiences regarding the child's self-esteem. Children realize the opportunities for support and empathy from friends. However, they also learn that other children might denigrate them in order to enhance their own self-esteem, or that they themselves can publicly and cruelly denigrate other children to enhance their own self-esteem. This is also the time of developing stereotypes, with pressure to adopt them in order not to suffer ostracism and disparagement.

Boys and girls develop their own ways of using the group to enhance self-esteem. Areas of commonality outweigh the differences, yet a significant percentage of boys' and girls' security operations are gender-specific by the end of grade school. For example, in factor-analytic studies of the classification of child psychopathology, Achenbach and Edelbrock (1978) found that the category of social cruelty was frequent enough to be included in their taxonomy, but only for girls in grades four through six. Anecdotes abound of the exclusive cliques that girls join over these years. Many boys find more physical ways to enhance their self-esteem through group participation, especially in aggressive competition in sports, on the playground or on the street. However, further research may show that such gender differences vary enormously by culture, by socioeconomic class, and by variety of gender role preference.

Children develop the cognitive ability of foresight, and they apply it in internal processes Sullivan terms the "spectator" and the "hearer." In these processes, children learn to recognize how they appear and sound to other children and adults. They guide much of their behavior with foresight regarding what elicits anxiety-provoking or security-enhancing responses.

Sometimes "social handicaps" make anxiety-provoking responses from others unavoidable. Among these handicaps, Sullivan included lack of popularity, poor ability at sports, lack of intelligence, shyness, physical disability, chronic illness, an alcoholic parent, or frequent moves.

In Sullivan's view, a school child's primary motivations are the need for the acceptance of peers and the need to avoid anxiety. There is one exception, namely the value of learning an orientation in living. Sullivan wrote that a child can emerge from this period oriented in living if he knows his needs and how to satisfy them without undue anxiety. Yet a healthy child will also know other "remote goals" for which he will forego the satisfaction of needs or prestige. Otherwise, children of grade school age might protect their self-esteem by excessive compromise, yielding on everything. Lacking an orientation in living, such children live only to please, to be liked, or to amuse. But Sullivan does not elaborate how these "remote goals" are developed.

In preadolescence, the need for the acceptance of peers is supplemented by the need for intimate exchange with a best friend. This chum, in Sullivan's terms, is a friend whose happiness, prestige, and self-worth matter to the child. A chumship is an intimate, one-to-one relation with a peer of about the same age and interests, and usually the same sex. Since a preadolescent child experiences a chum as important, the effort is to please the chum, to meet the chum's needs. Ideally this occurs before adolescence. Having a best friend prevents loneliness and alleviates anxiety, while also promoting social skills, competence, and status. There are long talks and largely uninhibited communication as close friends check each other's understanding about shared experiences and reach for a mutually validated consensus. A child is sensitive to the individual needs of a chum in a more particular way, beyond the need for compromise. Since this is mutual, an intimacy develops that allows a validation of each other's personal worth. Sullivan believed that without an experience of this kind of chumship, it is harder in later life to feel at ease and to enjoy experience with same-sex peers.

Preadolescent chumships interlock in the form of cliques or gangs. The most popular members are friendly with a large number of children and become the leaders of opinion or of influence. The gang develops its own opinions of each member's best friend. Different leaders emerge for different group activities. They can offer their peers reassurance, foresight, or a sense of certainty as to outcomes. Playing in groups also helps children experiment with other social roles—initiator, suggestor, critic, confuser, therapist, joiner, quitter, spoiler, savior, hero, villain, and so forth.

Sullivan emphasized the influence of the current interpersonal context on a child's continuing adjustment. Rather than to see character as fixed by the end of the oedipal period, this attribution of influence to relationships over the course of childhood leads to a more flexible picture. Children can be profoundly helped (or hurt) by their relations at all stages of development. For example, by affording a sensitivity and attunement to the child's needs and security, chumships in preadolescence can correct warped ideas about self and other. There are egocentric children with unlimited expectation of attention and services who often get avoided or even ostracized. Yet once they find a best friend, perhaps someone egocentric like themselves, they can get to know themselves as others see them. With a chum who cares about them and their prestige, they can learn to change. Of course, they can also go further, with their chums, in antisocial directions.

Malevolent children also find chums, usually in the context of a gang. Yet sometimes these children find that the experience of being treated tenderly (which Sullivan understood as the tendency to satisfy another person's needs) ameliorates their malevolence. After all, the conviction of living among enemies originally arose in the conviction that the need for tenderness would elicit only teasing and hurt, and chumship can overturn that conviction.

Vain children get to review their sense of entitlement to being universally admired, by comparing their real and imagined traits with a close friend. They can also more or less safely review their tendency to disparage others when they are inevitably disappointed in their expectation of admiration for their traits. As a consequence, their previous vanity can be mitigated. To look at oneself through one's close friend's eyes allows a great deal of repair, according to Sullivan.

Isolated school children may delay entering the chumships of preadolescence. But once such children make best friends, they can learn skills of social accommodation that they missed earlier, preventing a fuller schizoid development thereafter. Immature or irresponsible children, unwilling to adjust to life's necessities, may benefit as well. Gifted children realize the need to use their gifts tactfully and responsibly when relating to their best friends, so as to avoid having to confront their friends and themselves with occasions for unmitigated envy. Teachers' pets learn to enter more fully into peer society, through the chumship. Children with the various social handicaps described earlier can catch up, through a chumship, on opportunities for normal socialization they may have missed earlier on.

Sullivan describes some difficulties that can arise during the passage out of preadolescence and into adolescence. When a child who is ready for preadolescence and is searching for a chum finds a friend who has already developed into adolescence and is ready to sexualize the relation, serious misunderstandings can ensue—especially for preadolescents who lack an orientation in living as Sullivan defines it. For these children the intense need for intimacy, to overcome loneliness, leads to poor judgment in choice of friends.

Sullivan's description of the preadolescent chumship is quite idealized. In its seriousness, it also understates the playful aspects of friendship. In addition its universality has not been established. Nor is it certain that preadolescence is a critical period for fostering later intimate attachments. Central to our argument in this book is that the relational context remains vital (for movements toward psychopathology as well as toward mental health) throughout the life span. Neither the oedipal period nor preadolescence is so critical that later positive developments cannot undo injuries that are suffered during those periods.

COGNITIVE AND PSYCHOSEXUAL MODELS

A two-person model such as Sullivan's focuses on interpersonal relations as the proper locale in which to understand development, and sees development as organized by the interpersonal needs for security and intimacy. As mentioned earlier, other models, such as those for cognitive and psychosexual development, have focused on the child's mind as the locale for development. These one-person models see development as driven by internal forces such as adaptation (Piaget 1937) or libido (Anna Freud 1936, 1965). They are widespread in the literature on child development and therapy, and contribute detailed descriptions of impersonal processes and mechanisms that are seen as underlying behavior and experience. Since they organize a great deal of clinical data, they are summarized here.

Cognitive developmental frameworks are "one-person" models in which the growth of modes of thought is seen as something that occurs internally. In the cognitive model, children achieve the ability to represent reality, as well as simple relations within reality, by the time they begin school (Piaget 1937). This allows them an understanding of social roles, of people interacting in roles, and of people looking at one another from different perspectives. Over the course of later childhood, most children realize that trying to fulfill their own wishes occurs in the context of the goals of others. This leads to less egocentricity and more taking of perspective, a greater sensitivity to others' views and to others as reinforcers of the child's own behavior.

A cognitive reorganization occurs at the age of 7, plus or minus a year (Shapiro and Perry 1976). At this age, nerve myelinization advances, EEG alpha wave patterns stabilize, and there is a new spurt in growth in frontal areas of the brain. Laterality develops and attention span increases. Children become more capable of reality testing and planning (taking trial actions in thought). The stage of thought that Piaget described as concrete operations develops. In this stage, children become capable of cognitive capacities such as the understanding of the conservation of amount, weight, and volume. They also become capable of constructing complex solutions to problems in social perspective, such as recognizing how one person feels in relation to another person, or learning to identify with another person.

By the end of childhood (ages 10 to 12), the early stages of formal operations begin. With this development, children can develop hypotheses, construct abstractions, and generalize across concrete instances. However, these cognitive developments are uneven in speed, varying by child, situation, and culture. They are usually limited to particular content areas, rather than being available as general cognitive tools (Feldman and Elliott 1990).

The cognitive developments of early childhood provide the neurological capacity for the psychosexual reorganizations of the middle childhood period. This period is referred to as "latency" in the classic psychoanalytic literature, focusing on a supposedly quiet period in instinctual development. From this point of view, sexual as well as hostile interest in family members becomes repressed and sublimated into the capacity for fantasy and symbolization. These interests are also channeled into striving for success and mastery in reading, academic study, sports, and in the social environment in the school. Such repression and sublimation depend upon the achievement of cognitive distinctions between reality and fantasy, and concept and object. Although the concept of latency of conscious sexual feelings has been debunked (Constantine and Martinson 1981), the cognitive structure of latency is worth examining.

Sarnoff (1976), linking cognitive and psychosexual frameworks of development, described three cognitive organizing periods in the creation, maintenance, and dissolution of the "structure of latency." By ages 5 to 6, the new capacity for repression transforms simple metaphorical symbols into psychoanalytic ones. In this process, access to consciousness of anxiety-laden oedipal wishes and fears is denied by riveting attention to something else. The new object of conscious attention becomes the psychoanalytic symbol—a monster, ghost, fairy, or a vague looming figure. Imaginary companions also are present and continue to receive and express displaced, unacceptable impulses, affects, and wishes.

By ages 7 or 8, fantasy objects become more human-like and more culturally shared. There is a shift in thinking from fantasy objects to reality objects. This comes about with the maturation of concrete operations. There is also an improvement in memory. Children use names and labels more effectively to represent more complex ideas and references. Reading and writing give secondary-process elaboration to primary-process thoughts. Under the influence of repression, drawings often become more structured, less creative and individualistic. Finally, with greater perspective-taking ability, empathic ability develops, deepening friendships.

With preadolescence (ages 10 to 12) there is further growth in orientation to the knowledge of the world as it is and to the real qualities of one's peers. Fantasy now concerns real people rather than imaginary ones. Gradually the structure of latency crumbles under the pressures of puberty. Reality testing interferes with the use of fantasy as an outlet for intense longing for a sexual and intimate partner, since it becomes obvious that fantasy is not as satisfying as a real intimate relation. Adolescence begins.

Sarnoff's cognitive view of psychosexual development over the course of the grade school years can be compared to the classical psychosexual model of psychosexual development. Here the focus is on the libido, its drives and its compromises with the ego. In assessing normal and pathological development, Anna Freud (1965) examined sequences of libidinal development (oral, anal, phallic, genital, latency, adolescent) and ego development (progress in the sense of reality, in defensive activity, in morality). She built her concept of developmental lines with these ideas, noting the maturation of independence, eating, bladder and bowel control, other areas of body management, companionship, use of toys, and ability to work. Linking id and ego psychology, she described the relative progress, regression, and fixation of ego and drive along these developmental lines. She noted the effects of unevenness in the rate of progression between drive, ego, and superego development.

Anna Freud also explored what happened when the child regresses due to stress, moving backward along the various developmental lines she described. Children regress both in drive and in ego development. Regression in drive involves the concept of fixation. In this view, psychological drives develop via attaching themselves to objects that serve satisfaction at each libidinal stage. However, no way-station is ever fully outgrown. Portions of drive remain behind, stuck like drops of liquid in the side of a channel, fixated or tied to earlier aims and objects. Clinically relevant fixation of drive is caused by stress or trauma, either via excessive gratification or frustration. In this view, trauma blocks the forward motion of psychic energy, forcing it backward to an earlier fixation point. Then the clinical picture is typical of developmental functioning at that fixation point, and thereafter less drive energy is available "down the channel" for more advanced psychological functioning.

In this model, regression also occurs in the level of ego development. Some regression is seen as normal, such as occasional returns to more infantile behavior at bedtime, during illness, when "getting the giggles," or during unusual separations. Under chronic stress, regression can occur in the defenses, seen as one aspect of ego functioning. In denial, for example, the real world is seen less accurately; in repression, the inner world is attended to less; in reaction formation, anxiety-associated affect is replaced with its opposite; in projection, anxiety-arousing elements in one's image of self are attributed to the object world. Regression might be temporary, but (in this view) it can also last so long that the reinstatement of formerly reached levels will not occur without therapeutic intervention.

In the classical psychoanalytic view of psychosexual development, turmoil in normal children is due to different rates of progress along different developmental lines, and to unevenness due to various regressions. Pathology is understood intrapsychically, with less regard to a child's actual relationships. Pathology occurs when temporary regression becomes permanent through developmental fixation or arrest; when id derivatives increase in strength; when ego functions decrease in strength, as with chronic illness or strain; or when there are changes in the environmental opportunity for obtaining satisfaction (loss, separation, deprivation, trauma). Here environmental strain and support are finally acknowledged. However, the focus of this model is on an internal balance between the child's ego functioning and drive derivatives.

GROWTH IN THE SENSE OF SELF

Unlike the classical psychoanalytic model of child development, most models of the growth of the self over childhood are relational models. Cultural, family, and interpersonal settings are all seen as central in affecting this growth. Individualism, with its valuing of independence, autonomy, and self-reliance, is not always the norm in different cultures and subcultures (Weisner 1984; see also Chapter 5, this volume). There are culturally specific norms of power and control, of expectations of privacy, of gender roles, and of separation of various role performances. One culture might consider the social and public self to be a more real self than the private self. There, the public self and the consequent propensity for shame become internalized and normative. A culture that requires children to work in order to support the family might expect early compliance. It might use stern discipline and show less warmth or positive regard in child care. Such socialization practices would lead to different standards for normality than a culture that values positive regard, independence, and flexible discipline.

Within different cultural contexts, children grow in their conceptions of themselves, of themselves in relation to others, and in their sense of identity and emotional self-regard. Children come to define and recognize themselves in several ways. They distinguish themselves from others, moving from more concrete, ascribed characteristics (for example, name or gender) to more personal characteristics, beliefs, and identifications, such as the social groups they belong to (Markus and Nurius 1984). Next, children develop in their understanding of the social world and of their appropriate role and conduct in it. They come to understand the complexity of role relations ("I am my parent's child and my uncle's nephew"). They learn that people, including themselves, can be complicated and contradictory (for example, both nice and mean) at different times.

Children also develop in their sense of identity and in their emotional self-regard. As children develop a sense of self and of their place in a social world, they learn to distinguish subjective selves from objective selves. Subjectively, they learn what they feel, want, think, act, plan, and know; yet they also learn how they are defined and categorized objectively in the eyes of others. Over time, children learn to coordinate these two sets of selves into a growing sense of identity. For example, acquiring new skills allows a child to consider new domains for defining herself, especially as others acknowledge her new competence. Erikson (1959) found that children of school age identify themselves according to the achievements of their industriousness and their learning, as reflected by their parents and school. When this goes well, the child can say, "I am someone who can make and learn, like my peers and like the grownups," perhaps undoing feelings of inferiority and lack of control dating from the oedipal period.

As a child learns new skills, she finds that she is competent or inadequate at something particular, whereas before this, self-definition did not exist. The focus is on one's own ego mastery as reflected by others and internalized into one's identity, rather than on modes of handling discharge of internal tension, which was the focus of earlier models of psychoanalysis. The expressive modes of this period, according to a relational revision of Erikson's theory (Blatt and Blass 1990), are industry or lack of industriousness, with the associated self-feelings of confidence or inferiority. A child comes to know and feel herself as capable or incapable in her own eyes and in the eyes of others.

Self-esteem is the emotional aspect of reflected self-appraisals and self-expressions. When the child has coordinated subjective and external definitions of herself that are positive, she will feel good most of the time. When she appraises herself as better or worse than the view of herself held by those around her, she might feel misunderstood, anxious, mystified, undervalued, or resentful, with consequent behavior difficulties and emotional difficulties. When she and those around her agree that she is of low value, masochistic or depressive reactions might result. Alternately, she might be drawn into delinquent identifications with valued gang leaders.

MORAL DEVELOPMENT

Children develop moral standards for their own behavior among adults and peers, and develop strategies for controlling themselves according to these standards. Over the twentieth century there were various schemes of normative moral development proposed; we will review those of Freud, Bornstein, Piaget, and Kohlberg. Classical psychoanalytic theory limited itself to explaining moral development as the developmental outcome of certain rather rigid kinds of heterosexual gender role identifications. For example, Freud (1923) believed that the superego was the heir to the oedipus complex, meaning that a child comes to identify with the parents' rules after giving up the earlier, oedipal hope of possessing the opposite-sex parent and ousting the same-sex parent. From this point of view, morality is established by the beginning of the grade school years. Bornstein (1951), continuing the psychoanalytic description of the development of morality over childhood, found two stages. At first there is a harsh, rigid superego, aided by new defenses such as reaction formation (turning a libidinal interest into its opposite, such as transforming pleasure in messiness into disgust) or sublimation (deriving pleasure from culturally more acceptable forms of gratification, such as reading about romance or playing aggressive sports). In this first stage, there is an alternation between obedience, rebellion, and self-reproach. Guilt is hard to tolerate and is dealt with through moral masochism ("Spank me") or projection of guilt ("It's his fault, not mine").

In the second half of childhood the superego becomes less rigid, Bornstein found, and denial of unacceptable impulses becomes so effective that the child forgets large parts of his earlier childhood. Therefore, less energy has to be put into suppressing unacceptable impulses and guilt is more easily tolerated. New standards that derive more from the peer culture than from the family are internalized, and the superego becomes more autonomous of parental authority.

Piaget (1932) used a different, cognitive perspective in his four stages of the growth of morality over childhood. First, rules are solely external reactions. Next, the letter of the law is to be imposed regardless of its effect. Then, the spirit of the rule is understood and the child knows it should be obeyed, but the rule is still seen as emanating from external authority. Finally, the rule is internalized as a belief in respect and cooperation. From this point of view, morality is established only at the end of the grade school years.

Kohlberg (1969) developed a scheme of six stages of moral development. At first, the good is only what is rewarded. Next, good is whatever people can compromise on, distribute fairly, or agree to exchange, attending to the other's need only insofar as it interferes with one's own wishes. What is good is to put oneself in the other's position and to care about pleasing the other person. After that, good is conceived of as doing one's duty and obeying the law, which organizes the satisfaction of the interests of self and others. Later still, in this scheme of development, good is separated from social and conventional concerns, and is seen as arising out of basic rights that may conflict with societal laws. In the last stage, good derives from universal principles of justice that are the basis for societal law.

However, this last stage of morality was later dropped from Kohlberg's scheme as insupportable. Indeed, this whole influential system of a sequence of invariant stages of moral development was later criticized as culturally biased (Simpson 1974), gender biased (Gilligan 1982), ignoring the effect of the environment (Fischer and Bullock 1984), and obscuring distinctions between thought and action. Kohlberg's theory of moral development is particularly vulnerable to criticisms of developmental theories that are seen as a hierarchy of invariant stages, each superior to the one before it. While it is clear that certain advances in development require mastery of earlier stages, the assumption of relative value must be made much more carefully. It is first necessary to address issues of culture, gender, and the specific environment to which individuals must adapt, and then to judge the maturity of a particular moral attitude in that context.

PARENTAL DEVELOPMENT

Simultaneously with all these developments in the life of a school-age child, the parents are developing as well. Parenthood involves decades of new experiences, and it also evokes identifications and experiences from the parent's childhood. Experiences with one's child resonate with experiences the parent had at similar times in his or her own childhood. Partly consciously and mostly unconsciously, the original feelings from those experiences decades ago are revived over the course of parenthood. There is the chance, then, for parents to reconnect with their own experiences of being parented, and to rework those feelings from the new perspective of being the parent rather than the child. Thus, to have a child takes on old meanings as well as new. The integration of these meanings is a task that takes years, especially since the child keeps changing. As the child develops, the parental task changes, and so does the mixture of old and new meanings involved in parenting. Caring for children and growing through providing this care is the work of parenthood, the core of what Erikson (1959) described as generativity. To refer to these changing meanings, parenthood has been called a developmental phase (Benedek 1959) or a psychological process with critical periods (Benedek, 1970).

More recently, Shanok (1990) described growth over parenthood as different from the sequential unfolding of childhood development. Rather, it is a process that marks adult development by its continuing demands to adapt to the challenges of caring for children, affecting parents' identity (parenthood) and capacities for intimacy (parenting). From this point of view, the interpersonal context for a parent—the family—continues to be vital for growth and change over the lifespan, and potential is not seen as fixed by the experiences of early childhood.

In the area of sexual experience, parents of oedipal-age children must deal with their children's seductiveness, intrusiveness, and curiosity (Anthony 1970b). Parents' incestuous feelings are stirred by the child's physical touching, exhibitionism, and curiosity. Homosexual as well as heterosexual feelings are evoked, depending on the sex of the parent and child. The extremes of response are incestuous sexual abuse, on the one hand, and punishment of the child's sexuality, on the other. Parents' attitudes regarding modesty in the bedroom, nursery, bathroom, and hallway are re-examined, with old memories mixed with recent levels of comfort and discomfort in the pre-baby marriage. Through this process, the building blocks of parents' values and morals are revisited. There is the possibility for new levels of restraint or permission.

The parent's alliance with the spouse develops throughout the course of parenting. In a one-parent family, collaborative relations usually develop with some other partner in parenting (lover, paid babysitter, neighbor, grandparent, sibling, aunt). The degree of collaboration or conflict develops partially in identification with parenting images from the family of origin. Nonetheless, the "parenting alliance" (Cohen and Weissman 1984) is also a new adult experience, creating feelings of confirmation or rejection that are fundamental enough to alter a parent's mood and self-esteem profoundly and over the course of years. Feelings concerning the mixture of success and failure in the partnership reverberate with appraisals parents have made of their other most important endeavors. A parent's sense of identity is permanently expanded to include these new feelings.

The birth of a second or third child again challenges parents to new growth. Formerly, their love, concern, and projected images were directed to one child. Now the firstborn falls from grace as his or her aggression against the new baby is found unacceptable. If the parents had not yet imposed norms of fairness and sharing on the firstborn, they might now. Parents realize they are running a little government at home, playing the executive, legislative, and judicial roles all at once. There is further differentiation and connection in relation to early authority figures, as parents more definitively assume authority in their growing families.

As sons and daughters enter school, parents' attitudes continue to expand. Parents give up the familiar preschooler and get a new child, a pupil. Teachers give parents advice and opinions about their children's school performance. If it never happened before, parents come to feel as if their child is the product not just of their love but of their discipline. The child can become for parents a public sign of their moral values, their own assets and limitations (Kestenberg 1970). Parents themselves feel graded, tested, and judged through the teacher's reactions to their children. Since the school represents acceptable behavior and performance, parents' attitudes toward authority are called into question. Is the school right about the child's stated deficiencies and accomplishments? Is the school wrong, and the parents know better? Both are frequent reactions, and both are possible.

Since the answer is not obvious, parents are thrown back on their own judgment. Therefore, a parent's judgment itself is challenged, once it is compared with the teacher's judgment. Parental judgment has developmental origins, going back to early history of reality testing, consensual validation, and attitude toward consequences of actions. There is the chance to rework rigidity in judgment as the pressure to help the child in school opens up formerly closed ways of thinking.

Over the course of normal development, children hit, grab, trick, lie, cheat, and curse. Children monopolize the phone, the computer, or the bathroom. In response, parents socialize children. They must consider once again their own rights compared to those of others. Educational lessons to children concerning the proper way to behave may be relevant and useful. Simultaneously they may also be rationalizations for the parent's own tendency to feel entitled or submissive. There is the opportunity to review and modify these tendencies over time. The alternative is a greater rigidity in a parent's rules (leading the parent to feel isolated and embattled) unless the child develops character traits that allow the child to join the parent in this rigidity.

Parents react to their children's strengths. They watch their children love, support, and care for the parents themselves, and for their siblings and friends. They see their children learn, become more competent, and overcome former difficulties. To nurture, participate in, and merely to watch these experiences is highly affirming for parents. Capacities for reparation and concern (Klein 1975) get applied in new areas, softening old patterns of bitterness or depression. Tendencies to optimism can expand or even develop anew.

In preadolescence, children move into chumship intimacies, more noticeable periods of withdrawal from parents, and sexualized joking. Parents once again must readjust their experience of themselves as adults. What will the future bring? Signs of a child's puberty often coincide with a parent's own graying hair, balding, high blood pressure, cholesterol or back problems; with marital problems; or with the aging or dying of the parents' own parents. Gladness and love for the child's youth, vigor, and possibilities mix with envy and a sense of loss.

Considering their own adult development as they see their preadolescent children develop, parents can experience further differentiation of self and connection to others. For example, as parents nag and remind and suggest, their priorities are obvious. If these priorities do not match those of the child, conflict ensues. Seeing their preadolescent child's attachment to various friends, hobbies, or interests, the parents are reminded of their own interests. The parents have spent years regretting or being glad for their own patterns of relating, working, and playing, dating back to their childhood. Watching their sons and daughters grow up out of childhood, parents appraise their own childhood and its directions. Parents respond to their children's growing involvements with other people and interests by reviewing their own experience. There is a new chance for life review, for return to old interests and attachments and for the creation of new ones.

Throughout childhood, parents with a tendency to narcissistic rage, to moralistic intolerance, or to aggressive outbursts are at risk for child abuse, especially in relation to temperamentally difficult children. Discipline can take on self-righteous or sadomasochistic tones. Such parents react with horror against their children's messiness, greed, loudness, or directness—or against their own fascination with these impulses. If the parent feels intolerant of the child's behavior, the child can be hit or neglected. Consequent experiences—identification with the abused child, horror to be reminded perhaps of one's own childhood abuse, guilt and shame, rage to be made to feel all this—can escalate into a cycle of abuse, leading to longstanding alienation of child and parent and despair over parenthood as a chance for a new start.

On the other hand, love for the child often can elicit a healthy guilt and wish for reparation, and most parents struggle successfully to control this cycle. For these parents, overcoming their rage and narcissism is a great step forward into adulthood.

SUMMARY

All of these perspectives on children's development (interpersonal, cognitive, psychosexual, self, and moral) and parents' growth are useful in anticipating what might be expected and what might be unusual in the lives of children and parents in general. However, the fullest understanding of any particular clinical situation will arise out of the unique relational matrix in which those situations are embedded. We will elaborate further on this point of view in Chapters 6 and 7, when we examine childhood psychopathology. First, we turn to the parent–child relationship in the next chapter.

4

Love and Identification
between Parent and Child

This chapter attempts to articulate a relational view of the role of the parents in a child's emotional growth and development. It will not attempt a comprehensive account of the parent–child relationship, many aspects of which were dealt with in the previous chapter. Rather, it will explore especially the unconscious aspects of the parents' relationship to the child. More will be said about the parents' relationship with the young child, but we will also comment on this relationship as the child gets older.

PROVIDING SAFETY, SECURITY, AND
SECURE ATTACHMENT

Safety and security are among the most basic needs children have. Beyond simply protecting the child from danger and providing for essential physical needs, empirical research (Bowlby 1969, 1980) and clinical observation and theory (Fairbairn 1943, Sullivan 1953, Winnicott 1945) indicate the child's need for a primary attachment figure with whom the child can feel secure. Evidence suggests that such a relationship fosters the child's growth (Eagle 1995). When opportunity for attachment is grossly absent, even if physical needs are provided for, children may fail to thrive or even die (Spitz 1946).

In addition, from the beginning of extrauterine life, mother–child interaction and attachment patterns become part of the child's ways of regulating both its own arousal and affect, and the behavior of others (Beebe and Lachmann 1988, Brazelton et al. 1974, Hofer 1995, Stern 1985). These patterns also provide the basis for the child's evolving inner representations of self and others (Beebe and Lachmann 1994). The mother's contribution to the evolution of these patterns is, of course, informed by her own, already well-developed set of self- and other-representations, and the fantasies (conscious and unconscious) and identifications (both accepted and disavowed) that are a part of these inner representations. The effect of parental identifications on children will be discussed below.

HELPING THE CHILD FEEL LIKE
A WHOLE, REAL, INTEGRATED PERSON

Winnicott (1945) discussed how a child comes to feel like a whole person. In his view, being whole includes the child's sense of being real, living within his body, and feeling integrated. These are fostered by quiet experiences of bodily care given to the infant. Routines associated with care given primarily by a single caregiver also contribute to this sense of security. A parent listening to the child and witnessing his life, mirroring the child's self-expression, naming the child, and so on, are seen by Winnicott and others as a gathering together of various bits of the child's life, fostering a sense of personal integration. The infant's mother must also protect the child from stimulation that impinges: that is erratic, disturbing, disorganizing, or overwhelming, beyond the child's ability to tolerate, understand, and cope with. At the beginning of extrauterine life, this means that she must be highly attuned to the child's wishes, and provide the child just what the child wants, at just the right moment. Winnicott (1956) talked about how the mother's brief period of intense absorption in the infant during the first weeks of life—her "primary maternal preoccupation"—allows her to be so attentive and attuned to her child and to tolerate the strain of providing this near-perfect adaptation to her child. Ideally, this near-perfect adaptation gradually diminishes as the mother senses the child's growing ability to tolerate frustration (based on his ability to remember that the frustration will end) and cope using his own resources.

Frustration of the child's wishes by the parent, within manageable limits, helps the child accept the reality of the external world and accept that this world is beyond the child's magical control (Ferenczi 1913, Singer 1965, Winnicott 1956, 1969). This process is also helped when the mother can tolerate the child's rage with some equanimity (see Klein 1946, Winnicott 1969). The child then learns that the outside world cannot be destroyed by his feelings, and is therefore not under his or her omnipotent control.

PARENTAL LOVE AND PARENTAL IDENTIFICATION

A secure, intimate relationship with the parent is crucial for a child's development. As noted, a parent's love is often what makes this possible (Winnicott 1956). But what is parental love? Freud (1914) introduced the idea that there are two types of love: narcissistic and anaclitic. Narcissistic love is based on loving oneself: the love object stands for oneself, past, present, or potential. Anaclitic love is modeled on the child's love for the parent. How does a parent love a child?

A parent's anaclitic, altruistic love is, of course, highly important for the child. Parents are often called upon to put the child's welfare above their own. What does this teach the child about love, or responsibility, or the importance of valuing other people? Similar learning may take place when a parent demonstrates that she is capable of understanding the child, stepping aside from an egocentric perspective. Perhaps most basically, the child's sense of being loved by the parent contributes to the child's sense of security, the certainty of being protected and cared for (Main 1995).

However, a parent's love for a child is certainly also narcissistic—a point first made by Freud in his essay "On Narcissism" (1914). The child represents for the parent what the parent is, once was, or might have become. The parent identifies with her or his child. When Winnicott (1956) discussed "primary maternal preoccupation," he described the extent to which he believed such an identification was crucial during infancy.

But how does a parent's identification affect a child? Vygotsky (1962) and Stern (1995) suggest that a helpful parent often responds to her child not exactly as he is, but aims just slightly ahead of where the child is, essentially guiding the child toward the developmental achievement for which he is just now becoming ready. Vygotsky (1962) called this "working in the zone of proximal development." More recently, Trad (1992) has called this "previewing." It seems reasonable to believe that a parent's ability to do this is based not only on some type of access to her own early experience, which fosters an accurate identification and a sense of where the child is headed, but also on the mother's fantasy about the child. We may say that the mother's fantasy of who the child is becomes an important part of the child's environment—part of his roadmap, so to speak. One critique of Winnicott's work (e.g., Mitchell 1993) is that he portrays the true self as something that, ideally, takes its shape based completely on intrinsic factors. Its growth is nurtured, but not shaped, by interaction with its environment. A more relational or intersubjective view (Fairbairn 1943, Mitchell 1993, Stern 1985, Sullivan 1953) recognizes that such pristine development is not possible, and that every infant can only become a developed person in interaction with a specific environment. The point is that the parent's fantasy about the child inevitably becomes an important part of that environment, and an important influence on the child's developing personality.

The child is treated as he is perceived by the parent. Certain roles are assigned to the child, explicitly or implicitly. The more subjective aspects of the parent's perception of the child are strongly influenced by the parent's fantasies about the child, and are also necessary for the child. The child needs a parent who can see in the child, and respond to, potentials no one else can see (Vygotsky 1962).

Are we talking about projective identification—the parent treating the child not as an individual in his own right, but instead as a part of the parent's own self? Beyond a certain point, the parent's identification with the child no longer helps the parent to observe acutely and accurately where the child is at, and what the child needs. Instead, the parent's responses begin to violate the child's nature, or begin to exploit the child's abilities for the parent's benefit (Miller 1981). The child's needs have been forgotten. The parent's fantasies have become the basis of a coercive and destructive projective identification imposed on the child.

The parent also has transferences to the child; that is, the child represents figures from the parent's own past. Transferences are also identifications: identifications with the parent's internal objects rather than with the parent's self (cf. Racker 1968). Like other identifications, transferences can be damaging if they are rigid and excessive.

Universal events such as separation, independence, making friends, competition, and risk-taking have the potential to elicit strong identifications in a parent of any age child. Specific situations, such as a child's illness, fragility, or chronic pain, aside from their inherent impact on a child's experience, may also elicit different identifications in a parent. Such events, early in life, may color the parents' enduring perception of the child, and therefore the child's experience of himself. There are common situations in later childhood where highly loaded identifications by a parent are likely to occur. These include children's performing arts or sports activities. Examples can be seen as parents scream from the sidelines at any sports event while they watch their children play. In adolescence, a young person's developing sexual and romantic interests, or stronger challenges to a parent's authority, may elicit strong identifications in a parent.

Often, a mother and father will identify differently with a child, or respond differently to a shared identification with the child. Then the child may become a pawn in the parents' battle to define the child.

A 10-year-old boy has a father, an attorney, who, for various reasons, has doubts about his own adequacy, and often seeks out competition as a proving ground for himself. The father identifies this aspect of himself with his son and uses the same solutions he applies to himself: he fastens onto the son's softer qualities as evidence that the son is weak and a potential failure, and so reacts strongly to any hint of difficulty the son has. He tends to taunt his son when the son falters, pushes him hard to excel in every arena, and easily gets angry at his child. Not surprisingly, there is frequent and noisy conflict between father and son.

Mother, on the other hand, felt silenced and defeated as a child. One thing she loved about the father, when their relationship was new, was that he did not become resigned to difficulties but fought against them. She did not recognize that he sought out battles so that he could prove himself, due to his inner sense of inadequacy. One thing father liked about her was her admiration for him, her quiet manner, and her not challenging him. This mother has developed an identification with her son as someone who is vulnerable, as she had felt herself to be, and who easily could be hurt and defeated.

The result was that the more the father pushed and blew up at the boy, the more his mother saw him as vulnerable and in need of her care and protection. The more mother "babied" him, the more father tried to toughen him up, and demanded more of him. The child ended up angry at himself and unhappy much of the time, and put great pressure on himself to perform and succeed. He also did poorly in school, fulfilling the point of basic agreement between the parents—that he, like each of them, was inadequate.

On the other hand, despite the potential for problems, when a parent's fantasies (including narcissistic fantasies) about the child are less driven, less urgent, more responsive, and more interactive with what emanates from the child, they may be crucial for the child's healthy development.

WHEN IDENTIFICATION BECOMES URGENT: PSYCHOPATHOLOGY

Children identify with their parents, not only to an extreme degree in response to abuse (see Ferenczi 1933 on the concept of identification with the aggressor and Fairbairn 1943 on the concept of the moral defense; also Davies and Frawley 1994, and Herman 1992), but as part of normal development. Each parent has an attitude, often unarticulated, toward the child's identification with different aspects of herself. Some identifications are valued, some may be neutral, and others may be a source of conflict and anxiety, reflections of oneself a parent would rather not see. Some parents may reject or punish certain of these conflict-producing reflections, or simply extinguish them by ignoring them. A parent who is relatively accepting of herself, therefore, will foster the greatest freedom, spontaneity, and creativity in her developing child. In contrast, a parent who, with her own fantasies about, and identifications with, her child, encourages certain identifications or fantasies in the child, and then due to discomfort or conflict, rejects or punishes the child's response to these, creates inner conflict in the child. The "double bind" described in the family-systems literature by Bateson et al. (1956) is an outcome of this process. According to that concept, in addition to the contradictory demands placed on a child, there is an additional demand not to comment on or notice the dilemma in which the parent places the child.

This recalls Ferenczi's (1933) belief that parental hypocrisy—the self-protective denial of the child's trauma by the parent—was the key pathogenic element. There have been later incarnations of this idea. Sullivan (1953) introduced the idea of "selective inattention" and Levenson (1972), following Laing, talked about "mystification," both referring to the child's response when the parent requires that the child "not see" what disturbs him in his environment. This process is seen as a basic cause of psychopathology. Similarly, Bowlby (1980), integrating concepts from cognitive research, has described two memory systems that, in psychopathology, can contradict each other. The semantic memory system—the person's verbal story of what happened— may omit important aspects of what actually occurred, due to the parent's requirements. However, these omitted elements are stored in visual imagery in the episodic memory system. This is a pivotal element in the genesis of psychopathology.

Various theorists have talked about the destructive effects when parents require identification and compliance from their children. Many of these will be discussed at length in Chapter 7, "Different Ways of Thinking about Psychopathology." Briefly, however, Ferenczi (1933) used the term "identification with the aggressor" to refer to the traumatized child's compliance with the parent's wishes, and to describe the child's highly receptive psychic state, which allows him intuitively to understand and comply with precisely what is expected by the adult. Bowlby (1980) and Winnicott (1948) examined how parental depression also imposes requirements for compliance on the child. Winnicott's (1960) elaboration of the false-self organization also describes the child's compliance—

essentially, the child survives an impinging environment by suppressing his own direct perceptions, feelings, and initiative. Instead, the child responds reactively, fending off the parent's impingements, resulting in self-alienation. Fairbairn's (1943) idea of the "moral defense" is a description of another destructive aspect of the child's compliance with parental requirements. Here, the child takes onto himself the parent's badness, in order to hold onto the security of believing that he has a good parent. This recalls Ferenczi's (1933) earlier description of identification with the aggressor, and more specifically, what Ferenczi called introjection of the aggressor's guilt, which Ferenczi believed to be the most destructive effect of parental hypocrisy.

The phenomenon of splitting in the child's personality can be related to the child's identification with the parent's projections. Children who behave in highly contradictory ways—whose "little angel" behavior may coexist with a "little devil," for instance, with little integration or communication between the two—may also be expressing urgent but contradictory identifications with different parents, or different aspects of a single, disturbed parent.

More recently, Silverman and Lieberman (1999) have discussed the role of conscious parental attributions and unconscious projective identifications toward children. While they agree that both of these processes constitute normal, "fundamental mechanisms for mutual involvement" between parents and child, they say that when these processes are used excessively and defensively by a parent, the effect can be to "constrict the child's range of possible psychic and behavioral responses [including the ability to think] and coerce a compliance with these attributions because of the child's developmentally appropriate need to please the parent and to preserve the parent's love" (p. 179).

One aspect of parental attributions and projective identifications, which will not be elaborated here, is parents' transference onto their children. We all know of situations where a parent strongly identifies a child with one of the parent's own parents or siblings, or with an older child who has died. Bergmann and Jucovy (1982) have written about how Holocaust survivors often identify their children either with relatives who were killed in concentration camps or with the brutal camp guards—effectively perpetuating the destructive effects of the Holocaust for another generation.

INTERSUBJECTIVITY: THE PARENT
RECOGNIZES AND ASSERTS

Implicit in all that has been said so far is the notion of recognition (Benjamin 1988). Optimally, the parent responds to the child not simply as an object but as a source of subjectivity separate from herself, and values the particulars of the child's inner world. Children seek recognition. Without it, they feel alone. Lack of recognition can be traumatic, as it leaves the child alone with part of himself that he cannot make sense of or come to terms with on his own. The parent's recognition thus shapes the child's development (Frankel 1998b). The child will cultivate aspects of himself that the parent appreciates and is likely to stifle aspects that are ignored by the parent (unless she finds others who appreciate them).

Recognition allows the child to feel real and part of the world. It is the child's need for recognition that makes a parent's dissociation or hypocrisy so destructive: when the parent denies what the child knows to be true, the child's subjectivity is treated as unimportant, nonexistent. The child may feel profoundly alone, and also may doubt the reality of his own experience.

Not only does the parent recognize the child's needs, she has her own. It is important for the parent not to be too self-sacrificing. Not only can this create guilt in the child, but the child must also learn that others are real, and that the outside world is not a function of his own omnipotence (Ferenczi 1913, Singer 1965, Winnicott 1969). Therefore, the parent sets limits, reacts to the child selfishly at times, and in other ways represents the existence of an outer reality apart from the child's inner reality. Setting limits may also be a form of recognition (Frankel 1998b). Both Winnicott (1969) and Kohut (1971) talk about the importance of gradual disillusionment of the child's omnipotence. Benjamin (1990) talks about how the child develops a keen interest in the mother's subjectivity.

Related to this, Winnicott (1968) proposed from an essentially Kleinian point of view that for the child both to feel real, and to accept the existence of the other as real, he must gain the sense that he can "use the other": let the other "have it," direct one's impulses full force at the other, and find that the other survives this—meaning, the parent must not retaliate for the child's aggression. That is, the parent must survive as a parent, never forgetting about what the child needs.

5

Cultural and
Socioeconomic Influences

The developmental perspective, while useful and illuminating in many respects, contains a major pitfall: embedded in any developmental schema are values and norms, constitutive of our criteria for that which is defined as mature and immature, advanced and primitive. There are many potential problems here. Adam Phillips (1993) has argued that trying to fit a human life into any sort of predefined shape, including the shape imposed by developmental narratives of how a life ought to proceed, presumes that we know more than we can possibly know about life, on one hand, and, on the other, denudes our image of life of the unpredictability and surprise that makes it worth living.

A second problem, identified and described by feminist authors (e.g., Gilligan 1982), has to do with ways in which qualities culturally associated with masculinity get defined as "mature" in our developmental narratives. Our developmental schemata thus come to constitute unwitting reflections of a sexist society. For example, psychoanalytically informed developmental theories such as that of Mahler (Mahler et al. 1975) view early human development as proceeding from an undifferentiated state to a state of relative differentiation and independence. To the extent that this schema privileges independence and autonomy at the expense of dependence and relatedness, it replicates values that are at once Western European-North American and sexist. Independence is privileged, and associated with masculinity. As another example, Freud's developmental progression, tracing the development of the drives from oral through anal to phallic-genital, reflects a value system that privileges heterosexual intercourse above all other forms of sexual behavior.[1] Again, one can see here a "masculinist" and heterosexist bias in the preferred form of sexual behavior, that is, penis–vagina intercourse as the only normative sexual behavior. Benjamin (1988) gives a third example, showing how Freud's oedipal theory takes for granted gender complementarity, the mutual exclusivity of masculinity and femininity. In general, developmental theories that postulate a linear sequence of progression are in danger of enshrining culturally specific values and norms. These norms and values, as Foucault (1980) has pointed out, also tend to perpetuate the power arrangements in a given society.

Developmental theories arising from the British object relations schools tend not to postulate simple linear progressions. Thus, the problems of culture-boundedness are somewhat attentuated. For example, Melanie Klein's (1976) developmental schema consists of a paranoid-schizoid position and a depressive position. The word "position" as opposed to "stage" tends not to imply a linear sequence. Klein did believe that the paranoid-schizoid position arose prior to the depressive position, but that once the two positions were available, they coexisted. Let us take a brief detour into the details of this theory.

For Kleinians, aggression is inherent and primary. Infants, to a greater or lesser degree, are confronted with the problem of their own aggression at the very beginning of life. The earliest efforts to manage aggressive feelings, deriving from the death instinct, consist of the infant's attempts to rid himself of them by projecting them outward. The result is the creation of an external world experienced as persecu-

---

1. Consider how oral and anal sexual behavior have come to be defined as "foreplay." That is, thus defined, these behaviors have a place only as preparatory to heterosexual intercourse.

tory. Hence, the "paranoid" part of "paranoid-schizoid." The infant cannot bear to live in an unvaryingly persecutory world, however, and so he splits off a part of the world experienced as good. The word "schizoid" in "paranoid-schizoid" refers to this early splitting process.

The infant's world consists of the mother's body, in the Kleinian schema, so in the paranoid-schizoid position we are talking about a good breast and a bad, persecutory breast. In the depressive position, the infant comes to see the mother more as a whole person with good and bad features, realizing that his aggression is directed at a person whom he loves as well as hates. This realization gives rise to depressive guilt, and then to efforts at reparation.

Ogden (1986) has pointed out that the depressive position contains within it the basis for the "historical subject," the person who has a history. In the paranoid-schizoid position, history is rewritten each time there is a shift from the object as good to the object as bad, or vice versa. In this position, the bad object is only bad, and so was always bad, and similarly for the good object. History, as well as the depressive position, is born in the realization that today's bad object is the same person as yesterday's good object. Today's hating version of myself is the same self as yesterday's loving version of myself. For Ogden, the depressive position contributes self-consciousness and reflectiveness to the human repertoire, while the paranoid-schizoid position contributes passion and spontaneity (one cannot be too enraged or passionately loving if one is aware at the moment of all the other feelings one has had toward the same person).

The paranoid-schizoid and depressive positions, then, form a dialectic. Each makes an essential contribution to a human life. When one is in the foreground, the other is in the background. Thus, even though Klein has the depressive position developing later than the paranoid-schizoid position, being more mature in that sense, the depressive position on its own does not define maturity. In fact, without the passion and spontaneity contributed by the paranoid-schizoid position, an existence dominated by the depressive position would be drearily obsessional. Maturity, in the Kleinian schema, would have to consist of an optimal sort of interweaving of the two positions.

Let us return now to the question of the underlying value system or morality of developmental schemata. A "depressive-position morality," one that regards the depressive position as defining maturity, leads to the notion that self-reflectiveness, sometimes called "psychological mindedness," constitutes the highest virtue in a psychoanalytic or psychotherapy patient (not to mention the therapist). A less linear conception of Klein's schema takes account of the fact that patients who are only self-reflective can be overly compliant, not passionate enough to develop deeply felt transferential feelings, and so on. Depressive-position morality can lead to an overly compliant patient, collusive with the status quo inside and outside the treatment room. In short, a dialectical developmental schema, such as Klein's, is less prone to the enshrining of a culturally specific maturity-ethic than is a linear developmental schema.

Winnicott's (1975) developmental schema goes beyond the dialectic to what he calls the "paradoxical." One crucial aspect of Winnicott's developmental schema has to do with the interrelationship between the infant's immersion in subjective experience, and the recognition of external reality. Note that we are speaking of an interrelationship between experience in subjective reality and experience of objective reality, not a progression from one to the other, as is implied by Freud's concepts of the "pleasure" and "reality" principles. For Winnicott, the infant at the very beginning has a sense of total omnipotence, and there is no recognition of external reality. With time, what develops is "transitional" experience, best captured by the "transitional object" such as the teddy bear or "blankie." The transitional realm paradoxically unites subjective and objective experience. The "blankie" is simultaneously recognized as an object in the external world, a dirty old piece of cloth, and as the subjective creation of the child, the most precious thing in the world to the child. Winnicott brilliantly demonstrated how this most ordinary of phenomena (at least in certain cultures) goes a long way toward resolving the age-old problem of the relationship between the objective and the subjective in human experience. For Winnicott, human development leads to the ability to play and to be creative, the ability to bring internal, subjective experience together with recognition of objective, external reality in the transitional realm. For our purposes here, what is important to note is that the developmental schema does not postulate a linear progression, but rather an increasingly complex integration with respect to the individual's relationship to the world outside. There is thus no question, in Winnicott's theory, of a one-sided valorization of autonomy, independence, objectivity, or their opposites, for that matter.

Coates (1997) has proposed doing away with Anna Freud's (1965) concept of developmental lines, insofar as the concept implied that development is centrally organized (e.g., by drive development) to proceed in coordinated fashion across various domains. Coates advocates maintaining, nonetheless, the idea of a sequence of developmental steps, one building upon the other. We believe that the problem may lie more with the valuation of later developmental stages above earlier ones, rather than in the concept of sequential development per se. In our society, however, it is difficult to escape the implication that what is most advanced is also of greater value. The ethic of progress requires us to make a special effort to remember that earlier steps (such as nonverbal communication) may have a special value of their own.

Adrienne Harris (1999) has been working on a developmental model that avoids the various pitfalls associated with linear schemas. Harris notes that traditional developmental schemas tend to take the individual out of context, assuming that development is "hardwired" into the person, unfolding, under normal conditions, as it has been preprogrammed. Harris conceives of the individual as much more fully embedded in a social context, so she seeks a developmental model that will reflect this embeddedness. Harris, like Phillips, is also concerned that developmental models allow for the indeterminacy of how life unfolds. Drawing on the work of Thelen (Thelen and Smith 1994), Harris (1996) proposes a model of development "not as a concretized preformed ladder over which the individual scrambles, but as a multiple set of pathways whose particular forms and achievements are the outcome of emergent interactive process, not of hardwiring" (pp. 539–540). Harris envisions that in such a schema the individual is "not in a lockstep model toward higher functioning, but in an interactive variable patterning of experience that is emergent and shifting in a context" (p. 540). Bringing this sort of complexity into a developmental model tends to undermine any sort of simplistic and culture-bound notions of what constitutes maturity and immaturity. If our developmental model is to consider the individual in context, then we must take up culture and socioeconomic status as constituting two important elements in that context.

CULTURE

Generally speaking, culture can be defined as the meaning-systems generated by a group of people. Language is a major example of such a meaning-system. As an example of how culture works, consider how in many traditional cultures worldwide, especially in rural areas, children are not socialized for independence, as they are in the urban United States. Children, by and large, can be expected to stay in or near the village in which they were born. Male children can expect to work the family farm; female children can expect to have a marriage arranged for them by their families. Everyone stays pretty close to home. In the United States, however, it is normative for children to grow up and leave home. Children may leave home to go to college, or they may leave the family farm to work in the city, or they may simply go off in search of adventure and "self-discovery." In this context, consider the meaning attached to a child breastfeeding at age 2 or 3, or children sleeping in the same bed as parents at age 2 or 3 or 5. In the United States, such behavior would suggest an inappropriate degree of dependence between parents and child, while it is quite normative in village India, for example. In the United States, where children will need to leave the nest and make their own way in the world, it makes sense to prepare them from early on. Thus, we train infants to sleep in their own beds and to eat and drink on their own as soon as they develop the necessary motor skills. Such fostering of independence makes no sense in a traditional rural context.

Along the same lines, in the urban United States we reluctantly take a certain amount of adolescent and preadolescent defiance for granted as part of the process of evolving independence from parents. In a more traditional culture, such behavior might be considered more clearly inappropriate. One can see here, incidentally, a link between culturally syntonic attitudes toward authority and the fostering of independence in a particular culture. A culture in which independence is fostered in children can expect those children to develop a questioning, even skeptical, attitude toward the authority of their parents. Here we can also note how conflicts can be built into a cultural system. For example, parents in the United States may wish to socialize their children to be independent and to think for themselves, but may not wish to accept that their adolescent children question their authority. Consider the following clinical vignette that illustrates some of these cultural issues:

> In a traditional orthodox Jewish family, there was a 10-year-old boy, Yoni, who was brought to treatment because of encopresis. With some individual and family sessions, the encopresis quickly resolved. In more wide-ranging family discussions, however, it emerged that Yoni felt he received less positive attention and more negative attention than his nine siblings. In particular, he felt his next-younger sibling, a sister, was never chastised for her provocations of him, while his provocations of her were met with knee-jerk punishment from his parents. His next-older sibling, a brother named Moshe, was regarded in the family as out-of-control. He teased and tormented Yoni mercilessly. A brother older than Moshe was regarded as a model of intelligence and good behavior. The father, much to his own distress, responded with rage to the attacks of Moshe on Yoni, as well as to the attacks of Yoni on his sister. He felt that Yoni's provocation of his sister was his way of taking his frustration out on someone smaller than he, an undoing of the humiliation engendered in him by Moshe's mistreatment of him. The father was particularly sensitive to this dynamic, because he had felt victimized and humiliated by his own rageful father. The mother agreed with the father's assessment of the situation but added that she felt the father ought to spend more time with Yoni, that Yoni hungered for his attention in particular. Yoni's complaints, however, were more directed at his mother. For example, he tended to claim that his clothes were washed later than those of his siblings.
>
> For present purposes we wish to focus on two aspects of this clinical situation. First, the therapist, Jewish but not orthodox, could not help thinking: "With so many siblings, how can the older children in this family not feel neglected?" In fact, during the course of this treatment the mother became pregnant and gave birth to their tenth child. The therapist was sorely tempted to interpret Yoni's increasing complaints at a certain point as a response to his feeling that he would receive even less attention. The therapist recognized, however, that this family took the presence of this large number of children for granted and expected that children as they

got older would need their parents less, taking on caretaking roles with respect to the small children. There was a potential polarization here between the parents and the therapist. The therapist could have responded to the parents' expectation that Yoni would need them less as more siblings were born, with a championing of Yoni's legitimate right to feel deprived. Trying to avoid this polarization, however, the therapist began to feel constrained and inhibited. This particular logjam was broken when the therapist, through work within his own countertransference (he himself had been told that it was time to grow up, at age three, when his own brother was born), began to feel less judgmental, more accepting, of the parents' position. Then he felt more free to suggest to the parents that although Yoni might well take pride in his increasing capacity to take responsibility within the family, a part of him might feel that, at least temporarily, there was less attention for him. The parents accepted this formulation. A negotiation had occurred in which no one on either side had to give up his or her point of view, nor did anyone impose his or her point of view on anyone else.

On another occasion it seemed to the therapist that Yoni rebuffed his mother's efforts to reach out to him and see his point of view. The therapist suggested in a later session with the parents that Yoni might be uncomfortable with closeness with his mother, commenting that children often preferred distance as they approached adolescence. The parents initially looked confused, or blank. Then they said something to each other in Yiddish, which the therapist did not understand. When he inquired, the father interpreted that adolescence did not go this way in their community.

Cultures, of course, are not fixed entities. They change over time and influence each other. In addition, people are often affected by more than one culture. They may be immigrants, or the children or grandchildren of immigrants, involved in a process of acculturation, betwixt and between two or more cultures. A common example is the situation in which immigrant parents expect adolescent children to be compliant and respectful of their authority. The children, on the other hand, are exposed at school to peers who expect to have considerable autonomy and who are used to defying their parents. In such a case, therapists sometimes need to help parents negotiate the challenges of limit-setting while respecting a degree of autonomy for their children.

In one case, a mother, Clara, an immigrant from the Dominican Republic, was raising a 15-year-old son, Fernando, alone. Fernando was brought to treatment, on the advice of the school, because he was hanging out with a "bad crowd" and defying his mother's efforts to get him to come home at night, do his homework, and so on. The father had abandoned Clara while Fernando was an infant. Clara's mother lived in the neighborhood, but was quite elderly and ill. It seemed to the therapist, a man, that Clara took a very passive attitude toward limit setting. She complained that Fernando did not come home at night as she requested, but she seemed to make no authoritative efforts to influence him to do so.

The therapist, surmising that in Clara's traditional culture it would be the father's job to discipline the son (Fernando was a head taller than his mother), suggested to Clara that it seemed difficult for her to know how to be both mother and father to her son, to be both nurturer and limit-setter. Clara agreed, while Fernando listened. The therapist then organized a negotiation between mother and son as to what would be a reasonable curfew, and what would be the consequences (loss of TV privileges) if he came home late. This intervention seemed to have the desired effect, and Fernando started coming home more or less on time. It is possible that Clara's initial passivity in sessions represented a further example of deference to males, as well as, perhaps, a characterological trait notable even within the context of her culture. In any case, the therapeutic intervention seemed to free up Clara to take on some of the disciplinary function, likely to the relief of this out-of-control boy. It seemed important to involve Fernando in the discussion, to make it a negotiation, in an effort to respect both his need for attention and guidance from his mother and his need for respect and autonomy as a young man.

As people find themselves juggling behavioral patterns and meaning systems that may conflict and be mutually incompatible to some degree, there may be a tendency for cultural conflicts to join up with or coincide with psychic conflicts. Clara, for example, had been raised in the traditional culture of the rural Dominican Republic. Having moved to the United States, however, the influence of North American culture was everywhere and had to be dealt with in some way, even if only by being resisted. Clara had not learned English and she had not worked outside the home, but she might well have had friends who did, who brought into her world some of the ways of being self-sufficient, or of being a limit-setting parent, available to women in North America. The therapist's intervention, therefore, presumably did not come totally out of left field for her. Fernando, as much as he resisted his mother's control under the influence of peers who were used to considerable autonomy, was presumably significantly under the influence of the traditional value system of the Dominican culture in which children are to respect their elders. One could conceive, then, that Clara and Fernando became polarized with respect to the cultural differences and contradictions with which they were struggling. For example, one could imagine that Clara, feeling inhibited in her own independent strivings, might have secretly or preconsciously enjoyed Fernando's defiance and sense of freedom. Fernando, for his part, struggling with a sense of guilt over his independent strivings, might have resorted to a rigidly defiant position in order to deny these feelings. The therapist's intervention might be conceived of as an effort to undermine this polarization, to give Clara a somewhat more autonomous position, to give Fernando a somewhat more dependent position. One might say that Clara and Fernando were facing psychic as well as cultural dilemmas having to do with dependence and independence, passivity and activity, autonomy and embeddedness. They dealt with this by a splitting process in which, on gender and cultural grounds, Fernando took on the independent, active, autonomous side, while Clara took on the dependent, passive side. This particular split was unstable and untenable since, on a generational basis, Clara's parental functions were undermined. Gender and one aspect of the cultural situation (Fernando's relatively greater integration into the North American ethos of autonomy) pulled one way. Another aspect of the cultural situation (the expectation that parents will have a controlling function in relation to their children) pulled the other way. The therapist's intervention undermined, to a degree, this splitting by helping Clara move to a somewhat more active, controlling position in relation to Fernando, thus facilitating Fernando's move to a somewhat more dependent position in relation to Clara. In this process, each individual gained resources and flexibility in negotiating psychic and cultural dilemmas.[2]

It is clear from the example of Clara and Fernando that different cultures do not create wholly different psyches. Different cultures foreground and emphasize certain psychic characteristics, placing others in the background. When people meet, cultural differences can be seen as a special case of the intersubjective negotiation that takes place in any interpersonal interaction. When different meaning systems meet, or collide, the people involved try to make sense of each other in terms of their own meaning systems, sometimes stretching or even transforming their pre-existing systems in the process. The negotiations involved can be much like what occurs when a cultural anthropologist and a foreign culture try to make sense of each other (Schweder 1991). Culture informs the process of definition of self and other that occurs when two or more people engage with each other. This process can go awry when it is put in the service of anxiety-ridden efforts to rid oneself of unacceptable psychic characteristics by attributing them to the "other." Such projective processes, as they are known psychoanalytically, can occur between therapists and patients as well; recognizing and overcoming this kind of splitting as it can occur on cultural or other bases can have a therapeutic effect, as it did between Clara and Fernando.

Consider some common examples. Patients in inner-city public clinics commonly miss appointments without notice, or show up late. Sometimes this tendency is attributed, by therapists who tend to be from the North American mainstream culture, to a culturally based inattention to time. Such an attribution can shade into more pejorative form, such as "third-world patients lack a sense of responsibility." In psychoanalytic ego psychology, the pejorative quality can be cloaked in jargon: the patients have "ego deficits." They miss appointments because they are lacking in the tolerance for anxiety and frustration that would

---

2. In a traditional culture, a 15-year-old might well be considered an adult. He or she might already be married and a parent, and thus quite autonomous. There may also be a cultural conflict with respect to the degree to which a fifteen-year-old, a grown man or woman in many ways, needs parental guidance and control. In current North American society, adolescence is a time of moratorium, preadulthood, in which drugs and pregnancy are everpresent threats to the extended education that is supposed to be taking place.

make it possible to attend sessions in which anxiety-laden material is discussed without reassurance from the therapist. We would suggest that the pejorative quality enters when cultural difference is used, defensively, by the therapist to bolster a preferred self-image by projecting onto patients disowned and devalued psychic qualities such as inattention to time.

Taking a step back for a moment, one might say that rather than having an inattention to time, patients with traditional cultural backgrounds simply have a different sense of time. If we try to step outside of our own culture, we might be able to imagine how our own sense of time could be seen, again pejoratively, as quite rigid and compulsive, contributing to a "Type A" personality culture-wide. The psychotherapy session, in which patient and therapist have to start and stop talking when the clock says so, can be seen as a caricature of our obsession with time. Less pejoratively, one can conceive of simply different senses of time, each of which has advantages and disadvantages in various contexts. Rural people, for example, can develop a sense of time based on a longer time span, the rhythm of the day or the seasons, for example, while people working in an industrial and postindustrial context need to measure time out in smaller quantities. When two people with different backgrounds in this respect meet, in order to find a mutually respectful common ground, an effort of imagination is required to put one's own way of being into the context created by the other person's way of being.

How might it serve defensive purposes for a therapist simply to "assimilate" (Inhelder and Piaget 1964) a foreign sense of time into his or her own time-schema? For example, I might think that if I were to show up late for an appointment it would reflect irresponsibility, and therefore this patient who shows up late is irresponsible. Consider the element of rejection and abandonment that can enter into the experience of being kept waiting at an agreed-upon appointment time. Experiences of rejection and abandonment enter into all relationships, including therapeutic relationships. The patient in a public clinic can feel rejected when the therapist shortens the session because the patient showed up late, or the patient may expect (quite reasonably) that the therapist will rotate out of the clinic after six weeks or six months and leave the patient, or the patient may feel abandoned by the therapist's failure to understand some experience of importance to the patient. The patient may miss a session as an expression of anger after such an experience. Therapists, too, being human beings, can fear being abandoned by patients. Therapists can feel anxiety about failing their patients, can feel that their patients fail them, and so on. In this intersubjective context, the therapist's resorting to an explanation for a missed appointment based on the patient's inability to tolerate anxiety can mask the therapist's understandable difficulty in tolerating the anxiety aroused by the situation. The very act of attributing the inability to tolerate anxiety to the patient can be seen, from this point of view, as evidence of the therapist's failure to tolerate anxiety.

Note how culture is inducted into this essentially defensive process. The patient may realize, preconsciously, that the therapist's sense of time and responsibility makes lateness or absence a suitable way to express anger, or to transfer a sense of abandonment, to the therapist. The therapist counters by using a pejorative cultural stereotype to attribute a disowned psychic quality to the patient. There is, nonetheless, a real cultural difference between patient and therapist that needs to be recognized, on both sides, if the intersubjective contact is to be productive. The defensive use of the difference essentially aborts this process of meeting and recognizing another human being who is similar to oneself and also different from oneself.

These clinical examples are intended to illustrate the complexity that emerges when one reconsiders development in a cultural context. Concepts such as autonomy, dependence, tolerance for anxiety, and so on, look very different depending on the cultural meaning system within which we are operating.

SOCIOECONOMIC FACTORS

Socioeconomic status is another contextual factor that has a powerful impact on the development of individuals. Consider the effects of lower socioeconomic status on self-esteem, for example. Sennett and Cobb (1972) point out that the American myth that anyone can make it here economically leads individuals to see lower socioeconomic status as evidence of personal failure. The self-esteem of adults is thus undermined, leading to low morale, if not depression. The effects of societal racism often exacerbate the situation, as adults and children confront and internalize negative images of people like themselves in the media and elsewhere. The effects on parenting can be pernicious, with adults facing great difficulty in conveying a sense of pride and respect to their children. When parents are depressed, preoccupied, and overburdened, their parenting capacities are likely to suffer. This situation might well be considered an epidemic in our poorest communities.

Children growing up in poverty face a multitude of handicaps that work against their "making it," no matter what their personal attributes. Inadequate nutrition and substance abuse during pregnancy often leave children with several strikes against them before they are born. They are likely to attend overcrowded schools where they can receive little personal attention. To children, crime may appear to pay, given the fancy cars and jewelry worn by the local drug dealers. Adults who have prospered playing by the rules may be scarce. Parents in poverty are overwhelmed with anxiety related to basic survival. Societal support systems are tenuous. Safety nets such as welfare are no longer in place. Parenting is stressful enough when economic supports are in place, but extraordinary resources are necessary to give children the emotional support they need when parents themselves are unsupported in such basic ways. For a middle-class clinician working in poverty-stricken communities, it is important to try to imagine what it would be like to raise children under conditions of poverty, discrimination, and racism.

Nonetheless, the great majority of parents of lower socioeconomic status find within themselves, and in their environments, such resources. Extended family support is often more available than it is in middle-class communities. The church can be a major support. Research has also documented the resilience with which many people confront adversity (Neiman 1987, Rutter 1987).

Upper socioeconomic status can have a distorting effect on human development as well. Upper-middle-class parents can be distracted from parenting by their preoccupation with their work. The rich commonly leave childcare to employees. With so much already in place materially, school can seem quite irrelevant to children from wealthy families. These children can develop a sense of specialness and entitlement that can be a social handicap, creating complications in intimate relationships.

As is the case with race and culture, social class can contribute to structuring the interaction between patient and therapist. Images of self and other within the therapeutic relationship may draw on preconceptions based on socioeconomic status. Altman (1995) has described how some of these preconceptions may play out clinically. For example, he described how patients in inner-city public clinics may develop an "institutional transference" to the clinic and its therapists based on the clinic's place in the social service network composed of welfare, Medicaid, social security, and so on. These agencies are supposed to provide for the material needs of impoverished people, while in practice they may frustrate and humiliate aid recipients as much as they take care of them. The expectations that inner-city patients bring with them to the relationship with their therapist may thus fit the pattern of the "bad internal object" described by Fairbairn (1944/1952). Fairbairn felt that bad early experiences led to an internalization of the "bad object" in a split form—on the one hand, as an "exciting" object that promises gratification or nurturance, and on the other, a "rejecting" object that fails to deliver on this promise. Conceiving of the patient's image of the therapist along these lines can help to make sense of some common clinical situations.

For example, adult patients in public clinics commonly ask for help with various applications such as for housing or welfare recertification. Children may ask for money or food. Therapists may regard these requests as evidence that the patient does not understand the nature of the therapeutic relationship, even that the patient is not free enough of material needs to engage in a therapeutic relationship. If one thinks in terms of an "exciting-rejecting" object relationship, however, the patient's request can be thought to set up this transferential configuration. The therapist may well end up feeling that his or her only options are to deny the patient's request, thereby becoming a depriving object; or to accede to the patient's request, thereby leading the patient to expect more from the therapist than can possibly be delivered in the long term. The therapist in the process becomes the "exciting" object destined sooner or later to disappoint. This kind of situation may mobilize powerful countertransferential feelings in the therapist as well. Rescue fantasies, condemnatory responses to the patient's requests and manipulations arising from the therapist's defenses against his own greed, and denigrating, dismissive, or condescending feelings and attitudes are all examples of what can be stirred up in the therapist. Patients may consciously or unconsciously expect or perceive such feelings in the therapist. Requests for material help and support, seen in this way, are not distractions from the psychoanalytic enterprise; rather, they constitute one of the most powerful modes in which the transference–countertransference engagement can find expression. Socioeconomic status is in the background, organizing the expectations and perceptions of self and other of patient and therapist.

Socioeconomic status is an equally powerful organizer when the patient is of high status relative to the therapist. The therapist, for example, might feel intimidated by, envious of, or rivalrous with the patient. Patients may seek to evoke, or prevent, the emergence of such feelings in the therapist as part of their particular transferential engagement.

When the therapist is of higher socioeconomic status than the patient, social class can work in tandem with the status and power differential between patient and doctor/therapist to reinforce the "one down" position of the patient. Searles (1979) has written of how the "dedicated physician" who needs to be healthy, and thus "one up" relative to the patient, can reinforce the patient's pathology. The patient may feel the need to remain sick so as not to threaten the doctor's sense of security. The patient may also feel that becoming healthy may lead to the termination of the relationship with the doctor. Similarly, the patient of lower socioeconomic status may fear that upward moves socioeconomically can threaten the therapist's sense of superiority and lead to loss of the therapist's support. Clinical situations of this sort have been described in detail by Altman (1995).

PART TWO

Psychopathology from
a Relational Viewpoint

Looking at development in relational terms leads inevitably to the need to redefine psychopathology as a relational phenomenon. In the next two chapters, our effort is to develop a concept of psychopathology within a relational matrix. Rather than provide a new system of classifying children's difficulties—a new, relational taxonomy—these chapters will use the relational ideas discussed in earlier chapters to give the reader a more expansive view of children's psychopathology—a variety of overlapping and interconnected ways of thinking about children's difficulties and how they develop.

6

Three Assumptions about Psychopathology

We start with three interrelated assumptions about psychopathology. First, complex human behavior, including psychopathology, is always the result of the interaction of a child's constitution and his environment, and is never solely the result of one or the other. Second, psychopathology is usually not distinct from normal development but exists on a continuum with it, or as a variation of normal development. Third, what is defined as psychopathology depends to some extent on the cultural and personal values and outlook of the observer.

ASSUMPTION 1: THE INTERACTION BETWEEN CONSTITUTION AND ENVIRONMENT

Our relational perspective understands psychopathology as fundamentally interactional: a child's endowment interacts with his environment from the beginning of life. For every child, there are ways in which biological inheritance exerts a strong influence on the child's way of engaging the environment. Other aspects of behavior may be less biologically influenced and shaped more by the child's interpersonal environment.

We believe that there is no behavior that is a direct translation from the biological without being shaped in a meaningful way by a child's experience. Even when inherent constitutional or maturational factors are abnormal—what Greenspan (1992) calls regulatory disorders such as hypersensitivity or underreactivity to routine sensory experiences; difficulty regulating attention, affective state, anxiety, or physiological patterns; difficulty processing and integrating particular classes of sensory experiences—we believe that the child's ways of experiencing himself and others, and of engaging the world, are also significantly affected by his interactions with people in his environment. Regarding children with such inherent abnormalities, Greenspan (1992) says that "it is . . . recognized that early caregiving patterns can be influenced by *and exert considerable influence on* how these constitutional and maturational patterns develop and become part of the child's evolving personality" (p. 603; also see Crittenden 1995, p. 389).

While a child's environment always influences his personality, no behavior arises as a pure function of the child's environment without also having been influenced by the child's inherent capacities and tendencies. Children all have characteristic temperamental qualities, and they have strengths and weaknesses in various capacities. As Greenspan suggests in the above quote, the child's constitutional givens elicit particular reactions—attitudes, interpersonal patterns, other behavioral responses—from these children's caregivers, based upon the caregivers' own histories and personalities. One child may—in fact, always does— evoke a somewhat "different parent" than his sibling does, which in turn creates an environment for the child that is unique to him. A child always contributes his own unique, inherent characteristics to the interaction with his caregivers. It is in this mix that the child's personality, and personality difficulties, develop.

Specific Biological Influences

Biology can influence psychopathology directly (though always in interaction with environmental influences) through genetic defects, through deficient prenatal conditions such as maternal malnutrition or alcoholism, or through the child's illness or injury. There is evidence of genetic influence in some major psychiatric illnesses—for instance, in autism; its milder cousin, pervasive developmental disorder; schizophrenia; and in some major affective disorders—although there continues to be a voice for the influence of environmental factors in the latter two sets of disorders. We will not engage that debate in this chapter. Developmental disorders such as mental retardation or fetal alcohol syndrome can result from prenatal deficiencies. Specific cognitive or perceptual learning difficulties, certain language difficulties, or some attention or impulse disorders can result from one or more of these biological influences and may subsequently influence psychopathology, although some attention and impulse disorders can be primarily the result of environmental factors such as trauma (Crittenden 1995, Fish-Murray et al. 1987, Lyons-Ruth and Jacobvitz 1999).

On the positive side, a child's talents and special abilities can influence psychopathology; for instance, a gifted or very bright child may develop conflicts and inhibitions around expressing his gifts as a result of patterns of interaction with his parents.

We note that even in conditions that are strongly influenced by biology, the link between biological influence and pathological condition is negotiated by environment. Fouts (1997) gives a dramatic example in his discussion of his experiments in treating autistic children. His observations led him to believe that autistic children suffer from an inability to process auditory and visual stimulation simultaneously and to integrate information from both of these pathways (an ability known as "cross-modal transfer"). This deficit makes it very difficult for a child to learn spoken language, since that task requires associating visual images of objects in the world with the sounds of the words that refer to these objects; this deficit can also account for other symptoms of autism. To circumvent the deficit, Fouts taught autistic children American Sign Language, where visual images of objects in the world are associated with other visual images—hand signs—rather than with the sounds of spoken language. The autistic children Fouts worked with—who had previously learned virtually no spoken language—picked up sign language very quickly. Other symptoms also improved. (These children also soon began to use speech, due to certain facts of neural organization that are not relevant to our present argument.) The point, for our purposes, is that a biological deficit (in this case, in cross-modal transfer) may become pathology in a culture of spoken language, but not in a culture of signed language. Environment is a necessary part of the equation.

Temperament is an important way that biology influences personality. Temperament refers to a child's innate behavioral style, her "characteristic way of reacting to new persons or situations" (Chess 1980, p. 121). There is evidence, for example from studies that found a surprisingly low correlation between parents' personalities and the personalities of their adopted children, that a child's temperament is influenced by her genetic inheritance (Plomin 1986). Thomas and Chess (1977) have identified several interacting components of temperament, including the child's typical activity level; rhythmicity of such bodily functions as "hunger-feeding patterns, elimination, and the sleep–wake cycle" (p. 86); the child's tendency to approach or to withdraw from a new stimulus; the speed and ease with which the child can modify her behavior in response to a change in her environment; the child's typical mood; the typical level of energy with which the child responds; the typical level of stimulation required to evoke a child's response (threshhold); the child's level of distractibility; and the child's tendencies in the area of attention span and persistence.

From these dimensions, Thomas and Chess derived three typical profiles of children: the easy child, who is happy, engaged, and relaxed when facing a new situation; the child who is slow to warm up, who tends to withdraw and become mildly distressed when faced with unfamiliarity; and the difficult child, who tends to withdraw, to become irritable, to adapt poorly, and whose patterns are not very regular.

Kagan (1994) approached the notion of temperament more cautiously, criticizing Thomas and Chess's research methodology for its lack of rigor, and he relied to a greater extent on physiological data. Kagan believed the current data justified only one dimension of temperament, that of inhibited versus uninhibited people. This polarity roughly coincides with Thomas and Chess's "slow to warm up" versus "easy" categories. Kagan's behavioral categories are largely defined by the reactivity of the autonomic nervous system, with a more highly reactive nervous system leading to greater anxiety, reactivity, and social reticence, compared with that of less inhibited people. Temperament appears to be stable as children get older (Pedlow et al. 1993).

There seems little doubt that temperament influences psychopathology and personality difficulties (Kagan 1994). For instance, people who are more temperamentally reactive seem more likely to develop anxiety conditions, social inhibitions and withdrawal, posttraumatic stress disorders, and disorders like obsessions and compulsions that are designed to contain anxiety. Temperament has also been shown (along with caregiver availability, sensitivity, and responsiveness) to influence the degree of security of a child's attachment to caregivers (Seifer et al. 1996).

Temperament, along with environmental factors, also influences children's and adolescents' antisocial behavior (Ge et al. 1996, Henry et al. 1996). Further, while environment may be a stronger influence in nonviolent antisocial behavior, temperament becomes a more important predictor for violent antisocial behavior (Henry et al. 1996).

A closely related concept that is partly an aspect of temperament is resilience. Resilience is the ability to bounce back, to recover from adversity (Rak and Patterson 1996, Smith and Prior 1995). Resilience is a buffer against stress (Rutter 1987). Resilient children seem relatively resourceful and flexible, and are less vulnerable to events such as separation, loss, parental failure, or other trauma, and are more likely to continue to develop in spite of trauma.

Mishne (1992), Smith and Prior (1995), and Garmezy (1991) all propose that constitutional factors such as a relatively high activity level, and being easygoing and outgoing, are related to resilience. These constitutional factors also may interact with favorable early environmental circumstances to produce personality characteristics that are related to resilience. These environmentally related personality characteristics include secure attachment to caregivers (Mishne 1992, Worden 1996), reflectiveness (Fonagy et al. 1995), self-esteem and self-efficacy (Kobasa 1980, cited in Feinaur et al. 1996, Rutter 1987), and a positive attitude toward new experiences (Maddi and Kobasa 1991). Current environmental factors can also be important in children's being able to weather adversity. Influences from the child's current environment include families with flexible, effective problem-solving skills and open communication (Walsh 1996) that are supportive (Ge et al. 1994), warm, cohesive, and caring (Garmezy 1991); current influences also include extrafamilial support (Garmezy 1991).

Principles of Environmental Influence

All relational theorists focus on how the child's developing personality is shaped within his relationship with his parents. What follows is a brief statement of principles that seeks to explain this. Sullivan (1953) described how a child senses and shares his parents' anxiety through his empathic connection to them. Because anxiety is unpleasant, the child quickly learns to steer clear of expressing himself in ways that will evoke parental anxiety. Instead, he seeks out experiences that he has learned will evoke parental approval. His developing, internal model of social expectations, the biases and restrictions in his perceptual world in general (his "self-system," in Sullivan's language), and the social behavior that results from these, are thus shaped by his parents' anxieties. In this way, depending on the parents' personalities and personality difficulties, what looks like illness is in fact often "a pretty remarkable manifestation of human dexterity in living" (p. 11) based upon the person's adaptation to his caregivers. Sullivan's theory is our basic model of relational patterning.

Recent findings elaborate on Sullivan's ideas. Fonagy and colleagues (1995) found that young children's patterns of behavior were specific to the parent with whom they were interacting, suggesting that children's behavior is responsive to the particular ways that each parent interacts with them, and that children develop internal representational models of themselves with each parent that are independent of each other. In another example of how interpersonal experience determines internal models, Davies and Frawley (1994) describe how the experiential world of victims of sexual abuse becomes essentially limited to the roles in the traumatic situation: everyone—oneself and others—is either perpetrator, seducer, victim, or rescuer.

Bowlby (1980), similar to Sullivan (1953), posits attachment to other people as the primary human motivator, since it keeps children in touch with their caregivers and thus fosters survival. Guided by the goal of maintaining affectional bonds with attachment figures, people—especially infants, children, and adolescents—form "internal working models" of the self's capabilities and of relevant features of the environment. These internal models are enduring and resistant to influence. On the basis of these models, children develop patterns that organize their attachment behavior. Internal models may be based not only upon children's direct interaction with parents but also on their observation of parents' interactions with each other (Katz and Gottman 1993).

There are at least two ways in which inadequate models for maintaining attachments, for restoring attachments when they are disrupted, for coping with them when they are lost, or for developing attachments outside the family, are important bases for psychopathology. First, someone's internal model may not address a child's basic needs. For instance, if a child develops a model that disparages or undervalues the child's need for attachment to others (see Sullivan's [1953] idea of "malevolent transformation," concerning how the fear of tenderness transforms the personality), or if a child has a model that leads her to avoid self-assertion, or anger, or sexual feeling, then when these needs and impulses are evoked there are likely to be anxiety and complicated attempts to cope that may result in pathology. Second, the models a child develops may be out of synch with the larger culture in which she lives, perhaps leading to feelings of alienation and conflict with others, and to being perceived as aberrant.

A child's internal working models derive from her experience with attachment figures. The subsequent patterns of attachment behavior she develops in new interpersonal relationships, including those with peers (Cassidy et al. 1996) to a meaningful extent, are based upon working models that derive from her relationship with her caregivers. A child's inadequate or disturbed models and attachment patterns may be direct adaptations to the disturbed internal working models and attachment patterns of her caregivers (Beebe and Lachmann 1994, Crittenden 1995) and may also develop in response to discrete or ongoing trauma (Adam et al. 1995, Beebe and Lachmann 1994).

A few examples may suggest how disturbance in children can be a reaction or adaptation to disturbed attachment patterns in caregivers. Anxiety conditions result from ongoing experience with unpredictable caregivers. Abusive parents produce in their children a tense, clinging vigilance (e.g., Krugman 1987) or a turning away from all experience of need, vulnerability, and tenderness. Abuse can also result in deficits in attention focus, intellectual development, cognitive flexibility, and verbal and mathematical ability (Fish-Murray et al. 1987), and is implicated in dissociative disorders and borderline personality disorder (Herman and van der Kolk 1987). Parents who are submissive toward their children or who, in effect, beg for their children's acceptance may produce children who are overreliant on cognition or who use affect coercively (Crittenden 1995). Similarly, parents who, on the basis of their own attachment patterns, establish masochistic relationships with their children (among others in their lives) in which the parent feels dominated and powerless are likely to produce children who are coercive, pushy, or mean. Further, these children are likely to develop internal representational models that will lead to their manifesting these traits not only with parents but with peers (see Cassidy et al. 1996). Depression may be a consequence of "never having attained a stable and secure relationship with . . . parents despite having made repeated efforts to do so (Bowlby 1980, p. 247), resulting in a learned sense of helplessness and personal failure about one's ability to make and maintain affective relationships. Permanent loss of caregivers naturally leads to grief and mourning, but when an anxious attachment has developed as a result of a history of discontinuities or disturbed patterns of relationship with caregivers, the result is disordered mourning. Bowlby attributes much physical illness and psychopathology in children to disordered mourning, including impairments in maintaining intimate relationships and in organizing one's life, persistent fears about loved ones or oneself, "vehement self-sufficiency," persistent hope of reunion with a dead parent, irrational blame or guilt, distractibility, aggression, or identification with physical symptoms of the parent's illness. Specific attachment patterns and their associated pathology will be discussed in more detail later in this chapter.

Fonagy and colleagues (1995) suggest two principles by which a parent's mental functioning affects the quality of her infant's subsequent attachments: "The child is likely to be securely attached if (1) the parent's [preexisting] internal model of relationships is benign, dominated by favorable experiences, or (2) the parent's reflective function is of sufficient quality to prevent the activation of internal working models based on adverse experiences inappropriate to the child's mental state and to the current state of the relationship between child and caregiver" (p. 269). Psychopathology may occur when neither of these is the case.

Beebe and Lachmann (1994) have discussed principles by which mother–infant interaction patterns influence a child's internal models of himself and other people. They talk about three classes of events that lead to internalizations. These are: (1) ongoing, expectable interpersonal patterns, (2) disruptions and repairs of these patterns, and (3) single, highly affective events. Each of these classes of events may influence personality and psychopathology in different ways. For instance, in terms of ongoing patterns: an undependable parent may create expectations of undependability in others, with a consequent anxious, clinging personality, or else a vehemently self-sufficient one; an intrusive parent may set the stage for the child to experience people generally as intrusive and demanding, with the consequent chronic effort to escape others' demands. In terms of disruption and repair: a child may gain a particular sense of the adequacy of her own capacities depending on that child's experience with her efforts to repair disruptions in satisfactory, ongoing interpersonal patterns with a parent.

Finally, Bowlby's idea of discrete memory systems within a single person, which can simultaneously be active, either fully or partially, provides an additional basis with which to understand psychopathology from an attachment-theory perspective. Bowlby describes how episodic memory encodes autobiographical sensory experience, while semantic memory stores generic propositions—a narrative—about that experience. In some people, under certain circumstances, these two memory systems can be in severe conflict: the story by which we think about an event may not match the direct experiences we are trying to cope with, and this can lead to pathology. A mother may be remembered as a saint, yet her child may be angry all the time and not know why. In this case, the anger at the mother is out of awareness and may get displaced onto inappropriate people.

How Much Development Is Really "Hardwired"?

In recent decades, psychoanalytically oriented child therapists have generally used Anna Freud's (1965) "developmental lines" in order to assess children's difficulties. Children are seen as developing simultaneously in several areas, or lines, including drive, ego functions, and object relations. Each of these lines of development is a preprogrammed pathway, and each person is at a particular point or stage on the way toward an ideal of maturity. While there are certainly innate sequences in which development must occur (for instance, a child must be able to stand before he can run, and have the capacity for declarative thought before developing a narrative sense of himself), a scheme in which particular developments are expected at particular ages—a normative scheme—is likely to understate the complexity of development and especially its dependence on context (Coates 1997).

Similarly, as we have discussed in Chapters 1 and 5, we agree with Harris (1996) who, drawing on the work of Thelin, sees development:

> not as a concretized, preformed ladder over which the individual scrambles, but as a multiple set of pathways whose particular forms and achievements are the outcome of emergent interactive processes, not of hardwiring, [even for] such apparently constitutional features as infant locomotion and infant cry. [Development is] an open system in which feedback as the outcome of exploration creates new forms of relating and behaving. This is the alternative to the notion of error correction in terms of some preset map of behavior. [pp. 539–540]

For Harris, as for us, "the genres, styles, and idiosyncracies of human performance . . . are the surface registration of internal worlds" (p. 538).

Each developmental achievement occurs within a specific cultural context (see Chapter 5). From an evolutionary perspective, humans as a species are characterized by a great capacity for flexible adaptation, rather than relying on adaptive skills that are hardwired and preset. People can become socialized into the great variety of cultures, all of which draw upon different developmental potentials to different extents and in different ways. For instance, a child growing up in a hunter-gatherer society will perfect certain cognitive, perceptual, and motor skills relevant to survival in that society—for instance, visual, auditory, and olfactory scanning of the environment; simultaneous (as opposed to sequential) information processing, in order to maximize quick, adaptive responses to a complex sensory environment (see Fouts 1997); and gross motor skills related to hunting—while children in a post-industrial society are more likely to develop the fine motor skills and abstract, sequential thinking capacities relevant to the tasks required by that society.

Each developmental achievement also occurs within a particular family's subculture. Certain families value physical strength, toughness, and competence; others emphasize intellectual ability; still others may focus on emotional relatedness. The children raised in these families will adapt to these emphases, and different areas of their development will proceed or lag in response.

But children develop within an even more specific context. They arrive at a particular moment within a web of particular, interrelated self–other relationships, and are subject to specific attributions, projections, identifications, attachment patterns, and other personal responses and expectations based upon the internal representational models of their significant others. These are the particular social realities to which they must adapt. Children's developmental achievements are thus embedded in and take their meaning from all of these overlapping contexts. It would be an error to assess a child's level of development in any area (her degree of individuation, for instance) without also taking into account the child's current interpersonal and cultural contexts (Does the culture and, within it, the family value individuation?), the meaning and function of the relevant behavior for the child within those contexts based upon her history within similar contexts (What have been the consequences over her lifetime of her attempts to individuate from, for instance, her mother?), and the relationship of that behavior to other aspects of her development within that particular context (for example: How well developed are her speech, language, and motor abilities? Has each of these been more associated with individuation or intimacy with her mother? Has her mother been more responsive to her attempts at intimacy rather than independence? How has this affected the development of each of these abilities? How, in turn, has her competence in each of these areas affected her mother's perceptions of her?—and so on). Consistent with this viewpoint, there is evidence (Epstein 1979) that behavioral traits are situation-specific and do not generalize across situations. The girl in our example may have greater success individuating from her father than from her mother, and may consequently develop and demonstrate her gross motor abilities (but perhaps not her language abilities, which bring her closer to her mother) to a greater extent with father than mother.

One child may have difficulty "taming her drives" (to name one developmental line) with one parent but not with another, or only with one parent and only when a particular sibling is also present. Another child may be shy with adults but not with friends, or the reverse. A third child may be impulsive at home but not in school. With this "impulsive" child, viewing his impulsivity as a lack of having developed impulse control—a developmental failure—would be wrong. This child clearly can control his impulses—he has achieved that capability, though he does not always exercise it. We believe it is much more fruitful clinically to ask why he does or does not control his impulses at particular times, with particular people, in particular situations, under particular conditions, than to think in terms of developmental failure. What are the situations that evoke specific internal self–other representational models in which this child exerts, or does not exert, control over his impulses? Looking more closely, we also need to ask which impulses the child can control, or has difficulty controlling, in which situations. Our clinical approach seeks to understand particular behavior (which may be seen by other approaches as ego capacities or developmental achievements) in terms of the child's perceptual world (which is colored by her identifications and responses to the perceptual worlds of the important people around her). Even given that different capacities are more or less developed, what is the meaning this particular behavior has within that world at this moment, and what is the child trying to accomplish with it? What are the specific internal self–other representational models that are activated at that moment? Our approach emphasizes that most children's difficulties arise from personal struggles that occur at all ages, though in different forms based upon differences in maturity of the child's capabilities and in his social circumstances. Difficulties that appear specific to a particular developmental period, for instance "separation-anxiety disorder," may actually reflect a conflict that plagues people of all ages, though it yields different manifestations at different times of life.

In addition, if we are seeking to assess a particular developmental capacity, we must keep in mind that a child may be motivated, perhaps even most or all of the time, to mask his capability. He may also feel he must demonstrate a capacity precociously—to mimic something developmentally beyond him, or to force his own development in an unnatural and distorted way—as a way of coping with trauma (Ferenczi 1933). A gross example of this is a young child who has been sexually abused and who subsequently acts precociously sexually aroused. We understand this as an extension of what began as her identification and compliance with what is expected of her by her abuser, for the purpose of avoiding the feared consequences of not complying, such as emotional abandonment. This operates on a smaller scale with parents who do not abuse their child but who expect great accomplishments that do not match the child's developmental pace, abilities, or interests.

We believe that it is especially important to articulate our approach given trends in the larger psychiatric world and in our society as a whole, which are biased toward understanding behavior in terms of developmental achievements and skills. For instance, children who have difficulties in social relationships with other children are likely to be referred to a social skills group for "training" in "acquiring" social skills. From our relational point of view, it is quite possible that this child does not have any deficit in skills; rather, she exercises her social behavior within a perceptual world structured by her internal representational models, which are derived from her relationships with her significant others. She may, for example, be "naive" or "oblivious" or consistently fail to engage other children in a positive way as part of a role she has adopted in her efforts to cope with a particular parent, which she then has generalized to peer relationships (see Cassidy et al. 1996, on how children apply family-derived internal representational models to peer relationships).

ASSUMPTION 2: PSYCHOPATHOLOGY AS PART OF A CONTINUUM WITH, OR A VARIATION OF, NORMAL DEVELOPMENT

Certain conditions are unquestionably pathological. Psychosis, autism, severe forms of separation anxiety or selective mutism, or conduct disorder are examples. Yet none of these is discrete, qualitatively different from conditions that are less clearly pathological.

What principles can we use to distinguish pathology from normal development? Sometimes, it is simply a matter of degree as to whether a behavior is seen as pathology or an aspect of normal development. Some conflicts inherent in the human condition seem to turn pathological only when they reach more extreme proportions. For instance, all of us need relationships with other people, but we also need autonomy and distinctness from others. Yet in the extreme situation, any intimacy with others can feel claustrophobic and threaten the loss of self, and any autonomy or independence can threaten abandonment by others and profound isolation. In such a situation, more extreme schizoid isolation, or else what Guntrip called an "in and out programme" can result: here, a person always needs to be out with anyone he is in with, whether by alternating these positions, or undermining the relationship, or playing a balancing act between two different friends.

Other principles can also help us decide whether a particular child's behavior is acceptable or troubling. We can examine whether his personality is rigid, or whether it is flexible and allows for new learning and further development. This principle applies especially to a child's patterns of social relatedness, because this is a potential arena for so much new social learning, a place where living can provide a "natural" therapy. Another criterion for pathology might be the extent to which a child's personality organization cuts him off from experiencing aspects of himself. For instance, a child may not allow himself to act, or even feel, angry (or sad, or excited, or assertive and self-confident, or open and responsive to other people) if he has learned from his interactions with attachment figures that to do so will result, perhaps, in ridicule, emotional abandonment, or parental anxiety. We can ask whether a child's adaptation allows or helps him move forward in developing his modes of relatedness and expanding his experience of himself, or whether it prevents forward movement. All of these ways of deciding about the degree of pathology involve judgments on a continuum, not distinctions about qualitative differences. We can also ask how important it is to decide whether to label a child's adaptation as pathological. It seems more important to think through these principles assessing the adequacy of the child's adaptation, rather than to decide on a label.

We can explore the ambiguities between what is clearly illness and what might be thought of in a much more benign way, by examining a child who had been diagnosed with a mild case of Asperger's disorder. This autistic-like condition, which is generally described as a biologically based disorder, is characterized by a lack of empathic connection to other people; an alienation from the world of emotions; impaired ability to understand nonverbal communication, to interact with other children, or to form friendships; intense absorption with unusual, preoccupying topics; and physical clumsiness (Attwood 1998). In the extreme form, these children are unmistakable.

But there is a range of severity of Asperger's disorder.

Ten-year-old Billy has been diagnosed as having a mild case of Asperger's disorder. He is somewhat self-absorbed and socially clumsy. He often tends to have one-sided conversations, making little eye contact and speaking almost as if the other person were not present. He talks in a somewhat babyish, superficially cheerful way. Yet he also has some success socially. He has friendships that are important to him and that he can maintain, and he has strong, complex emotional relationships with members of his family. There are times that he is clearly more engaged with other people; he makes more eye contact, speaks more directly to them, and comes across more like a child his age rather than as someone younger. Billy also has a mildly preoccupying interest in fighter planes—not so unusual for a boy his age, in contrast to the more peculiar preoccupations of some other children who have been diagnosed with Asperger's disorder. Billy has trouble handling his hurt feelings and anger when he is upset, and he is prone to tantrums. But he is certainly not an alien in the world of emotions.

Does Billy's diagnosis of mild Asperger's disorder reflect an overly medicalized, inappropriately essentialist understanding of Billy, one that treats his difficulties largely as the result of a "hardwiring" problem? Pathologizing a child's problems in this way suggests that they are fixed into place by biology, and therefore are less subject to remedy. Is there a different way, or a complementary way, to understand Billy's problems? Consider the following formulation. On the "hardwiring" side, perhaps Billy has a relatively reactive autonomic nervous system, which results in his becoming easily anxious. Any interpersonal situations that add to Billy's level of stress or anxiety are likely to lead to his withdrawing from these situations, rather than engaging them, in order to reduce his anxiety to a more manageable level. In other words, Billy is likely to become socially withdrawn and shy as a way to regulate his high level of anxiety (see Kagan 1994; also see the literature on sensory integration difficulties, e.g., Ayres and Robbins 1991).

Billy's tendency to be anxious and therefore shy may lead to his developing more private interests, as shy children often do, in place of a livelier social life, and to his developing a more withdrawn interpersonal style in general. This would protect Billy against the anxiety that, for him, comes with social interaction, and from the sense of personal inadequacy and the expectation of rejection that are often part and parcel of the experience of anxiety (Sullivan 1953). Billy's manner of speaking, almost as if to himself rather than more directly to other people, may likewise be a self-protective move, designed to help him not notice the rejection he expects, and even to be able to disavow his humiliating, hopeless wish for acceptance from others when the dreaded rejection happens—after all, he never approached them directly, never asked for their acceptance. Billy's babyish cheerfulness may be an attempt to deny his anxieties and make himself feel happy. His poor social skills may be the result of his way of coping with anxiety. His avoidance of social interaction has deprived him of opportunities to learn these skills, and may also have had the unfortunate effect of alienating others.

Billy's interest in fighter planes may be his way of struggling with some of the feelings that he is not comfortable bringing spontaneously into his social interactions. The planes and battles may represent, on a symbolic level, his wish to assert himself, and perhaps angry feelings that he cannot simply express when he feels them. The need to inhibit his expression of feelings in general is likely to make him feel frustrated and angry. And for a shy child, a private interest is safer than one that requires or invites others to participate.

Other particulars of Billy's situation may add to his anxiety and sense that something is wrong with him. For instance, Billy was adopted at birth. It is common for adoptive parents to worry that their children are saddled with difficulties as a result of genetic or prenatal influences. Sullivan (1953) talked about anxiety as being "contagious," and also as being experienced as the feeling of inadequacy, and other relational writers (Ferenczi 1932, Lieberman 1992, Silverman and Lieberman 1999) have discussed how a parent's image of a child may be unconsciously communicated to and accepted by the child. It is possible that Billy's parents' worries that he was damaged may have contributed to Billy feeling that something was wrong with him. This perception might have intensified Billy's tendency to withdraw from other children, both out of anxiety and also from the sense that something was wrong with him and that he would therefore be rejected by others.

Billy's situation can help us to see that milder cases of "hardwiring" disorders may be more profitably understood as variations of normality, rather than overinterpreted as examples of "medical illness." As discussed in the previous section, all children's difficulties have a biological component—the particular givens of a child's neurological, endocrinological, anatomical makeup. But this does not mean that the child's difficulties reflect a hardwiring problem.

ASSUMPTION 3: THE DEFINITION OF PSYCHOPATHOLOGY DEPENDS ON THE CULTURAL AND PERSONAL VALUES OF THE OBSERVER

An article in a daily newspaper a few years ago (Dreger 1998) described how "psychosocial problems caused by stereotypes about anatomy are being 'fixed' by 'normalizing' the anatomy" (p. F4). The author gives as examples administering growth hormone to children with short stature and surgically altering those with unusual genitalia. She also gives as a humorous example those people who suffer from "Double-X Syndrome," whose physical symptoms include "bouts of pain and bleeding coming and going for decades [and] hair-growth patterns that obviously differ from 'normal' people's," and whose social consequences include "[being] more likely than others to live below the poverty line [and] more likely to be sexually assaulted" (p. F4). Double-X Syndrome, of course, means being a woman. The author's point, apropos for us, is that "one person's abnormality is another person's life." She says that she has found that, in her experience, most people with anatomical abnormalities, even conjoint ("Siamese") twins, would not trade their condition for "normality" (p. F4).

In the psychiatric realm, there are those (Hartmann 1997) who say that even attention-deficit hyperactivity disorder (to the extent that it is genetic) arose in the context of a prehistoric hunter-gatherer society. In such a society, being distracted by peripheral stimuli was an adaptive, even necessary, condition, since danger could arise at any moment, from any direction. Only in our very different society, where our schoolwork or occupational work is conducted in relatively safe environments and requires sitting still and focusing on a single task for an extended time, is such a "disorder" pathological. Depending on the society and the situation, most of what we see as deficits might be strengths. Altman (1995), like Erikson (1950) before him, makes clear to us that accurate judgments about people's behavior, including what motivates them and what constitutes and contributes to their psychopathology, cannot be made without understanding their culture.

On a more mundane level, a shy child is more likely to be accepted in a family of reticent people than in a louder, livelier, more outgoing one. The reverse is true of an active child. Many parents and child mental health professionals have come across situations where a teacher felt a child exhibited pathology, while a parent "had not noticed" it, or where a child does well with one teacher (or parent), yet continually comes into conflict with another teacher or parent. It is easy for adults, from their more socially powerful perch, to attribute their conflicts or differences with children to the child's "problem."

The therapist, like all the other adults in a child's life, is not a neutral observer. A therapist has no choice but to have values about what is best for a child and to make certain developmental presuppositions. Ideally, most of these values and presuppositions are well thought out and well grounded (within a scientific and philosophical perspective which itself has inevitable sociocultural biases). These facts recommend that a therapist be thoughtful in trying to clarify her premises (both intellectual and personal) in her work with a particular child, and also that she carry her theories about a particular child with humility, knowing there are inherent limitations to her perspective.

WHAT IS HEALTH?

This brings us to an explicit consideration of the role of norms and ideals and a further examination of the place of societal values in assessing a child. Do we measure the child in our office against an average child, to decide whether he requires treatment? Do we measure him against an exemplary child? Do we aim for conformity, for better adaptation and integration into a child's various social groups? Do we hope for higher levels of academic and social performance in the children we treat? Given all the caveats we have discussed, what do we think (from within our own cultural and intellectual biases) defines health, and what defines pathology?

We do not equate health with conformity and adaptation. Children's difficulties often reflect excellent adaptation to their families' limitations. Further, we see some of society's values as themselves troubling. For instance, the materialism and acquisitiveness that fuel our economy may not be such a blessing for those who buy into these values. The emptiness and despair that result from looking to material things to provide a sense of fulfilment is a commonplace. The objectification and commodification of other people and relationships, another outgrowth of capitalism, also undermines the possibility of realistic, intimate, fulfilling relationships and alienates people from each other and from their own inner lives (Fromm 1947). Exaggerated gender stereotypes foster a sense of personal inadequacy and also undermine intimate relationships, but they are pushed in a capitalist system because this feeling of inadequacy helps sell products that promise to deliver greater self-esteem. We strongly object to the idea that adaptation to the norms of society constitutes health. In this regard, see Fromm's (1941, 1980) critiques of adaptation as a measure of health.

We see personal maturity (ideally a goal of therapy and closely allied to health, in our view) as containing a strong dose of independent thinking, even skepticism (not cynicism). This includes the ability to disembed oneself, to an extent, from the values and expectations of one's family and culture, and to see other people and society through one's own eyes rather than buying into the simplified, idealized version that they are often selling. Using Levenson's (1972) language, we would call this "demystification." We also value participation in one's society and culture, but we believe that people should seek a way of participating that feels authentic, true to their complexity and personal sensibilities. While we all have had patients, adults as well as children and their parents, who have left therapy as satisfied customers, better adapted to socially expected roles, these successes are not as satisfying to us as those that include a patient developing a fuller relationship with himself.

Additionally, adaptation, especially under coercion or threat, may require sacrificing a sense of personal authenticity (Ferenczi 1933, Winnicott 1960). One may need to construct a false, socially adaptive self in order to function in an inhospitable world, and may lose access to what feels true within oneself, even when one is alone and away from requirements to adapt. Such dissociative developments typically occur in response to trauma, but they may also happen in situations where threat is at a lower level—for instance, when a parent's love or approval appears contingent upon the child's compliance. We see a child's access to a sense of personal authenticity, and (given an environment that will allow its expression) a child's being able to bring this sense of authenticity into his interpersonal relationships, as an important aspect of health.

These concepts may sound sophisticated, as if they apply mainly to adults, and only those who live in some "politically correct" world. But think of children who strive only for social acceptance or for academic achievement. It does not take a trained observer to see that they can be tense, stereotyped, false, or overly conventional. Their despair may show, along with alienation and even antagonism or fear toward many of their own feelings. Think of teenagers who must wear the latest fashion, who have learned to objectify themselves in order to gain social approval. Think of boys who must be tough and fear being vulnerable or smart, or of girls who avoid "showing off" their intelligence in class. These constrained ways of living represent the ultimate in "fitting in," but none of us would hold them up as ideals of healthy functioning children.

Our model of health includes access to a range of ways of being. In one sense, this means being able to adapt in flexible ways to changing situations, based upon having a variety of internal representational models, and each of these characterized by a freedom of action rather than a sense of urgency, desperation, or constriction. Ideally, health also includes a flexibility rather than a constriction regarding gender-role behavior. But it also means being able to balance this adaptive flexibility with a child's having a clear sense of her own needs, wishes, personal sensibility, and values, and being committed to them. This implies adaptation as a choice, not a reflex. In practice, this means that a child will have different ways of being with other people, including the ability to differentiate oneself from the group as well as to fit in, and to have a variety of ways to fit in or separate oneself. And fitting in should, as much as possible, be done in ways that feel true to oneself, ways that allow self-expansion, creativity, and personal freedom, not self-constraint and self-restriction.

The idea of flexibility also can be applied to one's experience of self. We see the capacity to let go of a fixed experience of self as an aspect of health. Sullivan (1953) discussed the self-system as a function of the personality that constricted perception in order to provide a more secure, but falsely restrictive, sense of self. Current relational theorists (Bromberg 1998, Mitchell 1993) have discussed the multiplicity of selves that constitutes each of us. We all live in different self-states at different times, and each of these comes with a different sense of the other with whom we are relating, different patterns of interaction, different affects and moods and patterns of thinking. Health, according to these writers, consists of tolerating, even enjoying this multiplicity—being able to "stand in the spaces" between these selves, owning all aspects of ourselves rather than rejecting some and hewing to an artificially coherent experience of ourselves. The latter may manifest in children as the inability to experience and express certain aspects of themselves.

Benjamin (1988, 1990) proposed the capacity for mutual recognition, or intersubjectivity, as an ideal for interpersonal relationships that are satisfying. This means finding a balance between being responsive to others and asserting one's own needs. And this suggests that health includes both valuing and acting on one's own perceptions and needs, and also recognizing the other as a center of subjectivity with his own perceptions and with inherent value. The idea that the capacity for intersubjectivity is intrinsic to health further suggests that the capacity to negotiate between one's own needs and those of others is also a key element in health (Frankel 1998b, Pizer 1998). Further, seeing other people as both inherently valuable and inevitably different from how one would like them to be suggests that another aspect of health is the ability to face the limits set by external reality and within oneself, and to accept that one cannot have everything that one wants; compromise, delay, and frustration are inevitable aspects of life.

Health is not just about one's relationships to other people but about one's relationship to oneself. Health includes the ability to be alone (Winnicott 1958a), and when alone, to find different states within oneself, to be enriched by them, and to be able to use what one finds in creative ways. Bromberg's (1996) idea of "standing in the spaces" between different experiences of self and others means being inside the experience yet having a perspective on it, not losing the broader sense of one's own possibilities. This is akin to reflectiveness, or having a sense of humor about oneself, not taking oneself too seriously. Along these lines, Freedman (1985) and Ogden (1986) have discussed health as coinciding with a capability to transcend the concreteness of particular self-states, to experience oneself as an active subject and creator of one's perceptions rather than as simply reactive —with a sense that one's perceptions of others are personal perceptions rather than unquestioned realities.

The capacity to transcend particular states and experience oneself as an active, creative subject is closely linked to the capacity to play. Play involves the simultaneous experience of different self-states, along with the freedom to actively experiment with one's experience of oneself and one's perceptions of others. In cops and robbers, I am "bad," but I know I am not really bad, and while I see you, the cop, as a threat to me within this game, I simultaneously feel safe with you, safe enough to play this game. Our roles within the game feel real, yet not real. Perhaps I have difficulty accepting my aggressive, "bad" aspects, and through playing this game with you I can learn to feel more comfortable with that side of myself. Play is a safe way of experimenting with possibilities within ourselves and in our relationships with other people, and is therefore a bridge to new, fuller, richer relationships with self and others. It adds a richness, an expansiveness, and an openness to new experience and growth. Especially for children, who play for much of their waking hours, playing is a key way of coping with and growing through developmental (First 1994) and personal challenges. As such, we view the capacity to play as a key element of health. We explore this theme further in Chapter 9.

A NOTE ABOUT DIAGNOSIS

Our three assumptions—that psychopathology is always the result of the interaction of a child's constitution and his environment, that it exists on a continuum with normal development, and that psychopathology can never be understood outside its personal and cultural context—suggest that diagnosis is not a matter of discovering the hidden anomaly behind a child's "illness." We believe that such an essentialist view is incorrect and a diagnosis made in this way is always oversimplified and misleading. It may even be damaging to a child. Placing a child within a reductionistic field of thinking, the child may feel objectified, deprived of experiencing his struggles as meaningful and himself as an active, creative agent in his world. His identification with constricting family or cultural perceptions of himself and others in the family may be perpetuated. Such an approach to diagnosis also inappropriately constricts the therapist's ideas about how he may helpfully approach a child and his world. Our field's tendency toward diagnostic "fads," especially with children, in which one child's complex problems may be boiled down to the label of attention-deficit hyperactivity disorder this year and Asperger's disorder the next, is an example of how such diagnostic tunnel vision can impair a child's treatment in the ways just discussed.

A very bright 14-year-old girl, Elaine, who had been a performing artist for years, whose parents were both performing artists, and who was in her first year at a very demanding performing arts high school, one day suddenly developed dramatic symptoms. She had absentmindedly left a journal of her own poetry in a classroom. While in her next class, she suddenly realized she was missing her journal, and remembered where it was. Elaine ran back to her previous classroom, to discover the journal as she had left it, open to a page that displayed an explicitly erotic poem she'd written. The classroom was empty except for the teacher, a critical woman who looked at her in a way that she thought indicated that the teacher had read the poem and disapproved of it. Upset but relieved that she had rescued her book, Elaine ran back to the classroom she was supposed to be in.

Immediately, her thoughts began to race, and she began to speak so quickly others had a hard time understanding her speech. She could not slow her speech down. After a little while, she started to stutter badly. She went to the school nurse's office to try to relax and slow down.

When I saw her later that day for her usual Thursday evening appointment, she was very upset, thoughts racing, and stuttering badly. We tried to reconstruct the events of earlier in the day, and to explore the thoughts and emotional reactions she had had in response to these events. It seemed likely to me that some combination of sexual arousal, feeling harshly judged, and feeling pressured by high expectations from home and school had led to these dramatic symptoms. I also knew that this girl often struggled with the sense that her parents did not take her emotional needs and anxieties seriously, even as she presented herself in a mature, poised way that seemed to tell people that they did not need to worry about her. Moreover, she had a dramatic personality, and in the past had found other dramatic ways to communicate her distress and despair when she felt people were not paying attention. In brief, it seemed likely to me that she was exhibiting an hysterical conversion reaction—her symptoms communicating dramatically, but unconsciously, something she did not feel she could say openly.

However, I was also concerned about her suffering, and I wanted to short-circuit any symptoms before they began to have any staying power. I suggested a psychiatric consultation, thinking to find for her some antianxiety medication that hopefully would put an end to her symptoms in short order. I found a child psychiatrist who could see her the following day. I should note that I also took her crisis as an indication that I, like her parents, was not taking her needs and conflicts seriously enough. At this point, Elaine and I decided to increase our frequency to two sessions per week, and to include her parents in many of her sessions.

After her consultation, the psychiatrist called me. "I think Elaine is manic," the psychiatrist said. The psychiatrist thought this was the first presentation of a bipolar disorder—what used to be called manic-depressive illness—and that she required long-term use of a mood stabilizing medication such as lithium. The absence of grandiosity, expansiveness, or an elevated mood, or the fact that these symptoms had been present less than twenty-four hours, did not deter the psychiatrist from her diagnosis. These symptoms can be absent in an adolescent presentation of mania, she said. Elaine's "sexual preoccupations" (Is this so unusual in a fourteen-year-old?) and dramatic presentation (despite Elaine's having been socialized in a performing arts family and culture) supported the diagnosis. The psychiatrist knew of an adolescent lithium-efficacy study being conducted by a colleague of hers—a specialist in adolescent mood disorders—that would require a short period of hospitalization in order for blood levels to be monitored. The researcher, another psychiatrist, could see Elaine the following day, Saturday.

Until she could be evaluated for this study, the first psychiatrist prescribed risperdol, a very potent anziolytic medication often used to treat psychotic symptoms. This medicine put Elaine to sleep, even at half the prescribed dosage. However, a quarter pill did help her symptoms without knocking her out.

I was horrified. Symptoms that seemed to me to be meaningful, communicative, and almost certainly transient, and personality characteristics that were developmentally and situationally appropriate, in a girl I had known for several years (since a previous episode of treatment), were being seen by someone who had just met Elaine as evidence of a chronic, biological illness that would require long-term medication. Elaine was about to be swallowed up by the medical-pharmaceutical complex, to be transformed into a chronic mental patient!

Elaine's parents were also upset by the diagnosis and reluctant to accept it. Yet they wanted to consult with the mood-disorder specialist to see what she said. The specialist agreed with first psychiatrist. Wisely (I think), the parents did not follow through with her advice, and accepted my recommendation to consult with yet another (now, the third) psychiatrist. In the meantime, I had found someone who was medically competent, yet also more psychodynamically informed.

The third psychiatrist saw her on Monday. He was not sure of the diagnosis, but thought it was likely that Elaine's symptoms represented something more transient, more along the lines of my own thinking. He certainly thought it was early (now four days after the initial presentation of the symptoms) to make a diagnosis of a chronic mood disorder. He left Elaine on her self-prescribed dosage of risperdol, one quarter of a pill, which did seem to be helping. Elaine said he was the first of the psychiatrists who actually seemed interest in getting to know her.

In my next session with Elaine, now five days after her symptoms first presented themselves (she and I, and also her parents and I, had had daily phone contact in the interim), Elaine's symptoms were much reduced. We explored further the situation surrounding the emergence of her symptoms. When I asked Elaine what her symptoms would say if they could talk, she said, "They would tell everybody: 'Give me peace, stop expecting so much of me, I can't do everything you want me to do.'" It was clear at this point, to me and to Elaine, that her symptoms had meaning in the context in which they arose, and that they were a way of communicating with and influencing the people around her. In a few more days, Elaine's symptoms were gone. She stopped the medication, and the symptoms did not return.

Why had Elaine's first two psychiatrists been so quick and certain of their diagnosis of a mood disorder? It seems to us that psychiatry, including child psychiatry, is rapidly moving toward a more biochemical view of psychopathology, in which all human difficulties can be boiled down to "disorders," each of which has a set of medications which constitutes the treatment. The complexity of influences, especially familial and other environmental influences, and the sense that the child is an active agent trying to cope with a difficult situation, are devalued and ignored, despite the scientific support for psychological and emotional influences. With this approach, psychiatrists may feel more like physicians, more a part of the "neuroscience revolution," and less likely to run afoul of insurance companies who require an illness model and who demand the shortest-term treatment. They may also be able to see more patients and make more money. The fact that they respond to economic and cultural influences does not mean they do not also believe in this approach. But it continues to shock us that at the present time, a professional can spend time with a troubled child and her family and be oblivious of the overpowering human dimension of the child's problems. And it troubles us greatly how this biochemical bias can damage a child's sense of herself as a healthy, active, creative agent; can severely undermine her belief that her own experience makes sense and has meaning; and can dismiss and disparage the child's efforts to help herself, rather than understand and appreciate them and help her be more effective in her own cause.

In contrast to the essentialist position that Elaine's first two psychiatrists exemplify, we see diagnosis as heuristic and multidimensional, a continuous process of constructing and revising a complex set of interrelated, evolving understandings about a child's difficulties. The therapist's view must encompass various converging influences on a child's functioning and various possible ways of understanding those influences, and at least equally important, seeing the child as an active (if conflicted, inconsistent, and ineffective) agent in coping with his difficult inner and outer realities. In our view, the therapist must approach his working hypotheses with humility, since his understanding will always be incomplete, and with self-reflectiveness, since he can never fully escape his own preconceptions and personal (often unconsciously determined) biases. We believe that such an approach broadens and enriches a therapist's view of how he may approach a child and the child's world; it tends to foster a mutually creative process involving child, family, and therapist; and it conveys greater respect for the child's and family's own resources and essential health.

Additionally, a therapist is never an objective observer (a fact that is increasingly appreciated in adult analytic therapy but less so with children) and is therefore hardly in a position to offer an authoritative and complete diagnosis. There are two reasons why objectivity is impossible for a therapist. First, she has her own countertransference. The child's appearance, personality, family, and difficulties all have personal meaning to the therapist in terms of her own history and internal representational models. Further, she will undoubtedly be drawn into the child's family dynamics as these impact on her own anxieties, vulnerabilities, and identifications. The therapist can never completely escape her own perceptual schemas and biases, nor her professional identifications, nor her inevitable subjective involvement in the interpersonal field, as she interacts with and assesses a child.

Second, the child's awareness of the therapist, and the meaning of the therapist and the therapy situation in terms of the child's perceptual schemas, all mean that the child never presents himself to the therapist fully and objectively—without memory or desire, to borrow Bion's (1967) term. The child's transference, based on his own internal models of self–other relationships, means that he hides aspects of himself and highlights others; he hopes for certain responses or gifts from the therapist, and fears and tries to avoid other responses. Additionally, the child's actual experience with the therapist (whose behavior the child and family have inevitably influenced) affects his perceptions of her and the situation. Further, the therapist has a place in the dynamics of the child's family. She may be valued, idealized, disparaged, or dismissed by the parents. Each parent, grandparent, or sibling may respond differently to the therapist, or to the idea of the therapist. The idea of the therapist and the therapy itself may become pawns in conflicts among family members. The child's own loyalties, identifications, and role in the family and its conflicts will influence the child's perception and response to the therapist. The child is involved in a negotiation with his therapist as he perceives her, and may be involved in negotiations with himself about who the therapist is. The child's presentation of himself to the therapist is shaped within this perceptual field. A child may act "good" or provocative, stupid or capable, open or afraid and avoidant, stuck in a particular role or more multidimensional, based upon his perceptions of the therapist. The therapist is left with a picture of the child that is never the whole story.

Children come to our offices as active and creative agents. The process of diagnosis can easily have the effect of restricting rather than broadening our understanding of a child. It tends to objectify the child while at the same time subtly enhancing the stature of the therapist, who becomes the active agent, the expert. If the therapist takes herself too seriously, believes too much in her formulations as correct and true (rather than provisional, always incomplete and evolving, and inevitably somewhat biased), then the process of diagnosis both limits and fixes the therapist's understanding of a child, and tends to reify in her mind her perceptions of a child's limitations. Her understanding of the child as capable, creative, purposive, multidimensional, essentially healthy, may get lost, and this will certainly affect her approach to the child and the course of the treatment. Our three assumptions suggest a treatment that (1) must approach the child primarily as agent, not reactor—a person whose perceptions and motives determine his difficulties and will drive his treatment; (2) is relatively accepting of a given child's particular ways of being in the world, rather than measuring him against a preconceived ideal; (3) treats the processes of play and negotiation as inherently therapeutic; and (4) views the entire social field of which the child is a part as a legitimate focus of therapeutic interest and attention. Further, even when biology plays a prominent role in psychopathology, the fact that the child's significant others perceive and respond to these givens in a particular way, which then influences the meaning a child attributes to these aspects of himself, suggests that psychotherapy can be an effective approach in such cases.

7

Different Ways of Thinking
about Psychopathology

In our view, there are three broad ways of understanding psychological difficulties. These are overlapping, and most children's difficulties can be understood in all three ways. The first view of psychopathology involves patterns of attachment and relatedness. The second view
involves patterns of subjective experience. The third involves self-
regulation. We want to be clear that we are not splitting off the interpersonal from the intrapsychic: there is always an interpersonal aspect
to inner difficulties and a private aspect to interpersonal problems, both
as cause and effect.

PATTERNS OF ATTACHMENT AND RELATEDNESS

Our various theoretical bases for understanding attachment patterns—whether from interpersonal psychoanalysis, object relations
theory, or attachment theory itself—all involve the construction of
inner representational models of the interpersonal world that guide each

person's interactions with others. All these viewpoints try to explain how our experience with important other people influences the ways we subsequently experience ourselves and other people, and the expectations we have in our social interactions.

Disturbed patterns of relatedness can be roughly divided into several subcategories:

1. insecure patterns of attachment (potentially involving any interpersonal relationships)
2. problems with identification and confusion (which generally apply to a child's relationships with adults and with children who are seen as authorities or as frightening)
3. problems with interpersonal negotiation (the impact of these is often felt most keenly in a child's relationships with other children)
4. disturbed patterns of achievement, which we understand as generally related, at least in part, to parental ideals and values

Insecure and Disturbed Attachment Patterns

Several broad attachment patterns have been identified within populations at various stages of the lifespan (see Goldberg 1995 and Crittenden 1995, whose work provides a basis for the following discussion). Securely attached infants use their caregivers as a secure base from which to freely explore their environments. They seek contact with caregivers when in distress, find comfort in this contact, and generally have a positive approach toward caregivers. In middle childhood, these children seem relaxed and happy and are able to focus on tasks. As adults, they are "autonomous," capable of intimate relationships, and are self-reflective. There is evidence that maternal sensitivity (essentially a mother's attunement and responsiveness to her child) is related to the security of a child's attachment (Ainsworth et al. 1978), although other factors such as temperament also influence the quality of a child's attachment (e.g., see Seifer et al. 1996).

There are several less adequate, or "insecure," attachment patterns. First among these is "avoidant attachment." As infants, these individuals seem uninterested in their mothers and snub them. As these children get older, they continue to be seen as defended and to avoid freer interaction with their parents. They try to please and comply with adults and make few demands. They are obedient, overcontrolled, often overachieving, and hide anger and unhappiness. Later, as "dismissing" adults, they minimize the importance of intimate relationships and may be cut off from feelings related to these; they may also idealize their parents, yet their descriptions of their parents will be thin and two-dimensional—that is, they are not reflective about themselves and other people.

Children who are "ambivalent or resistant," the second insecure attachment pattern, have difficulty separating from caregivers as babies; they are easily distressed and not easily comforted, and their play is impoverished. They may also have problems separating from parents as they begin school. These children's "ambivalence" may be a response to parents who act submissively toward their children (Crittenden 1995). Children who have more prolonged difficulty leaving home and staying in school may be responding to a mother's anxiety or fears about her child's separation (Bowlby, 1973, Chapter 18), or to the child's own worries about his parents' depression, vulnerability, or suffering (Bowlby 1973, Ferenczi 1933). These children are often seen as dependent later in childhood; they may act whiny, contentious, and disruptive, or coy, helpless, and victimized. Personal responsibility is rejected. Others are made responsible for their well-being, and immediate gratification is often demanded. Such children may coerce attention from others, either through their behavior or through physiological problems that require attention. As adults they seem preoccupied, and as continuing to be entangled in early struggles with parents, with little reflective understanding of these; they may also be angry or passive.

This coercive, blaming way of engaging other people has overtones of what in adults is labeled as an hysterical or even "borderline" personality style: the display of one's own emotions and playing upon the emotional responses of others are ways the person uses to get what he wants. Implied here is the idea that other people have what you want and that you can get them to give it to you. Other people may be seen as omnipotent; certainly, they have the power in one's relationship with them. Despite these people's active, even manipulative, influence on other people, they deny their own agency: the sense that they are responsible in meaningful ways for how they experience themselves and other people. They may feel essentially passive and helpless. Yet their own disavowed sense of omnipotence and their sense of entitlement is reflected in a refusal to acknowledge both that external reality can set limits on them and that internal conflict can be a source of their difficulties. In a sense, this attachment pattern reflects a refusal to mourn the loss of omnipotence that typically occurs during the oedipal period, when some desires must be faced as inherently impossible to gratify—because the inherent limitations of reality or conflicting wishes present unavoidable obstacles to getting what one wants—and when accommodating to frustration or delay becomes more accepted as an unavoidable part of human life.

The third insecure attachment pattern identified by attachment researchers, more associated with frank psychiatric disturbance, is "disorganized/disoriented." These infants do not seem to have an organized strategy to manage distress; their behavior may seem odd, and they seem to be afraid of, or confused by, their caregivers. As older children, this disorganization may continue, and the child may also attempt to control the parent through overachievement, by working to entertain the parents, or by acting in a condescending and humiliating way toward the parents. In adulthood, there may be lapses in appropriate distance and orientation when discussing loss or traumatic events.

Psychoanalytic writers working with traumatized patients have described what amount to other attachment patterns. Ferenczi (1933), Fairbairn (1943), and Davies and Frawley (1994) described how children of abusive parents typically are loyal, protective, and tenaciously attached to their parents, and will deny or minimize the abuse; they also discussed how these children are likely to use dissociative mechanisms, both by feeling detached from the world they share with other people and living more in a private world even as they may appear to be socially engaged, and by detaching from the capacity to experience or show certain feelings, such as fear, pain, or vulnerability, which are associated with their abuse. People who have been abused also may experience a constriction in their perception of interpersonal relationships, and in their own possible roles in their relationships with other people; everyone, including oneself, is seen as either victim, seducer, aggressor, rescuer, or witness to abuse (Davies and Frawley 1994; also see Ferenczi 1932, 1933).

Overidentification and Confusion

Unconsciously purposeful confusion about others' motives and actions, and overidentification with other people or with their perceptions or expectations, are often two sides of the same coin.

Sullivan (1953) described how all children intuitively pick up their parents' anxieties and thus learn to avoid acting, feeling, and perceiving in ways that are "out of bounds" in their families. The result is a systematic selective inattention toward perceptions that the child has learned are likely to provoke anxiety in significant other people.

When a child has grown up among highly disapproving, critical, or anxious parents, there will be large areas of experience to be avoided, with the result of significant personality restrictions and a poor ability to adapt to and learn from current life experience. When the restricted areas of experience include some of the child's basic needs, or when many of the actual possibilities of the child's interpersonal world are proscribed, there are likely to be "disastrous distortions which will manifest themselves . . . in the whole subsequent development of personality" (Sullivan 1953, pp. 170–171).

Children construct their ways of perceiving the world—their internal representational models—based on the models communicated by their parents. When children need to tailor their experience of the world to fit their parents' very restricted or distorted viewpoints, many types of experience become closed off to them. For instance, they may become unable to feel that others are benevolent or to trust them (see Sullivan's [1953] concept of malevolent transformation); or, conversely, they may always give others the benefit of the doubt, even when there is good reason not to. They may become inhibited in expressing joy, or unable to show anger.

Children not only model their perceptions based on their parents' unconscious communication, they also accept many types of roles that their parents unconsciously assign them. They may become caregivers to parents who always seem frail or nervous (Ferenczi 1933, Miller 1981). They may become excessively responsible or self-sufficient, and may learn to deny all feelings of anxiety, dependency, vulnerability, or uncertainty, if that is who they are expected to be. Or else they may become "helpless," perennially anxious, and plagued with problems, if that is the parents' unconscious design for them. They may become "identified patients," behaving in a troubled or disturbed way, becoming the repository of other family members' disavowed psychiatric difficulties or emotional conflicts. Traumatized parents may show no gross evidence of posttraumatic difficulties, yet their children may carry the mantle of trauma, showing the symptoms that are absent in the parent (Abraham and Torok 1994, Lyons-Ruth et al. 2000; also see Main and Hesse 1990, Seligman 1999, pp. 138–139). Families who were victims of the Holocaust show posttraumatic reactions not only in the generation that experienced this firsthand, but in later generations as well (Bergmann and Jucovy 1982).

Children's efforts to fit themselves into their parents' view of the world and deny their own contradictory perceptions may be enforced by an anxiety that responds to a parent's (often implicit) threat of rejection, even emotional abandonment (Ferenczi 1933), if the child does not comply. In a related move, identification (including compliance with a parent's perceptions) may be a way to feel close to a parent when the parent is emotionally unavailable (Freud 1917 and Bowlby 1980 discussed pathological identification in response to loss, and Ferenczi described identification in response to the trauma of emotional abandonment [see Frankel 1998a]). We must emphasize, however, that identification is universal and not simply a response to the trauma of loss or isolation. Identification plays an essential role in children's identity formation and in the establishment and growth of all their important interpersonal relationships, good and bad.

Some children reject these assigned roles. Often in such situations, there is an important relationship with another family member, or with some other important person such as a teacher, which helps the child cleave to a healthier, less restrictive adaptation than the parent presses for. Even in these cases, however, there is a price to pay. These children may feel alienated or even rejected by their families, and may end up with a high level of inner conflict. More commonly, many children develop in such ways that make their parents uncomfortable at certain points, that challenge the restrictions in their parents' personalities. Some children may try to be what their parents want, yet assert themselves in passive or subtle ways. Ironically, it is often at times when children struggle with more expansive aspects of themselves than their parents are comfortable with that parents bring their children to psychotherapists.

Levenson extended Sullivan's ideas about selective inattention to the concepts of mystification and semiotic competence. Like Sullivan, Levenson (1983) understands pathology as the result of "being indoctrinated into a world where people act to maintain their own social stability" (p. 40). In order for some children to maintain their own sense of security and integration with this interpersonal world, they may not develop adequate semiotic skills—that is, skills at being able "to read and interpret the world, to grasp nuance, and to operate with sufficient skill to affect the people around them" (p. 40). Children may lose their ability to deal with other people in an appropriately discriminating way.

One typical way that children (and adults) systematically distort their perception of other people is to idealize them. Abused children, for instance, often continue to love and esteem their abusive parents, and wish to return to them even after being taken away for their own safety (e.g., Fairbairn 1943). They also typically feel guilty and responsible for the abuse they have suffered, despite the lack of any objective reason for doing so. This is often partly because they believe what their abusive parents tell them: that they are to blame for provoking the abuse, that the abuse is the result of their being seductive or behaving badly (Ferenczi 1933). On an even more basic level, children are often ashamed of being abused. Due to a combination of immaturity and parental pathology, they may not fully differentiate their parents from themselves. If their parents are bad, then they are bad. And if something makes them feel bad, they are in fact bad (Fairbairn 1943).

Taking on the parent's badness is not limited to feeling bad. Children often behave badly, precisely to prove their own badness and justify their parents' mistreatment of them (Ferenczi 1933). Freud (1916) first discussed such maneuvers in a section of his paper "Some Character Types Met with in Psychoanalytic Work," where he proposed that criminals did not feel guilty because they had done something bad, but did bad things in order to concretize a feeling of guilt that had unconscious roots.

Idealizing one's parents at one's own expense is not limited to abused children. Many children display this kind of exaggerated, self-effacing "loyalty" to their parents, making efforts to see the parent as strong and not weak, or good and not bad. Often, this is a result of worry about a parent. The child will believe that the parent, who is seen as vulnerable, needs such propping up. The child may believe this about the parent because of actual circumstances of parental illness or hard times (see Bowlby 1973). The child is likely to feel that it is imperative to see the parent as strong because not to do so would threaten the child's own sense of feeling secure and protected.

However, one possible key type of parental vulnerability that may contribute to a child's need to idealize the parent is the parent's inability to own up to his own vulnerability. Such an inability suggests that the parent feels so weak or overwhelmed that the parent cannot even bear to talk about his difficulties, perhaps not even think about them.

The child may also feel compelled to collude with the parent in "not noticing" a parent's "badness" toward the child or others. This is likely to occur out of fear, even if the fear is not based on having experienced abuse. The child may sense the parent's suppressed or unconscious rage and feel afraid or insecure (though these feelings are also likely to remain unconscious). The result is that the child may deny that the bad things the parent does are in fact bad, or he may excuse the parent, blaming either some third party—someone outside the family, or perhaps the other parent—or blaming himself. The parent's image as "good" is protected, because to see the parent as bad would also threaten the child's sense of security.

Similarly, children collude with their emotionally disturbed parents' need to feel sane and stable, because to admit to a parent's unpredictability would likewise open the door to intolerable insecurity. On a milder level, parents involved in an acrimonious divorce often lose their reason and objectivity and become swept up in anger and bitterness. Children caught in such a struggle may be under great pressure to identify with the parent whose emotional storms they feel most subject to—many times the parent they live with—and these children often end up sharing that parent's feelings and perceptions.

The costs to children of needing to deny what they unconsciously know include a diminished sense of being able to know what is really happening between people ("semiotic incompetence"); a lack of conviction and a mistrust in regard to their own perceptions and beliefs, and confused ideas about personal responsibility (see Ferenczi 1933, p. 162); the projection of the parent's badness, weakness, or unpredictability onto other people, with the consequent experience of people in general as bad, weak, or crazy (see Fairbairn's [1943] discussion of "the repression and return of bad objects"); and the child's own identification with these denied qualities in the parent, resulting in the child feeling that he himself is bad, weak, or disturbed (Fairbairn 1943, Ferenczi 1933).

Some children largely accept their parents' definition of the parent–child relationship and have difficulty defining the relationship on their own terms. Obsessive and compulsive symptoms may result from a child's anxiety about separating from a parent in this way. One 8-year-old boy suffering from compulsive rituals, intrusive thoughts, and a feeling that he needed to be excessively good, came to his session one day saying that his father had told him to talk with the therapist about a particular behavior of the boy's that concerned the father. The therapist asked whether the boy wanted to talk about that—a surprising question for the boy. This led to therapist and child articulating the boy's constant sense that his father was sitting on his shoulder, looking into his mind. The boy felt he had no right to own the contents of his mind, to think what he wanted, or to keep his thoughts private. The therapist's questioning these assumptions was striking to the boy. The idea that the boy owned his own mind, and the therapist's sponsorship of his being able to think and feel what he wanted regardless of what others wanted him to think or feel and of his being able to keep the contents of his mind as separate from other people as he wished, seemed crucial in the resolution of his obsessive and compulsive symptoms, including a lifting of his personality constriction, which followed shortly after these sessions.

Problems with Interpersonal Negotiation

Many children have difficulty with certain types of interpersonal transactions. Sullivan (1953) spoke about learning cooperation and competition as the primary social tasks of middle childhood. Similarly, Benjamin (1988, 1990) has discussed psychological health as requiring both the ability to assert oneself and simultaneously recognizing the other as a valuable person and a source of experience—a state she calls intersubjectivity. Some children have difficulty doing these things: they may be able to assert themselves but are not very responsive or interested in others, or they are quite attentive to others but are reluctant to assert themselves in these areas. Children who have trouble asserting themselves and competing may become withdrawn. In a more limited way, they may become tongue-tied when in the spotlight, or even be quite sociable, but only under more cooperative circumstances. These children can give but they cannot take.

Other children have difficulty appreciating and cooperating with others. They can take but not give. They must always be the leader, or must be in opposition to someone else. They may be provocative in order to prevent too much good feeling from developing. Sullivan (1953) spoke about what he called the "malevolent transformation": When children learn that their need for tenderness will be met with rebuff, ridicule, or pain, they come to associate the need for tenderness with anxiety; subsequently, in any situation that tends to evoke the need for tenderness, the child will instead act "bad." This "badness" can look like aggression or it can take a more passive-aggressive form. Such a child "makes it practically impossible for anyone to feel tenderly toward him or to treat him kindly; he beats them to it, so to speak, by the display of his attitude" (Sullivan 1953, p. 214).

Anger can feel like quite a useful substitute for other difficult feelings as well, such as anxiety, uncertainty, or vulnerability. Unlike these more painful feelings, in which a sense of powerlessness is inherent, anger comes with a feeling of power and certainty. It gets rid of insecurity and anxiety (Sullivan 1953). Many children, when they are feeling particularly vulnerable or upset, will rage or have a tantrum. Other children will act tough, as if they are invulnerable, untouchable, or don't care about anything.

Unfortunately, despite getting rid of disturbing feelings, the inappropriate substitution of anger generally interferes with better adaptation. Freud's (1926) concept of signal anxiety is useful in understanding this. Freud suggested that anxiety acts as a signal for psychological defenses. Therefore, the ability to tolerate anxiety rather than to act quickly to get rid of it using defenses—for instance anger—helps us to adapt more appropriately and responsively to a situation. Winnicott (1960) suggested that the capacity to tolerate vulnerability is a mark of psychological health. Being able to tolerate anxiety and vulnerability, rather than immediately turn it into anger, allows us to think and reflect on our current situation and on our responses to it, and to act with consideration for other people's feelings even if they conflict with our own.

In the extreme case, Fonagy et al. (1995) describe how the failure to be able to "mentalize—to picture the mental states of the other" (p. 488)—is related to feeling detached from other people and from one's own motivations and actions, and can lead both to self-harm and to mindless assaults. It seems also that such a lack of empathic capacity makes it hard to test the reality of what other people are really like, and easy to experience them as old, bad objects.

Problems with Achievement

Children may "overachieve," or more accurately achieve under pressure at a cost to themselves, for various, often overlapping reasons— all anxiety-based. Children who have developed avoidant attachment patterns may choose to devote themselves to achieving things in place of having relationships with other people or experiencing feelings. They may focus on achievement as a way of pulling themselves out of their disturbing families and finding connections outside the family, for instance at school, with teachers or other children with similar interests. Other children may feel they need to achieve in order to engage or hold the interest of otherwise preoccupied parents, or to please and disarm potentially rageful parents. The latter especially applies when parents value achievement. Children may also achieve in compliance with parental pressure, but this is likely to run against a resistance to doing so, and the result may be that, in any given instance, this child's efforts to achieve will be short-lived or vulnerable to interruption (Ferenczi 1930–1932; see Frankel 1998a, p. 55).

Other children underachieve, not working up to their potential. This is often a way of expressing resentment and refusal to fulfill the expectations of ambitious or demanding parents, and it can be a way of protecting a sense of autonomy or personal integrity that feels threatened by complying with these demands. Allan Sillitoe's (1959) novel *The Loneliness of the Long-Distance Runner* portrays beautifully how a young person can protect his integrity by failing. The hero, an inmate at an institution for delinquent boys, is exploited by the school because he is a fast runner and can bring glory to the school in athletic competitions. As he approaches the finish line, leading in a big race, he simply stops. He feels that to win would be to collude in his own exploitation and to sacrifice his sense of personal integrity.

DISTURBED PATTERNS OF SUBJECTIVE EXPERIENCE: PROBLEMS FEELING REAL, AUTHENTIC, AND OWNING ALL ASPECTS OF ONESELF

Whereas the first type of psychopathology that we see in a relational perspective emphasizes difficulties in attachment, the second type focuses more on disturbed patterns of subjective experience. For example, dissociation has been a focus of all major relational theorists (though some object-relations theorists have used terms such as schizoid, narcissistic split, or false self). Dissociation entails emotional detachment from aspects of one's own experience. It may involve lack of awareness of particular motivational systems involving emotions such as anger or affection. It can affect all aspects of a child's experience: certain perceptions, emotions, or thoughts; her body or parts of it; certain actions or aspects of relationships with other people—any or all may feel unreal, false, or not a part of her.

Dissociation is universal, and we can think of it as occurring along a continuum. On the mildest level, dissociation is an aspect of a normal developmental process of integrating various aspects of ourselves. Different emotions, different interpersonal relationships, different situations may all call forth from us experiences of self so different from each other that we feel as if we are different people from one self-state to another, perhaps even unable to feel a continuity from one state to another. As we grow, we struggle with this sense of inner discontinuity as we gradually build up an integrated, increasingly complex sense of who we are.

Some people rely more extensively on dissociation as an ongoing aspect of personality. If they learn, for instance, that certain aspects of self are unacceptable or that within their families certain emotions always bring anxiety, these may become walled off in a more rigid way (Sullivan 1953). Even parts of one's body may come to feel alien, based upon the meaning that has become associated with that body part. As life progresses, these people will have less access to the kinds of inner experience, and to the aspects of social behavior associated with these experiences, that they have learned are unwelcome. Such processes are to an extent universal and not necessarily pathological; everyone's personality is shaped by the reception their various potentials and qualities receive from their caregivers—which feelings or behaviors are welcomed and appreciated, which are frowned upon, which bring forth more extreme and upsetting responses. Sullivan (1953) discussed the consequences of this in terms of three aspects of the self: the parts that constitute "good-me," those that become "bad-me," and those that evoke such awful responses that they become "not-me": that is, they are dissociated. Everyone may have some area of "not-me," though childhood experience determines the extent of the personality that is dissociated into the "not-me" realm.

Dissociation is a natural response to trauma, whether that trauma consists of violence, violation, or the quieter trauma of not being adequately loved by one's parents. Some theorists (Fairbairn 1952, Guntrip 1969) also discuss dissociative developments as an attempted solution to the conflict between the need for other people, which threatens engulfment and loss of self, and the wish for autonomy, which threatens abandonment and profound isolation. This conflict is inherent in the human condition, but a difficult mother–child relationship can intensify it. In its more extreme forms, it typically leads to detachment or less than full participation in interpersonal relationships.

Dissociation can extend from a profound sense of one's experiences and the world not feeling real—even being unaware of oneself at all during a traumatic event—to being out of touch with more delimited areas of experience. As an example of the latter, a child traumatized by his parents' lack of response to his need for tenderness may become unaware of this need in himself and devalue all tenderness he finds in any interpersonal relationship. A child who has been regularly beaten may become unable to feel pain or fear at times. Other children may feel unable to be angry or forceful.

Dissociation may also be experienced as feeling lost and without direction, feeling disconnected from one's past or one's future, feeling that one's actions are simply automatic responses to events and do not reflect one's personal perceptions or choices, feeling a lack of conviction in one's decisions, a lack of commitment to one's relationships, or a lack of real participation in one's activities, feeling detached from other people, or feeling that one's life or other people's lives lack meaning. Mindless assaults on others may be enactments toward others of traumas that were inflicted on oneself, conducted in a state in which one's body, one's motives, and one's emotions are all dissociated; they may also be attempts to provide oneself with a sense of containment, cohesiveness, and reality—that is, with attempts to undo the dissociation (see Fonagy et al. 1995, Grand 1997).

Such mental states can have a variety of outward appearances. Children may look depressed, withdrawn, emotionally detached, somewhat mechanical in their way of interacting, or "unreadable." In others, an apparent social engagement and emotionality can mask underlying feelings of detachment or unreality. Some children who dissociate more tender or vulnerable feelings act smug, superior, or contemptuous, as if they have an advantage over children who can feel more than they can. Dissociative mental states can also manifest themselves as various forms of aggression and violence—indeed, such states may make violence possible.

Grand (1997) discusses how perpetrators of abuse can be guilty yet disown—dissociate—their actions and feel innocent. One of her emphases is on adhesive modes of relatedness, which are characterized by the experience of fragmented, diffuse sensory and affective states. There is no sense of agency, of history, or of the other as a subject. The other has no greater importance than simply being a "second skin" that one seeks in order to give one a sense of one's own chaos being contained. These ideas also can help us understand how some young people commit self-destructive acts apparently without thinking about them, and are resistant to reason about their behavior.

Playing is an important activity for children (and for adults in a different form), and disturbances in play can be thought of as a special form of this dissociative pathology. Play involves a positive attitude toward new situations, and fosters exploration, spontaneity, novel behavior, and creativity (e.g., Bruner 1972). As such, play is essential for children (and adults) in exploring developing capacities and gaining instrumental and social skills, in learning to solve personal and interpersonal problems and in approaching new or anxiety-laden kinds of interpersonal relationships, in developing creative solutions to difficult tasks, and in gaining a clearer sense of one's own feelings and one's evolving identity. The capacity to play, therefore, is crucial for healthy emotional development.

Play involves interaction between children, but it also is an inner negotiation between different aspects of a child's self. The playing child is both a reality self who knows that his play is not real, and equally a fantasy self for whom the character he is playing is very real indeed. Play requires such a duality of experience. It also requires a tentative, experimental approach to aspects of oneself: I am fully identified with the character I am playing, and in the next moment I can change my character or drop him totally and go on to being someone entirely new.

When the sense of duality is lost, a child may become overabsorbed in fantasy and undervalue the mundane, pragmatic reality in which he must live; or else he may cling to concrete reality and become afraid of his inner life. In the latter case, the child loses access to his imagination as a resource for coping with life's inner and outer difficulties. He loses a sense of himself as a multidimensional, creative agent with a particular outlook on the world. He becomes literal-minded: what he experiences is what is, he believes, and there is no other way to see things. He is without a sense of perspective or a sense of humor, and feels simply reactive to events.

Similar to the latter case, when the child's sense of experimentation is lost, the child loses his sense of humor and his flexibility. He cannot bend and may feel that any self-assertion by someone else is a threat to his own place and sense of security. His self-esteem is always on the line. Such a child will easily get upset and may readily get into fights.

PROBLEMS OF SELF-REGULATION

Beebe and Lachmann (1988) have demonstrated how self-regulation and regulating one's relationships with others are inextricably intertwined. Disturbances of self-regulation include disturbances in regulating one's inner experience, behavior, or most probably, both. Children who are trauma victims may be likely to develop a rigid, less adaptable character (Ferenczi 1932), to have difficulty regulating arousal levels (van der Kolk and Greenberg 1987), and to experience increased alertness and sensitivity to possible future trauma (Bowlby 1980). They may also achieve at excessive levels or become excessively "good" in an effort to control their circumstances (Ferenczi 1932). Or else, like many other people who have learned that more direct expressions of anger and assertion are unwelcome, they may underachieve.

Winnicott, in his 1974 paper "Fear of Breakdown," suggests that the fear of future breakdown is really a displacement of a memory of an actual breakdown from the past into the future; this suggests that other fears and apprehensions, not only those related to breakdown, may also actually be memories that are not experienced as past events but as future possibilities.

Children traumatized by unresponsive parents are likely to become depressed and to develop a learned sense of helplessness and personal failure about their ability to make and maintain affective relationships. Children whose parents are anxious about tenderness and intimacy are likely to have difficulty tolerating these emotions; the effect in their interpersonal relationships is likely to be that they will sabotage and spoil positive relationships with people (Sullivan 1953). Bowlby (1980) includes difficulties with intimate relationships as one of the consequences of disordered mourning, suggesting, like Sullivan, that certain interpersonal experiences will undermine the capacity to tolerate emotions related to intimacy. Crittenden (1995) discusses how insecure attachment can lead to children relying too heavily either on cognition at the expense of affect, or on affect, used coercively, at the expense of adequate cognitive functioning. Such strategies can lead to "conduct and attentional disorders, disorders of intimate and sexual relationships, depression, and, in the extreme, addiction to substances and suicide" or even to psychopathy (p. 402).

A NOTE ABOUT DIAGNOSTIC MANUALS

Diagnostic manuals such as the DSM-IV (American Psychiatric Association 1994) are increasingly oriented toward classifying psychiatric difficulties on the basis of observable signs and symptoms. As such, they seem to assume that similar signs and symptoms indicate similar underlying processes. Increasingly, this assumption is being extended to treatment, suggesting that people with similar presentations should receive similar, standardized therapeutic protocols.

We object to this orientation for several reasons. First, this orientation sees people as passive, as victims of conditions that befall them.

In contrast, we see people—including children—as active agents in their own lives. Each child sees and experiences the world in her own particular way, based on her innate capacities—her temperament and her perceptual, motor, intellectual, and emotional capacities—and on her personal, family, and cultural history. A person's way of seeing the world leads her to think, feel, and behave in ways that make sense, given her perceptions and capacities. We believe it is much more helpful— and accurate—to try to understand someone's behavior, including behavior that may seem pathological, in these individualized terms rather than as evidence of some alien, inner condition—some "psychological bacterium"—that is lodged inside her. The latter is an essentialist position that denies the complexity, the personal uniqueness, and the active and interactive nature of psychopathology.

Second, the essentialist position that we object to implies an illness, something that makes the sufferer qualitatively different from those not afflicted. Our assumption that psychopathology is usually not distinct from normal development but exists on a continuum with it, or as a variation of normal development—an assumption we have discussed and demonstrated—stands in stark contrast to such an "illness" model.

Third, the essentialist position taken by current diagnostic manuals denies the fact that what is defined as psychopathology depends, to some extent, on the cultural and personal values and outlook of the observer. While diagnostic manuals may appear to remove the doctor's own subjective influences from the diagnostic process by setting forth a standardized set of diagnostic criteria, in fact these criteria reflect an unexamined (and thus ignored) set of cultural biases. Further, this illusion of objectivity discourages the doctor from attending to his own, personal biases and responses as they influence his perception of, and influence on, the patient he is diagnosing. How many patients have told us of previous therapists or psychiatric consultants whose off-putting characteristics profoundly influenced how and what the patients presented to these professionals?

Manualized, medicalized approaches to psychopathology omit the crucial influence of perceptions—of the sufferer and of the observer— and replace it with a false essentialist assumption. The unhappy results are, at the least, that the patient is misunderstood and dehumanized, and is encouraged to discount and discard her own experiences and see herself, falsely, as passive. Often, such a manualized approach deprives the patient of the individualized treatment that is required by our viewpoint, substituting a standardized, and standardizing, treatment protocol, and stifling the child's own growth. Additionally, pigeon-holing a patient into a diagnostic-manual category would seem to prematurely terminate what we understand as a continuous, evolving process of ever-deepening understanding of someone's difficulties.

A FINAL WORD ABOUT PSYCHOPATHOLOGY

Any child's difficulties are likely to cover most or all of the bases discussed in these chapters. There will be temperamental and other constitutional influences as well as environmental influences. His difficulties are likely to involve his patterns of relating to other people, his feelings of what it is like to be himself, and his ability to regulate his own inner states. He is likely to have some confusion about others' actions as well as some exaggerated identifications with others. He is likely to have problems negotiating his relationships with other people, some rigidity and compromises in his ability to learn and adapt, and he will probably misunderstand certain of his emotions and feel helpless in dealing with some of them.

Most important, his difficulties do not separate him from the rest of the human race, though he may feel they do; his active struggles to come to terms with his endowments and his relationships with the influential people in his life constitute his unique variation of the human condition. As Sullivan (1953) said: "Everyone is much more simply human than otherwise" (p. 32, original in italics).

PART THREE

Conceiving of Treatment

The beginning of any child therapy in effect is a process of assessment. How specific, formal, and delineated it is from the treatment depends on the style of the clinician and on the nature of the case. Even the clinician who jumps right into treatment will be assessing the case, if only inadvertently. When the clinician decides to bring the parent into the session because the child is out of control, or mentions the possibility of medication, he or she is involved in an assessment. We do not believe that an exhaustive, definitive assessment is always either desirable or possible prior to treatment, but we do believe that the more thoughtful the clinician can be about his or her reasons for adopting a particular approach, the better. We believe that the clinician's curiosity about the case and willingness to maintain an open mind about what will be most helpful are critically important positive attributes.

8

Assessment and Treatment Planning

To set the stage, we present an overview of an initial assessment. Then we examine the processes of assessment, choice of treatment modalities, and revisions of treatment plans in the early phases of treatment.

A CLINICAL EXAMPLE

Ellen, a 7-year-old girl in second grade, was masturbating in class. This masturbation was not unobtrusive. It involved standing by the corner of her desk and moving against it, looking distracted. When asked, Ellen usually could not say what she was thinking about while she was masturbating. Once she told her mother that she was thinking about babies. She and the teacher had worked out a system where Ellen got stickers for every hour there was no masturbation. When the teacher asked her to stop she would do so, but then would start again shortly thereafter. Her parents had told her masturbation was fine but should be done in private; she wanted to stop but could not.

Her parents consulted with a psychologist whom they had heard was an expert in parent–child relations. The psychologist believed that Ellen should be seen individually and that the parents should be seen in couple therapy. He was ready to work with the parents, and referred the parents to Dr. T for individual therapy for Ellen. However the parents, each in individual therapy themselves, refused couple therapy at that time. They accepted the referral for individual therapy for their daughter, agreeing to meet regularly with Dr. T but only around parenting issues.

The assessment period lasted a month. During that time Dr. T met with the parents once, with Ellen four times, with the family once, and then with the mother (father was out of town on business) to tell her his impressions and recommendations. The paternal grandfather, who lived out of state, also died during that month, and Dr. T sent a letter of condolence to the father. He spoke with the teacher as well, who was frustrated and concerned.

In the initial consultation with the parents, the therapist learned that there was a considerable degree of nudity and sexual tension at home. Ellen had three sisters. Her father occasionally showered with the 12-year-old sister, and Ellen was also interested in this sister's changing body. Ellen and her 6-year-old sister used to play doctor, and the mother was nursing and changing the 4-month-old baby. The referring psychologist had also learned this, and had told the parents that all the nudity was overstimulating to Ellen. He advised the father to stop showering with the older sister. When Dr. T met alone with the parents, he repeated this advice. They assured him that this indeed had stopped, although they had not seen much wrong with it before their meeting with the referring psychologist. Dr. T asked about any experience Ellen may have had of molestation or sexual abuse, but they knew of none. Their lack of visible embarrassment or anxiety at these questions was similar to Ellen's apparent attitude toward her masturbation, aside from her quiet refusal to discuss it much.

Ellen attended a competitive private school that put a premium on speaking up and achieving social and academic success. Her younger sister, well-behaved and easily social, also attended this school and thrived there. Ellen, however, was fidgety, shy, and quiet, keeping her feelings to herself except for occasional explosions of anger. She had a few friends whom she guarded jealously lest her younger sister take over. She did well academically.

The parents' relationship was stormy, with frequent verbal arguments. Father was a commanding executive with a big voice who got into frequent loud arguments with his wife and oldest daughter. Ellen's mother resented his control and criticism and had a temper herself. In her own therapy she was learning to be less long-suffering and more assertive, even threatening separation; the father resented this. There was a particularly upsetting period about nine months before therapy began, during which the parents had told the children that they would be divorcing. Ellen's masturbation had become more frequent and less controllable since then. The parents also reported that Ellen had revealed that she was distressed by her father shouting at her mother or older sister. The referring psychologist wondered if Ellen were jealous of all the attention father gave the older sister, whether negative or positive, especially now that mother was distracted by the baby.

In individual sessions Ellen was quiet, spoke little, and made no move toward the toys. Sensing the need for a playful and nonverbal structure within which to relate, the therapist suggested doll play, but Ellen was not interested. Then he introduced the squiggle game (Winnicott 1971b). She loved this game and asked to play it at every session during the evaluation and for weeks after that. In this game, the therapist and child take turns making a squiggle (a scribble on paper) and then having the other person turn it into something. Ellen was much more expressive on paper than with words. Her squiggles, and the stories they led to, indicated anger at other girls, jealousy of her older sister, and explosive feelings. She left sessions gleefully, quite unlike the quiet, inhibited girl who used to come in at the start of the session.

When Dr. T met with the family, the tensions were palpable. The parents were cooperative but strained. The older sister was very concerned not to upset father in his grief over his own father's death. Ellen fidgeted, chewed on her belt, and was mostly silent as her younger sister chattered. Mother and father both occasionally yelled, which upset Ellen as well as her sisters. Ellen, despite her silence, followed everything, and felt obliged somehow to fix people's feelings after there was yelling.

By the time the therapist met the mother to tell her his impressions and recommendations, the masturbation at school had diminished dramatically. In addition, Ellen was more expressive at home. This improvement was probably a temporary reaction to the gratification of the evaluation period itself. The squiggle game had given her a way to express herself; and for the time being she had gained in Dr. T a man of her own to have a special relation with, allowing her to ignore for a while her intense feelings about her family.

The therapist presented a formulation to the mother of Ellen's masturbation. It was a sign of feelings of anger, sexual tension and overstimulation, guilt, and jealousy, especially of the intensity (negative as well as positive) between her father and her oldest sister, as well as her resentment of the middle sister's greater social ease. She could not speak about those feelings directly, but they distracted her, claimed her attention, and led to the uncontrolled masturbation. Dr. T linked those feelings to various relationships in her family, and explained her feelings about some of her classmates in light of these family feelings as well.

This kind of formulation is interpersonal. We assume that children will sometimes use their bodies for expression of feelings about their relationships—feelings about real situations they experience with others, and feelings concerning the memory and image of those situations as they review them in their reveries.

Expecting Ellen's symptoms to recur, the therapist recommended that his involvement continue beyond the assessment period. He wanted to intervene at four levels of relationship: Ellen's internal fantasy world, her family interaction, her relations with friends, and her relation with the teacher and school. Therefore, he recommended weekly individual therapy with Ellen; marital therapy as soon as the parents were willing; at least monthly meetings with the parents regarding Ellen's therapy; and permission to speak with the teacher to get and receive advice and information as it seemed helpful. These recommendations were accepted, and the therapy was launched.

THE ASSESSMENT PROCESS

For the relational therapist, the assessment process can be daunting. Unlike the family therapist who a priori chooses the family as the system or entity to treat, and unlike the more traditional individual therapist who is equally clear that the individual child will be the focus of treatment, the relational therapist does not begin with an already developed idea about whom he is going to see or in what combinations. More important, however, relational therapists believe that at the heart of the work is an unfolding and a discovery. This process depends upon whatever the child comes to feel comfortable expressing and doing in the consulting room, thereby determining what the therapist and the child can learn about the child's less conscious concerns and conflicts. It also includes what the child and the therapist do with their relationship, what potential it includes for creative transformation. They cannot know with much certainty how the treatment will go before it actually happens. In the case previously described, for example, the clinician considers family treatment but also discovers the patient's capacity to make excellent use of a play process.

There is a contemporary emphasis in diagnosis and treatment planning on the attempt to identify a discrete syndrome that characterizes the child, such as attention-deficit hyperactivity disorder (ADHD), posttraumatic stress disorder, a specific learning disability, or obsessive-compulsive disorder (OCD). The goal is to formulate a particular type of treatment intervention appropriate to the specific diagnosis. There is much to be said for the effort to discover relationships between particular syndromes and specific interventions that may aid in the treatment. Relational therapists adapt the treatment approach to the strengths and deficit areas of the individual child. For example, these adaptations may include modifications in the structure and conduct of the session for children with attention difficulties that would allow them to focus more fully on certain materials or certain topics.

This diagnosis-specific way of approaching treatment is especially popular among managed care companies, in that it lends legitimacy to the idea that one can predetermine the number of sessions required to treat each disorder. In addition, the more specific one can be about the nature of the problem and the particular intervention required, then presumably the more efficient the treatment and the less lengthy it will be. It allows the managed care companies to require a specific prediction from the therapist and to strictly limit the company's responsibilities for reimbursement. This approach can also appeal to parents. They can have legitimate concerns about what they understand to be open-ended treatment that they fear could go on indefinitely. Parents are also often reassured by being offered a specific answer as to what is wrong with their child, especially if it is an explanation that may relieve them of continual anxieties or fears about what harm they may have done.

Therapists thus often face demands for specific diagnoses from the managed care reviewers after their initial contact with the case, including diagnostic codes from the Diagnostic and Statistical Manual (*DSM-IV*) published by the American Psychiatric Association, which assesses the child on five different "axes." Therapists also face anxious requests from parents for the therapist to tell them what he or she thinks is wrong with their child, how it can be treated, and how long it will take. Often the therapist can make some preliminary observations after the first meeting, and at the same time tell the parents the questions he or she has that will be the basis for the ongoing evaluation. The therapist may also have to comply with the requirements of the managed care company by offering at least a preliminary diagnosis.

Nevertheless we have reservations about an approach that attempts to formulate a one-to-one correlation between the child, as representative of a particular syndrome, and a single treatment approach. Ironically, as the popularity of placing children in a set of discrete diagnostic categories grows, what started out as an effort to be more specific has resulted in an overgeneralization and loss of specificity. Currently many therapists, parents, and other professionals identify a wide swath of childhood behavior as characteristic of a small set of syndromes. Thus a tendency toward daydreaming, a capacity for independent play, intense concentration in one area and forgetfulness in others, can all be seen as symptoms of ADHD. There is a danger that children who are markedly different from one another except for sharing certain specific symptoms may be subjected to the same treatment protocol in ways that may not be appropriate. There is a danger that children's unique strengths and personal characteristics will be pathologized and seen as part of a syndrome. Similar, even identical patterns of behavior in children can arise from vastly different causes, and thus require different treatment strategies and lead to different understandings.

The emphasis on the syndrome may obscure what is truly meaningful and important to the child, and therefore what the therapy should address. The clinician who is overly focused on identifying and treating a syndrome may never discover where the child's pain lies and how to help him or her with it. When the therapist approaches the treatment with a particular program in mind, then the therapy loses its open-ended, experimental nature, and it deprives the child of the chance to use the play situation as an opportunity for self-directed exploration.

Our approach differs in being more holistic, and in putting an emphasis on the whole child and his or her relationship with his significant environment. The holistic orientation does not neglect specific syndromes that may characterize the child's difficulties, but rather includes such matters in the overall approach. Although some conflict or tension may inevitably exist between the approach we are advocating and the more concrete, specific one of identifying the particular diagnosis and its related treatment regimen, we believe that the more inclusive and thorough the therapist is in attempting to understand the child and his family, then the better equipped he or she will be in addressing the concerns and questions both of insurers and of parents.

Carey is an 8-year-old girl whom her parents had attempted to engage in individual therapy, which she resisted vigorously. After several sessions, they discontinued the effort. The parents described Carey as moody, demanding, often angry, and very rigid. Nighttime with her was a horror, as she frequently demanded ongoing attention and had great trouble going to sleep. The parents were very eager to identify the nature of Carey's problem and to find the best treatment approach. They had done some reading on some of the behavior Carey was showing and on various treatment approaches. It appeared to them that Carey suffered from OCD. They had read about cognitive-behavioral therapy for such difficulties. They were hoping to find a therapist who would tell them what Carey's problem was, what the goal of the treatment would be, and how long it would take.

But in the course of a careful, detailed exploration of what Carey's behavior was like and what might be affecting her, several things became clear. Carey had become bitterly envious of her younger sister, who had been diagnosed with ADHD and had commanded a great deal of her mother's attentions over the past two years. Further, it became clear that Carey was disturbed by any separation from either parent, and during such moments, she would become tense and rigid in her behavior. Carey's mother responded to these tense moments with anxiety and considerable rage, so that it was not often clear where the anger started. Carey missed having consistent contact with her dad, who traveled a lot and was not a regular presence during the most stressful moments in the children's lives. Dad, who had grown up in a family with much conflict and fights among siblings, was less troubled and less thrown by how his daughters interacted. The mom, who was an only child, found the children's behavior very troubling and felt at a loss in the face of it.

As these issues were identified through the therapist's questions, it became clear that Carey's distress might have a number of different sources and that it would require the parents' participation in making efforts to reduce or eliminate some of them. Although Carey did show signs of rigidity that could point toward an incipient OCD syndrome, as well as signs of depression, it seemed unlikely that any clearer formulation of what might afflict her could be reached until the parents began some work on how they were dealing with both children and handling the rivalry between them, and before there was a more successful effort in engaging Carey in some type of treatment relationship.

Although the parents were eager to find an answer from a book, or from the clinician, when they reviewed the range of possible factors in the clinical interview, they began to see that a different process was required of them. We often find that when a case is described fully and sensitively to either the parents of a child or the managed care reviewer, the case speaks for itself, and in some respects makes the task of assigning it to a specific diagnostic category less compelling and less essential. While we argue that assigning a child to a specific diagnostic category may not always be warranted, we do believe that it is the responsibility of the therapist to offer the parents a clear and concise statement of his or her observations concerning the child.

CHOICE OF TREATMENT MODALITY

Therapists see parents and children in various combinations, depending on the needs and availability of the child and parent, as well as on the child's age and stage of development. For example, therapists may see parents regularly while also working with the child (Chethik 1989, Hoffman 1984); or alone without any child therapy (Chethik 1989, Furman 1957); or conjointly with their child in dyadic therapy (Bergmann 1993, Elkisch 1953, Fraiberg et al. 1975); or in individual therapy concurrent with family therapy (Shapiro 1977). More than one therapist is often involved. It may be judged preferable for an adolescent or preadolescent to see one therapist and for the parents to see someone else for support and guidance around their difficult teenager. Chazan (1995) describes a different approach to the simultaneous treatment of parent and child, in which the fact of one therapist earning the trust of both parent and child is used to facilitate the therapy. Yet it also may be judged preferable for someone else to see the child, so that, for example, intrusive parents don't overwhelm the boundaries of the child's therapy. Or a therapist may see a parent in analysis while someone else works with the child (Kris 1981).

It would be counterproductive and contrary to our interpersonal focus for the therapist to impose a treatment plan on an individual patient or a family. The therapist may have a strong recommendation to make, but nonetheless needs to solicit the patients' reaction to the recommendation and engage in a dialogue with them about the recommendation and about any alternative suggestions they may have. In this way, our approach diverges from a traditional medical model in which the therapist is the expert, solely responsible for determining the treatment that is indicated. We recognize that the therapist has an expertise, but that the therapeutic process is inevitably a two-way street. Even in strictly medical treatments, patients are heard from, if only by their noncompliance with the expert's recommendations.

Typically, treatment planning needs to take account of a family's limitations with respect to time and money. Therapists, with their own limitations, cannot intervene at all levels, nor can they always predict or control developments at various levels of a system. Treatment planning is essentially the process of deciding the level at which we will focus our interventions, and how we will take account of developments at other levels of the system. We may pay most attention to the child as a person, let us say. But we do our best to keep an eye on the child's biochemical and medical status as well, and on the family, the school, and the community, to monitor events at these levels and to influence them as best we can to further our therapeutic project. Nonetheless, when a child is presented for treatment, there is usually a need for parent guidance, if not couple or family therapy as well.

Contemporary children are often as tightly scheduled as a busy professional person, and needless to say, so are their parents. Money is also typically an issue, especially if the therapist's fees are high. This situation has led to even classically trained psychoanalysts settling for once- and twice-weekly treatments with many of their child patients. When there are family-systemic problems as well, the therapist and family may need to prioritize the treatments. Most often, one ends up feeling like a juggler, trying to keep two or more balls in the air simultaneously. For example, a therapist might do individual treatment with a child while trying to help the parents function together as parents (thus intervening in a marital system) in occasional "parent guidance" sessions.

Although we approach the treatment of a child from a relational and psychoanalytic perspective, it should be clear that we do not insist on seeing a child a minimum of three times per week, as is often the case in more traditional psychoanalytic approaches. We are advocating an approach that we believe can apply usefully in clinic settings where children may not be seen more than once per week.

We do believe, however, that in most cases, when seeing the child individually, the greater frequency has several advantages. The greater frequency requires a higher level of commitment on the part of the parents and the child. It also encourages a fuller involvement and commitment on the therapist's part. The greater frequency is likely to deepen the emotional engagement between the child and the therapist and to generate fuller opportunities for exploration of transference and countertransference. Greater frequency may mean that more far-reaching work of more significant impact can occur in what may prove to be a shorter period of time than would be possible at once per week.

The decision about how often to see the child will be affected by the arrangements the therapist makes for meeting with the parents as well. If the therapist begins by meeting with the parents exclusively, such sessions may be worth continuing even if the therapist chooses to start seeing the child individually. When the therapist decides to work with the child primarily, it is certainly desirable to have meetings with the parents on a somewhat regular basis. When a child is being seen twice a week, one of these sessions could be used for parent meetings if cost and schedule pose obstacles to adding another meeting time.

It is a common arrangement in clinic settings for the therapist to divide a weekly session between a parent and a child, and to see the child for forty-five minutes and then meet with the parent for fifteen minutes. This arrangement may be necessary when it is important to keep the cost to a minimum and where transportation, scheduling, and child care arrangements prohibit more frequent contact. While such an arrangement can be workable, it has several disadvantages. Sharing the session can undermine the child's experience that the therapist is there for her or him and can heighten the child's concerns about boundaries, privacy, and confidentiality. In addition, such an arrangement puts a heavy burden on the therapist for whom the fifteen-minute parent contact often does not allow him or her to raise important parenting issues and to explore the parent's participation in the child's particular conflicts. Such brief contacts more often than not become vehicles for conveying parental anxieties and complaints, rather than being vehicles for introducing the parent to the role of being a patient. Of course, such brief contacts do offer the therapist a chance to learn more about what is going on in the child's life and to learn more about the parent. Under these circumstances, the therapist might consider supplementing these contacts with a regularly scheduled telephone session with the parent and possibly the use of e-mail exchange to further develop the parent–therapist dialogue.

When the family is willing, we tend to favor working with the family or couple before starting with an individual child. It is generally relatively uncomplicated to continue an individual treatment after a family or couple intervention has been made; it is often not feasible to include other family members once an alliance is made with an individual member. Furthermore, it is more likely that an individual's symptoms will be resolved by a systemic intervention, than that a systemic dysfunction will clear up as a result of an individual treatment. An exception to this general principle is that it is sometimes possible for parents to work on personal problems via, or on behalf of, their child in a way that they would not do on their own behalf. The following case illustrates a shift in parental participation that occurred most likely as a result of a systemic intervention.

Joey was a 6-year-old boy who had been saying that he was, or wished to be, a girl, since he was 3 years old. Joey had a sensitive and shy temperament, and avoided rough and tumble play with other boys. He loved to put on his mother's or sister's clothing, make-up, and perfume. His father, Mr. A, was a highly successful attorney who described himself as very aggressive in his work and in his athletic career in college. Mr. A's own father had been very demanding with him, and was at times verbally abusive when Mr. A failed to live up to his standards academically and athletically. The therapist, who was male, had the impression that Mr. A had a sensitive side to him, which he revealed in unguarded moments, but that he seemed determined to present himself as very tough. He spent little time with Joey, claiming that Joey was so different from him that he did not know how to connect with him. Mr. A spent his days off watching sports on TV, which did not interest Joey. Joey liked fantasy play, which did not interest his father. He resisted the urging of his wife and the therapist in sessions that he find ways to spend time with Joey. But outside of sessions, and without acknowledging that he was doing so, he began to explore activities he could share with him. Mr. A loved golf, which previously he had played only with business associates. Now, he and Joey started playing miniature golf together, which they both enjoyed. Mr. A began reading Joey stories in the evenings and even sometimes became part of the bedtime routine.

It was the therapist's impression that Mr. A, based on his own history, had excluded his own more gentle and sensitive side from his overt behavior, and perhaps from his own awareness. Joey may have represented for his father a part of his own personality for which there had been no space in his family of origin. Mr. A may have avoided Joey as he avoided his own more sensitive side. The therapist, as a man who could play with children, perhaps modeled a new way of being a man for Mr. A. In any case, on behalf of his son, Mr. A, as he found a face-saving way to build a bond with Joey, did some reworking of his own masculinity that he might never have done on his own behalf.

The principle of attempting a systemic intervention before attempting an individual treatment makes most sense when individual treatment is conceived of as nonsystemic, that is, when a child treatment is thought to involve only the child as an isolated, autonomous individual. Our own approach to child work, which involves parents in a central way, is inevitably systemic, so that the distinction tends to break down in practice.

Here is a clinical illustration of treatment planning, in which the choice was made to conduct a primary intervention with the child and a secondary intervention with the parents.

A male therapist is consulted because a 4-year-old boy is experiencing severe separation anxiety at school. The therapist learns that the mother has a traumatic background, with parental neglect and abuse. In her effort to protect her child from what happened to her, she has difficulty disengaging from her child, or in trusting other people, including her husband as well as outsiders such as teachers, to care for her child. Her husband resents being left out of his wife's life as she focuses so heavily on the child. He withdraws from involvement with his son. The nursery school staff get frustrated with the mother, as she resists their efforts to help her leave her son with them. Some days, the child resists leaving home to go to school, and his mother decides to give him a day off. But then she feels overwhelmed by the child's needs, unable to have a life of her own. The nursery school staff have been trying to get her to take her son to a therapist, which has made her feel all the more that they do not like or understand him, and thus cannot be trusted to take care of him. Finally, she agrees to consult a therapist with the idea that she needs help deciding whether to withdraw him from the school.

In this case, the therapist recommended that the child be seen individually to help him with his separation anxiety. The focus was on the child because the parents seemed to be focusing minimally if at all on their own participation in the separation difficulty, and it was felt that they could best be engaged if the child was the focus. It seemed enough at the time that the school was no longer perceived as the only problem. The therapist recognized, however, that the parents' participation would be crucial to the success of this treatment. He recommended every-other-week meetings with the parents. They objected that this frequency would put a strain on their own schedules, and seemed unwarranted. The therapist agreed to monthly meetings, as long as he could touch base with a parent on the phone briefly once a week. The therapist occasionally described the nature of the play activities that took place between him and the child, and the ways in which he understood the child's mental life as revealed therein. The mother would occasionally tell the therapist that she felt he was getting something wrong, and the therapist would appreciate the mother's input. He felt that it was important that the mother feel she could participate in the child's therapy in this way.

In both classical Freudian and Kleinian psychoanalytic treatment of children, the custom was for one therapist to see the child, while another therapist saw the parents for "parent guidance." If the parents required more intensive intervention, they would be referred to another therapist for individual treatment or treatments. The rationale for such planning grew out of a one-person psychology, where the therapist in each case should be focusing on the intrapsychic life of each individual. To see a family member or other collateral individual was to break the boundary around the individual treatment. Although our own approach is interpersonal and systemic, we do believe that there may be times when such a treatment plan is desirable. For example, when a parent is in a pre-existing individual treatment and the parent's therapist makes a referral of the child based on what she is hearing from the parent, it often seems appropriate to see the child individually. Collateral meetings between a parent and child therapist may also result in a parent's becoming curious or concerned about himself or herself enough to seek out individual treatment. In such cases, we believe that it can be crucial that all therapists be in communication with each other to provide a coordinated and integrated approach to the various participants at the individual and family systemic levels. There are times when the failure of such communication can threaten to create therapeutic impasses. The decision to attempt such communication is a complex one, however. Considerations regarding boundaries and privacy must be weighed against the potential advantages.

We use the word "intervention" as distinct from therapy, to characterize the therapist's initial contact with the child and his family, to indicate that at the outset, it is not always clear that what the child needs, at least at first, is therapy at all. In the evaluative phase, the most important function of the therapist is to raise questions, often ones not considered prior to treatment. In so doing, the therapist may frustrate the parents' need for answers and may not necessarily support the initial recommendation of the referring clinician. The questions that the therapist considers will form the skeletal structure for the initial sequence of interventions.

The referral came from a pediatrician. Roy, a 12-year-old boy, had been having trouble getting to sleep for over a year. Medical causes had been ruled out and the pediatrician suggested a psychotherapy consultation, after a brief conference with the parents.

When the parents called, the therapist told them that he usually meets first with the parents alone, but sometimes with young teenagers it is important to include them from the beginning. He asked what they thought would be appropriate in their child's case. Most parents traverse this issue fairly quickly, but Roy's mother became very confused and vacillated back and forth obsessively. Mrs. C said that she could not decide because she thought that it would be good for her and her husband to talk without Roy, but she also feared that she would not do justice to Roy's point of view if he were absent. The therapist suggested that based upon that feeling that Roy's point of view was key, it might be best to have Roy attend the first session.

The C family was striking at the first meeting. The parents were pleasant and very positive with their son. Roy was small for his age, overweight, and very anxious. At first all three of them were seen together. After gathering some factual information from Roy for a standard cover sheet, the therapist asked them who would like to start and tell what brought them to a psychologist's office.

To the therapist's surprise, Roy volunteered and told about his sleep issues.

Roy described a situation each night where he was afraid to fall asleep because he feared that "something bad will happen." "Such as . . . ?" the therapist asked. Roy replied, "Someone breaking in or someone getting sick or hurt, or some other emergency. I have had these fears ever since a weekend camping trip, over a year ago." Nothing remarkable was remembered about this trip to initiate sleep difficulties. His mother chimed in to help him out: "Wasn't there a movie scene that scared you and that you keep remembering?" "Oh yeah." Roy said. "I think about a scene in the movie *Apollo 13* where they realized that they could get stuck floating in space forever, until they died of starvation. I know that's stupid." The therapist said that it sounded pretty scary to him, and his parents quickly agreed. The father added, "We keep reassuring him that the odds of his being trapped in some situation where he would helplessly starve to death were minimal, but it doesn't seem to calm him." "I know it's stupid," Roy said again. All three adults found themselves telling Roy that the problem was definitely not about stupid thoughts but scary ones. The family problem was alive in the room at this moment: Roy being afraid and feeling ashamed about it, and all the adults quickly coming to his rescue and solicitously telling him not to feel bad. The therapist made this observation, and the parents agreed that this was a part of the situation.

The therapist then asked the parents what they would like to add. The mother added that her father died last year and that Roy was very close to him. Roy later told the therapist that he missed his grandfather and that he had the same birthday as his grandfather. Also, Roy's first baby-sitter, whom he had had since birth, had to quit last year since she was ill. Finally, the father of Roy's friend had died in a car accident also within the past year.

The father added that Roy comes into the den late at night while he is watching television and wants to cuddle with him. Then in a slightly embarrassed but straightforward way, the father also remembered that Roy came into the parents' bedroom one night and saw the two of them naked in bed in a "compromising position."

[We would like to mention here that in some family consultations, flexibility, within the session, as to who is present is desirable. The goal is to help family members articulate what they need to say to the therapist. Sometimes this requires that a child leave the consulting room or a parent, or parents, leave the room. The goal of aiding in family understanding is stressed. In this case, Roy's parents felt that they would prefer if Roy were not present while they discussed some issues that turned out to be of a sexual nature. Roy did not object to being asked to leave for a few minutes. Later the therapist can check in to see how the child processed the request that he leave.]

Back to the session, later the father told the therapist, when Roy was not present, that he wondered if Roy came in on purpose because he heard noise and wanted to see if they were making love. The father added that Roy had never come into their room before without knocking, but this time he just barged in, looked at them and left. The parents claimed that this had not affected their subsequent private time together, but they were not convincing in an interview that had otherwise seemed more forthright and honest. The therapist asked the father what sexual information Roy had. Mr. C said that he did not know, but he knew that Roy sometimes looks at pornography on the Internet. The therapist asked how they were handling this, and another crack in the parent's cohesive presentation appeared. The father said he told him that he "shouldn't look at pornography because it was disrespectful to women." The mother felt that this had been too harsh, and then the father quickly added that he didn't know what else to do since it caught him so off guard. The therapist remarked that whether sex is dirty or not has plagued teenage boys (and lots of adults) for centuries. The parents laughed.

Also during the first session it was learned that Roy was maturing slowly, and according to the father he was "a foot shorter than the other boys on his basketball team." After questioning them, it was learned that the father was also a late maturer and that this had been a source of shame for him. The therapist asked if the father had told Roy that, because it might relieve him a bit. It could also be related to whatever transpired at the camping trip, since he was with boys his age at the time. The father said that he had not told him but he would, because this late maturing issue seemed to be an important piece to Roy and he felt that they did not pay enough attention to it.

Diagnostically this boy appeared to be experiencing some separation fears that were based partly upon fears that he would not be able to handle the responsibilities of adult men, as he saw them. He was anxious over separating from his parents, which was now represented by sleep; facing his fears of death, recently brought on by an unusual string of tragedies, as calmly as Apollo 13 astronauts; fearing the loss of his parents to cancer or some accident; wondering whether he would mature physically into manhood; having respectful sexual feelings and activities with women, as he feels his father must have, instead of his "dirty" thoughts; unresolved "boyish" feelings of closeness to his mother and their implications for his impending manhood. Also there was some familial anxiety about sexual matters that was being acted out by the three of them. This was evidenced in the late night patrols Roy would take, perhaps to put restrictions on his parents' sex life.

Ordinarily at the end of such a session with a 12-year-old boy, arrangements would be made to see the boy individually. However, in this case, the family did such an impressive job of facing all of these complicated issues that it seemed that such an option would foreclose the potential productivity of continuing as a family. The family agreed when the therapist voiced these thoughts aloud, and they scheduled to meet as a family the next week. The treatment plan had become an ongoing negotiation among the four of them. This example illustrates the provisional, continuous nature of treatment planning as distinct from an approach in which a definitive decision is made at the outset.

Even though such a treatment plan was effective, the therapist thought it was still necessary to examine why he had diverged from his normal course of action. He realized that he liked this family; it was hard to find pathology even though he thought that they were looking for him to "tell it like it is" and to give them an expertly presented course of treatment. The treatment continued in this collaborative way with family sessions, parent sessions, and individual child psychotherapy, alternating weekly.

There are several key issues that the therapist will wish to consider. When a case is first referred to a relational therapist, he or she asks at what level or in what sphere are there disturbances in a child's life, and are there appropriate interventions for the therapist or for others to make. The child may be suffering from difficulties at the somatic, intrapsychic, familial, peer environment, school environment, and community levels. Does the child have a physical illness? Does it sound like the child is genuinely grappling with a psychological problem? Alternatively, do others have a problem with the child? Is the school or class a poor match for the child, and therefore is he or she not flourishing in that environment? Is the child adapting poorly to the situation, or is he or she doing the best one could expect given the challenges of that environment? Just because the child is the one referred does not necessarily mean that the child is the one in need of help.

Consistent with the relational approach, it is critical that the therapist engage in a process that will give her or him the opportunity to consider the range of issues just outlined. Generally speaking, this involves an initial meeting or even series of meetings with the child's parents to begin to understand their view of their child and the child's difficulties, and to make an assessment of the parental relationship and the role it may play. In certain instances, the therapist may choose to see the parents for an extended period before meeting with the child, and in some cases may choose not to see the child at all.

In his or her contact with the parents, the therapist will address questions regarding the parents' relationship to their child, including their own expectations, fantasies, and unconscious attitudes, the parents' personalities and how they may impact on and are shaped by their child, and what role the child may play in both the couple relationship and in the family system. The therapist is also interested in assessing the parents' psychological resources and capacity to help the child.

During the course of this evaluative work, assuming that it appears that the child is in need of treatment, can the therapist rely on a sufficiently supportive caretaking system to conduct the work? Specifically, can the parents support the treatment, emotionally and financially? Can the parents in combination with other resources (the school, extended family, nanny, child protective services, and others) support the treatment? Alternatively, does it seem likely that the therapist can engage in meaningful work with the child in the absence of support from the caretaking system, and possibly in the face of parental undermining of the process? This latter is usually only likely in the case of the older child with considerable autonomy and sense of self.

In one particular treatment of a 10-year-old boy, the child's mother, who was divorced from the father, was in favor of the treatment, but was so overwhelmed by personal and family problems that she devoted very little time and attention to her son. The father, who was more available to the son and saw him more, was adamantly opposed to the whole idea of treatment. He demanded detailed records and justifications for the therapy from the therapist, and often threatened the therapist with legal action. In addition, he warned his son that therapy would make a cripple of him by promoting an unnatural and destructive dependence, an illusion that others were responsible for one's problems and that you could rely on others to solve them. He read long passages to his son from texts purporting to debunk therapy. The son listened to all this, but would then secretly bring these books into therapy. He would ask the therapist to help him understand what these ideas meant, and to help him with the conflict between his own experience of therapy and what his father had to say about it. These questions served as a valuable context in which to explore his feeling of being a tennis ball batted back and forth between his parents, and his wish to develop his own ideas about things. He used the time with the therapist to help him develop his beliefs, and to come to terms with the authoritarian way his father dealt with him. This boy had an unusual capacity to form an independent and effective engagement with the therapist, in the face of his father's very active attempts to undermine it.

After one meeting or a series of meetings with the parents, the therapist will decide if it makes sense to go ahead and meet with the child alone. As is the case in meeting with the parents, the therapist may choose to meet with the child once or twice as part of the initial assessment, or may settle on a series of meetings. In either case, it is desirable that the therapist have an opportunity to observe the child in interaction with both his parents and siblings.

In actual practice, it can often be difficult to arrange such meetings. Siblings or one parent or another may refuse to participate in the assessment process. This is often the case, for example, in families with a single parent, in families with considerably older siblings, with stepsiblings, and with blended families. The therapist then faces a decision concerning how to proceed. Particularly, how critical does he or she believe such contact is to the conduct of an effective assessment and treatment? Even when the therapist decides that a particular compromise is necessary and possible, it is important that he or she consider what loss of therapeutic leverage is involved and under what degree of disadvantage one may be working.

There are a variety of circumstances and settings that may require the therapist to compromise his or her preferred way to carry out the assessment of a case. These settings can include schools, clinics, or hospitals. Circumstances that can challenge the clinician include court referrals, children in foster care, children being considered for adoption, children who are the subjects of an ongoing abuse or neglect evaluation, children who have experienced trauma that is the basis for legal intervention, and children whose parents are in the process of divorce.

In many child treatments, there is a tendency for the referring person and the parents to give the child into the care of the therapist and to breathe a sigh of relief that someone is assuming responsibility for the problems at hand. This tendency is often particularly pronounced in the kinds of circumstances just enumerated. Of course, each therapist has to decide how much responsibility he or she feels able and willing to assume. But we are particularly interested in encouraging the therapist to be wary of assuming excessive responsibility. This can be a dreadful quagmire for the therapist! By stressing the need for an overall system of therapeutic support, and the need for an appropriate context in which to conduct treatment, the relational therapist can improve the odds in favor of a more successful treatment process.

After meeting with the parents and the child, the therapist may then wish to consider the need for additional ancillary steps in the assessment process. He or she may decide that psychological, neuropsychological, or learning disabilities testing would be indicated. In such cases, it is often best to make such plans in conjunction with the child's school (more about this below). In addition, the therapist may think that medication could be an important adjunct to the treatment. The therapist may wish to consider either a referral for a psychiatric consultation, or, if the therapist is a psychiatrist, decide if he or she wants to make that determination as part of his or her own assessment procedure. It is best to consider this question after an initial assessment of the child and the family, and before settling on an overall treatment plan.

We will return to the individual assessment of the child, which is the heart of the process, but it is important for the therapist to look outward to the world that surrounds the child. As we have already described, the child's life unfolds in a context with which he or she is in continual interaction. The family is certainly the immediate context, but the therapist must look beyond the family in attempting to assess what challenges the child is facing. The therapist may choose to use the parents as his or her source of information regarding the child's school experiences, involvement with peers, and difficulties and opportunities presented by the wider community. Alternatively the therapist may choose to communicate directly with school personnel, pediatrician, coaches, baby-sitters, extended family members, and other key people in the child's life.

When the child is involved in any medical treatment, remedial services, or other significant interventions, these may play a powerful part in the child's emotional state, and need to be actively considered by the therapist. In a similar vein, the therapist needs to consider any outstanding difficulties that confront the child, and any outstanding strengths or talents.

In cases where the child's well-being has become a matter for legal intervention, including children who are the object of custody disputes, who are in foster placement, or who are in protective custody, the therapist will inevitably need to speak with representatives of the custodial system, including (but not limited to) the protective service worker, an attorney for the child, family relations officers, the judge, foster parent or parents, parent aides, and others.

In these cases, the therapist can benefit from the interventions and efforts of others, and can be of potential help to others in this system, but the therapist may also find it challenging to preserve her or his separate, independent relationship with the child, while participating in a larger caregiving system. One of the therapist's goals in making an initial assessment is to evaluate if there is an appropriate place for her or him in the current system of caregivers. Some have argued, for example, that when a child is in temporary foster placement, or involved in an adoption process, it may not make sense to begin individual treatment at that point.

Some therapists also choose to defer individual treatment in the context of a custody dispute. It can often be difficult in custody battles for the therapist to avoid developing an advocacy position that may compromise the therapist's ability to deal with the child's feelings of conflicting loyalty. Generally speaking, in situations where there are significant questions regarding who should care for the child and under what circumstances, the therapist will come under considerable pressure to offer opinions about such matters. If the treatment has been mandated by a court proceeding, the therapist may find that he or she is simultaneously deprived of autonomy in treatment planning and also accorded an excessive, unrealistic authority.

In cases where the child has suffered significant trauma, particularly of a type that has involved other children, other forms of treatment intervention may already be in place at the time of the therapist's intervention. In these circumstances, the therapist must consider how his or her role will fit and contribute to an overall systemic intervention. If such treatment efforts are not already in place, the therapist must then consider what combination of interventions may be necessary in addition to whatever he or she may be prepared to offer. These additional interventions may include support groups, day treatment services, big brother or sister, foster care, and so forth. A critical part of the therapist's assessment is to consider the inherent limitations of what he or she can offer, and not to attempt too much or claim too much for psychotherapy, whether of the child, the parents, or the family. It is obvious, for example, that to offer only play therapy to a child who is being actively abused is not only not therapeutic, but can also constitute a form of abuse in and of itself.

In sum, as a key part of the assessment process, the therapist needs to consider the need for and the existence of therapeutic interventions in the child's larger life, and how any projected therapy may fit into this larger picture. It would be a serious mistake for a therapist to launch an uncovering type of play therapy with a child who has no stabilizing support in his life. It would be a mistake to consider that individual therapy alone or even in combination with family therapy would be sufficient to help a child who is out of control in his school setting, or who is engaged in an antisocial pattern of destructive behavior. When a child is actively involved in a larger system of intervention, then the therapist must consider how his proposed intervention may fit in with what is already in place. The therapist must consider if he can negotiate a treatment arrangement that can work in positive combination with other existing services in a way that preserves the autonomy of the treatment process.

In actual practice, therapists frequently deal with cases where they have an active question regarding the viability of the treatment. In the course of the evaluation, in certain instances the therapist develops a fairly clear conviction regarding the viability of the case, or at least can create conditions in the treatment that will help to clarify whether a viable treatment relationship is possible.

A family was referred for treatment to help them to deal with an impending adoption by the parents of four foster children who had been living with the parents. Based on the initial meeting with the parents, the therapist concluded that the parents appeared to have little interest in treatment, but were willing to comply with the request of those involved in the adoption that they seek some therapy for the children. The therapist was struck by the couple's apparent lack of concern or anxiety about the adoption process and its potential effect on the children. The parents took the explicit position that everything would be okay and they did not really see the need for therapy. They did not believe that the four children, all siblings from a very poor background, would have any problem with this change.

The therapist doubted that any useful work could be done with the children alone in light of the parents' attitude. She therefore recommended a period of couple treatment to help resolve questions concerning the parents' motivation regarding the adoption, and how realistic they were concerning its complexities and potential difficulties. Unfortunately, in this instance, the couple turned down the recommendation, and expressed anger that the therapist was placing what they viewed as obstacles in the way of complying with the requirements of the adoption agency. While the outcome was unfortunate, it saved the therapist from engaging the children in what very likely would have been a frustrating process that was unlikely to lead to a genuine therapy.

Here is another example of a therapy that turned out not to be viable.

Two children were referred for treatment following a six-month period of placement in foster care. They had been removed from the parental home by child protective services following complaints from neighbors and school personnel that the children were being neglected. After removal and following investigation by child protective services and a suit by the parents claiming that the allegations were false, the children were returned to the parents. The court found that there was insufficient ground to remove them from the home. The children were referred to treatment to help them deal with the trauma of the foster placement and the resultant disruption of their lives.

At first, the parents seemed very interested in pursuing the treatment and appeared to be very much in support of the idea that their children needed therapeutic help in dealing with what happened. The therapists to whom they were referred were participating in a training program and were very eager to take on cases that would contribute to their own learning. The children also showed an openness to the treatment process and appeared able to get involved in play. The therapy thus began on a positive and optimistic note. After several sessions with the parents, however, the therapist working with them became distressed by the lack of progress in the work. It was her impression that whenever she would raise questions about what the children were like at home, or how they were dealing with the task of reintegrating everyone into family life, she got either evasive responses or questions and challenges regarding the nature of her interest. By contrast, the children would talk with some freedom about their current life, but became quite mute when the topic of their foster experience or the period preceding their foster experience emerged.

While the parents did seem to have some concern about the children and some desire to help them, their unwillingness to open up and to look at the whole experience more freely became increasingly evident. After a number of sessions with the parents, the therapists concluded that they were focused on a suit they were pursuing against the city for their children's placement in foster care, and that they were motivated to pursue therapy at least in part so that they would give the appearance of being devoted responsible parents. At the same time they did not want to offer any information that might in any way compromise their case, anything that might allow someone to think that they were anything but perfect parents. In addition, they harbored a rage toward all professionals who purported to know more than they did about how to raise their children, and who had any intention of intruding on their private family life.

After a few weeks of treatment, several things became clear to the therapists. While the decision to remove the children from the family was probably unwarranted and in part the result of a vendetta by hostile neighbors, the parents were in fact quite lax in their attention to the children and were not offering them either the structure or the protection that the therapists felt would be helpful. It was equally clear that the parents would not tolerate any discussion of these issues. The parents needed the therapists to validate them as decent parents, and while they showed some genuine concern about their kids, they were very suspicious and resentful toward the therapists. They were not in a position to help the children deal with the painful feelings around the placement itself. It was also clear to the therapists that both children had made a good connection to them and were deriving some benefit from the sessions, although limited by the circumstances of the case. In this instance, the therapy continued for several months with marginal benefit to the children, but was ultimately abruptly terminated by the parents when the therapy no longer served their purpose in connection with the court case.

Had the therapists been more experienced, or had they not been in a training program and therefore in need of cases, it is quite possible that they might have concluded fairly near the beginning of the treatment, in what we would consider the evaluative phase, that they could not make a viable effort here and may have recommended that the treatment stop, perhaps until after the conclusion of all court related actions.

In her initial contact with the child, the therapist wants to learn as much as she can about what is troubling the child, and how available the child may be to a treatment relationship. If the therapist believes that the child is struggling with a very focused experience or situation, such as a specific trauma, a specific defined area of difficulty such as mistreatment by peers, or the psychological consequences of a learning disability, the therapist may choose to focus directly on these issues and test out the child's capacity to talk about them directly. Of course, this depends upon the age of the child. No certain generalizations can be made about age because children vary so much regarding their capacity and willingness to articulate their experience in words. The therapist should be prepared to develop a direct dialogue with the child or to move into a play approach, and also be prepared to move freely from one to the other.

If the therapist finds that the child can become engaged in either a play process or a verbal exchange, and that the parents can offer a general support to the process of therapy, then the therapist may choose to proceed with individual sessions. The individual sessions may be combined with less frequent parent sessions. In the course of this work, the therapist may discover that important conflicts exist between parent and child, or significant misunderstandings that warrant sessions that include both parent and child. We think of different treatment arrangements as available options for the therapist to combine in an overall treatment sequence. We do not believe that once committed to a particular approach, the therapist should not feel free to modify the approach along the way.

Traditionally, analytically oriented child therapists often kept their contact with parents to a minimum. The concern was that frequent and more extensive contact between the child's therapist and the parents could jeopardize the child's treatment in several ways, including the reality that the child might fear that his or her privacy and confidentiality would not be respected. It would also increase the likelihood that the parents could influence the treatment or at least the content of what was discussed by reporting various events to the therapist. Some therapists took the position that they wanted to know nothing about the child's actual life. In these cases the parents would be seen by another therapist who would serve as a buffer between the parents and the child's therapist. There are times when such an approach is valuable. It is certainly not uncommon for the child's therapist to refer the parents for parental counseling or couple therapy with someone else.

It is our view, however, that from the start it makes sense that the child's therapist have contact with all the relevant people in the child's family. Since the child's relationships with his family are a key factor in his conflicts, we believe the therapist needs to learn about these relationships firsthand right from the outset. If she determines that additional therapeutic modalities may be indicated, such a recommendation can be made when appropriate. See Chapter 14, for further attention to the necessary work with the parents.

In the following example, the therapist began by working with the child, but saw the mother as part of the evaluation. As the case proceeded, the therapist came to believe that the most important area of work was with the mother.

> Mary was a 3-year-old child who had suffered a specific trauma. In the course of changing her diaper in a public restroom, a hinge holding the changing table had caught Mary's finger and sliced off its tip. She was terrified and in considerable pain at the time, and later experienced more pain and sensitivity in her finger. She was required to undergo surgery in an attempt to reduce the effect of the damage and its disfiguring nature. Subsequently she experienced social withdrawal from other children, considerable apprehension, and would alternate between making disparaging remarks about her finger and identifying it as something special about her. She was seen for an evaluation at the instigation of an attorney who was helping the parents with a suit against the establishment where the accident occurred. She was initially seen in individual play therapy, during which she acted out themes of injury and healing, as well as scenes of accidents in a dollhouse she used for play.
>
> In the course of ancillary contacts with the mother regarding the treatment, it became apparent that her mother was struggling with depression. At the time of the accident, her mother had been

so distraught in the face of the injury, and what she experienced as her failure as a parent, that she was unable to comfort her daughter. In exploring these issues, it became clear that the mother experienced considerable ambivalence about becoming a mother and giving up a particular career she had been pursuing. This ambivalence played a very important part in her feelings of guilt about the accident, in her depression, and in her inability to help her daughter with her own feelings. These revelations made it clear that an effective treatment for the daughter must include a regular treatment involvement on the mother's part as well. This change in the treatment plan proved to be enormously helpful to both mother and daughter.

In some therapies, the therapist is wise to change the treatment plan midstream. In the following case, mother–son sessions were very helpful at first, but later the central need was for individual sessions in order to work through issues about the father.

Sammy was a 12-year-old boy, an only child, who lived alone with his mother. He had what appeared to be a pathologically enmeshed relationship with her. His parents had separated when he was very young, and the father had been absent or undependable in his involvement with Sammy.

Sammy was referred to therapy by his mother due to his poor school performance and defiance toward his teacher, as well as his escalating, "out of control," defiant, sometimes even frightening behavior at home. Sammy would sometimes throw furniture around his room when he was angry with his mother, and would act toward her in threatening ways when he did not get what he wanted. Once he pulled a knife and threatened to stab her, though he did not follow through on his threat. Sammy would posture belligerently toward his mother, insulted at being treated as a child and not as her co-equal, and refusing to comply with her authority. Sammy's school problems seemed to reflect a modified version of this same set of feelings.

Initially, Sammy was seen both individually and with his mother. In individual sessions Sammy would show off, would need to be in the know and always right about everything. Yet his bluster seemed to coexist with a genuine interest in an affectionate relationship with the therapist, a man. When talking about his difficulties and anger at his mother, Sammy always blamed her for her own temper tantrums, unreasonable decisions, and selfishness.

In sessions with both Sammy and mother together, the therapist helped them negotiate a peace treaty. Sammy was direct about his sensing that mother did not take his feelings and concerns seriously, and was preoccupied with her own troubles. Mother was able to hear Sammy and respond constructively. Their relationship at home clearly changed as a result of these discussions, and their problems improved markedly.

Meanwhile, Sammy became increasingly interested in talking about his father rather than his mother, with whom his relationship had improved. Mother had recently made yet one more effort to reinstitute visits between Sammy and his father, who lived in another city. After a surprisingly good visit, father failed to call or to show up for future visits. Sammy was upset, angry, and disappointed. He would spend some time in each session talking angrily about his father.

As this occurred, Sammy's behavior in sessions changed. He became softer and seemed less of a show-off. He was increasingly able to listen and take in, rather than posture and bluster. He wished that the therapist could be a participant in his life beyond the sessions—he asked the therapist to go with him to a baseball game—although he was able to live with the limits of the situation. It became clear that he was developing affectionate, filial feelings toward his therapist.

While early in therapy, the task might have been defined as addressing the mother–son dynamics that underlay his school and home behavior problems, at this point Sammy seemed to be "working on" his disappointments and longings in his relationship with his father. In his transference to the therapist, and in the therapist's complementary countertransference to him, Sammy seemed to be bringing up, testing out, attempting to renegotiate and to grow beyond being stuck in his heretofore unresolvable feelings toward his father. At this point in the therapy, individual sessions were clearly the main arena in which Sammy could work out the problems that were most pressing for him.

As this case illustrates, the assessment process is a critical beginning step in any treatment. When the therapist sees himself in an evaluative position, he will consider a wider range of options, and also feel less obligated to pursue therapy in the face of untenable conditions. But in another sense, the assessment phase is never definitively over; each turn in the treatment process requires reevaluation and a possible shift in modalities and in strategies for intervention.

PART FOUR

Child and Therapist
in the Treatment Room

In this section of the book, we begin our focus on psychotherapy by looking at the core elements of the treatment process, namely play, transference, and countertransference, through the lens of our theory as developed in earlier chapters. We see play as interactive between therapist and child, both on the level of behavior and on the level of the interaction of the fantasy productions of both participants. We track the development of the concepts of transference and countertransference from their one-person roots in Freudian theory to contemporary notions of the interaction between transference and countertransference in the here-and-now, as they apply to child treatment. Finally, we address how parents and other family members can be considered to form part of the transference–countertransference field.

9

Play in Child Treatment

THE PLACE OF PLAY IN CHILD TREATMENT

Historically, play has been at the heart of most child treatment. Therapeutic work with children originated in the efforts of early psychoanalysts such as Anna Freud (1946), Melanie Klein (1955), and Donald Winnicott (1958b) to apply the understandings of psychoanalysis to the concerns of childhood. For all of the early psychoanalytic clinicians, play was the central medium of exchange in their work. Traditionally, play was seen as analogous to the material generated by dreams and free association in adults, and provided a glimpse into the inner unconscious content of the child's world. To misuse Hamlet's oft-quoted words, play was the thing with which to catch the unconscious of the child.

Within the psychoanalytic tradition, children's play has also been a rich source of data and inspiration for generating theories of childhood development. As already described in previous chapters, psychoanalytic developmental theory, specifically Kleinian and Freudian stage theories, became the basis for understanding and interpreting children's play. This framework was an enormous help in attempting to decode the fluid and often ambiguous play of a child in sessions. For example, in a case used to illustrate play disruption, psychoanalyst and noted play theorist Erik Erikson (1950) described a 3-year-old girl who used a doll to push objects, and who held the object below her abdomen and repeatedly dropped it to the floor. Based on several additional observations, he suggested that the child saw the penis as an aggressive pushing tool, and that she was dramatizing her lack of such a tool.

Erikson thus employed psychoanalytic developmental theory regarding the importance of genitalia to the child and related concerns about castration to illuminate a particular play sequence. Of course, today we would note the highly phallocentric nature of this idea. Play sequences were also in part the basis for formulating some of these psychoanalytic developmental ideas. Psychoanalytic psychotherapy with children not only has been the original source of play as a therapeutic device, but also has provided the theoretical base for much of our understanding of play.

Play has also been an essential process in the client-centered approaches to child treatment (Axline 1969), as we have already noted. Within this tradition, play itself is seen as having a developmentally forwarding, curative effect. Erikson (1950) also stressed this aspect of play. For him it was both a form of self-healing and the earliest form of human problem solving. For clinicians such as Axline, it is the therapist's task to create an atmosphere of unconditional regard and support within which the child can evolve his or her own self-curative processes.

More recently, a number of clinicians have attempted to combine play with more structured treatment approaches, including greater explicit direction from the therapist (Gardner 1971). Knell (1997) has developed what she defines as a combined cognitive behavioral play therapy that draws on certain aspects of traditional play therapy in conjunction with more structured, explicit direction from the clinician.

CONTEMPORARY APPROACHES TO CHILD TREATMENT

In contemporary child treatment, play therapy is only one of a number of possible interventions clinicians consider. A survey of other forms of treatment would include, for example, behavioral therapy, cognitive therapy, client-centered treatment, family treatment, and supportive counseling. There have also been efforts to link quite specific treatment interventions with discrete, narrowly defined syndromes. These might include social-skills training for children with various relationship problems, such as Pervasive Developmental Delay, Asperger's Disorder, or less severe disorders like problems with impulse control or excessive aggressiveness. Specific cognitive behavioral interventions are often employed for children identified as having attention-deficit hyperactivity disorder (ADHD) or obsessive-compulsive disorder (OCD).

Although play is central to the treatment approach described in this work, open-ended, symbolic play therapy is also only one of a number of options that a relational therapist considers when evaluating what would be appropriate to do in any individual case. The relational therapist, who inherently views clinical situations from a systems perspective, will ask himself what is the most useful and appropriate level of intervention, and what type of intervention best fits the requirements of the case. Should the child be seen alone, or possibly in combination with one or more parents? Should the parents be the main focus of the work, with perhaps minimal or no contact with the child? To what extent is the clinician's primary task to intervene with the school system, or other institutions and agencies that directly affect the child's life? Of course, the clinician actively considers all of these questions not only at the outset of treatment but throughout the course of the work.

Even in those treatment situations where the clinician has determined that open-ended play therapy is the treatment of choice, he may experience intense pressure to conduct a brief, focused therapy. Pressure may come from parents who are desperate for relief or from the school, or from the insurance company or managed care entity. This pressure has in part fueled the effort to develop more directed, problem-focused approaches. It takes a certain courage and willingness to swim against the current to conduct longer term, open-ended symbolic play therapy with a child. Play therapists sometimes give voice to their own uneasiness in comments such as "I can't believe that they are paying me to play." In one particular case, a child's mother gave credence to such uneasiness on the part of therapists when she fired the psychiatrist who was seeing her son after she overheard patient and therapist discussing the best designs for paper airplanes.

The ability of the therapist both to help parents understand the value of an open-ended play therapy and to feel a sense of comfort in conducting such treatment depends upon the therapist's own understanding of its profound value. One of the purposes of this book is to articulate the range of therapeutic benefit such an effort offers. This is a theme that runs through the following chapters.

BROAD AND NARROW DEFINITIONS OF PLAY

When we think of play in connection with child treatment, it brings to mind toys such as dolls, puppets, or action figures used by the child in a free improvisational way. The child and the therapist identify what they are both doing as play. We might call this make-believe play. Such play is understood to be symbolic: it paints a picture of the child's inner concerns—wishes and anxieties—in a way that the therapist can "read" and may choose to interpret. This type of activity is what we might call the narrow or specific definition of play.

Play is also a much broader, more inclusive term. In fact, play may well be the most inclusive concept in the English language to denote a particular range of human activity. A slight detour into a consideration of the activities that constitute play may be of some help in understanding its function in the therapy of children. It includes such diverse events as sports, religious and secular ceremonies and festivals, various artistic performances and creative endeavors, literature, stock speculation, sex, computer games, play fighting, tickling, and many others. Sutton-Smith (1995), a play scholar and researcher, has attempted to group play into a number of different categories. These include mind play or subjective play like daydreaming, solitary play like hobbies or writing, informal social play like dancing or going to malls, vicarious audience play like movies, and performance play like the piano, celebrations, and festivals.

Sutton-Smith argues that, historically, this vast domain called play has evoked a wide range of attitudes or philosophical positions toward it. In addition, certain types of play closely fit these attitudes. He calls these attitudes rhetorics and distinguishes seven of them. These are: progress, fate, frivolity, power, imagination, self-experience, and identity. He argues that the rhetoric of progress, the idea that individuals and societies develop in a positive direction over time, has been the dominant contemporary view of play, particularly as it concerns children, and the young of any species. Thus play is seen as facilitative of personal, psychological development in the way that Erikson claims, and as a form of practicing that helps in the mastery of basic personal and social skills. Sutton-Smith summarizes a whole body of research, including ethological studies and the work of developmental psychologists such as Kagan (1984) and others, that either attempts to demonstrate this aspect of play or include it as a basic assumption in the work. While Sutton-Smith does not dispute the plausibility of this view of play, he argues that it is a far from proven claim.

In designating seven rhetorics of play, Sutton-Smith makes the argument that there are other culturally significant views that are equally meaningful and in some respects contradict the view of play as progress. The coexistence of these multiple views accounts for the complexity and ambiguity of the concept. For example, in Sutton-Smith's view, the rhetoric of fate emphasizes the chancy and external nature of events, beyond our own individual control, evident in gambling, the belief in magic, and the play of the gods. This type of play diminishes our sense of the capacity to affect our lives and the world around us. The rhetoric of frivolity emphasizes the meaninglessness of play, and play's ability to upset the established sense of meaning and value in any culture or organization. Frivolous play can question and undermine, and turn on its head any notion of progress. Child therapists generally don't want to be seen as conducting frivolous play. They are usually highly earnest in their play and want to see it as all directed toward a worthwhile purpose. At times this may require them to stretch the bounds of credulity in assigning a larger meaning—for example, when the child suddenly starts flicking spitballs out of the consulting room window.

The rhetoric of power emphasizes the competitive, agonistic aspects of play, and the way in which play functions to establish a certain civilized power structure. The noted cultural historian and play theorist Huizinga (1955) stressed the way in which play, through competitive contests, games, and rituals, helps to bring order to society and to civilize a range of human impulses. But play as an exercise in power relationships also includes rebellious, mischievous, and defiant acts typically carried out by an underclass or subjugated group, whether they are adolescents in a classroom or political activists. A politician in

Serbia who was leading the movement to install an alternative government to that of Milosevic asked that his supporters come to a public park with wine and food because a rebellion needs to be fun (Erlanger 1999). In a biology class on the topic of aging, after discussing how in traditional Eskimo society the aged and weak were left to die, a group of adolescent students started joking and fantasizing about how they would eliminate their grandparents: "Sorry, Grandma, but your time has come."

Viewed from the perspective of play as power, we may consider the way in which play in child therapy consists of the therapist's effort to civilize the child through play. It raises questions concerning who decides that play is going to occur, and who sets the rules for the play process. It also alerts us to the competitive aspect of play and the elements of mischief and rebelliousness. When a child suddenly changes the rules in a game of chess in a way that works to the child's advantage, is this an indication that the child is having difficulty, let's say, mastering the stage of concrete operations? Does it reflect an egocentric orientation, a struggle with oedipal conflict, or does it reflect the child's assertion of power in a subjugated position? Why should the child agree to play with us in the first place? He or she didn't choose us as a playmate. And why should the child go along with rules set by the larger society of which we are representatives?

MAKE BELIEVE AND IN-EARNEST ACTIVITIES

We think of play and real action, or play and serious activity, as denoting distinct and in ways opposing realms of engagement. Thus play fighting is harmless fun, and real fighting is dangerous. The virtue of play as a therapeutic pursuit, among other virtues, is its freedom from real consequences and thus its apparent safety as a vehicle for self-expression. Play is characterized by a metacommunication about itself to the effect that what we are doing is not entirely real or serious (Bateson 1955).

According to Bateson, in nonplay interaction, a nip between two animals stands for or signals an actual bite. Bateson states that a nip is a signal of a bite, but not a bite itself. But in play mode, a nip is not a signal of a bite; in fact, in play the bite itself does not exist except as a fictional construction. Thus, play is what Bateson calls a paradoxical frame. Play is a type of activity that can appear to be fully real and meant, and yet includes a comment on itself to the effect that it is not serious or meant. According to Bateson and Sutton-Smith, because of the paradoxical nature of play, a tension always exists between the way in which play does or does not signal something truly meant. For example, Bateson cites the Andaman islanders who conclude a peace by allowing each side to strike the other ceremonially. This ritual is susceptible to failure when the frame "this is play" or "this is ritual" is lost and the ritual blow is taken as a real blow; then combat erupts from a peace-making ceremony. It is common among playing children that the frame "this is play" can be lost.

Play that is sometimes called deep play or high-risk play illustrates play's paradoxical nature. In certain extreme sports or daredevil play there are real risks involved and potential for serious loss, even death, although the activity is defined as just a game or just play.

Play has two faces. On the one hand, it serves as a vehicle for confirming and extending traditional societal and cultural values through reassuring and predictable rituals. Society's games and traditional pastimes create a world that is make believe and yet involves some of the things that matter most to people. It is often through games that we give meaning to our lives and create its emotional importance. The other face of play is change and innovation. In playing with things or playing at them, we make discoveries, develop new practices and new ways of understanding our experience. In play we can try out new forms of behavior, new roles, new solutions, and can create new understanding and knowledge.

By introducing novelty through the fiction of play, it also becomes a mechanism for at times radical social change. Play can suggest ideas without making too firm and absolute a claim for them. Unusual subversive or frightening notions can be given life in play, and can thus be tolerated without being fully acknowledged. We can allow them to inhabit a region of ambiguity. The paradox of play lies in its being an inconsequential activity (just playing) and in its being a characteristic of our most profound endeavors.

Many of life's most creative endeavors combine great seriousness with play. Bruner (1972b) has argued that a capacity for play is a characteristic of all great leaders. Because of play's ability to incorporate a

sense of high purpose and seriousness with no actual or real consequence, it allows for a freedom of experimentation through which new
behaviors and new roles can be explored.

PSYCHOTHERAPY AS A PLAY PROCESS

In our view, analytic psychotherapy in general, not just child treatment, can be characterized by these essential qualities of play that we
have been describing. Does that mean that psychoanalytic psychotherapy is play? This notion that psychoanalytic treatment is a play
process may strike many as odd and incongruous if not simply incorrect. Certainly psychoanalytic treatment is a profoundly serious effort,
and what does that have to do with play?

In her book on play in psychoanalysis, Sanville (1991) reported
on an exchange with a noted analyst in a seminar she was taking. In
response to a description he gave of how he often offered interpretations to patients, she commented that she liked what he said because
it had a playful note. Apparently he replied with some indignation that
psychoanalysis was a serious undertaking.

Of course psychoanalytic treatment is a serious undertaking. It is
an effort to address both profound personal pain and bedeviling personal
conflicts, which we don't routinely associate with play. As relational
psychoanalysts we also see the interpersonal experience as being at the
core of the work. But the paradox we have already described as defining play is also at the heart of any psychoanalytic treatment. It is both
profoundly serious, fully in earnest, and an act of play.

What are the characteristics of analytic treatment that are common to play? First, it has a distinct beginning, middle, and end, defined
by both participants. It occurs at a set place and time, on an established
field. In these respects, it has a certain ritualistic character. Second,
there are quite distinct rules of engagement that shape each person's
participation. Third, both participants get together in this particular,
artificially constructed manner in order for something to happen between them that would not happen otherwise. Fourth, what happens
between them, however genuine and real, also stays at a level of simulation. For example, although the relationship could develop a powerful mother–child dimension and set of experiences, therapist and pa-

tient do not become a mother and a child. If they fall in love, they do not become lovers. However intense their relationship, it will not continue to the end of their lives. Fifth, the rules of the treatment, like the rules of any game, limit it in ways that clearly say, this is not reality in its full unbridled form. We are both limited from the potential fullness of experience that a nonplay relationship could offer and we are protected from its potentially harmful consequences.

Of Sutton-Smith's seven play rhetorics, at least three of them appear to be defining characteristics of the process of a psychoanalytic psychotherapy. These are (1) the rhetoric of imagination, which includes processes characterized by imagination, flexibility, and creativity; (2) the rhetoric of the self, which includes desirable experiences of the self such as fun, relaxation, and aesthetic satisfaction; and (3) the rhetoric of identity, which has to do with processes that connect individuals with a larger community.

In the processes that give shape to an analytic treatment, we can see the elements that Sutton-Smith identifies. The patient is invited to play with the therapist. She is encouraged to surrender her concrete view of things, to loosen her hold on reality, and to attend to a much wider range of emotion and experience. She is asked to free associate, to capture fleeting thoughts and images, to report dreams and to offer reactions to them. The therapist's effort is toward the development of an imaginative process. Similarly, the therapist attempts to allow his own thoughts and reactions to develop freely, and to attend to them without limiting or editing or prematurely judging. The therapist also attempts to make an imaginative connection to the patient, to conjure up a vision of the patient's life experience, to put himself in the patient's shoes and get a feel for what it is like inside the other's skin. These are essentially play processes that depend on the quality and vitality of the patient's and the therapist's imagination.

In transference interactions, the therapist and the patient become involved in a range of play interactions or imaginative interactions that at times may have the force of reality, but are essentially fictional roles that evolve in the "playground" of the therapy. The therapist often feels out the role or roles assigned by the patient, and reacts to them or against them consonant with his own role definitions. These interactions can be defined or characterized by the same terms that describe creative, symbolic play. Levenson has described the analytic process as the continual expansion of material, arguing that the curative benefit lies in this very expansion. If play is that activity in which one entertains possibilities, carries out possible sequences of actions, explores and expands the universe of the possible, then Levenson's (1983) characterization fits well with the notion of therapy as play.

Many of the psychoanalytic writers from a relational orientation have emphasized playfulness as both a crucial ingredient in the process and one of the important goals. For example, Mitchell (1993), in describing the shift in our understanding of the goals of such treatment, argues that the goal of contemporary psychoanalysis is an enriching and authentic personal reality achieved through a process of imaginative play.

We believe there are distinct ways and degrees to which the term "play" can be applied to psychoanalytic psychotherapy. As we have already indicated, analytic psychotherapy shares much in common with the concept of play in its broadest meaning. But what about the fact that for many analytic therapists, although not for all, the aim or the goal of the work (as opposed to the play) is to have a meaningful impact on the patient's actual life? For many play activities, it is the very lack of any actual implication or impact, its freedom from actual consequences, that carries the appeal. Sutton-Smith notes that perhaps it is the pure exercise of a pleasurable capacity that is at the heart of play. Of course, these distinctions tend to break down. A person can become despondent for days, as a result of a football game. And there are infamous examples of violence and death that have occurred in the context of a soccer game. As Bateson points out, the paradox of play can break down. Nevertheless, analytic treatment probably straddles the play/nonplay distinction the way that certain other simulated experiences do, such as flight simulation or war games. Analytic treatment thus is both play and not play in countless ambiguous ways.

Analytic treatment can also be described as playful. The term "playful" suggests an approach or a stance toward some endeavor. Thus, one can be playful about matters that might seem to have little to do with play, such as family life, career, social relationships, or politics. Playfulness then refers to the inclusion of certain playlike attitudes suggesting lightheartedness, humor, spontaneity, and creativity. Equally, there are various types of play that are not necessarily playful. Certain forms of competition or sports and certain high-risk play or games may occur with an intensity and pressure that hardly suggests playfulness.

Psychoanalytic psychotherapy in general has many features that would define it as a play activity, but that does not necessarily make it playful. One central goal of a relational approach is the development of a playful engagement between the therapist and the patient. When the patient is a child, this playful engagement may include the evolution of a make-believe, symbolic play process.

PLAY AS A COMPONENT
OF RELATIONAL CHILD TREATMENT

If all psychoanalytic psychotherapy has play as a core component, then the more specific, make-believe play conducted in therapy with a child is really a play within play. At the beginning of treatment, the therapist and the child, who are negotiating a play process, may choose to participate in certain play scenarios with dolls, puppets, or other figures that constitute a specific play sequence within the larger play relationship. Alternatively they may choose to talk, play some sports activity, or the like. The therapist generally has in mind the idea of conducting play therapy along certain lines. The child may or may not find the therapist's ideas congenial with his own ideas of what he wants to do.

What ensues is an interpersonal negotiation between the two participants regarding how the sessions are going to go, including the nature of the activities that the therapist and child will pursue. The open-ended, analytically oriented therapist will give the child great latitude in choosing the direction of the sessions within certain limits. Nevertheless, such a therapist will have some ideas about the kind of play that she imagines will be conducive to therapeutic work. Sutton-Smith's identification of seven play rhetorics becomes useful in thinking about this negotiation between the child and the therapist. For example, the child who comes to therapy under duress, dragged in by a parent or referred by Child Protective Services, may wish to engage in pranks or mischief to thwart those in the position of power, including the therapist. Alternatively, the child from whom much is demanded by anxious or ambitious parents may have a strong desire for frivolous play, or may become drawn to the play of chance, the sense of having little control or direction over one's fate. Other children may wish to engage the therapist in high-risk play in which there is some actual chance that one or the other of the participants will be hurt. Some of these initiatives on the child's part may seem decidedly not playlike to the therapist, who has a more specific vision of play therapy.

The specific symbolic play that emerges in the course of child therapy, the themes that the child develops with puppets, dolls, or other figures, may well parallel and thus illuminate the nature of the play negotiation between the child and the therapist, or in other terms express the particular transference issues that the prospect of playing concretizes.

By looking at therapy as a playful interaction within which a more specific make-believe play can occur if both parties consent to it, the therapist is more likely to notice how the child is playing with him in ways he might not initially understand to be play. For the relational therapist this specific play, the play within the larger play relationship, is not, strictly speaking, a means to an end, as it tends to be with more traditional psychodynamic therapies where play becomes the medium for interpretation.

If the relational therapist's general goal is to develop a playful interaction or engagement between himself or herself and the child, then playing, in the narrower sense, may either be a means to that end, or in some other cases, may be a sign that the therapy has achieved its purpose. For example, if some children who are either very withdrawn or guarded finally develop the ability and willingness to sit on the floor and play with the therapist, this may be both a sign of the progress they have made and an indication that the treatment is near its end.

The relational therapist does not view play in the narrow sense as an end in itself. Rather, she is concerned with how the child's ability to participate in a relationship is a key factor in the child's capacity for full and effective living. Play as a general attitude and as a specific treatment activity is seen as facilitative. In this regard, relational play therapy differs from some other approaches to play therapy such as that advocated by Axline, in which the play itself, independent of the relationship dimension, is seen as both the goal and the curative process. The relational approach also differs from a cognitive approach in which the therapist employs certain play interactions with a child as a means to influence the child toward a changed cognitive organization of material. The relational therapist may employ such an approach under certain circumstances, but it is not generally characteristic of relational therapy.

Instead, play is at once an essential defining feature of any creative, open-ended exploration of one's life, and also a form for connecting with another person that can parallel and hopefully facilitate a more direct, discursive mode of exchange. The relational therapist wants to encourage play and playful interaction, but also wants to encourage direct, declarative talk.

PLAY AS INTERACTION

In child therapy, play is essentially an interactional process, particularly in the mind of the relational therapist. Admittedly there are children who are either so withdrawn, so solitary, or so unresponsive that it is difficult to describe what takes place as an interactional process. Some children simply refuse to play, or if they do, they become involved in an activity that largely excludes the therapist as a participant. But with the exception of highly withdrawn children, there is usually some implicit or explicit agreement to play, what Bateson (1955) called a metacommunication signal that what we are doing is in some sense not real or not fully intended. The child and the therapist strike an implicit deal that they are going to make believe, to make things up.

TO PLAY OR NOT TO PLAY

The therapist's decision to try actively to involve the child in play in the narrow or specific sense will depend on a number of factors. For very young children, the therapist may have no choice but to engage in play. The older child of, say, 9 or 10, may refuse to play, experiencing it as too childish. Older children may prefer board games or simply talking. These positions, of course, can and often do change in the course of the work. Children who have suffered trauma either may lack the capacity for play or may require a treatment approach that focuses much more specifically on the particular traumatic experiences they have suffered. Such treatments may require the therapist to offer quite specific cognitive interventions to help the child reduce excessive fears and anxieties. In these instances, the therapist may encourage the playing out of certain specific events as a vehicle for helping to clarify what the child has experienced and to put it in a context that will aid in re-ducing the child's fears. Under these circumstances, the therapist may use play less as a process of open-ended exploration and more as a means for addressing quite specific anxieties that the child exhibits.

WHEN IS PLAY PLAY, AND WHEN IS IT NOT?

If therapy by its very nature is a form of play, then in the broader sense what takes place between a child and a therapist in a session is never not play. But if the therapist's goal is to develop a play relation-ship, this can happen to varying degrees. Certain activities include more of the therapeutic, interactional elements of play, open-ended and cre-ative, while other play activities may be solitary, repetitive, and devoid of any obvious symbolic or emotional meaning. The elements that seem particularly important from a therapeutic point of view include its par-ticipatory nature, its open-endedness or receptivity to learning and change, and recognition of its pretend or symbolic nature in which the play activity stands for or represents something beyond itself. Certain activities in a therapy session may have the appearance of this type of play. For example, the child may use dolls or action figures, but may employ them in a repetitive, stereotyped pattern that either lacks sym-bolic or metaphorical significance, or is so exclusionary as to preclude any interaction with the therapist around the child's activities.

Frequently child therapists who opt for an open-ended play ap-proach to treatment find themselves either engaged in or observing some activity that feels as if it lacks any emotional import. Of course, the therapist who attempts a much more focused, cognitive approach to treatment may find himself faced with the same dilemma, because children will participate only to the extent and in the ways that allow them to feel comfortable. The relational therapist has an advantage in such situations by recognizing that, regardless of the activity, the child is engaged in a certain type of interpersonal relating of importance. The therapist and the child are most likely involved in a kind of play that is both worthy of note and an important element in what the therapy is supposed to be all about.

It is one of the challenges of the therapy for the therapist to dis-cover or create what is therapeutically meaningful in the interaction, including his or her role, and to discover the particular activities that engage the child. Certain activities that would appear to lack either symbolic value or meaning as an expression of internal conflict may be the very medium through which the child can come to express herself and the issues with which she struggles. For example, the child may choose to play basketball because she is a good basketball player and wants to experience her competence, or she may choose it because it reflects a powerful wish regarding what she would like to be, or a crucial identification with some other figure in her life.

Activities that have no obvious play elements may become a type of play as it evolves between the child and the therapist. In this type of evolution, the therapist can play a crucial role in the development of a playfulness between himself and the child.

One particular child would only talk about cars in his sessions. Otherwise he was totally mute. His conversations about cars were quite specific, including the relative merits of different models, their specific design features, comparative costs, and performance. He had some pretty well-developed opinions based on considerable research and observation. He appeared to stay with a very concrete, realistic topic that he discussed with great earnestness. But when he and the therapist got involved in these exchanges, they took on some play aspects. The therapist and the boy began to speak like potential purchasers of a car, which was not true for either of them.

The exchange was an opportunity for a very depressed and withdrawn boy to become engaged with someone and to practice having a conversation. As their talk continued, they were able to explore some of the emotional meaning of it—the appeal of cars in general, what particular cars meant to this boy, the history of cars in his family, and what they represented in his life. In the course of these exchanges, the boy had a dream about going into a field with his dog, and how the dog dug up a car that had been buried in a grave, one of his favorite cars from a younger period in his childhood. That car represented a happy time in his life, before his parents separated and divorced, and before his own life fell apart. The conversations about cars became a means for the boy to give shape to his complex and painful feelings about his parents' divorce and about himself. The therapist was able to make observations and encourage him to consider certain ways of understanding his experience through their talk. It was also through these conversations that the boy became able to employ humor and some playfulness in the sessions.

THE AIMLESSNESS OF PLAY OR
THE NONPRODUCTIVENESS OF PLAY

As noted before, play is a paradoxical activity in that, as Bruner, Erikson, and others have suggested, it serves as an important medium in the evolution of an individual's creative, problem-solving, and imaginative processes. It also serves as a useful attitude or stance in looking at a variety of life experiences. Yet in another sense, play is aimless in that it has no goal, no specific aim, and no product. Many parents find it difficult to play with children because it feels nonproductive, a waste of time and inconsistent with getting things done, with accomplishing things. Such parents may view play from what Sutton-Smith calls the rhetoric of frivolity and see it as having no particular value for their child. More and more, in contemporary life, the thrust is on accomplishing things, whether in school or on the athletic fields. When parents bring their children for treatment, they also expect results. The current emphasis on goal-directed, short-term treatment only gives greater weight to the value of "getting results." Therapists may feel either apologetic or vaguely clandestine in "playing aimlessly" with a child. Such play may conflict with their own sense of professional purpose. The therapist's discomfort with the paradox of play may prompt him to find ways to make it useful, either by interpretation or some other means. But it is important for the therapist to recognize that aimless or frivolous play can have an important place in a child's life, and in the therapy. Therapist and child work toward some level of mutual comfort regarding the nature of the play that characterizes their sessions. This may well clash with parents' highly productive, goal-oriented values, as well as their wish to know they are getting something for their time and/or money. The therapist thus is challenged not only to find his own comfort with the paradox of play, but also to help parents with the same dilemma. This can often be an important turning point in the course of treatment.

Mary, a 5-year-old girl, was initially referred for treatment at the age of 3, one year after she had been involved in an accident while with her mother that severed a small part of a finger (see Chapter 8). Following the accident, it appeared that she withdrew from social contact, became unwilling to play with other children, and voiced negative feelings about herself. After an initial evaluation, she was seen for a brief period. In sessions, she played in a markedly aimless way. She would set up play figures in different scenarios but would not develop the arrangement in any particular way. She would switch abruptly from solitary exploration of the playroom to brief exchanges with the therapist that included short episodes of hide and seek.

During this period, Mary's mother kept pressing the therapist to learn if, in sessions, her daughter had said or expressed anything concerning either her accident or her relationship with other children that was illuminating. The therapist was having difficulty making any sense of Mary's play, and her mom's questions only added to his anxiety. After further discussions with Mary's mother, he discovered that she actually disliked playing with her daughter because it seemed to her to be such a waste of time, and therefore she did very little of it. Mary's mom felt a high level of frustration regarding her own sense of productivity in her life. In addition, she had never experienced a playful engagement with her own mother, someone who seemed unwilling to pursue any interest or agenda other than her own. Over time, Mary's mother came to understand some of the ways she had been depriving herself and her daughter of a more playful, enriching engagement. The therapist learned to be more tolerant of Mary's fits and starts in play and its apparent disconnectedness. Not surprisingly, Mary's play began to evolve with more sustained and relevant themes.

PLAYFUL EXPLORATION OF SPACE

Much of Mary's initial activity in the playroom consisted of exploring the space and its contents. She flitted from object to object and from one part of the room to another. She liked to zip behind chairs and play hide and seek. Loewald, in an article on children's use of space in play therapy (1987), draws on the work of Bachelard (1994) concerning the importance of creating a particular kind of space of safety for creative work. In Mary's case, perhaps it was no accident that her mother, who disliked play and saw no value in it, was also fastidious in the extreme as a housekeeper. No shoes could be worn in the house and every mess was cleaned up the minute it was made. It is reasonable to think that Mary's aimless play in the beginning phase of treatment was in part a response to her mother's highly goal-directed stance and her discomfort with any disorder. The positive effects of the treatment for Mary probably had much to do with her discovery of a space in which she could explore with minimal demands and make something of a mess with no aversive consequences.

How children use the space of the treatment room, and the therapist's attitude toward the child's use of space, is a critical issue in the course of the treatment. For example, some children happily confine themselves to the limits of the treatment room, while others appear to need a larger compass and do best when sessions can be conducted in a larger space, even outside. In the case Loewald describes in her article, the child she was treating appeared to gain a more confident kinesthetic sense of self in his exploration of the treatment room and in his exploration of space with his therapist.

PLAY'S FLUID RELATIONSHIP TO WHAT IS REAL

The fluidity and ambiguity of play as already described allow it to encompass actions that are realistic and actually occur but for their categorization as play, as well as actions that are highly opaque and fantastical. For example, the child who screams at the therapist the way his mother screams at him in reality is telling the therapist something very specific about his actual experience, but in a way that doesn't require him to acknowledge it directly. In this type of interaction, reality is treated as play, perhaps in order to render it less painful and less humiliating. In this sense, play allows for many degrees of acknowledgment regarding certain conflicts. The child may direct the therapist to play the part that the child is unwilling to acknowledge, or even if acknowledged, that the child is too anxious to play himself. The concept of projective identification would fall into this range. By contrast, a child who invents a hybrid creature he calls a "cidracasafile" with its own special dance, and invites the therapist to learn how to do this dance, is attempting to give shape to highly complex inner experiences that very likely can only be so captured through a type of symbolic or metaphorical process. In this case, the issue of acknowledgment or "ownership" of the experience may be less of concern. Rather it is more a question of giving existence to an experience. We will say more about this below. This fluidity allows the child potentially great freedom of expression and experimentation. This intermingling of play and reality in the treatment process is part of what allows the child to entertain and ultimately accept new realities.

THE CREATION OF NEW MEANING IN THE PLAY PROCESS

Through the mutual creativity of the child and the therapist, the play sequence may come to constitute a newly developed self or self-and-other experience for the child. This can occur in two ways. As just mentioned, the child may add a new repertoire to his behavior or way of interacting with another person that can go through various degrees of personal acknowledgment. This was the case, for example, in the treatment of a very timid child mentioned elsewhere who learned to yell in his relationship with the therapist. The child, in his play, can bring forth a new or different sense of himself and others. The child is free to try out possibilities, express fears, hatreds, and desires that may be prohibited, censured, or the source of shame in daily life. The play can concretize and make manifest possibilities for self and self–other experience that the therapist can help to forge and confirm. The emergence of new truths can include new desires and competencies, new possibilities for self–other interaction, and new relationships to the child's space and physical environment.

In its most radical and creative aspect, play therapy can help a child synthesize or create a new experience, a new reality. This synthesis occurs through the creation of new metaphors about the self. In this regard play, like dreams, creates a structure using what Fromm (1982) called the forgotten language. Fromm was referring to the way in which language or images or metaphorical actions represent emotional states, attitudes, and conflicts. When language or action is used in this way, it includes an experiential state or is part of an experiential state, rather than abstractly referring to something in the way that words are used to convey information.

The child's creation of play sequences, a particular configuration of metaphors, produces a concrete emotional structure that is a metaphor for an important aspect of the child's experience. In this way, a play sequence can be very much like a poem or other works or art that create such structures (Langer 1967). The ability to create new truths through interactional play is dependent upon its metaphorical nature. Metaphor is central to the creation of emotional truth. Lakoff and Johnson (1980) argue that metaphor is integral to the way in which the human mind structures experience. We give our experience shape and substance by defining it in physical and sensory terms. Our somatosensory reactions give us a vocabulary and a set of commonly held experiences through which we can give shape and definition to our inner emotional lives. New experience, new ways of viewing ourselves and others, gain reality and meaning through metaphor. It places a previously undefined experience within a world of meaning and signification.

Cavell (1993) argues that all knowledge about the world and about ourselves develops out of an interpersonal exchange. The interpersonal process through which two people come to understand that they each mean the same thing or refer to the same experience when they use the same word in common is at the heart of our knowledge about ourselves. In the metaphor of play, the child is able to concretize for herself and for the therapist aspects of her emotional experience. While metaphor is intrinsically ambiguous and can capture a range of emotional experience, it allows the therapist and the patient important common ground. They begin to develop common knowledge about the child's emotional life.

In a particularly innovative, improvisational mode, a child created a scenario of a mad ambulance driver who would take patients on highly risky and dangerous rides to the hospital. The play scenes changed rapidly and unpredictably, and in this play he seemed to be spinning out novel ways of viewing himself and the dilemmas he faced. This expressed a complex truth about his own relationship to important people in his life, his aggressive, violent urges, his feared and desired loss of control, his need for help, his desire to rescue and be rescued, and his own grandiosity. In the play he was in the role of the rescuer, rushing people (undoubtedly in part himself) to the hospital. He was also the madman, both menacing and at times destroying others. The driver, however, would always rise from the ashes of his own destruction. No simple declarative statement or interpretation could express this complex emotional truth.

Such emotional experiences may represent trial possibilities a child is playing out in her engagement with the therapist. In play the child can explore possibilities without having to fully own them.

A child with a gender-identity disorder created the play scene of a canyon with high sides and a river running through it. On one side of the canyon were boys and on the other side were girls. He positioned himself and the therapist in varying degrees of proximity to the edge of the boy's side (he much closer to the edge). Then he allowed one character (himself) to swim in the river between the two sides, which included both the sense that he could stay afloat with his own mixed identity and even enjoy himself, but also that it was a very steep and high wall to climb to be distinctly on one side or the other. This concrete play representation expressed more about his relationship to the question of gender than could any logical, verbal explanation.

THE SAFETY AND REASSURANCE OF THE FAMILIAR

Having just made a claim for the value of the innovative and creative in the therapist's participation, it is important to note that the therapist is also often a protector of the status quo. She may be called on to reassure the child that she will not be overly disruptive or challenging concerning the child's need for the safety and comfort of familiar routines. As noted earlier, play faces in two directions. One face is that of tradition, ritual, and the reassurance of the familiar. Aries (1962) has noted how play often includes centuries-old cultural and religious symbolism. The following vignette illustrates a child's use of play to create a reassuringly familiar emotional structure.

> A child engaged the therapist in the repeated play of building a fortified castle with moats. The play was routine, predictable, and drew on traditional symbols and objects. In large part this play seemed to serve the purpose of establishing that the therapist would respect the child's need for a fortified castle and would not attempt an invasion. The structure of this play appeared to lay the groundwork for later quite daring and dramatic revelations.

The therapist comes to know the child's need for the reassuring, familiar routines of play, and also develops a sense regarding when it is possible to encourage new exploration.

THE PLACE OF INTERPRETATION IN PLAY

In traditional psychoanalytic play therapy, interpretation has been seen as the primary vehicle for therapeutic change. Of course, no unanimity exists concerning what constitutes an interpretation, toward what is it directed, and what are its presumed effects. For some clinicians, any comment on the child's play, particularly one that makes an assertion about its emotional meaning, constitutes an interpretation. For others an interpretation must include not only a comment on the child's emotional state, but also on its presumed cause, either in the immediate present or in reference to past historical events.

Clinicians differ regarding what they attempt to interpret. Freudians have generally followed the rule that one interprets the defense first, moving from more surface concerns to deeper ones. Kleinians, on the other hand, have emphasized in-depth interpretations of underlying basic impulses. Further differences exist concerning the relationship between the metaphor of the play and its interpretation. Some clinicians choose to interpret the play in light of the child's direct, actual life circumstances and presumed concerns, whereas others advocate keeping the interpretation within the metaphor of the play itself (Spiegel 1989).

In our view, all of these approaches to interpretation can be useful in a given treatment with its own particular features. Matters of timing and circumstance may dictate when one approach is likely to be more effective than the others. But the overall approach to child treatment that we have been describing places much less emphasis on interpretation as the key element in the process. We hope that we have made clear in the preceding pages that the shape of the interaction itself—the particular negotiations between therapist and child, and what the two participants in the play process create—is the essential element in the therapeutic action of child treatment (see the following chapters on therapeutic action).

We also believe that child treatment stimulates discoveries that are not reducible to any interpretive statement: a child's play remains inherently ambiguous, as distinct from the more traditional view that the child's play may be "read" for its specific meaning along certain well-established developmental lines.

Few child therapists would question the curative value of play itself. Most would agree that the therapist's initial task is to provide a safe, structured environment with limits that are conducive to the play process. But many children who enter therapy show an inability to engage in spontaneous, metaphorical play. Their inability to play is often an aspect of the difficulty that brought them into treatment. Erikson claims that the difficulties of most children seen in therapy result from play disruption in their lives as a result of feelings of fear or hatred toward those figures in their life that are in a position to protect their play.

In this light, interpretation can be a helpful intervention for freeing up the play process. This is the case when the therapist can point out the child's concerns or anxieties in ways that help the child to see that he is safe to express himself more freely. It is also true, however, that nothing works quite so well as a concrete experience of greater freedom or playfulness between the child and the therapist. In fact, to the extent that the clinician restricts herself to interpretation, that very role itself could well inhibit the child's more spontaneous playful involvement. Thus, the first task of the interpersonal child therapist is to promote the child's playful, creative engagement, and her willingness and freedom to use her imagination. The specific meaning of any given play sequence is far less compelling than is the quality of the child's playful participation, how that participation engages the therapist, and what the structure of the play tells us about the dilemmas of this particular child.

One of the important challenges for the clinician in play therapy is to develop a sense regarding when an interpretive observation will further the process and when it is likely to inhibit it. For some children, carrying on an interaction with the therapist in the denotative, declarative mode required by interpretation while at the same time engaging in symbolic play is quite comfortable and facilitative. Saying what the play "means" does not appear to inhibit the play itself and may enhance it. But for other children an interpretive comment, even the mere suggestion that the play may "mean" something, is the kiss of death, and may suppress any play for some time afterward. These same observations apply to the question of whether one restricts interpretive comments to the realm of metaphor or makes direct links to the child's life. These are understandings of the work that can develop only through the direct experience with an individual child.

When we speak about interpretation, we mean what the therapist chooses to put into explicit statements to the child. The therapist very likely will be interpreting to himself continually throughout the work. Several of our case illustrations give instances of that process. These interpretations to oneself then influence the therapist's subsequent interactions with the child—what he chooses to move toward or away from, or to show interest in. Sometimes, the therapist will only discover his own interpretation after the fact, so to speak, by observing his own behavior and what it suggests was on his mind.

It also bears repeating to say that many important understandings that emerge in the play process, particularly those involving the creating of new meanings and new self-understandings, are not necessarily reducible to verbal formulation. The play image or metaphor may be the best representation for such experiences. To the extent that these new meanings inhere in new senses of self, the interaction with the therapist enacts these new self-experiences and quite possibly can be expressed in no other way.

TELLING IT LIKE IT IS

The child's direct statement of feeling or concern, and a give-and-take between the therapist and the child about those concerns, can be very powerful and valuable. While it is true that there are certain understandings that can be created only through the metaphor of play, there are other experiences that can only be conveyed in such direct, denotative statements. And it is certainly a general goal of child therapy to help the child in her ability to say directly what she wants, what she feels, and what she thinks. Much of the art of relational child treatment lies in the child's and the therapist's ability to create a dialogue that incorporates the more imaginative and playful processes with direct declarative expressions regarding the child's struggles in her own life.

WHO TAKES THE LEAD IN THE PLAY

Commonly, in writings on psychoanalytically informed play therapy, the therapist is seen as having a relatively passive role, either observing the child's play and commenting on it, or at most accepting certain roles explicitly assigned by the child. In some more cognitively based therapies, by contrast, the therapist, having decided on a particular intervention, will assume an active stance dictated by the particular issue or point of view the therapist wishes to emphasize.

The relational therapist will attend to the particular type of interaction that she and the child are developing. This interaction may or may not lead to play in the narrow sense as we have defined it. This will depend on how they evolve together as players. If the child's sense of play consists of thwarting or opposing the adult authority, this may remain the focus of their relationship. The therapist may find it necessary to take an active, initiating role. For example, if the child is particularly inhibited, the therapist may take the lead in developing a play process. The therapist not only has to be alert for the play potential in her exchanges with the child, but she may also have to assume the lead or the initiative in stimulating a playful exchange. This step requires the clinician to depart from the more usual role of observer and more passive participant, and to incur the risk of actively influencing her patient. It is also an approach that de-emphasizes the meaning of the specific content of play and emphasizes the play process itself. It is easy for a therapist who engages a child in this manner to fear that she has abandoned all professional responsibility and has simply surrendered to her own regressive desire to have fun.

Even in cases where the child is quite active in play, the therapist may find himself drawn to a particular way of participating. In these instances, the therapist may be enacting disowned aspects of the child's own fantasies or desires. For example, in the case of a highly inhibited, timid child, the therapist might find himself playing out the part of a highly aggressive, defiant character at the child's direction, and to the child's utter delight. The therapist's understandable concern in these situations is in the possibility of moving the therapy in a direction profoundly influenced by the therapist's issues, or by the therapist's beliefs about what is important in the child's experience. The therapist may take some comfort from the theory that he may be moved by internal states that are an instance of so-called projective identification, and has taken on feelings or attitudes projected onto him by the child.

Whatever the source of the therapist's motivation to interact in a particular way with the child, if one views the play as an evolving dialogue in which both participants learn from each other, then if the therapist's participation at any point is not responsive to the child's issues or needs, this will probably become evident. It is our contention that the therapist who is willing to take a chance and actively participates with the child in the play dialogue will come to understand the child in a more intimate way, and will be contributing to a process between them that is most likely to support the emergence of new insights and new experiences of self.

PLAY IN THERAPEUTIC WORK WITH PARENTS

In working with the parents of children in therapy, the clinician usually confronts their embeddedness in a particular view of their child, the child's problems, the part they play or don't play, how they envision a solution, and the therapist's function. The therapist may invite the parents to relinquish some of their closely held assumptions about these matters, and to consider ideas that might seem anywhere from improbable to absurd. These ideas include the willingness to tolerate the notion that their child may have no specific diagnosis such as ADHD, that the child's problems may in some respects be important strengths, that the pattern of family interaction, including their own unconscious longings and conflicts, may figure prominently in their child's functioning, and that a desirable outcome may be impossible to define. The therapist will thus ask the parents to suspend their own perhaps rigidly held views of reality and to play with new possibilities, to open themselves to new ways of experiencing their child.

More specifically, as the treatment proceeds, the therapist may discover that the parents and the child have never really developed a play process between themselves. As the therapist gains the confidence of the parents and the trust of the child, he may become an active facilitator of play between one parent or both parents and the child, either through direct suggestion, general encouragement, or modeling in a parent–child or family session.

10

Transference and Countertransference in Child Treatment

In the play of child treatment, therapist and child get caught up in a host of feelings toward each other. These feelings are the "stuff" of their transference and countertransference relationships that can then guide the therapist's interventions. Whether to be active or more passive, to interpret or to avoid comment, are all choices the therapist will make largely on the basis of his experience and his understanding of the transference–countertransference relationship.

SOME COMPARISONS

Before exploring transference issues with children, a brief description of adult transferences will serve as a foundation for comparison. Sigmund Freud (Breuer and Freud 1893–1895) came upon the concept of transference while working primarily with adult female hysterics. He found that these Victorian female patients were developing strong feelings about their male doctors that he felt were based on some distorted or "misaligned" perceptions of the actual person of the doctor. It is from these earliest beginnings that psychoanalysts have come to see transference today as the predilection to allow our unconscious projections of earlier relationships to influence perceptions of the people with whom we come in contact in our daily life. This transferential tendency was felt by Freud to be heightened in the presence of the psychoanalyst if the analyst kept to a minimum any obstacles that would preclude the projections of patients' past relationships onto their current one.

Other concepts also have been developed in relation to the transference with adult analysands that affect our general thinking about child transferences, specifically the repetition compulsion, neutrality, and abstinence (Freud 1912). Briefly, the theory is that the unconscious tendency to work through or to recreate specific, familiar (albeit problematic), and unresolved childhood situations is so strong that one will repeat such situations with others, often oblivious to the inappropriateness of these interactions. This is true especially in the ambiguous situation of psychoanalytic treatment where typically not much is known by the patient about the therapist's life and personal issues. Therefore, the opportunity is ripe to project or superimpose one's childhood scenarios onto the therapist and the therapeutic milieu. Freud saw this ambiguous situation as highly conducive to the treatment, so he instructed therapists to remain affectively neutral and personally abstinent in order to facilitate such transferential projections and repetitions. That is, the therapist does not try to influence the unfolding of the unconscious material by taking a position or revealing personal information that would guide or influence the projections and displacements. Psychoanalysis was designed to provide maximal opportunity for the patient to project characteristics of significant parental figures, in particular, onto the person of the analyst. The analyst, in turn, studies her personal reactions in order to be aware of her countertransferences toward the patient.

Altman (1992) delineates three ways in which this adult model is not an exact fit when applied to the transferences of children patients. First, he reminds us of Anna Freud's (1927 [1926], 1946) point that children are so involved with and attached to their parents on a daily basis that their need to transfer onto a therapist and work through issues with a therapist is not so compelling. They have the original objects in vivo to deal with on a daily basis. Second, the concepts of abstinence and neutrality are basically unworkable with children, since direct engagement is usually a necessary piece of the work with children. Finally, Altman sees transference interpretations as too cognitively complex for the child therapist to depend upon as the primary means of reaching children on transference issues.

Even though there are problems in applying an adult, classical model of transference directly to child work, this has not been reflected sufficiently in the literature. Many descriptions of psychoanalytic work with children automatically accept such principles as neutrality in spite of the difficulties this created. Transference and countertransference, however, are as constant a part of the work with children as they are with adults. This is particularly relevant to a relational perspective, since it provides an avenue for exploring the ways interactions in the present day are connected in varying degrees to internalized representations of past relationships.

The adult literature on transference and countertransference has been undergoing exciting changes and innovations during the last two decades. The classic view of transference and countertransference has been modified by modern Freudians, object relations, interpersonal, and relational theorists to place more emphasis upon the here-and-now aspects of the patient's relational repertoire as they manifest themselves with the actual therapist, and less of an emphasis on the distortion of the therapist to fit into the previous molds of the past. For example, a child may focus angrily on the limits set by the therapist. While it would not be incorrect for the therapist to focus on how this is a manifestation of transference feelings for the parents from the past, the relational child therapist would also want to explore and understand these feelings of the child toward the therapist's rules as an in vivo experiencing of a problematic situation for this child. It has been amply demonstrated in the adult literature that a focus on the immediate manifestations of the transference and countertransference in the patient–analyst dyad has potent therapeutic value that may be lost if references to the past are routinely given. A brief guide to this literature would begin with the work of Aron 1996, Gill 1982, 1994, Jacobs 1991, Joseph 1985, Levenson 1983, Mitchell 1997, and Sullivan 1953. In many cases, it may cool the therapeutic heat of the here-and-now moment to adhere to some theoretical sequence of analyzing the past instead of keeping the focus on the present situation. Of course, at other times such interpretations to past relationships may be where the heat is, but the emphasis in a relational perspective is not to leave the heated present material by delving into the past as a matter of rote procedure.

The same is true is for countertransference in the adult relational model. The analyst's countertransferences are examined for their value in understanding the current patient–analyst relationship, warts and all. Such awareness is not confined to seeing what it was like to be the patient's mother, or even to seeing it as manifestations of the analyst's psychopathology, as Freud had thought. The therapist's countertransferences are also seen as data from the immediate experience of the two participants that is helpful in piecing together the essential issues of the work together (Aron 1996, Bollas 1987, Ehrenberg 1992, Epstein and Feiner 1983, Mitchell 1997).

With child patients there is one additional and important factor in the assessment of the transference and countertransference, namely that the parents in particular (and even teachers in certain instances) have a certain stake in remaining in contact with the therapist. They have news to report and they believe, with good reason in most cases, that the therapist would never find out some significant information without their input. Thus the analyst has to include ways of dealing with information about the child that comes from outside the sessions with the child herself. Sarnoff (1976) called this the "alterego" function of the parents. Similarly, countertransferences may originate in the session from the contact with the parents as well, and must be handled in a way that informs the work with the child.

HISTORICAL CONTEXT

The history of applying psychoanalytic concepts developed in the work with adults to working with child patients in psychoanalytically oriented treatment had very strong, yet theoretically quite different, proponents in Melanie Klein and Anna Freud. These two women came to head two different schools of child psychoanalysis, Kleinian object relations and Freudian classical. Eventually as this division unfolded, Winnicott emerged as an "independent" voice, using both theories as the springboard for his own seminal contributions to the child psychotherapy literature.

Melanie Klein

When one surveys Klein's work with children, one is left with paradoxical conclusions. On the one hand, Klein left a legacy of technical considerations in child treatment that are standard operating procedure today, due to their respectful approach toward the child's presented material. This permissive and understanding stance, however, stands in stark contrast to the clinical transcripts of her work with child patients, which are shocking in the directness and verbal candor of her interpretations. This shock is especially apparent in comparison to the more neutral interactions that Anna Freud (who was developing her theory in the same time period) had with her child patients, as reported in her clinical examples.

Let's begin with her innovative contributions. Klein (1975) discovered that the play of children in psychotherapy sessions was relatively comparable to the free association and dream material of adults. While this seems obvious to our modern sensibilities about child's play, no analyst had approached child's play in this meaning-laden manner before. For instance, the Freudian camp was simultaneously developing a technique of working with children that was more educational and didactic. Klein likened the technical procedures of working with children's play to the handling of free associations and dreams in the analyses of adults. That is, the analyst's role is to facilitate the expansion of the material that the child is producing and to see it as unconscious manifestations of the issues that the child is working through. Anna Freud, in her writings on transference with children, credits Klein with establishing this method of working with children. She originally called it the "Kleinian play technique" (1927[1926]).

Differences between Klein and Anna Freud become apparent, however, when one considers that Klein in her object relations theory of psychoanalysis (as it was practiced by her and her colleagues) believed in making interpretations immediately to the patient at the "deep" level of unconscious meaning, whether the patient was an adult or a child (Elmhirst 1988, Klein 1959, Segal 1964). Her rationale for this with child patients included the observation that the connection between the unconscious and the conscious in children is traversed easier and more frequently than in adults because of the child's early position in personality development. Thus Klein believed that children are ready to hear interpretations directed to the unconscious material from the start of psychotherapy and are not harmed by these "insights" (Klein 1975).

Hence for Klein, the transference with child patients was handled much as it would be managed with adult patients. Interpretations were given by Klein when she had some understanding of the child that had been garnered from the child's play and other communications. These interpretations were formulated for delivery to the patient in terms of the child's relationship with his parents of the past, that is, as introjects (Segal 1964, Warshaw 1992). The introjected representations of the parents of the past were considered to be the child's unconscious and biased version of the parent upon which the transference, and thereby the free associative play, were constructed by the child (Klein 1975). Here is an example of Klein (1961) interpreting to a 10-year-old boy in the thirty-second session of child analysis:

> Mrs. K interpreted when still in the room, his wish to keep the playroom standing for her and Mummy, intact. Touching and liking the beads, which were similar to his mother's, expressed his wish to keep Mummy's breast safe and undamaged, and to make sure it was there; the playroom also should be kept safe against intruders, which meant that Mummy and Mrs. K should be protected against the intruding and dangerous father, Paul, and himself. [p.156]

Klein did not include reality factors, such as those concerning the present-day parents for example, since (as in her work with adults) she believed that the changes in the external world followed from insight into the internal world through genetic interpretations. In fact, Klein had little place for the actual parents in her interpretations or in the interpretive process of child psychotherapy. After initially explaining the process of child analysis, she hoped to have minimal contact with the parents. She "refused absolutely" to talk to them about the treatment (Klein 1975). She even preferred that they not sit in the waiting room. Although she thought that some of the information that parents could provide was worthwhile, she chose not to procure it if it caused her any difficulty. In this regard Klein (1975) said: "Although valuable, it is not indispensable" (p. 77). The parents were asked to be cooperative logistically, and they were told that they could eventually secure relief from their concerns when they saw that their child was improving.

Another contribution of Klein's to transference–countertransference work centers about her concept of projective identification, which was described earlier in the infancy section of this book. Klein (1946) detailed her belief that preverbal infants rid themselves of unwanted and overpowering negative affects by projecting them into a receptive caregiver. But it was Klein's followers who have redefined and reconceived projective identification as the study of the transmission of feeling states, usually unconsciously, between people. Thus while there is still an interest in the intricate communication between infants and mothers, there is now an equally important focus on the implications of such interactions in other relationships, particularly between patient and therapist (Beebe and Lachmann 1988, Bion 1959, Joseph 1987, Ogden 1982, Seligman 1999).

Silverman and Lieberman (1999) provide a compelling example of how "negative maternal attributions" through projective identification have been transmitted intergenerationally across three generations: from a girl's grandmother to the girl's mother, when the mother was a girl, and then again one generation later from the mother to her own young daughter. They are part of a revolutionary revision of the Kleinian concept of projective identification in which they study the process of projective identification and examine how the mother sends her split-off feelings to reside in the infant, instead of the more typical example of infant projecting into the mother. "It was under the guise of protecting her daughter that the most direct repetitions of Laura's [the mother's] violent childhood experiences were re-enacted with her own child" (p. 163). Specifically, while the mother's conscious agenda was to protect her child, the mother's exposure of the daughter to aggression in the world, in her misguided attempt to instill caution, actually backfired. The daughter frequently placed herself in dangerous situations in a way that was compatible with the "negative maternal attributions" of which the mother had little awareness. The authors describe how they believe the mother's projective identifications were transmitted to her child (Isabelle):

First, Laura perceived Isabelle in a biased way directly linked to her [the mother's] early childhood traumatic experience. . . . Second, Laura responded to Isabelle in ways that corresponded with her negative attributions. . . . The third stage of the process is that Isabelle behaved in a distracted and un-selfprotective manner. . . . consistent with her mother's attributions. [Silverman and Lieberman 1999, p. 180]

Child therapists in such situations as described above are working in a complex situation where incompatible conscious and unconscious agendas are simultaneously operating in the mother–child relationship. Additionally, the child therapist is just as likely to be the host of the continued pattern of transmitting these harmful attributions unconsciously, as he enters into a relationship with the child patient and her mother. Thus while we must be attuned to the transmission of these attributions in the child's family, in a similar fashion during psychotherapy sessions the therapist can attune himself to the emotional climate in the room between himself and the child (or also the mother) as another avenue of understanding the directions that the transference and countertransference are taking.

For example, a therapist may note the difference in his own feelings when two different children play with the toys in a careless way. For the first child it may signal a lack of valuing of the self, which the therapist may become aware of by noticing his feelings of concern about the child and her play. In contrast, with the second child this carelessness may elicit feelings of irritation in the therapist more likely to emanate from angry feelings in the child and himself. This second child unconsciously acts out his anger by his disregard for the consequences of his actions with the toys. The therapist may unconsciously act out his anger at this carelessness by being more strict with limits than he typically is. In these two cases a transference–countertransference correspondence signals to the therapist that he and the child patient may be enacting some relational pattern that the child therapist must be alert to, in order to process his inner experience and to attempt to transform it therapeutically in his subsequent interactions with the child. Once the child therapist has recognized his unwitting participation in the enactment of a psychopathogenic relational pattern, it is as if a wash has come over the treatment. From that moment on, the therapist has the capacity to be a new object (Altman 1992, Greenberg 1991) in the patient's life and to handle the situation in a different and therapeutic manner (Ogden 1982).

Anna Freud

Although Anna Freud utilized Klein's technique, her position on transference with child patients differed from the emerging Kleinian model and even from the pre-existing Freudian one taken with adults (Altman 1992, A. Freud 1927 [1926], 1946, Sandler et al. 1980, Warshaw 1992). In her earliest writings, Anna Freud described a treatment for child patients that began with a preparatory period in which her first goal with the child was to establish an "affectionate attachment" (A. Freud 1946) or positive transference. This step was deemed to be necessary because of her view that children only listen to, and take risks with, people whom they love and with whom they feel loved. Ekstein (1966), in support of this position, stated that the ego of the disturbed child is particularly sensitive to transference feelings and that the child will withdraw into a defensive posture if the ego is threatened by the content of the interpreted material. This is a reflection both of ego psychology's careful attention to the child's ego functioning and of its movement away from Sigmund Freud's more id-focused approach. In addition, ego psychologists of Anna Freud's era (Hug-Hellmuth 1921) did not subscribe to the Kleinian stance of immediate and deep (and also shocking, according to many non-Kleinians) transference interpretations.

Another of Anna Freud's innovations in working with children was her attempt to resolve negative transferential reactions as quickly as possible, due to her belief that they had a mainly disruptive impact on the treatment of children. This was, of course, quite different from the accepted classical practice with adults or that of the Kleinians with children and adults. Anna Freud was less concerned with observing the provisions of neutrality or abstinence with children than she was with adults. In fact, Anna Freud gives a clinical example in her early paper on transference with children (1927[1926]) in which she visits a 6-year-old female patient in her home and even stays for the evening bath, barely a neutral event. The child psychoanalyst was seen as an ego-enhancing agent.

One notices, once again, the stark contrast between Klein and Anna Freud when one considers the development historically of an empathic stance toward the child patient as an integral part of the therapeutic situation. In Anna Freud's later thinking (Sandler et al.

1980), the preparatory period, mentioned above, and its emphasis on positive transference, is replaced by the concept of a "treatment alliance" and of "liking the therapist." Anna Freud is clear in spelling out the need to have the child "like" the therapist as a necessary prerequisite to successful treatment. Modern child therapists find it hard to argue with the wisdom of this basic concept.

Once this treatment alliance has been established, that is, once the child likes the therapist and the treatment sessions, the transference work with children still differs from adult psychoanalyses in other ways. According to Anna Freud, since children have an ongoing relationship with their parents while in therapy, it becomes difficult for the therapist to distinguish whether the child is merely reacting to the therapist now (following the successful attainment of a positive treatment alliance) as he would any beloved adult at that point in his life, or if, in fact, the behavior is a repetition of earlier childhood experiences with a parent of the past, acted out within the treatment setting (Altman 1992, A. Freud 1946, Sandler et al. 1980). Since the parents are an active part of the child patient's daily life, Anna Freud postulated that the child still attempts to work through her issues with her parents in a quotidian manner at home, rather than saving them for her sessions, even though the child may comprehend that the stated purpose of her therapy is to provide a forum in which to work through these issues. Ekstein (1966) described this as the child's fear that if she loves the therapist too much, there will not be enough love left for her parents. The relational orientation is less concerned with whether the play is mainly derivative of repressed childhood material, and more concerned with whether the child feels free enough to use the session to express herself regarding whatever is on her mind, regardless of the origin. If the child utilizes this freedom, then meaningful play and interactions will result as the relational therapist tries to stay warm on the trail of the play.

Donald Winnicott

It was after World War II, when the disagreements between Anna Freud and Klein were at their peak, that Donald Winnicott began his synthesizing of these two influences on his work with child patients. Winnicott's theory is a curious and respectful mixture of both Klein's and Anna Freud's theories (see Greenberg and Mitchell 1983 for a detailed description of Winnicott's hybrid and sometimes contradictory blending of opposite points of view).

With regard to their respective theories, briefly, Winnicott combined Anna Freud's emphasis on ego functioning with Klein's focus on the dynamics of the first year of life. In the clinical applications of these two theories, one finds a compelling admixture that has proven to be very influential. Winnicott agreed with Klein that technically, child and adult analyses were similar. That is, the analyst aids child patients to capitalize on their "genetic tendency" (1958c, p. 116) toward mental health or a "true self," as they would with their adult patients. Although he addressed the same material as Klein, such as current manifestations of infantile ties to internalized objects, Winnicott had a decidedly softer touch in the presentation of interpretations. He did not aim to reach the unconscious directly through "deep" interpretations of the ilk that Klein and her followers were using with children at that time. In this use of a softer touch, he agreed with Anna Freud. He too believed that a warm and essentially positive relationship with a focus on ego strengths was a necessity with child patients. To these concepts of Klein's and Anna Freud's, Winnicott (1971a) added his own innovative contributions, including the value of play and playfulness. Winnicott also stressed, more than his female predecessors, the importance of the mother's role, developmentally in terms of personality formation (as she nurtures her child through the various stages of childhood, particularly infancy) as well as clinically (where the mother's role can serve as a model for the therapeutic relationship). He involved parents in the treatment to the extent that it was possible and did not hesitate to involve significant others from the child's environment (Warshaw 1992).

In keeping with his tendency to bridge the Kleinian and Freudian schools, Winnicott gave two-part advice regarding the handling of the transference. First, he relied on transference interpretations meted out according to the analyst's accumulated perceptions of unconscious tendencies and timed for optimal acceptance. Second, Winnicott emphasized a relational aspect of the transference with child patients that he called the holding environment: "What matters to the patient is not the accuracy of the interpretations so much as the willingness of the analyst to help, the analyst's capacity to identify with the patient and so to believe in what is needed and to meet the need as soon as the need is indicated verbally or in nonverbal or preverbal language" (1958c, p. 122).

Winnicott realized that a prime factor in the treatment of children (and adults) was the analyst's participation (Altman 1992) in the process. He wrote honestly and movingly about how he gauged his involvement. He attempted, as the above quote demonstrates, to monitor the affective shifts and needs of the patient so that he could be responsive to them.

Winnicott (1958) interpreted early in the treatment, in keeping with Klein, but this did not stop him from quickly involving himself positively with the child, à la Anna Freud. He wanted both to "orientate" the child to an analytic model (and thereby demonstrate the benefits of the treatment) as well as to provide a "holding environment." For example, in *The Piggle* (1977), Winnicott's record of his psychoanalysis of Gabriella from age 2½ to 5, he good-naturedly played any role she assigned him and willingly answered questions about himself such as how old he was. He also interpreted psychological material directly as it arose, including such issues as the Piggle's (Gabriella's nickname) fear of object loss. After the Piggle angrily said that she wanted to eat Winnicott during a session prior to his vacation, he replied: "If you eat me that would be taking me away inside you, and then you would not mind going" (1977, p. 101). Here Winnicott alludes to the oral incorporative wish à la Klein, but with his light touch. Moreover, in his work with the Piggle, one is particularly impressed with how carefully Winnicott monitored the relationship he had with Gabriella in terms of the holding environment, even though he also demonstrated how deft he was with interpretations based upon either the Kleinian or ego-psychological theory. Not surprisingly, Winnicott's work has become a beacon to child therapists today since his warmth and openness have an almost magnetic appeal to those of us who struggle in our work with children to find a place for our countertransferential tendency (or wish or need) to have warm and fulfilling relationships with our child patients while also being respectful of an interpretive psychoanalytic tradition.

RELATIONAL PERSPECTIVE ON TRANSFERENCE AND COUNTERTRANSFERENCE

Thus Winnicott's influence is strongly felt in the practice of child psychotherapy today particularly in the aforementioned beliefs in

(1) an endogenous striving toward health, that is, toward the "true self," as well as (2) an interest in the actual influence of the real (not introjected) mother and family (Altman 1992, Winnicott 1956, 1960). This shift in emphasis onto the vicissitudes of the actual mother–child relationship heralded a sea change in the way child (and adult) psychoanalysts began to theorize about the workings of child development and hence child psychotherapy. Now the shift was more toward the mother–child relationship as the key clinical paradigm instead of the oedipal triangle, and toward interpersonal life as a basis for personality instead of an exclusive focus on the introjected intrapsychic world. Theories proffered by Bowlby in England (attachment theory) and Sullivan in the United States (interpersonal theory) continued in this trend toward recognizing interpersonal relatedness as a key building block of personality functioning and therefore significant to any exploration of the therapeutic relationship in a clinical setting.

Mitchell (1997), in his updated exposition of a relational position, amplified the interpersonal nature of psychological functioning when he stated "what actually happened matters" both in early life and in the session. This statement of Mitchell's echoes an earlier question of Levenson's (1972, 1983) who, in delineating his interpersonal position, said that he asks himself during a session, "What's going on around here?" Thus, in pursuing the lead of adult relational theorists, the child therapist follows the trail of the child's play in psychotherapy. This play informs the therapist how the child has incorporated various relational patterns (Mitchell 1997) learned throughout her young life as her primary means of adapting to her environment, including the psychotherapy sessions. How adaptive or maladaptive, flexible or rigid, active or passive, are the play patterns? This information tells not only about the child's adaptive struggles but also how these same struggles are acted out interpersonally with others, including the therapist.

Thus the transference and countertransference inform the therapist about old objects (parents in daily life and in introjected objects) and new objects (the relationship to the therapist). Current relational thinking about the transference does not leave out the typical process whereby the therapist enters the child's psychological life as an old object who becomes the vehicle for projections. What is added by a relational perspective about transference and countertransference is that the therapist eventually must become a new object for the therapy to have its optimal therapeutic value. As the therapist demonstrates therapeutic handling of problematic situations in both the child's life and her interactions with the therapist, the child's psyche makes room for the new and healthier experiences that therapy provides for her— experiences that run counter to many of the prior relational patterns. The therapist is simultaneously an old object and a new object and thereby positioned to be a therapeutic force in the child's life (Altman 1992, Greenberg 1991).

The following clinical vignette illustrates the intertwining of transference and countertransference, along with the internalization of interpersonal patterns in the family and how these get replicated in the treatment room. The vignette also shows how therapeutic intervention, from a relational point of view, can interrupt the internalization of pathological interpersonal patterns.

A 5-year-old girl, Jennifer, was being seen individually for provocative and disruptive behavior at home and at school. The father worked long hours, while the mother was a rather passive woman who was also busy caring for a toddler-aged boy. Jennifer would poke at the brother, refuse to clean up messes that she made, and in a thousand ways make an annoyance of herself at home. The mother, overwhelmed with her behavior and the demands of caring for two children alone, threatened her by saying the father would punish her when he got home. The father would arrive home exhausted, quickly becoming resentful of his wife's demand that he now take care of Jennifer's misbehavior. One day, this normally nonabusive man, fed up, kicked Jennifer when she refused to clean up her room as mother had been asking her all day. The therapist was informed of this event the next day, shortly before he was due to see Jennifer.

Jennifer entered her session in an agitated state, behaving more provocatively than usual. By the time the session was coming to an end, every toy in the room was strewn over the floor and Jennifer was refusing to stop throwing them around. The therapist, of course, had another patient waiting. He was getting increasingly irritated as he contemplated running late for the rest of the day because of the need to clean up this formidable mess. At one point, he found himself standing over Jennifer, who was lying on her back on the floor in passive-aggressive fashion, surrounded by a chaos of toys. The fantasy of kicking her alerted him to the context of the father's kicking her the night before. He relaxed and said: "I'll bet you're wondering if I'm going to kick you like your father did last night." Jennifer smiled, and got up. A moment later, she began to clean up the room. As she left the session, she ran up to her mother and said, "I helped Dr. X clean up today!"

This vignette, unprecedently magical in its outcome, should not be taken as a paradigm for what usually happens in child treatment. It does, however, serve to illustrate many points. First, one can see the very beginnings of how a traumatic relational event gets internalized through repetition outside the original context. Then, one can see how the other person's subjective reaction to the child (the therapist's reaction, in this case) gets inducted into the process. The therapist's rage at the child is fully his own (the therapist felt responsible for not having set limits earlier in the session, and for the tension level he felt about keeping the next patient waiting, for example), even as it is induced by the child. Countertransference, in this sense, always feels like any other subjective reaction for which the therapist is entirely responsible, even as it seems to be induced by the patient and to replicate a relational pattern that was already there in the patient. This synchronization of subjectivities constitutes the great mystery of transference/countertransference; it is what makes psychoanalytic work within the transference/countertransference matrix, perhaps all deep human relatedness, possible.

But the rage at Jennifer was not the entirety of the therapist's reaction. At a certain point, a certain perspective, the effort to understand from a therapeutic vantage point, came into the foreground. The therapist was able to metacommunicate about the entanglement he and Jennifer had co-created in a way that freed both of them from the sense of necessity associated with it. In the end, the therapist's having gotten temporarily "sucked in" to the enactment proved useful; without anger having been felt powerfully on both sides, the therapist's ultimately thoughtful and boundary-defining intervention would not have had the same impact. The therapist said to the patient, in effect, "You are making me angry; I am affected by what you are doing. But I am not going to stop with being angry with you, and I will not hurt you. I know that although you mean to make me angry, that is not all you mean to do. I will do my best to think about how you are communicating to me about the situation with your father, and how it feels to you and to him to be involved with each other in this way." The value to the child of this intervention is that it provided a new, in the sense of unexpected, relational experience in the context of a potentially self-defeating repetition of a traumatic experience. The patient gave a smile of recognition when she and the therapist together discovered the nature of the evolving engagement, as well as a way out. This sequence of events also promoted her self-observing capacity and her capacity to symbolize her experience verbally. In microcosm, one can see here one way, at least, in which psychoanalytically oriented work with children can forestall pathological developments and lead to change in patterns in the process of being internalized.

11

Launching the Therapy
with the Child

In these two chapters we address nuts-and-bolts aspects of work with children and parents. Our effort is to develop an approach to technique that goes beyond interpretation toward a full engagement with child and parents. We see the therapist as always responding to a unique clinical situation, though guided by general principles applied flexibly. Throughout, we consider how therapeutic change takes place within an interaction in which there is mutual influence between patient and therapist, both of whom have personalities, needs, and desires.

The core element in the approach we wish to describe is a playful engagement of the child and the therapist. In our view, the entire therapeutic process has an important play dimension, and that includes the work with parents, siblings or the whole family. In this section, however, we wish to focus on the specific challenge of developing a creative and private play space for the therapist and the child.

WHAT KIND OF PLAY AND TO WHAT END?

We use the term *playful engagement* rather than play, play therapy, or symbolic play therapy in order to emphasize the interactional nature of the process and the spirit of playfulness that we feel is critical. Call it a broad attitude or stance that can infuse a wide range of different activities. This playful engagement may consist of mutual play, symbolic play, active games like basketball, board games such as "Life"™ or "Battleship,"™ card games, chess, or conversation. The particular medium that forms the basis of the interaction is less important than the development of such a therapeutic process. The child may warm to certain types of engagement and not to others, depending upon the child's age, developmental status, and specific concerns. Similarly, the therapist may choose to emphasize certain forms of interaction depending upon what she feels would serve her therapeutic purposes best.

TO DIRECT OR NOT DIRECT

Traditionally, play therapists have done little to direct or shape the process, and have restricted their role to observing and interpreting the child's play. The interpersonal relational therapist is generally more willing to become directly involved as an active participant, believing that it is the relationship between therapist and child that is key to the therapeutic effect of the work. This more active involvement on the part of the relational therapist, however, usually occurs in the context of the work as it unfolds. In general the relational therapist will approach the child's participation with relatively few preformed notions about how to proceed. In this regard, the relational therapist's approach differs from that of cognitive-behavioral therapists or family therapists who often have a specific strategy for the direction they want the interaction to take.

Nevertheless, there are circumstances in which the relational therapists may choose a more directive approach. In the case of children whose treatment may grow out of certain specific circumstances, such as children with HIV or children of parents with HIV, children who have suffered significant personal losses or family illness, children who have been physically or sexually abused, and children who have experienced other forms of trauma, the therapist may choose to be more directive about the selection of play materials or in the type of exploration he or she encourages. For example, certain therapists may suggest that the child paint or draw a picture concerning a particular experience. Others might view such directedness as contrary to the very processes that play therapy should encourage, namely an open-ended, autonomous exploration of the child's inner world, akin to the process of free association in adult treatment. For example, some therapists find Richard Gardner's (1971) "Talking, Feeling, Doing" game to be a useful tool to generate certain kinds of expression in the therapy, while others find it anathema to the whole purpose of play therapy. In our view, the clinician need not feel it necessary to adopt either the more directed play approach nor the entirely open-ended approach exclusively. These choices will depend very much on the child, the nature of the task the therapy confronts, the setting of the therapy—school, clinic, private office—and on such factors as the length of the therapy that can be anticipated, the particular stage the therapy has reached, and the therapist's sense of timing.

In the case of the traumatized child, the therapist may weigh the value of encouraging the child to explore specific themes related to the trauma, whether in play or verbally, against the possible risk of over-stimulation and re-experiencing of the traumatic situation. In working with children who present regulatory dysfunctions, such as impulsive children or those with difficulties in self-regulation or self-soothing, the therapist may also choose to focus his interaction on these aspects of the child's functioning. The therapist may choose to work on such processes in conjunction with an occupational therapist as part of the overall treatment arrangement.

In the current managed care climate, the therapist's choices may be either to see the child for a strictly limited number of sessions or not to see the child at all. The therapist must think strategically about whether anything can be accomplished in a brief time period. If the therapist decides that a therapeutic intervention may be worthwhile, he may choose to take a more directive role in shaping the play process.

EXPECT THE UNEXPECTED

Whatever particular ideas a therapist may have in mind regarding the treatment he would like to conduct, the first five minutes in the room with the child will usually convince the therapist that one's ideas have relatively little relationship to the actual experience that develops. Children described as wild and unruly may appear subdued and reticent. Others described as depressed or fearful may become rambunctious and playful. The therapist who feels committed to the idea of encouraging a play process with the child may be startled and unnerved when the child sits down and begins to talk directly about his difficulties with no prompting.

Nevertheless, the therapist will feel more secure if armed with some general guidelines before entering the treatment room. Children up to the age of 4 or 5 often will play very readily and will also equally readily tell you what the play is about. For example, one young boy in session put a figure of a child on a chair, over another figure beneath it on the floor. When the therapist made some oblique suggestions regarding the scene, he quickly explained that he was the figure on the chair and he was peeing on his mother's boyfriend whom he hated and who had wrecked his life. Somewhat older children (up to 8 or 9) will usually take to play fairly easily, but they are usually more reticent to ascribe any particular meaning to their play.

Older children (8 to 12) will often prefer some type of game or activity to play and will sometimes show a willingness to talk about things. Timid children will often be slow to engage in any play and prefer solitary activities. Aggressive children, on the other hand, may become overstimulated by an array of play materials and raise havoc with them. Children with impulsive behavior and with attention problems can also pose challenges in their manipulation of play materials. Abused or otherwise traumatized children may avoid play altogether or become excessively agitated. Some may enact certain specific scenes of their own abuse that have a rigid stereotyped quality.

Either from the outset or as the therapist develops hypotheses in the evaluative phase, she faces a decision regarding what she sees as the purpose play may serve in the process. If it appears to the therapist that the child is inhibited in his capacity for play, or has lacked both opportunity and encouragement to play in his life, then the therapist may decide that play is a critical capacity or function to help develop. On the other hand, if the therapist feels that the child has receded into play or has used play to avoid what may be anticipated as painful or frightening human interaction, the therapist may be thinking about encouraging the child to move more toward direct, discursive interaction.

THE BEGINNING SESSIONS

The remarks that follow about engaging the child in play are meant to apply generally. We will offer examples to give a sense of the variation required by different ages and circumstances. In addition, we note specific situations that may warrant a significant deviation from the more standard approach to engaging the child in the beginning sessions.

In beginning to work with a child, the therapist hopes that the treatment room will become a special place (Loewald 1987) in which the child experiences the safety and the freedom to express himself, as well as to reorganize his experience, his attitudes and feelings, and the behavioral possibilities that he considers. But at the beginning, the child's view of things may be very far from the state of mind that the therapist hopes for. Such safety and freedom can only be achieved with experience over time. There are no short cuts.

Each child will bring his own particular concerns and ways of operating into the room. Certain children may be brimming with requests or pent up frustrations, such as the boy who immediately complained that his father insists he address him as "sir." Others will be silent, timid, wary, or sullen. Still others will react to their anxiety by treating both the room and the therapist as one big jungle gym. In the face of such a variety of behaviors, the therapist has to find a stance that is relatively comfortable across situations.

To begin, it is important to ask what the child's understanding is of why he has come. Of course, the therapist should spend some time on this question with the parents before meeting with the child. In general, it is useful for the parents to introduce the idea to their child by referring to concerns that the child may have or that they may have about the child. If it is a question of school difficulties, the parents may mention that the child has been unhappy in school or frustrated about schoolwork. If it is about peers, the parents may choose to mention the child's sadness about friends or feeling that others do not like him. If it is about divorce, they may want to identify the unhappiness or anger their child, and in fact all children, feel in such circumstances.

In spite of the therapist's best efforts to the contrary, parents frequently give children very little idea as to why they are there. When the parents have prepared the child, it is often instructive to learn what they have said, or at least what the child believes they have said. The therapist must then offer the child some understanding regarding the purpose of their meeting. The therapist may begin with a general comment that he is someone who meets with kids and helps them with their feelings. He may add something that pertains to the child's particular circumstances. In general the therapist will let the child know that he believes the child has some distress in his life—feelings of pain, sadness, anger—with which he may need some help. The therapist then explains to the child that in the therapy room he is free to play and to talk. It is important that the therapist introduce the notion of play and the opportunity to play from the outset.

The therapist can then show the child the play materials at hand, and may ask the child what toys or materials she uses at home or elsewhere. Beyond such a general introduction, however, the therapist has to be prepared to meet the child in whatever way the child is willing to become engaged. Once in a while a child simply seems born to the consulting room, but generally few children take to therapy enthusiastically. Most will tolerate being brought (there are the exceptions that strap themselves to the legs of the dining room table to avoid being brought in), but their initial willingness may go no further than getting through the door.

The child who decides she doesn't want to be there may sit in absolute silence, or possibly challenge the whole premise of the treatment. As one 7-year-old girl said to her therapist: "I know what you are doing. You expect me to play with those toys to show you my problems. But don't think you can treat me like an infant." The child who is drawn to the toys but finds the presence of the therapist disturbing may settle into a type of play that neither requires nor invites any participation or even comment. Some children will become involved in rather elaborate fantasy creations that draw the therapist in while others may take on some very concrete task, like building something, that would appear to have very little emotional relevance or power.

Typically, if the child does not volunteer anything or become engaged in any particular activity, the therapist may make one or two suggestions, and perhaps make a gesture of playing with certain figures (puppets, dolls, action figures), and then may wait to read the child's response. Some children need to be left alone for a considerable period before they will accept any direct comment or suggestion from the therapist. Children whose visit to the therapist is the final step in a sequence of meetings with concerned adults may want nothing more than to be left alone. The therapist's need to feel useful or to feel reassured that she is "doing well" with the child can become a major obstacle to developing a good connection. Creating a nonintrusive, quiet space may be the first task of the treatment. Other children will only become more uncomfortable if left in silence. The therapist must read whatever marginal signs or clues the child offers as to whether or not she is on the right track. The therapist will try to engage the child with comments and suggestions without crowding or overwhelming him.

Keep in mind that play therapy is always an experimental process. While being attuned to the child is a desirable goal, there is no reason for the therapist to expect herself to be on target consistently, particularly so at the beginning of treatment. This is why it is especially important to follow closely the child's response to any comments or interventions one makes, or the child's response to the absence of interventions.

The therapist's challenge in the beginning sessions is to convey to the child a desire and a capacity to engage him empathically and to introduce a note of hopefulness concerning the things that pain him. The therapist attempts to engage the child, but in a way that gives him plenty of space and respect for the child's wariness, skepticism, or outright rejection of the whole enterprise.

It can be helpful to the therapist who is eager to engage the child in a play process to keep in mind that, broadly speaking, her initial task is diagnosis or evaluation. Thus any particular way the child chooses to respond to the session is of value, and can become the basis for subsequent interventions. The shy child who is fearful of his own aggression and that of others may be reluctant to engage in play at all. This reluctance may characterize the depressed child as well. The child who has difficulty self-regulating may start off playing quietly but will then show a pattern of heightening agitation and self-arousal that requires the therapist to intervene in order to calm him or to limit him. The child who constantly seeks the approbation and reassurance of others may immediately try to engage the therapist either in conversation or in play, whereas the child who is fearful of any emotional contact may maintain a detached, self-sufficient stance toward the play.

If we keep in mind the complex nature of play as outlined by Sutton-Smith (1995), we will also be asking ourselves: What is the particular type of play this child appears to prefer? Is it solitary, imaginative, competitive, frivolous, challenging? It is important for the therapist to stay open to the child's sense of play and what he may choose to create in the therapy room.

THE ROLE OF ANXIETY

In all of these variations, the therapist must pay particular attention to the course of the child's anxiety. As already noted, too much talk or attempted engagement can greatly heighten anxiety. Equally, any prolonged period of silence, even more than half a minute, can be terrifying to some children. A child may begin a play activity that then becomes overstimulating for the child, begins to touch on difficult experiences, or requires too much involvement with the therapist. At these points the child may abruptly shift gears, or the child may even get stuck in the activity and need the therapist's help in moving away from it. The therapist's ability to read and respond to the child's anxiety level will play a major role in how the relationship develops.

The therapist must pay equal attention to parental anxieties. Although sometimes initially less obvious, parental anxieties may in fact dominate what takes place in the sessions. Their influence may be subtle, in the form of offhand remarks or comments made to the child, or quite overt, such as the parent who positions himself immediately outside the consulting room door and strives to pick up any snatches of conversation.

A 5-year-old boy refused to enter the therapy room by himself. The therapist invited the mother in as well, and the therapy began with the mother as an observer. After several sessions, the therapist sensed that the boy was ready to be there on his own. When he suggested to the mother that she could step out, she declined. After two more sessions with the mother in the room, the therapist met with her to discuss it. The mother then told the therapist that as a young child she had been molested by a physician, and did not trust her son alone in a room with a stranger. After that meeting, the mother allowed the therapist and the boy to meet alone.

INVOLVEMENT OF THE PARENTS IN THE SESSIONS

It is often a good idea, especially with young children, to include the parent in the session initially. The therapist may wish to prepare the parent for this possibility by explaining that he may ask the parent to sit in, and that the parent's role will be as an observer. The therapist generally will not direct himself to the parent, but will focus his attention on the child. Of course, there may be situations in which the therapist chooses to make the parent an active part of the play, depending on the nature of the work being done, but this is not likely to be the case at the beginning. The need for a parental presence in the sessions may fluctuate, and flexibility on the therapist's part in this regard is very important. At times it is useful to have a parent sit in the waiting area and keep the playroom door ajar. Erikson (1950) describes a case in which a young child left the consulting room with her mother, and then began to play a game in which she would not let Erikson into the waiting area, but kept opening and closing the door between the two rooms.

TALKING ABOUT PRIVACY

Near the beginning of the therapy, it is important for the therapist to introduce the concept of privacy and confidentiality to the child in a way that is appropriate for the child's age. A child's sense of privacy is, of course, dependent upon his or her age and developmental status. For very young children it may have no meaning, whereas it can assume powerful importance for the preadolescent child. The family values and culture will shape the child's notion of privacy, as will the child's own level of autonomy and sense of separateness. In some instances, the idea of privacy may be confused with secrecy, and can be the occasion for feelings of guilt and conflicting loyalties. Under these circumstances, the issue of privacy may become a crucial aspect of the treatment, and may gather together many of the important strands that the child and the therapist must confront together. For any child, the simple declaration that what happens in the sessions is private will not settle the issue. What privacy means will be shaped over the course of the treatment. The level of privacy that is appropriate for any given treatment is never an entirely clear or settled issue, even perhaps for the therapist, and it may evolve or change over the course of the work. Clearly in a therapy where the parent is in and out of the room, there is little that could be considered strictly private. Even in that context, however, the therapist may decide to introduce the idea. In fact, the therapist may choose to establish an agreement that what happens in the sessions among the three—therapist, parent, and child—should be treated as private. This may be particularly important in situations where the parent might not naturally respect the child's privacy, and might cause the child humiliation or embarrassment in front of siblings. Ultimately, it is important for the therapist to help the child develop a sense that what he or she and the therapist do is private and protected, that the space they inhabit together is unique in its protections and privacy. The idea of privacy is often an unfamiliar concept to children. This sense of privacy and its attendant safety is absolutely crucial to the evolution of the play process.

COMMUNICATIONS FROM THE PARENTS OR FROM OTHER INTERESTED PARTIES

The therapist not only must decide what to do with information or revelations from the child, he must also deal with reports and requests made by the parents or by others, such as school personnel. Some therapists choose to meet with a parent immediately preceding or following a session with the child, and may create a context for a parent to communicate concerns and pass on information. The session with the child will inevitably be shaped by this exchange. Even without such regular contact, parents or others may provide the therapist with reports or requests by telephone. These can range from useful information that is helpful for the therapists to know, to impetuous demands that the therapist confront the child on certain issues or resolve certain specific conflicts ("You must talk with Fred about pouring water on his teacher and make sure he understands the consequences"). In Chapter 14 we say more about how the therapist can attempt to navigate these sometimes complicated relationships, but for the moment we are concerned with their impact on the play process.

At the start of the treatment in particular, it is best for the therapist to protect her developing relationship with the child from much outside intrusion. The therapist, having discussed the reasons the child is in treatment, may add an observation here and there from parental reports, but it is important to avoid becoming an agent of parental or school concerns, and to create a separate sphere. For the child to experience a freedom to play in safety, she must come to know that his inner world can expand into the play space with minimal restriction or outside influence. This is what is so unique about the therapeutic situation and about the play process in particular. Part of the therapist's task at the beginning is to help the parents understand the child's need for such a space, for the therapist to serve as a buffer from the anxieties and demands of the child's world in a way that does not leave the parents feeling excluded or rejected.

RULES AND STRUCTURE FOR THE CONDUCT OF THE SESSIONS

Each therapist has his ideas about the structure that is necessary to conduct a session. Elements of this structure may include arriving and departing at agreed upon times, staying in a specified space, no physical violence, restraint from destruction of property or misuse of equipment, no behavior that poses a risk of physical harm, and respecting the use of adjoining space by others.

Entering and Leaving the Consulting Room

How sessions begin and end is both very important and often a matter of uncertainty for the clinician. Essentially, however, the child is the responsibility of the parent or parent surrogate up until the beginning of the session and at the point of its ending. In between, the child is the therapist's responsibility, unless the child is unable or unwilling to comply with certain basic requirements the therapist has for conducting a session. When a child refuses to enter the treatment room, the therapist has several options. He can invite child and parent together into the room. Alternatively, the therapist can wait for the parent and child to resolve the impasse. In certain cases, it may be appropriate to invite the parent in if the child refuses to enter and then to wait for the child to join, if she chooses to do so. In other instances, if it is practically possible, the therapist might choose to use the waiting area as the space for the therapy, and go to the child. On some occasions it may be possible to go for a walk with a child who refuses to enter the consulting room. No one of these approaches is the right one for every case, and some would clearly be a mistake under certain circumstances. For example, in the case of a child who seems to be in doubt (or at least to be questioning) as to whether the therapist is her person, or the parent's, or fears that the therapist and parent are ganging up together, it would not be a good idea to invite the parent in alone. If the child is impulsive and has difficulty with self-regulation, then proposing a walk is unlikely to be a wise solution. The important points to keep in mind are that the therapist is working on a relationship or within a relationship in which his requirements for conducting therapy shape how he approaches the child's and the parent's capacities and willingness to participate. The resulting interaction should include the therapist's own structure and his willingness to exercise flexibility. Under these circumstances, the therapist need not experience the need to conduct the session in the waiting room as a defeat. Equally, the therapist should not assume full responsibility for bringing the child into the session.

Challenges to the Therapist's Structure

The more action-oriented or more enactment-oriented children are likely to pose challenges to whatever order or structure the therapist is attempting to maintain. Whatever rules the therapist has, either explicit or implicit, may be challenged or questioned. What happens when the child damages play materials? Can the child take materials from the therapy room? Is the child asked to clean up? Can the child bring in her own supplies or play materials? Are there any limits? Can the child bring in books, homework, tapes, discmen, and so forth? What if the child refuses to leave, or tries to sneak toys and materials out of the room?

There are no answers to these questions that apply consistently from therapist to therapist and from child to child. Therapists work differently, and often equally effectively with considerably different rules. Similarly, the nature of the circumstances and the nature of the child will call for different responses. Regardless of these variations, however, it is the therapist's responsibility to develop and maintain a structure with reasonable consistency. It is a hallmark of the relational interpersonal approach to accept the notion of considerable individual variation, and the idea that each therapist–patient dyad may develop rules or ways of working together that are specific to its particular relationship. It is crucial at the outset that the therapist think through what his policies are regarding these questions, even though they may evolve over time. While no amount of forethought will prepare the therapist for every question or challenge that a child may introduce ("Can I bring my dog into the session?" or "If I knock down that picture on your wall, that should be good for six points"), still it is better to be prepared at the outset.

Generally the play materials should stay in the treatment room and not go home with the child. This can be explained simply as necessary so that other children will be able to use the toys as well. It is also generally best if the child does not start bringing in his or her whole armamentarium of toys from home. An occasional item that he or she may want to show the therapist can be helpful, but it is best to limit this practice. Deliberately breaking toys should not be allowed, and if the child's play is too rough to safely use certain toys without risk of destruction, the therapist may choose to withdraw those from the available repertoire until the child can use them more appropriately. While some latitude may be allowed, it is not conducive to therapy to have the child destroying materials and the therapist either anxious or resentful.

What if the child refuses to leave at the end of the session? The therapist might take some momentary satisfaction in the child's quick attachment to the space, the toys, or the therapist—until he considers what is next on his schedule. If the therapist has exhausted the usual reminders (the session is over, we will meet next week and play some more, everything will be here when you return, your mother or father is waiting) to no avail, then more dramatic measures may be required. At the point when the session is over, the responsibility for the child reverts to the parent or parent surrogate who has brought the child to session. This means that the therapist can usefully involve the parent at this point. Of course this generalization, like any other, needs to be qualified by a consideration of who the parent is and how the parent may react. In most cases, however, the therapist may well choose to involve the parent at this point. One therapist described how he and the patient's mother managed to move the child out of the consulting room much like the way in which Robin and Piglet removed Winnie the Pooh from Piglet's home after he had eaten too much honey: one pushing from behind and the other pulling from the front. Together, they can usually impress upon the child the need to leave the room. It is sensible in this regard, particularly when seeing a child for the first time, to leave ample time to make this transition and to not feel crowded by an imminent appointment.

As already noted, it is a good rule of thumb when working with children to expect the unexpected. No matter how carefully one plans or schedules, the therapist will undoubtedly face a situation where he has one child waiting to see him and another, whom a parent or other childcare person has failed to pick up on time, requiring his attention. The role of the child therapist requires flexibility.

If the therapist keeps in mind his ultimate goal of a therapeutic connection with the child, he can allow flexibility regarding the composition of the sessions and even their location. In some instances, it may be necessary to include one or more parents in the room. In other instances, the therapist may have to conduct the session in the waiting room or possibly outside. All of these variations can work, as long as the therapist is able to maintain a viable therapeutic involvement with the child.

Play Materials

Therapists vary regarding the array of play materials they choose to present to children at the outset. Some favor extensive projective play materials such as dolls, puppets, animal figures, dollhouses, toy soldiers, and action figures, while others may emphasize manipulative materials such as clay, paints, drawing materials, wood, tools, and so forth. Some include construction materials like Legos,™ while others avoid them. Water play is favored by many therapists. Others work with sandboxes. Still others use tools and building materials. These choices depend upon personal preferences and available resources. But the therapist should never feel that she does not have enough. Even a minimum of materials will do.

For the relational, interpersonal therapist, it is important that the play materials not come between the therapist and the child. If the consulting room is too much like a toy store, the child can get lost in the materials, and can use them to distance from his feelings and his relationships to the therapist. While it is valuable to have a range of materials that will appeal to different ages and to children of differing styles, generally less is preferable to too much. For some therapists, a bag of a few items can be sufficient. It can also be helpful to hold some materials in reserve. It may be best to keep board games and other structured activities out of the way until they seem necessary. With more aggressive or more distractible children, a minimum of toys is best, offering the least opportunity for distraction or the least need for the therapist to continually set limits on the use of materials. By keeping toys to a minimum, the therapist can also explore with the child what kinds of play objects he enjoys and uses at home, and through that exploration, consider what they might choose to do with each other.

Therapy happens with the materials at hand. Clinics and hospitals sometimes provide child therapy rooms with minimal play material, or with toys that appear and disappear from week to week as different therapists use the rooms. Under these circumstances the atmosphere is one of scarcity, and themes of deprivation and unreliability are encouraged by such an environment. Similarly, a richly stocked playroom can provoke themes of greed, envy, satiation, and associated feelings.

If the child is not responsive to an encouragement toward either more expressive or projective play, and seems unwilling or unable to talk, the therapist can always resort to board games and other similarly structured activities, or sports activities such as basketball. Some therapists even include such resources as tools and carpentry supplies. There is virtually no limit to the number of activities that can lend themselves to an interpersonal exchange with elements of play. Of course, some are more suited to the particular elements of symbolic or metaphoric expression and exploration, such as symbolic figures—puppets, dolls—and materials that can serve a personal artistic expression—crayons, paints, clay—but virtually anything can come to serve that purpose in the course of the work.

Regardless of what array of toys the therapist offers, the child may choose to ignore them all and fasten on something that seems entirely unlikely as an object of interest. For example, the 7-year-old girl mentioned earlier, who disdainfully rejected both the available toys and the therapist's transparent attempt to learn about her through play, eventually developed a whole unacknowledged play exchange with the therapist involving the use of a pillow.

If the child starts out by playing, then the therapist's task becomes one of deciding how she might fit into that process. Does the child look to the therapist for participation? Does he ignore the therapist and plunge right into play themes? Does the child use the play materials in a generally appropriate way (for example, the child does not use the anatomically correct doll as a baseball bat, or the Play Doh™ as snow balls)? As long as the child begins to play in a way that is not dangerous or particularly destructive, the therapist can afford to feel her way into the process.

THE THERAPIST'S PART IN THE PLAY

If the child chooses to explore play materials, or develop play themes by herself, the therapist may feel excluded or superfluous. The therapist may be tempted to insert himself into the play in a way that the child may experience as intrusive. The therapist can best serve the process by considering what the situation presents to him. Why does the child prefer to play in isolation? Is the child using the play opportunity to explore, in symbolic fashion, a set of internal struggles that either does not require the therapist's participation or may be hindered or restricted by the therapist's participation?

John was a 4-year-old child with divorced parents who were continually in conflict in ways that inevitably drew him in. He made use of the play materials to act out themes of intrusiveness and control and to express his own rage in ways that depended on the therapist to simply leave him alone.

While, from a relational perspective, we see all activities in therapy as having an interpersonal dimension, it is also true that the most useful therapeutic process at any particular point may be that of a rather solitary intrapsychic exploration. For John in particular, given his family interactions, it was essential for him to experience the therapist's respect for his boundaries and for his need, in Winnicott's (1958a) phrase, "to be alone in the presence of another."

Conversely, is the child's solitary play the perpetuation of an isolated, disconnected way of being in the world that may ward off certain terrors regarding personal interaction? If so, can the therapist help to forge a safe avenue for mutual or collaborative exploration of interpersonally frightening experience?

One young girl, a double amputee who had lost both legs just below the knee, had been profoundly traumatized by her contact with hospitals and doctors. She was terrified by such people and wanted nothing to do with them. In addition, she vigorously denied that there was anything wrong with her legs and refused to participate in a range of activities with others that might stimulate any curiosity or questions about them. She wanted to stay as far away as possible from an inquisitive or intrusive therapist. Yet part of her difficulty concerned her denial of her physical condition that required her to stay socially isolated. In the beginning of the therapy she explored play materials very much on her own. She balked at even the most tentative offers to participate on the part of the therapist, who continually but gently looked for openings to expand their interaction. Over time, the child warmed to these nonintrusive overtures, and increasingly let the therapist in on her play.

The therapist may have to sit for a while before developing a sense of how she may join more in the process. For less verbal children, it may be helpful for the therapist to introduce a verbal dimension to the child's activity by question or comment. For children who are more inhibited about their actions, it may be helpful for the therapist to offer some type of participatory response.

One very inhibited boy made repetitive drawings of a clock. At one point he looked up at a clock on the wall of the consulting room and pretended to shoot it with a gun. The therapist chose to imitate his behavior. The boy noticed, smiled, and did it again. This beginning exchange was followed by a whole series of such interactions in which child and therapist copied each other's behavior.

Of course, other children will immediately enlist the therapist in the play, assign him a part, and expect the therapist to follow directions. Although the therapist may feel a bit like a human puppet, it is best to lend oneself to this process, at least initially. Alternatively, the therapist may be actively enlisted to play but given wide latitude regarding how to participate, what to do, and what to say. Under these circumstances the therapist has to decide how much initiative to take, and to consider the question of whose therapy it actually is.

Some children will simply refuse to play. They may sit quietly in the treatment room. Or they may talk in an animated way without playing. The therapist may be gratified that the child talks so readily, and yet feel that he really should be playing. How the therapist may choose to respond will depend upon the age of the child. With children up to the age of 8 or 9, it is noteworthy if they show no interest in playing. Here too there is no absolute rule, and sometimes very young children simply have a lot on their mind and make use of the opportunity to express it. But if a relatively young child shows an apparent unwillingness or inability to play, it is probably of diagnostic importance, and tells the therapist that the child experiences an excessive restriction or inhibition. Helping the child learn to play may become an important treatment goal. There is no special magic or technique to facilitate play with a child. In large part, it depends upon the therapist's own interest in play, willingness to be flexible, and readiness to seize or create opportunities when they emerge.

In one case, when a child momentarily made a pillow into a character, the therapist took advantage of that opportunity and spoke in the voice of this pillow character, which filled the child with giggles. In subsequent sessions, the child developed more elaborate pillow play that the therapist joined, all this in spite of the fact that the room had a complete array of more usual play materials.

Where the child is reluctant to play, the therapist can often play a facilitating role. It is more important at this stage that play take place than it is to understand the play or construct interpretations regarding its meaning.

Of course, the therapist may also be confronted with a child who is too eager to play, that is, who only wants to play, or wants to play so aggressively that the therapist gets caught up with questions of damage control. The child who treats the therapy room as a playground, and the therapist as either a playmate or the coordinator of fun activities, may well be running away from any painful material or experiences from which he is suffering. The child's eagerness to play is a strong advantage at the beginning, and therapists need not worry that they are not doing their job by joining in and letting the play develop. As this process unfolds, the therapist also pays attention to the child's family circumstance, social experience, and school experience to learn more about the child's behavior with the therapist. Children who feel a hunger for companionship, and children who feel deprived of attention, may have such an overriding need for contact and direct involvement that any explicit use of the therapy or the play to explore issues may simply be out of the question. As the child comes to feel more assured of the therapist's continuing involvement and interest, he may allow for a more complex interactional process, and tolerate the movements into more self-reflective exchanges.

In a different way, the child who continually requires the therapist to set limits and structure the sessions may lack such an experience outside of the therapy room. The child's experience of the therapist's ability to set limits in a reasonable and respectful manner may be the most important therapeutic effect of their time together, at least at the beginning of the work.

ENACTMENT AND PHYSICAL CONTACT

Enactment is the word most commonly used to characterize those moments when the child appears to be doing something either directly to the therapist or in relation to the therapist that is neither a verbal representation of an experience, wish, or conflict nor an imaginary or pretend recreation. In traditional terms, an enactment is the manifestation or expression in behavior of an unconscious conflict. For example, Hertzog (personal communication) describes a child who defecated before every session. He viewed it as an enactment of the child's unconscious conflict. Such enactments are thought to characterize the process of therapy with traumatized children in particular. Within relational, interpersonal adult psychoanalysis, enactment has acquired a broader definition. It encompasses virtually all therapeutic interactions, particularly those that are seen as reflecting the particular transference and countertransference paradigm that characterizes the relationship.

In child treatment, the concept of enactment takes on a different character. To the extent that play is a matter of doing something and not simply talking about it, one might argue that it is inevitably enactment. On the other hand, the traditional use of the word enactment implies that the behavior is not essentially pretend in nature, but instead is the actual carrying out, even if symbolically, of an internal conflict, albeit unconsciously. A related but not necessarily identical concept is that of the boundaries of play. For example, it is acceptable to pretend to hit the therapist but not to actually hit him. If the child does in fact hit the therapist, is that necessarily an enactment?

If we adopt the more restrictive, traditional use of the term enactment, we might argue that a child may hit a therapist in a fit of anger that is not unconscious and not necessarily conflictual and therefore not an enactment, even though it is a boundary violation. Alternatively, the child may hit the therapist in a moment of enthusiastic immersion in play that is no less imaginary and pretend for the child in spite of its very real manifestation.

If we adopt the broader, relational use of the term enactment, we might come to define all play interaction as enactments, whether they are boundary violations or not, or whether they include or are devoid of the element of play. The problem with this approach is that the term loses any real discriminating power in being so inclusive. There appear to be quite useful distinctions between behavior that falls within the boundaries acceptable to the therapist and those that fall outside, and between behaviors that are essentially play in nature and those that are not, although the latter distinction may sometimes be hard to make.

The value of placing clear limits on the activities that are acceptable within the play therapy room is that the therapist is not burdened with the task of evaluating the significance or meaning of the behavior in the moment. If hitting is not allowed, then that is clear and simple. If the therapist discourages physical contact, the child sitting in one's lap, and so forth, then it is relatively easy to follow that guideline. If, on the other hand, the therapist attempts to evaluate the behavior and determine its appropriateness on the basis of its meaning, the task is much more complex and uncertain in outcome. If we take the view that all play is at some level an enactment, then in the course of it, the therapist will not know exactly what he is participating in and what it means for the child.

In the case of Mary, the 7-year-old girl mentioned earlier, it seemed to the therapist that it was important, perhaps necessary, for her to make certain physical assaults on the therapist, including grabbing his arm and his shoulders, and hitting him with a pillow. These assaults did not pose a threat of physical harm nor did they usher in a sequence of uncontrolled behavior. The therapist therefore felt he could tolerate them, and that they constituted a way for this highly verbal child to enact and ultimately deal with some very powerful conflicts. He felt there was value in their dealing directly with the concrete manifestations of the sadness and rage she felt about her parent's divorce and the deep hostility she felt toward her brother who treated her with sadistically controlling behavior.

In tolerating a certain amount of her physical aggression, he was relying on his own intuitive feel for what the behavior represented, along with his general clinical understanding of her. His belief was that by making room for the concrete manifestation of her struggle within the play therapy relationship, he and she would be much more able to grapple with it directly. In making this choice he ran the risk that his tolerance might heighten her aggressiveness, possibly overstimulate her, and convey a general permissiveness that could increase her aggressiveness toward others. Of course, there was also the possibility that her physical contact with him served both nurturant and erotic wishes that by allowing limited gratification in their interaction, might have strengthened inappropriate behavior on her part.

There is another consideration regarding mess, damage, or even injury. In acting destructively, the child can be testing to see if the therapist will prevent injury or damage from occurring. This is a test of the therapist's caring and of the therapist's ability to control hostility. A depressed or suicidal child might act in a destructive way toward materials or belongings that the child in fact values highly. Here the therapist would do well to prevent this in order to protect the child from her own aggression, saying at the same time, "I know how angry you are with yourself. But I also know you will regret damaging this later on, because you care about it, and that's why I want to protect it for you."

The therapist's overall challenge is to allow the child to be present in the therapy in the way that the child chooses, while at the same time maintaining a level of structure, regularity, and safety that makes sense to the therapist. The clearer the therapist is at the outset regarding what he is trying to accomplish, and what limits and structure seem appropriate, the more able the therapist will be to exercise the flexibility that is often required to engage the child.

12

Interaction in Child Psychotherapy

The terms *transference* and *countertransference* have been handed down from adult psychoanalysis to psychoanalytically oriented child psychotherapy with both positive and negative consequences. To begin with the positive, the usage of the terms brings child psychotherapy within the family of all forms of insight-oriented therapies in which attention is paid to the patient's relationship with the therapist and the therapist's monitoring of her own feelings. As such, the therapist serves at times, in the traditional sense of the term transference, as a screen for the patient's projections of significant people from his life, including but not limited to parents. The therapist is not just a blank screen, however, but also someone who brings her own personality to bear on the process and to whom the patient reacts personally as well as transferentially. Interpersonal issues arise between them and produce another aspect of the transference, that is, here-and-now transference in which issues (whether their derivation is a replay of the past or whether their origin lies in the current relationship) are enacted in the present (Gill 1982, Levenson 1983). Issues that arise from the here-and-now relationship with the therapist might involve whether the therapist is sufficiently sensitive to the needs of the patient, attentive, interactive, and so forth.

This brings us also into the realm of the therapist's countertransference. Traditionally this has referred to the therapist's unfinished psychological business that gets visited unjustly upon the patient during their interactions. The modern revision of the term countertransference takes into account that the therapist has her own particular reactions to each patient that shift over time and that derive not from psychopathology (in most cases) but from immersement in the relationship. The awareness of these individualized states of being with each patient contributes to the fund of information about each therapeutic relationship. For example, a young female patient's presence in the therapy office was often accompanied by unexplained feelings of sadness in the therapist, even when the content of the play or discussion was not sad at all. The therapist was alerted to be aware of what was going on in their interactions when she found herself as the holder of sad feelings. What caused the therapist to feel that way with this particular child patient? Were the feelings being denied by the patient but being felt by the therapist? Were these feelings springing from the memories of the therapist and if so, why now with this girl? These are typical of the issues which are pursued when the individualized nature of each countertransference is examined.

Using the same terms, transference and countertransference, for the relationship that both adults and children have to their therapists, however, blurs some important and conspicuous distinctions. Working with children in psychotherapy produces some situations unique onto themselves. The following vignette illustrates some issues of transference and countertransference with children and how they converge with, and diverge from, those with adults.

This message was left on a therapist's telephone answering machine: "This is Mrs. D. I know that I shouldn't call you like this, but I couldn't wait until our next session to talk to you. Doug stole money from my purse again and I just can't stand it anymore. I told him that I was going to tell you and he got pretty mad about it. So I don't know what's going to happen when he gets to your office this afternoon."

Following the ominous message from his mother, the Doug who entered his therapist's office was not the same Doug who had left at the end of his prior session. Subsequent to that message, he and his therapist were both transported to a place in their relationship where Doug's position was one of being in trouble with his mother, and in his mind, probably with the therapist, too. One of his presenting symptoms, stealing from his mother's purse, would definitely be in the front of his mind as he entered the therapist's office. The guilt and shame that he felt in relation to the stealing would either be painfully present or staunchly defended against. The therapist's stance toward him was also now altered to one where he was curious to hear Doug's side of the story, whether Doug wanted to tell him or not. Countertransferentially the therapist was upset with Doug's mother for not waiting until the next parent session to talk about this incident, and the therapist was also perturbed with Doug for stealing again and thereby setting off this whole chain of events. It was under this set of circumstances that the next session began.

Thus to obtain a reasonably valid picture of transferences and countertransferences with children, they must be considered as involving the child patient within the context of his family especially, but also his school and daily environment. This is in addition to the usual focus of whatever transpires in the psychotherapy between the patient and the therapist. That is, the extratherapeutic reality of the child, such as in the clinical example of the message on the telephone answering machine about Doug stealing, has its share of impact on the form that the transference and countertransference will take and it must be considered when the therapist either assesses or intervenes interactively.

The questions for child therapists to ask are: Does a definition of transference, as derived from work with adults, fit well into our collective experiences as child psychotherapists, in our psychotherapeutic work with children?, and, In what ways can we work with the indispensable involvement of the parents so that it augments the treatment of their child, specifically the interactions between the therapist and patient? A conceptualization of the psychotherapeutic process with child patients, one that recognizes that child transferences are not merely a younger variation on the older themes of adult psychoanalysis, needs to include some familiar factors but also some factors unique to child psychotherapy.

The child's presentation in individual psychotherapy sessions is influenced strongly, more so than an adult's (because of the presence in the child's life of parents), by what has occurred between sessions in his daily life. This must be taken into account by the child therapist in his work with the child as well as with his parents. While this may have a tauto-logical ring to it, there are some who continue to propose that child psy-chotherapy can function in isolation from the child's daily milieu. It be-hooves us as child therapists to "conceptualize a point of view, a way of understanding the parents' request for help, that will broaden our under-standing and therefore help us in our responses" (Hoffman 1984).

There is an expanding literature that reflects this aspect of the psychotherapeutic work with children. Sarnoff (1976) called the col-laborative work with the parents "necessary." Chethik (1989) describes the work with parents as "absolutely central" and the pivotal factor in the satisfactory progress of most cases. Spiegel (1989) cites it as "in the interest of the most effective treatment for the child." To many con-temporary child therapists, banishing the parents from the child's treatment seems like avoiding one of the sticky but crucial aspects of the child's life and psychopathology. Integrating the parents into the treatment and the transference, however, requires some adjustment to the traditional concepts of adult psychoanalysis and raises its own countertransferences.

Sandler, Kennedy and Tyson (1980), in their delineation of an Anna Freudian approach with children, and Chethik (1989), follow-ing the lead provided by Anna Freud, divide the child's transference into several parts that take into account the multiple levels that the thera-pist must consider when formulating an understanding of the child's object world. One of these factors deals specifically with the dilemma of considering the reality issues in the transferences. Sandler and col-leagues (1980) refer to the child's ongoing perception of the role of the analyst as a sort of go-between for the child and his parents. Chethik (1989) labels these issues "transferences of current relationships" (p. 122). Under this classification are grouped the factors that impinge on the child's day-to-day functioning and, therefore, obviously appear in some form in his treatment. Essentially, Chethik describes "reality conflicts" that involve issues with the child's daily life with the parents, and difficulties that center about the "current developmental phase" of the child. Negotiating such issues as bedtime, allowances, and so forth in conjunction with the parents facilitates and models good communication. It may not be necessary for the child therapist, in all cases, to wait until the issue is worked through in the play and in the projected transference. Sometimes working with the actual parents, who are both real figures and internal objects for the child, promotes psychological growth in a more integrated manner than through individual sessions with the child alone. In individual sessions with the child, "rehearsals" of how a child may deal with the imagined parents provide both the tools for the child and also a window for the therapist into how the child portrays the parents. When this is followed by actual interactions by both the child and therapist with the parents, either in a family session or between sessions with the child, valuable information or progress may result.

To resume with the case of Doug, he was at the time of the aforementioned phone machine message an 11-year-old, with the symptoms of multiple learning disabilities, enuresis, and Attention-Deficit Hyperactivity Disorder. He also demonstrated symptoms of a childhood borderline disorder that had its origins in a history of early neglect, abandonment, and probable physical and possible sexual abuse during his first three years, when he lived with his biological parents, and eventually with foster parents. He was adopted at the age of 3, along with his older brother, by a middle-class couple with an entirely different ethnic background. These parents were divorced, and Doug and his brother were currently living alternate weeks in each parent's home under a joint-custody agreement. Doug had multiple evaluations both psychological and psychiatric, and was in special schools for the past few years. This was his first time in individual psychoanalytically oriented psychotherapy. He was in twice-weekly play therapy and his parents were seen on a regular basis. Doug had been taking Ritalin for several years, but at the therapist's request, Doug took only his morning dose on the days that he had psychotherapy, because it occasionally made him sleepy in the late afternoon.

When he arrived for the session subsequent to his mother's phone message, he began playing as he usually did during that particular phase of therapy with families of small, rubber, wild animals. While he typically had played with them within a family context, he fantasized about them now, as he had only once before, by having members of families hunt and kill each other for food. The therapist commented on the difference in the way the family members were relating to each other and wondered if anything were going on in the jungle to precipitate such violence within each family. Doug answered that there was not enough food in the jungle anymore and that animals had to resort to eating members of their own families in order to survive. The therapist wondered what had happened to all the food. Doug told him that it just ran out. Then he added: "Don't you think they have anything better to do all day than to keep feeding their babies?" The therapist felt somewhat hurt and angry at this sudden outburst in his direction. The more he thought about it, however, it sounded remarkably like something a frustrated mother might say to her child, and he said so. Doug agreed. The therapist felt like this was his opening to address the phone call that they both knew had occurred. He said to Doug that he had been called by his mother and that she had left a message about his stealing and that she had been very angry. Doug said that he knew because his mother told him that she called.

The therapist interpreted that he must have felt that he might not have gotten what he wanted from his mother if he asked, so he just took some money and that made him feel better, until he got caught. Doug nodded in agreement. The therapist asked what he wanted. He said angrily that he wanted his cookie restriction to be lifted. Apparently, he had been disciplined for eating an entire box of cookies, by not being allowed to eat any cookies, his usual after-school snack. This was the first that the therapist had been told of this recent incident. Now the therapist had heard both and different sides of the same sequence of events. He reminded Doug of a theme that they had discussed many times before, of how his parents had found him undernourished when they adopted him, and how as a consequence of this some foods, especially sweets, were very important to him.

Doug had continued his aggressive play with the wild animals during this interchange but without the usual sound effects or expansive arena of play. The therapist told him that when he first heard that he had stolen this time, he was upset with him for stealing again, but now that they had talked about it, he felt sad. He reminded Doug that when he had talked to his mother in the past and told her that he was afraid that he would not get enough sweets, she usually felt sad, instead of mad. Doug said nothing. He ultimately requested that they play chess, which they both saw as his most mature level of play in our sessions. Was he avoiding the issue or calming down? This time it seemed that he was digesting all of this material, and the therapist accepted without interruption his request to remain silently in contact with him. He played chess the rest of the session.

The transference was occurring on at least three levels with the additional channel of countertransferential reactions during the session. First, Doug was playing out his experience of omnivorous and violent family interactions, particularly with a maternal figure. This is the piece that involved, to some degree, his perception of his current familial reality, including his present relationship with a mother who is angry with him. But of course, this angry set of interactions had a history in their relationship, which it was also felt to be necessary to call to Doug's attention since, as with many children, he tended to see these as isolated events. Second, on a genetic level, Doug had special issues around food and nurturance, since he experienced some degree of neglect during his first three years. The interpretation of the value of sweets to him was more in keeping with a transference interpretation where the theoretical construct was that early experiences with parents color the current-day perceptions of, and interpersonal relationships with, other parental figures. Third, there was also the level of the here-and-now transference to the therapist as the potentially angry and depriving parent. It was important for the therapist to address their common knowledge of the phone message and give Doug the opportunity to deal directly with his therapist.

Finally, countertransference during the session helped to inform the therapist's interventions as he became aware of his own feeling of being hurt and angry, when Doug snapped at him while talking about there not being enough food. This was consistent with Racker's (1968) description of concordant countertransference in the adult literature, which is when the therapist identifies his own feelings with how the patient might also be feeling at that time. When Doug began to tell the story of the cookie restriction, the therapist's affect moved from irritation to one of sadness, which helped him to hear the deprivation behind the acting-out. Doug's response to all this? Not a word. His attempt to play chess was sufficient communication, within the métier of play, that he felt more organized and was able to interact in session in a more typical and mature fashion. The question always exists in child treatment as to whether the transference and countertransference should be discussed to the extent that they would be in adult psychotherapy. Doug had been remarkably able to handle the discussion up to this point and it was a judgment call on the therapist's part that respecting his silence and not pursuing it further verbally was the right choice and might give him the space to utilize this material as well as he was able, on his own.

INTERACTIONAL CONTEXT
FOR CHILD TRANSFERENCES

In a typical session of play therapy such as the one above, the child plays imaginatively with the materials provided in the therapist's office, while the therapist observes attentively and participates in the play, usually unobtrusively. The therapist makes relevant comments or interpretations as warranted by the nature of the child's play in that session. For instance, if the child is playing imaginatively and enthusiastically, while also expressing relevant themes in the therapist's judgment, then few substantive comments may be necessary by the therapist. If the child's play is inhibited, repetitive, or uncontrolled, the therapist may be called upon to facilitate play that aids in the symbolic expression of the child's needs or to wait patiently if the child requires such "potential space" (Ogden 1986, Slade 1994, Winnicott 1971a). The therapist attempts to apprehend the unconscious trail of the play that the child has introduced and to comment or to interpret strategically about the "meaning" of the play in terms of his understanding of the relationship between the child's play and the issues with which he struggles in his life.

This therapeutic model is based mainly upon ego-psychological principles of development and psychopathology. The focus at such moments is on the intrapsychic workings of the child. The emphasis is usually on the unfolding of the child's inner life, with only a slight nod to the workings of the particular patterns of the transference-countertransference in the therapeutic dyad. As with adult psychoanalytic treatment, there is undeniably, however, a here-and-now, in addition to the then-and-there, of the relating patient in the presence of a feeling and experiencing analyst. Dealing with the here-and-now need not be avoided with child patients even though they often resist it. One subset of these comments on the here-and-now would be rightly labeled as transferential and countertransferential. That is, these comments would serve to enhance and to explore the child's unfolding of his projections onto the therapist and onto the play characters.

Many of the child patients that we see in individual psychotherapy fit well enough, and most of the time, into the standard model of child psychoanalytic treatment. However, we have also learned from those moments with children that do not fit so well or easily into our standard model, moments that force us to consider other possibilities. Particularly, this section will focus upon the moments of here-and-now interaction, where relationally oriented, direct transference–countertransference work, as one may utilize with an adult, is not only possible but indicated.

Before we address the utility of the here-and-now relationship in child psychotherapy, we must recognize some good reasons for this reluctance to enter into the here-and-now dialogue with the child patient. For example, we are all aware that many child patients balk at direct references to their problems or to the relationship with the therapist. A sure way to destroy an intimate moment of play therapy with a child is to ask him how his problems with his little brother are going, even though he may be pulverizing the little brother figure in your office doll house. Just as useless would be an attempt to make here-and-now transference references as one would exactly in the treatment of adults. For instance, it is hard to imagine an occasion when the following would be the proper technical choice with a child: "I notice that the way you are talking to that teddy bear is similar to how you talk to me when I don't understand you." At best, the child is likely to respond with some token acknowledgment and then lead you directly back to the imaginative play at hand.

So what is the other side of the story? On many occasions the here-and-now statements of the child can be seen as an indication from the child that he wants to have contact with the therapist in the context of their relationship. Since the child literature is less than helpful in describing these moments, due to its usual concentration upon symbolic play and the metaphor, we must examine what the adult psychoanalytic literature and practice have to teach us in this regard. Currently the corresponding adult model of treatment has been enriched by theorists of all orientations who advocate (1) a greater emphasis on the interplay of the here-and-now transference–countertransference relationship (Aron 1996, Gill 1982, Hoffman 1998, Levenson 1983, Mitchell 1988); (2) utilizing the impact of the analyst's participation (Ehrenberg 1992); and (3) greater awareness on the therapist's part of the forms of nonverbal communication such as mutual regulation (Beebe and Lachmann, 1988, 1992) and projective identification (Ogden 1979, 1982).

An example may serve to demonstrate the value of occasional here-and-now transferential dialogue with child patients.

> The first thing an 8-year-old boy said in the first session when his therapist asked him about beginning treatment was: "The whole problem that I am having is that both of my parents are overachievers and they won't leave me alone. They don't lay off ever even for a minute and I get all upset about it."

An enactment (in the here-and-now) had begun. The therapist had expected this boy to use the métier of play, as is typical of boys his age. He, however, was prepared to talk as both his parents and his older brother did with their therapists. Perhaps this boy was now overachieving with the therapist, as if he had the same high expectations for himself that his parents apparently do. The therapist quickly floated the hypothesis in his mind that treatment had to provide this boy with a place where he could be 8 years old and not have to be so mature and responsible. To implement such a plan immediately, however, without acknowledging what had just happened between them seemed to ignore a potentially rich source of material in their here-and-now relationship, that is, the enactment that had just occurred. While describing his problem, the patient actually was in the process of acting it out in the here-and-now transference (Bromberg 1999). The therapist believed that this enactment contained material that could be useful to their therapeutic relationship, if it were understood more thoroughly. Once the child therapist reaches the point of wishing to utilize his countertransference, the models of adult psychoanalysis offer him many choices with regard to actual technique. The therapist could self-analyze into his own past like Jacobs (1991), or he could examine the nuances of his experience like Ogden (1982), or he could present a distillation of his affective experiences like Bollas (1987) and other British independents (Casement 1985), or he could process the projective identifications like the Kleinians (Joseph 1987, Ogden 1982), or he could directly express his experience of the patient like Ehrenberg (1992). These technical interventions are eminently utilizable in work with children, as they are in work with adults.

To continue the clinical example with the 8-year-old boy, the therapist found that one of his first conscious countertransferential thoughts was: "Were my expectations that he play with toys inappropriate for this boy?" Eventually the boy demonstrated that he loved to play with the cars and trucks in the therapy office, but in that first session he was trying hard to be the patient that he felt that his parents wanted him to be. The thought occurred to the therapist that his experience of feeling the boy to be pushing himself was related to something that the boy may have unconsciously wanted the therapist to feel, and that it would be beneficial to explore that dynamic. Here the therapist was using a model of projective identification to understand his experience. The therapist found that the boy wanted him to know how it felt to be impressed with one's maturity and at a loss as to what to do with it, all at the same time. Both the boy and the therapist were feeling different versions of the same issue. The therapist began to realize that the problem for this boy might be how to be a mature and intelligent 8-year-old boy with his particular set of pressuring parents. The issue in the therapeutic interaction, in turn, was a recreation of this same dynamic—that is, how to be 8 years old and interested in play but to also talk in an appropriate way about his awareness of his difficulties.

The therapist's complementary countertransference evolved into wondering how to treat an 8 year old who was talking like an adult but definitely signaling that doing so was not entirely natural. On the one hand, moving him toward play would have been ignoring his opening salvo of "talking about his problems." On the other hand, a serious discussion about his own strivings or his parents' wishes may have only furthered the enactment.

Drawing upon the adult model of interacting around the information supplied in one's countertransferential reaction, the therapist went with his immediate confusion since, as best as he could reconstruct it, that was his strongest experience.

The therapist said: "Boy, I'm not sure what to say to that. You look exactly like an 8-year-old boy, but you sound just like a grownup patient in a psychologist's office. I don' t know whether to pull out toys as I do with other kids or to just sit and talk like I do with grownups." The boy replied: "You don't know what to do?" The therapist said: "No. I'm not sure." "I can't believe you are saying that," was the boy's response. "Why does that surprise you?" "Because you're supposed to help me with my problems with my parents." Following a lengthy discussion, the therapist then proposed a solution that they work on getting to know each other better and then it would be easier to know what to do together. With reluctance and excitement, the boy agreed.

USING INTERACTIONAL DATA AND COUNTERTRANSFERENTIAL REACTIONS

It is never possible to provide a therapeutic situation that is devoid of interpersonal influences, and this is particularly true in one's work with children because of the compelling presence of the parents, and even teachers, in the child's everyday life. Thus the relational child therapist attempts to make productive use of the inevitable and inextricable familial and social world of the child in individual psychotherapy (see Part 5 for a fuller exploration of the context of child psychotherapy). These others not only exert a strong influence on the daily life of the child, but also affect the therapist's perceptions of the child and her behavior between and during sessions. While it is rare for the significant others to participate in an adult's individual psychotherapy, this is commonly the situation with children where many concerned adults would be more than happy to provide their particular take on the child patient's situation to the therapist (Pantone 2000).

This information is sometimes eye-opening and clarifying; yet sometimes it is also confusing and contradictory. In our view, however, eventually and usually it is found to be useful and pertinent. The concerned parent provides not only her view of some episode with her child, but she also provides an in vivo experience for the therapist of how she deals with the child when she speaks to the therapist directly. For example, if a mother was angry and punitive with the child on some occasion between sessions, how does she address the same issue with the therapist? If the mother were to evidence the same anger toward the therapist as she did with the child, it may be very useful in understanding the daily life of the child for the therapist to be on the receiving end of the mother's anger. Conversely it would be equally instructive if the mother described the same angry episode with the child in a concerned way so that the therapist got a window into the mother's concern about her angry interactions with her child. The same would hold true for a father who has insufficient contact with the child. After the father's avoiding several appointments with the therapist and being relatively inaccessible by telephone, the therapist would need to explore if he really were that uninvolved, or if he were anxious and avoidant about his role of father with his daughter.

Such material, garnered from experiences with the parents, can be referenced by the therapist internally and silently while in session with the child. Additionally, this material could be used directly in a question from the therapist to the child, such as "What's been going on with you and your mom about your little brother?" Or the therapist could utilize the information during symbolic play with the child: "Boy, that tiger really is angry at her little brother. No matter how hard she tries, he is always getting in her way." We believe that trying not to use the interactional data that the therapist is accumulating from the parents, in the service of keeping the individual child psychotherapy sessions pure, is short-sighted, not to mention impossible.

Another channel of collecting data about the child's psychological life for the relational therapist is assessing her own countertransferential feelings during her interactions with the child. For example, is it easy to feel concerned about the child patient whose mother is angry at her, or does the therapist feel punitive toward the child too and enact the same pathogenic relational patterns (Mitchell 1988)? A therapist could say, "Please! Be careful with the toys this time," instead of, "Let me help you with that toy. It's kind of delicate and I worry that it may break." As another example of being aware of one's countertransference, there is the child who may be so accustomed to an uninvolved father that she does not expect or facilitate interaction with the therapist: "What are you playing?" No response. "Can I help you with that?" No response. "You seem used to playing by yourself." No response. The therapist needs to assess her internal reactions to see if the child's demeanor feels like schizoid avoidance or passive-aggressive provocative behavior. Sometimes with verbally nonexpressive and withdrawn children, the countertransference becomes a chief channel through which sense is made of the child's world. The therapist's building frustration at being ignored in the above examples serves to inform the therapist about aspects of the child's object world. Using the therapist's own feelings is one example of assessing how the child has an impact on others. The child's world may be peopled, at times, with incontrovertibly angry others whom she tries to hurt through passive-aggressive means such as breaking a delicate toy, but this is obviously beyond her conscious awareness. The therapist learns this gradually in her own consciousness by being aware of her feelings of being angry with this child's persistent carelessness. In the second example, the avoidant child seems to know no way of relating initially to the therapist other than isolated play. The therapist's countertransference of feeling isolated and lonely while with the child helps her to distinguish between a schizoid-like orientation or willful avoidance on the part of the child.

If both the child patient and the therapist are dealing with the problem of an angry mother and/or an uninvolved father in the child's life, then the child may feel understood and the therapist will have a greater sense of what it is like to be the child of one of these parents. Finding oneself in empathic connectedness with the child is a truly gratifying aspect of being a child therapist. It is the reason that many of us wanted to do this work in the first place. This type of countertransference has been called concordant by Racker (1968) because the therapist's reactions are in harmony with those of the patient.

The picture is not always that rosy. Child psychotherapists also experience the other type of countertransference that Racker described, complementary countertransference. While this type is not necessarily negative, this is the situation where the therapist's feelings are more consistent with the other objects in the child patient's life, instead of with the child herself. For example, a therapist's sympathies often may lie with the parents when the child is trying, hyperactive, or difficult to be with for even an hour—"I wouldn't want to be with that kid for twenty-four hours, seven days a week." This dilemma of a somewhat negative feeling during the work with the child can also be a useful position for the therapist to find herself in, if she can use it to broaden her base of understanding with the patient—"What this boy needs is patience, but he makes it so hard to sustain that position with him for a prolonged period of time." Once a negative feeling is acknowledged and after an attempt is made to analyze it, there may ultimately be a transformation of both the therapist's feeling as well as the milieu of the therapeutic hour. Thus empathizing with the parents does not necessarily mean that the therapist is out of touch with the child. The therapist finds herself in a position of knowing how the child pulls the other to conform to some pathogenic relational pattern rather than engendering some more positive, and perhaps unfortunately unfamiliar, mode of interaction.

THE INTENSITY OF CHILD TRANSFERENCE

Anna Freud (1946) has stated that the transference with children is quantitatively lessened, in comparison to those of adults, because of the daily presence of the parents. Nonetheless, in her theory of clinical work with children, the repetition compulsion is believed to be so strongly experienced in child patients that they recreate the necessary conditions in the transference to have an acutely powerful relationship with the therapist, one that dwarfs, in many cases, the transferences of their older counterparts. Thus, in many cases, the child is not stopped by the presence of his parents in his daily life, or in collaborative sessions with the therapist, from using the therapist as a new object, recreating his issues in the transference, and eventually, in many cases, to play and/or to talk freely during the sessions. Whatever drawbacks may be encountered in the complicated world of working psychoanalytically with the child within the context of his family, they are often capable of being dealt with in the child's psychotherapy sessions mainly because of the intense transference with the therapist that the child is willing to have. The child is willing to enter into such intense transference relations with the therapist because of the unique empathy with which the therapist receives him.

For example, in an article about working with borderline children, Donnellan (1989) describes a phase of the psychotherapy where the child's transference to the therapist takes on a highly intense quality in spite of the presence of the parents in the child's life. The therapist, Donnellan suggests, through a focus in his interpretations on emotional content, enables the child to have a powerful transference that is directed unconsciously by the child's freedom to express more of the affective material. Donnellan describes how the child has the dual experience of seeing the therapist as invested and benevolent on the one hand, and as the dreaded and psychopathogenic transference figure on the other. By the time this development has occurred in the treatment, the child has also probably entered into the countertransference of the therapist in such a way that the therapist can now have a personal take on what the design of the child's psychopathology actually is, through his firsthand affective responses.

13

Using Countertransference and Participation in Handling Impasses

The traditional child psychotherapy literature described the use of fantasy by relating material from the child's play or dreams, interpreting the material to the reader, and then telling of progress in therapy (Bornstein 1951, 1953). The unstated assumption was that something about the material, its expression or the therapist's response, led to the progress. More detailed accounts (Winnicott 1977) included the therapist's interpretations to the child, with the assumption that these led to therapeutic change. Therapeutic neutrality was valued, leaving verbal interpretations as the only "legitimate" way in which the therapist could be involved in the therapy and bring about therapeutic change.

Relational accounts of the use of fantasy in child psychotherapy have paid closer attention to the source of the therapeutic effect in the use of the child's fantasy material. A number of authors (Caspary 1993, Frankel 1998b, Gensler 1994, Krimendahl 1998, Lewis and O'Brien 1991, Spiegel 1989) offer case vignettes. In all these vignettes, the therapist's participation in the play communication is critical to the therapeutic effect. In particular, the therapeutic effect does not rely specifically on verbal interpretations of the child's metaphorical communications. A therapist participates in play communication in many ways other than by interpreting its meaning to the child. First, the therapist may initiate play (as in introducing a new puppet to represent a healthier point of view, or in giving voice to an unspoken point of view of one aspect of the child). The therapist might also respond to the child's invitation to play. Such therapeutic responses are sometimes under the child's control ("Have your guy hit my guy"), but at other times require the therapist to offer her own dialogue, humor, affect, and action. Third, the therapist visibly judges the play. She does so by means of the degree, enthusiasm, and nature of her participation; by nonverbal utterances showing her own affective response to the play themes; and by occasional verbal comments. The therapist also participates privately in the play by her own countertransference. It is a source of information about hitherto excluded selves and others in the child's life that clamor for expression but have not yet been invited onto the playground of the child's fantasy expression.

Here is a simple example of the use of countertransference in response to expressive fantasy material, to guide the therapist's response to the child's fantasy material.

A 5-year-old boy with a history of ear surgery and moderate articulation difficulties has recently started to stutter, especially upon first starting a sentence. The parents love their son and also are achievement oriented, verbal, and anxious people. The boy draws in air and keeps his first word poised on its first consonant, his breath held and his mind seeming to work at composing the whole thought and sentence before he begins to speak. As a consequence he speaks very slowly, trying the patience of listeners even while they respond with compassion to his struggle to speak. The family has been counseled to reduce speech demands, to accept speech in accents or in baby talk, and to encourage nonverbal modes of expression. The parents wonder whether feelings about his recent ear surgery, or his grandfather's death over a year ago, are bothering him.

In the course of a particular session, these issues do not seem relevant to him. He starts to draw a landscape. He draws very slowly. He plans the scene with intelligence and is careful to color things as he chooses. His slow, deliberate pace causes the therapist some impatience; she is eager to return to talking about the boy's hospital experiences. Her mild impatience reminds her of the family's reaction. She becomes interested in her reaction, calms down, and becomes curious about the function of the boy's pace as he draws. Now it is easy to engage him in discussions of speed, planning, and delivery. His way of drawing is not really a metaphor for how he speaks. Rather, the tempo both of his speech and his drawing indicate a cognitive style of slow deliberation. This style is easily discussed with the boy, who becomes interested. He can even think about its use and drawbacks. The therapist and boy are now fully engaged.

The therapist has used her countertransferential response to include the family's reaction to the boy's slow pace, and to include the boy's internalized self-critical reaction to his own slow pace, broadening the discussion with her patient while making it more relevant to him.

Sometimes children in therapy alternate rigidly between antagonism to being in therapy at all, and insistence on making the therapist into a play partner who is completely under their control. The countertransference might be one of helplessness, as well as resentment at being used and controlled. These feelings, once recognized by the therapist, are a useful signal of the child's own feelings of impotence and resentment over his actual family or school situation. The therapist would not be in a position to receive this signal if she were not ready to enter into play with the child on the child's own terms. Once the signal is registered as a countertransferential message of the child's feelings of helplessness to improve internally on his own, the therapist is in a position to realize the need to make external modifications in the child's environment so that the child can feel more control. These could include recommendations for medication, for changes in the child's school day, for a change in class or school placement, for therapy for the parents, and so forth.

A boy with attention-deficit hyperactivity disorder (ADHD), also temperamentally difficult and with labile moods, needed more than the psychostimulant medication that he was taking. He felt guilty and self-critical after an incident in which he upset someone he cared about. He had impulsively slugged a friend after school after mishearing something, thinking the friend had insulted him. He often stubbornly refused to cooperate in getting to school on time in the morning, even though he knew it made his mother late for her own medical appointment. Certainly, his lack of cooperation had its unconscious motivation based on magical thinking ("If she can't see the doctor, she doesn't have lupus"). It also revealed his passive-aggressive expression of resentment at her illness and her occasional need to put herself first. However, despite these factors it was also much harder for him to control himself when he was in a "bratty" mood, which occurred unpredictably. Perhaps psychiatric medication for affective disorder of some sort should be tried. The therapist learned of this need by sensing the boy's inability to get out of a bad mood (defensive, sullen, silent, combative, picky) on his own. The therapist also recognized the boy's readiness to do so when given the external support of an offer to toss a ball around, or an invitation to joke around.

How did this happen? In this case, the therapist found himself feeling hopeless about helping the boy, identifying with his and his family's despair over the boy's impulsive outbursts. Once he was aware of the hopeless feeling, he could consider its contradictory relation to the hope he felt because of the various strengths in the family and in the child. Then, realizing the presence of countertransference, he could experiment with the hopeless mood by introducing external supports (change of medicine or class placement) to help this boy use his strengths to counter his helplessness against his moodiness.

All child therapists are familiar with the occasional need to make some unusual intervention, whether in play therapy, in work with the parents, or at the school level. But when to intervene? At what level of the child's systems of living—in the play? With his parents? At school? And when to go no further than to facilitate play therapy, and to stop there? One orientation to these questions is to identify obstacles to a child's fuller communication or healthier development, and plan a strategy to remove those barriers or to go around them. The key is to identify the obstacles, to judge which are capable of transformation, and to find ways to intervene in that direction. This can occur at the school level through creating an alliance with the teacher, changing the child's class placement, or working with the parents to advocate in these ways more effectively for their child. At other times in therapy, the therapist could identify obstacles at the family level and seek to overcome them there, via work with parents or family. At other times still, the obstacles can occur in the therapist–child dyad, through the child's limitations or resistance or through the therapist's countertransference.

Here is an example of intervening within the play therapy dyad, using a countertransferential sleepiness as a sign of a problem in the child's forward growth.

An 8-year-old boy, the son of divorced parents, is in twice-weekly treatment. He is so immersed in his fantasy world that he is losing ground in school and alienating other children. The parents see the therapist once every two weeks. The boy lives with his mother and visits his father regularly; his parents frequently fight with each other verbally and (rarely) physically. The boy is schizoid, occasionally enuretic, and anxious. With his fantasy world, he sometimes appears schizophrenic, except that he always knows that his companions are imaginary.

In therapy he plunges into his fantasy play, talking to his companions and having them talk to each other, with little regard to the coherence or intelligibility of the story to the listener, his therapist. The fantasy narrative rarely changes, involving a world of diminutive cuddly creatures, a special friend, the friend's nanny, and the evil king who persecutes the creatures. The plot is told with no regard for the audience or for narrative coherence, and with great energy. The therapist's comments are met with silence or with impatient explanations. The therapist's exclamations, understanding, or interest are ignored.

The therapist becomes intensely sleepy. It is nearly impossible to keep his eyelids open. If he were driving, he would have to pull off the road. He struggles to keep thinking, not to sleep, and realizes he is forcefully being put to sleep. He decides to stop the process, judging the situation to be one in which he is being deadened in order to spare his patient having to feel things more clearly. He interrupts the patient, apologizing and explaining that he is having terrible trouble following the story. Would the patient please pause and help the therapist catch up? The boy agrees. The therapist summarizes the play as he has understood it; the boy corrects and adds to the parts that the therapist missed. The therapist, feeling more awake and related now, says to the boy, "Before you continue, I just realized that this story reminds me of something your parents told me last week. If you were as powerful in real life, and as free of any feelings of guilt, as the evil king is in the story, you would never have to deal with the trouble at home that your parents told me about. You could just cut off their heads and make everybody else bow down to you."

Now, after the therapist inserted himself, his feelings and needs, into the session, he was more emotionally present. The boy felt this and became more emotionally present as well, answering, "That's exactly what I would do!" The rest of the session involved a more flexible flow between fantasy and reality, on the same themes, and education regarding the connection between fantasy and reality.

The therapist had interrupted the fantasy in relation to his own need not to be deadened. He processed it in terms of its possible relation to reality. This helped the boy become alive too, and a real connection was made between fantasy and reality.

When the transferential bond with the therapist is weak, the therapist has less leverage interpersonally with the child. At such times, the countertransference is all the more important in resolving therapeutic impasses.

An 8-year-old boy had been seen in individual play therapy for several weeks, while his parents were seen once every other week in collaborative sessions. The boy played with little enthusiasm or pleasure. Mostly he sat idly and pouted. He said that he did not want or need therapy. He claimed his "angry" behavior, which had been a problem at home, in school, and in Bible classes, was over and therefore the therapy was no longer necessary. Every adult from the parents to the Bible teacher insisted that this boy would not be able to continue in his current school or church activities without treatment. They needed to feel some hope. The therapist also was starting to feel that he was never going to establish any rapport with this boy. Thus the external conditions of the boy's life had been recreated and enacted in the therapeutic relationship: a frustrating boy and a frustrated and hopeless authority figure.

The boy earnestly insisted that he be allowed to come to the sessions with his parents, so he could plead his case with them for him to quit individual therapy. The therapist, who felt at the end of his rope with this boy, agreed partly because the boy was so driven and partly out of frustration. After acknowledging his frustration, the therapist was also able to see that the boy was seemingly heartfelt and focused in his appeals, in a way he had never shown before in sessions. The parents were informed of the agenda, as the boy had requested. At the first of these sessions, the boy presented his side of the story so movingly that both of his parents were crying and claiming that they had never seen him so contrite and convincing. The therapist, for the first time in a while, felt positive about a session with this boy and quite relieved that the boy was able to devise this successful treatment plan. The boy thanked the therapist at the end of this session for allowing him to persuade his parents to stop treatment, in what was surely the first time he expressed a positive emotion while in the therapist's office. Family sessions continued for a few weeks and progress ensued at a level that made the parents hopeful that they, as a family, had turned a corner. They stopped treatment at the request of their son and with the agreement of the therapist. The motivation for individual contact with the therapist had never convincingly evidenced itself. Subsequently the boy never initiated contact with the therapist, but the parents often did.

This boy was sufficiently attached to his parents and so pained in his relationship to them that even at his young age he preferred and needed to work through his issues with them directly, rather than through play (at home or in a therapist's office) or with a third party. He was insulted and hurt that a "stranger" had been called in to help. Perhaps the positive transference and countertransference between the parents and the therapist was the crucial factor even though the child was the identified patient, and enabled the treatment to find a new "port of entry" (Stern 1995) into the family system.

Therapists participate in the therapeutic relationship and its outcome through such use of countertransference. They also supply the play area for their child patients, and continually make choices in doing so.

A hyperactive child won't just sit and talk. He needs to move. Expression occurs more easily when he is engaged with his whole being. If he is expected to suppress his intense impulse to motor expression, he is deeply distracted from what he genuinely has to talk about. Once he can move physically in the session, then his issues around self-control, self-criticism, and self-esteem arise much more naturally. His physical movement must be welcomed. This is not neutrality, but interpersonal participation.

One boy's therapy was actually more effective on days when he missed his second, noontime dose of psychostimulant medication. His therapist had supplied the room with a basketball hoop and net, along with a nerf ball. The boy came into his session one day racing about, impulsive, tripping over himself in his rush to play basketball. He knew that the therapist would call a "time-out" if he threw or batted the ball into something potentially breakable, and he hated time-out. This boy steadily had refused to speak about anything outside of the basketball play. Then he blocked a ball with tremendous force, batting it into the venetian blinds. Time-out was imposed. Frustrated and angry, he shouted, "I can't help it, I'm hyperactive!" This was a statement of helplessness and also a bid to manipulate the therapist to drop the time-out. It became invaluable for later sessions. The therapist coached the child in ways to make sure he didn't get a time-out in the future, acknowledging how unfair and how hard it was to control himself given the hyperactivity. This child, who previously had refused all verbalization about his issues, was now more open to such coaching and talking.

The progress occurred because the therapist had supplied the means for expression, the permission to use it, the limit-setting of time-out, and the coaching after the boy had shouted out his dilemma. This degree of therapist involvement is normal and necessary, from a relational point of view.

REQUESTS AND QUESTIONS

Therapists can supply games or play materials that children ask for. But this kind of giving has its own effect, because it makes the therapist an actually generous and responsive person in the child's life, evoking feelings regarding provision and deprivation. Neutrality is not the goal from a relational point of view; rather, the goal is to understand the child's reaction to the therapist's considered, interpersonal participation.

Children make requests and therapists are not free to ignore them. Requests must be responded to in terms of their individual meaning to the child in relation to the therapist. For example, if a child wants to take a toy home, the answer depends on many factors. A relational therapist does not uniformly apply a rule such as "Do not gratify, analyze," because to do so is itself participating with the child (as a withholding person) without analyzing the participation. Is the child testing the therapist's limits, which should then be upheld? Is the child so needy or narcissistic that she could not understand an explanation that the toy should stay in the office for others to use, and so perhaps something should be allowed home? If the child uses materials to make a work of art or a construction of some sort, and then asks to take it home, the answer may be a test of the therapist's valuing of the child. Does the child hope that the therapist wants to keep the artwork as a special production of the child? Or is the request a test of the therapist's control over the child, with the child setting up a conflict over who owns the work? Is it a test of the therapist's willingness to remain no more than a mirroring or need-satisfying object? If the child wants to take unused materials home (tape, paper, pipe cleaners), is it because the child, lacking full object constancy, has no confidence that the relation with the therapist will last until the next session? Is the child emotionally starving, ready to deplete all the therapist's supplies by the end of each session? Or does the child want to take something home because she is jealous of the last child patient, who left as she was coming in, and is trying to establish a sense of being special because of intense sibling issues? As discussed in Chapter 9, therapists must make judgments for each individual situation, based on their best estimate of how to participate productively in the relation with the child, given the child's and the therapist's needs.

Children in therapy may ask for help in a project that would bring the therapist beyond the frame of an individual therapy and into the child's social world. A child may ask the therapist to tell his parents something, or to make phone calls to other people to sell tickets for a school fundraising event. The framework of therapy, and the use and limits of the therapist's role, should be respected. The answer to the request need not be given right away. Indeed, exploration of the fantasies regarding how the therapist would be useful; exploration of the reasons why the child can't do it herself; exploration of the fears that others might not be helpful; exploration of the feelings that the child anticipates she would feel if the therapist agreed or refused—all might do away with the need to answer the request at all. But if the child presses for an answer to her request, one should be given.

One therapist's answer is not another therapist's answer. However restrictive or liberal, the answer to the request must feel comfortable to the therapist. Otherwise, by the process of anxiety contagion described by Sullivan (1953), the therapist's discomfort would flood the child and disrupt the therapy. In addition, such domination by the child of the therapist would not provide a model to the child of a different kind of relationship, one that aimed for the possibility of mutual recognition. While the therapist offers the child a safe playground (Winnicott 1971a) and a substantial degree of containment (Ogden 1982) for the child's anger and testing of limits, these must be limited by the therapist's actual needs in tolerating the situation. Finally, once an answer is given, and a request granted or not, there should be more exploration (in play or in conversation, as the child can handle it) regarding the child's experience of the way in which the therapist was willing to take up such a real role in her life.

Since the child lives with his family, the therapist must always keep in mind the effect on the child of participating in such problem-solving. Can the child be encouraged to turn to parents or others for this help? Or would this be a denial of the child's real isolation and therefore a foolish rejection of the child's legitimate needs?

This kind of request, for help in the child's daily life, involves taking action. Other requests are for advice. Problem-solving is an adaptive, rational ego capacity; when there is a conflict of values, moral judgment is a human dilemma. Even if a child does not ask, therapists might be tempted to see a situation as an opportunity to suggest to the child that problem-solving or moral judgment is necessary. It may or may not be appropriate for a therapist to act on this temptation. For a child who is overwhelmed by the intrusions of others or by his own punitive superego, therapy would best be a place to let the child develop themes at his own pace and with his own voice. But for a child dealing with emotional abandonment or reasonable mistrust of hurtful family members, the situation is different. There, a therapist would do well to guide the child into recognizing the need to solve problems or to consider conflicting values.

Children ask personal questions that have many meanings. There is no rule about how to respond. Children often ask if the therapist is married or has children. They might ask for the therapist's age, religion, street address, or e-mail address. Sometimes a question requires a simple answer, followed by inquiry into the reason for the child's curiosity. Such a response, given in a matter-of-fact way, keeps the line of thought open without interruption. At other times, it is better to defer answering the question and to inquire what the child thinks. This can occur under different circumstances. For example, it may be appropriate not to answer, when answering the question would violate the therapist's sense of privacy, when the question is loaded with meaning or anxiety and a quick answer would close off further inquiry, when the answer would violate other patients' confidentiality, or when the therapist believes that knowing the answer to the question would be more hurtful to the child than not knowing. If the question is part of a curiosity that has become intrusive because of aggressive or oedipal significance, it is better explored than answered right away. However, it is important to give answers to children who are emotionally too needy or developmentally too immature to feel other than rejected, when a question is not answered.

DREAMS AND STORIES

Children sometimes tell their therapist about nighttime dreams or daytime fantasies, about imaginary companions or about scary monsters. Therapists show that they value talk about such images. Children might speak of these images spontaneously, or because the therapist has asked about them. As a child learns that the therapist values hearing about such images, the therapist's interest comes to have its own influence (Gensler 1994). Thereafter, speaking about these images reflects not only the child's wish to tell, but also her fantasies or knowledge about the therapist's interest. The child may simply feel encouraged to look further into her dream images. Or a child may report them more often out of the plea-sure of pleasing the therapist, whether or not the child is interested her-self in introspecting or talking about these images. Or the child may ward off the therapist's interest so as not to have to face the anxiety involved in some of these images. Then the child may resent the therapist's inter-est, ignore it, or refuse to cooperate with it. The child may also take the therapist's interest as a chance to tease or provoke the therapist, by with-holding the images the therapist seems to value.

All these reactions to dream and fantasy material are usefully un-derstood as defenses against the anxiety built into the imagery itself, as in the classical theory. However, they also arise in the context of the therapist's real interest, taking their meaning in comparison to the nature of the interest (or lack of interest) of other significant people in the child's life.

The therapist is frustrated by a cynical, detached, bored 12-year-old patient. The boy is contemptuous of therapy. He has been evicted from private school for not doing his work. He also tor-ments his twin sister, showing no remorse and seeming to enjoy the trouble he is causing. At one point the therapist feels hope-less, ready to give up on this case, and sorry he ever went into the field of child psychotherapy. He recognizes that reaction, a famil-iar sign of countertransference. Then he realizes he feels alone and needs help, probably the way the boy is feeling. He seeks help from the unconscious and asks if the boy remembers any dreams. An-swering readily, the boy tells about a recurrent dream. He, a friend, and a benign and powerful stranger are assaulted by an overwhelm-ing force and eventually defeat it. For the first time, the therapist and the boy are discussing a genuine interest of the boy's, namely these dreams, and also some of the intricacies in his relations with his male friends. Asking for his dreams allowed the therapist to bring out what was important to the boy, rather than to his par-ents. This child did not want to talk about his provocative behav-ior to his sister, or his refusal to do any classwork or homework. His own concerns dealt with the feeling that he had no adults around to help him, only a friend and a magic figure, against dan-gerously violent odds.

When these concerns were brought up in a family meeting, with the boy's permission, the family started to review a period of parental physical abuse against both children, ending two years previously. This period of abuse had not been revealed in earlier reviews of the family's history. The children and parents related the fear, anger, and guilt involved. The therapy had advanced.

The therapist's interpersonal involvement here was in simply asking for dreams, showing an interest in finding something that the child perhaps genuinely cared about. This involvement of the therapist is appropriate in child therapy, rather than to feel constrained by notions of neutrality and therefore to have to wait for material to emerge.

Like dreams, stories can be encouraged as a way to help inhibited children express themselves, or to break out of therapeutic impasses (Gardner 1971, Wachtel 1994). For example, the child is encouraged to tell a fantasy story that is tape recorded. Then the therapist responds with one of her own, also tape recorded, which begins the same way as the child's story but ends differently. The therapist tries to identify key problems, feelings, or defensive reactions inherent in the child's story, but ends her story with a more adaptive reaction, a more realistic response from the adults, a more clear expression of the feelings, or a more effective solution to the problem. The therapist and child listen to the recordings and use the contrast between the two endings to play with the feelings and relationships shown in the two stories. The point is to facilitate a process that fosters a playful attitude toward the dilemma depicted in the child's story, bringing in the freedom of play to consider alternative narratives and outcomes. As in many other instances of fantasy expression, there is usually no need to translate the dilemma into the explicit dilemmas the child is facing; children work most comfortably for extended periods of time in the metaphor of symbolic play (Krimendahl 1998, Spiegel 1989). Within the metaphor of the play, the therapist is encouraging the child to broaden her outlook, to express her feelings, to seek help, and to be more accepting of herself. These ways of participating in the therapy are not interpretive; they are diverse, textured interpersonal responses to the child, calibrated to her current individual needs.

SUMMARY

The emphasis in this chapter has been on the therapist's use of his or her own countertransference, interest, and imagination. With these as tools, the therapist can join in with the child's troubled experience and create a mutually constructed arena, the "playground" that Winnicott (1971a) refers to, for visualizing, feeling, and enacting the child's dilemmas. The genuine fact that the playground was mutually constructed, balancing the therapist's and the child's contributions according to the needs of the child, makes the child feel a sense of ownership and belonging in the therapeutic relationship. This has two effects—it allows the child to imagine feeling that way in his other relations, and it affords him the opportunity to come to terms with the dilemmas he faces in a safe and supportive atmosphere.

PART FIVE

The Context of Child Psychotherapy

A field theoretical approach to child treatment, such as we have developed in this book, leads to a consideration of the interaction between the therapist, the child, the parents, and the various other professional interventions that may be occurring in the child's life. Children are involved not only with their parents and family, but also with teachers, tutors, social service caseworkers, and various others in the community. Chapter 14 examines the therapist's relations with the parents as a key component to the work with the child. Chapter 15 addresses the negotiations the child therapist may have with other professionals in which there is a potential for splitting and disruptive conflict, as well as integration of various points of view in the interests of the child and family. Chapter 16 develops more fully the concept of the therapist as mediator or negotiator in the external and internal worlds of the child. We see the therapist's integrative function with respect to various aspects of the child, and with respect to the various people who are involved with the child, as key to her therapeutic efficacy.

General systems theory views systems as forming a hierarchy, with less complex systems subsumed by the larger systems of which they form a part, and which, in part, define their function. Looking downward in the hierarchy, a cell is an organized system of chemical molecules. Looking upward in the hierarchy, it is part of an organized system of cells that form an organ. The organs, in turn, form the organized system that we call an organism. Organisms may form families, communities, and so on. The structure and function of entities at any level of a system take their character from the larger system that they constitute, and that constitutes them. At the same time, the characteristics of a subsystem have an impact on the larger systems in which they are embedded. Subordinate and superordinate systems influence each other in circular fashion. While systems at the various levels are continually influencing each other, it is equally true that a system at a given level has its own integrity and can be considered as an autonomous entity for some purposes. A subsystem is always an autonomous entity (a system in its own right) from one perspective, while also dependent upon the lower-level systems that compose it, and embedded in the higher-level systems of which it forms a part.

Constituents of a system are organized in a way that creates an equilibrium, a way of working together in the service of the function of the larger system. Disequilibrating events occur from time to time that result in a realignment of the system so as to produce a new equilibrium. The feedback process that results in this ongoing maintenance of a system is called "cybernetic."

A child can be considered from the point of view of her various constituent systems, and of the larger systems of which the child is a constituent. The child can be viewed from various levels of analysis, from the biochemical to the cultural. A given child's behavior may be seen as reflecting a biochemical peculiarity, but it must also be seen in the context of the dynamics of the family in which the child is embedded. That family, in turn, must be seen in the context of a culture, a community, a society.

While the child's behavior can be seen as a function of her biochemistry, and/or of her place in a family or community, it is equally true that the child's personality has its own integrity and autonomy. It can have a major impact on her biochemistry, on her family system, and even on various communities such as her classroom. The child, her biochemistry, the family, the school, and so on, continually influence each other.

The various therapeutic modalities target systems at various lev-els, regarding them as autonomous entities to some degree. The child therapist takes the child as an autonomous entity, while the family therapist does so with the family system, as the psychopharmacologist does with the child's nervous system. Since a child's dependence on his parents, family, and community makes him a system that is very much open, with considerable mutual regulation occurring among child, fam-ily, and larger community, we have been arguing in this book for an approach that takes into account as many levels as possible of the sys-tems that interact with a child.

Child therapists who keep an eye on the various systems that in-terface with the child may feel inclined to take a relatively interven-tionist approach to the work. They are also likely to feel quite over-whelmed by the number of things that need to be attended to. The child therapist who chooses to engage the larger system that shapes the child's life—family, extended family, school, community, other caregivers—can be entangled in a dizzying network of alliances, boundaries, and conflicting interests. Often the child therapist looks with envy to the relative simplicity of the adult therapist's role and its finite demands. Interventions with the family, the school, in the community, often seem necessary and promise to be helpful to the child. While much thera-peutic leverage may be gained by such interventions, the child thera-pist must balance attention to these various forces in the child's life, with priorities that are established as a function of the primary treat-ment modality—for our purposes, individual child therapy. It must also be kept in mind that no therapist can do everything; therapeutic wis-dom and maturity often consist in accepting that no therapeutic effort touches every base and that therapeutic outcomes are, at best, partially successful.

A therapist is called to intervene in a child's life when at some level there is a disequilibrium in the child or in the systems of which the child is a part. There may be family conflict, school failure, or dis-ruptive anxiety in one or several people. The therapist is called on in an effort to restore equilibrium, but at first there is a further destabili-zation of various systems, because a new person has been added to the mix. The therapist must be accommodated in some way. A new system comes into being that had not existed before because a new element has been added. In our view, the therapist must attend to the ways in which systems are realigning in order to accommodate her. She must also attend to the ways in which her own behavior is influencing this process. A child therapist's intervention with the child will have effects that ripple out into the family and beyond. These interventions may set in motion throughout the system sequelae with which she may or may not be prepared to deal directly. Parent guidance sessions may bring to the surface marital tension, or giving a teacher advice may put the teacher in conflict with her supervisor or the child's parents. The ultimate effect of that intervention will depend on the way in which these ripples unsettle various structures, and how the structures reconstitute themselves. The therapist who does not keep an eye on these developments risks unleashing forces willy-nilly that may undermine the attainment of therapeutic goals.

For example, there may be transference complications in the work with the child consequent to the therapist intervening with the parents, siblings, or school, transference complications that render these interventions undesirable, on balance. On the other hand, interventions with a child may change the equilibrium in the family, possibly bringing marital tensions to the surface. In such cases, the child therapist needs to pay attention to such unintended consequences of his work with the child, sending the parents for couple therapy or doing a limited intervention himself. The therapist may need to strike a balance between more and less interventionist approaches, keeping many considerations in mind, as will be illustrated in a clinical example later in this section.

14

Including Parents
in the Psychotherapy

A relational approach to working with children recognizes that parents are as important as the child in a therapist's thoughts and activities. The child's internal world of object relations, the child's current relationships, the concrete support of the treatment, the help or harm rendered to the child outside of therapy, the webs of transference and countertransference that are spun, all involve the parents. A parent is variously partner to the therapy, adversary to the therapy, part of the system, source of guidance as well as resistance for the therapist to respond to, a patient of the therapist, and the employer of the therapist. The therapist's power to influence the child and the parent is in the therapist's technique only insofar as the therapist uses this technique to potentiate the factors for growth in the child and in the parents.

Why are not significant others equally involved in the psychotherapy of adults? Just like a parent with a child's therapy, similarly, a lover, spouse, boss, sibling, or parent can undercut an adult's therapy. Their lack of empathy or hostility can be unhelpful, they have potentially useful information about daily occurrences in the patient's life, and so forth. Further, although children do not usually bring themselves to therapy, there are similar occasions when someone else determines whether or not an adult goes to therapy. This occurs when adults are pressured into therapy by their spouse, or when they are mandated to therapy from prison, a drug detoxification unit, an employee assistance program, or the court. Sometimes the adult patient even lives with the referral source, as when a wife insists her husband enter therapy. Like children in therapy, these patients may resist therapy. They may neither recognize a problem, nor care to seek a cure, nor share the referral source's goals for treatment. Yet the therapist of an adult patient referred from such settings still does not conceive of the necessity for regular "boss guidance" or "spouse guidance" (except for marital therapy), and the therapist does not work with the person from the referring setting in any regular way. What is the difference?

Parents are children's referral sources, and engage a therapist for their child in order to serve their own goals for their child's development, just as the court or an employer does for the adult patients it refers. However, unlike these referral sources, parents care about the outcome and recognize their own responsibility to such an extent that they usually physically bring the child to the therapist and pay for the treatment. This depth of concern and assumption of responsibility arises from deep within the parent's identity as a parent, and also in recognition of the child's developmental immaturity. Parents recognize the child's inability to engage in therapy without help. They are concerned for the child, they feel intolerant of the symptoms, and they want to act in accord with their identity as parents.

Further, children themselves usually do not know that there is a helping profession. Nor is their sense of reciprocity and relatedness usually developed sufficiently to realize from the start that a therapist needs to be paid and to have control of the hour. Children usually do not have the means to pay for therapy (or to assure payment through third-party reimbursement) nor to get to and from therapy. To occur, child therapy requires sufficient involvement from a parent or guardian to work within these considerations.

When they can, then, therapists take advantage of the necessity and nature of the parents' involvement to attempt to do what usually cannot be done in adult therapy—to help people central in the patient's life (in child therapy, it is the parents) to increase their understanding and to conduct themselves more empathically, facilitating the child's growth. The closest analogy in adult psychotherapy is the ongoing nourishing of a therapeutic milieu in inpatient settings, a point Ornstein (1976) makes explicitly.

Child therapists who are psychoanalytically oriented and work with parents have sometimes been hampered by traditional definitions of neutrality. When neutrality is understood as not directing, therapists working with parents can feel uncomfortable about aspects of their work with parents, such as reassuring, or giving hope or advice. From this point of view, the purity of the child's transference is compromised. The therapist would let himself be perceived not only as a projection or externalization of family images, but also as another real parental figure. However, a relational approach to psychotherapy with children holds that there is no treatment that is devoid of the therapist's participation. In this approach, the interpersonal nature of the work is one central theme rather than secondary or problematic. Taking a position with the parents as part of the work, then, is no longer an interference with the purity of the child's therapy. Rather, it is an inevitable and useful part of the work, to be handled as thoughtfully as possible.

Therapists may choose to involve themselves with parents in a variety of ways. These may range from the development of a positive alliance with the parents to allay their anxieties about treatment and reduce the likelihood that they will undermine it, to rather intensive therapeutic work on certain of the parents' personal conflicts. This range of possibilities includes parent guidance and education, serving as a model or mentor in parenting, helping parents overcome difficulties that interfere with their parenting, and helping with specific, problematic parent–child interactions. A child's therapy is enhanced when parents can be helped to create a more facilitating environment or a therapeutic milieu for the child in the home (Ornstein 1976, Winnicott 1963); when parents can learn skills for better parenting; when parents can get useful advice (Arnold 1978); and when parents can report daily occurrences in the child's life to the therapist.

Parent work is also helpful in getting the parent not to undercut the treatment. Parents can be ambivalent about turning to a professional for help with their child (Glenn et al. 1978) due to jealousy of the therapist, a sense of being threatened or vulnerably exposed, feelings of envy or inferiority, or resentment over the time and expense of therapy. An alliance with the parents keeps this ambivalence from leading the parents to remove their child from therapy.

Child rearing is new for most parents, and they need to learn how to do it. Many parents need information or advice on how to handle problems related to discipline, fears, or sibling relations. This kind of work, called parent education, includes giving a general understanding of child development, or a specific understanding of the child's symptoms.

> Carlos, 7½, was crossing a street on the way to church with his mother when they were both knocked down by a hit-and-run driver. The boy was struck twice and run over the second time. He suffered a concussion with mild neurological aftereffects (headaches, compromised balance), which diminished as the weeks went on. The mother's leg was broken. The boy's father and uncle, both police officers, were furious but unable to find the perpetrator.
>
> In therapy, the boy played and replayed a family peacefully minding its own business and then interrupted by overwhelming intruders whom he felt compelled to challenge. He put intense energy into this play. Prominent issues included being macho, wishing guiltily that he had been "man" enough to push his mother out of the way, and the unfairness and vulnerability of his life (he had had a previous eye operation, and his younger sister had recently been hospitalized for croupe). When the therapist let father know that Carlos was in conflict over showing his feelings of vulnerability, father reminded his son that he, the father, had cried in upset over the accident. The play therapy, and father's empathic support for Carlos' feelings, let Carlos relax visibly as the sessions went by.
>
> Carlos' presenting problems—fear of crossing the street and inability to talk about the accident with his mother—abated quickly after two months of therapy. But he remained more high-strung, irritable, and emotionally sensitive than he had been before the accident. The therapist told his parents about acute stress reactions, normalizing this kind of heightened reactivity under such circumstances. They were relieved to learn that this was a normal reaction that would probably diminish (as indeed it did), especially since the presenting problems had resolved.

Besides parent education, Chethik (1989) describes "transference parenting" (pp. 233–238), a way of supporting the parent so that the parent can support the child and the therapy; "treatment of the parent–child relationship" (pp. 239–250) a limited form of insight therapy or "sector therapy" (p. 241) in which the unconscious meanings of a child for the parent can become more evident; and "treatment of the child via the parent" (pp. 251–269) in which the therapist helps parents to do the therapeutic work directly with their young child (see also Freud 1909, Furman 1957, 1969, Lieberman and Pawl 1984).

PSYCHOTHERAPY WITH PARENTS

Therapy with parents deals with parents' concern and empathy for their child, with their identity, development, and moral values as parents, and with the meaning the child has for them, including positive and negative identifications. Many parents hold ambivalent feelings about primary people in their life, and identify their children with these people (Schwartz 1984). This interferes with their ability to perceive their children accurately and empathize with their children as individuals (Paul 1970). A child's therapy is more likely to succeed when parents work through such negative identifications in parent guidance or other psychotherapeutic work.

Mary, 11, came into therapy feeling depressed and low about herself, longing to be friends with girls who rejected her. Her occasionally silly and spirited self disappeared after other girls teased her. Whenever she got angry at her father, he would become overtly morose and self-critical, as he used to when his own parents got angry at him, to the point of suggesting that the family would be better off without him. Mary would then feel guilty, but also angry and helpless not to have her feelings accepted. Father was an immigrant and disapproved of American values of individuality and self-expression. He was the coach of Mary's soccer team and wished she would show him more respect. Mother tried to mediate ineffectively.

Therapy lasted eighteen months until the family moved out of town. At termination, Mary was confident and socializing happily, though anxious about the move and sad to lose her friends. The individual therapy had allowed her room to explore her feelings without being made to feel guilty. She never before had spoken about feeling burdened with the responsibility of managing her father's feelings, especially his readiness to feel abandoned when she expressed her wish for independence.

Meetings with parents and family clarified the patterns of family interaction and allowed the father to realize and admit to Mary his part in Mary's trouble (even though that made the father feel guiltier). Meetings with mother were particularly helpful when mother was then able to tell Mary that father would not change, and that it was all right for Mary to be mad at him nonetheless. Mary felt less guilty over the intensity of her feelings for her father and was able to become more assertive with her friends as well.

Parent meetings were one crucial component of this progress, especially when father admitted how he induced Mary's guilt, after realizing how similarly his own parents had induced guilt in him. This was a limited working through, what Chethik calls sector psychotherapy.

PARENTS' DESIRE TO BE INVOLVED IN TREATMENT

Many parents want and expect to be involved. Consciously they have a goal for the therapy—to undo the presenting problems and to change the child's behavior, mood, or attitude. Psychotherapy with parents often includes guidance of the therapist. Parents try to advise the professional regarding the nature of the problem, as they seek help regarding these problems. Unconsciously parents are ready to engage in a transference relation to the therapist. They may identify with or depend on their child's therapist. Alternately they may withhold from, mistrust, control, blame, defend against, or compete with the therapist.

Parents' involvement with their children's therapy is also related to their own stage of parenthood, with issues particular to each stage of their child's development. Also, real situational obstacles (e.g., chronic painful medical illness in the child) may interfere with the parents' wish to be good parents who can protect their children (Birch 1993). Therapy addresses the emotional consequences of facing these obstacles.

In turn, therapists react to parents unconsciously and consciously. Unconscious reactions derive from countertransference (e.g., blaming or exonerating parents, competing with parents, or seeking praise from them), from over-identification with parents, from efforts to compensate for parents' inadequacy, or from the parents' real positive and negative attributes (Glenn et al. 1978).

Overtly the therapist undertaking a child therapy makes an informal contract with the parents to try to achieve some of the parents' conscious and verbally expressed goals. Yet a therapist may have a private strategy for the work with parents, which supplements the parents' stated goals for their meetings with their child's therapist. Therapists want to secure the parents' support for the child's therapy, and to help parents to parent more effectively. Therapists try to accomplish this aim through increasing parental empathy and attunement (Paul 1970), easing negative identifications with the child and strengthening positive ones (Schwartz 1984), and creating more of a therapeutic environment in the home (Ornstein 1976).

Whatever the therapist's overall strategy for treatment, parents judge therapy by its progress toward their own goals, and by its cost in money, time, and emotional involvement. The success of therapy depends fundamentally on the parents' approval and support. This dependence is direct, since the parents can stop therapy when they choose. It is also indirect, since a child feels a parent's faith in the process, or the parent's resistance to the process, and the child is influenced by it.

So the therapy is certainly defined by the child's and the therapist's involvement. Yet it is equally defined by its meaning to the parents. This holds true regardless of frequency of sessions with child or parent. Work with parents is not "extra-analytic" (Sandler et al. 1980) or "secondary" (Glenn et al. 1978), as the classical child analysts have written. Rather, it is central to the treatment.

WHEN THE PARENTS ARE NOT INVOLVED

With no involvement, parents may interfere with therapy, or keep it from accomplishing its goals. Or the therapist may lose sight of the parents' goals for the therapy. If the therapist conceives of child therapy as something to do with the child alone, with little involvement with the parents—or if the parents won't get involved—the therapist has to help the child react to unhelpful aspects of the parents (or to parents' unhelpful reactions to the therapy) without being able to help the parent change in a way that is more helpful to the child and the therapy. Sometimes this can work; sometimes, if the parents are not involved, it is necessary. But it is harder.

The therapist confronts a variety of circumstances in which parental involvement is difficult or impossible. There are parents who are pressured to bring their child to therapy by the school, the court, or the foster care system. There are parents who do not involve themselves in their child's therapy because they are unable to come (they may be ill, working, or taking care of a baby or an elderly parent at home). There are parents who do not involve themselves in their child's therapy because they are too busy or preoccupied to have time to attend sessions. They may see the therapist as a child care expert to minister to the child without their involvement. Other parents are too drug-addicted, abusive, or unconcerned to become involved.

The therapist has the dilemma of deciding how much pressure to apply and how much to accept the resistance. The therapist's stance here toward the parents also becomes a vital element in his relation to the child. Both therapist and child develop attitudes regarding the parents' resistance. The therapist's attitude toward the parents can be influenced by the child's attitude toward the parents, and it can also contribute to the child's attitude. Therapists find a balance between acknowledging to the child the reality of the parents' limitations, and staying empathically within the child's subjective experience of these limitations. There is the danger that if a child tells parents who are minimally committed to the therapy that the therapist "agrees you are mean to me," the parents will end the treatment.

THERAPISTS AND PARENTS ADVOCATING FOR CHILDREN

When a child's therapy is working, parents develop as well. There is much growth in achieving a greater understanding of the child's problems, in freeing oneself from having to identify the child with other difficult people in the parent's own life, and in accepting the need to care for and love the child as he is. This growth includes advances in the ability to reflect on feelings, to contain difficult and conflicting feelings, to integrate past and present self-images, and to gain more flexibility in the use of defense mechanisms. Traditionally these areas of growth have been attributed to the ego.

Parents also grow in their judgment, restraint, and ability to act on their child's behalf. They become clearer about their values, what they care about and what they will not tolerate, as parents. The parental superego, a term from a one-person model, or the parents' internal and interpersonal patterns of advocacy and guidance regarding their children, as a relational model might conceive of it, have the chance for further growth over the course of a child's therapy.

Parents have ultimate responsibility for their children, and a child therapist cannot ignore the way in which they do and do not guide and advocate for their children. Some parents resent having to shoulder the responsibility of looking out for the child's best interests; others are excessively solicitous. A child therapist needs to pay attention to a parent's actions and inactions on behalf of a child, as another important aspect of the parent's identity and relationship with the child.

Parents ask for advice. Therapists also offer it, solicited or not, via advocacy and suggestion. So the therapist is not only paying attention to the parents' moral concerns for the child—"What should I do?"— but also actively assuming the role of a guide and an advocate on behalf of the child.

Therapists will vary in their degree of advocacy. At the extreme, therapists will not try to influence the parents' efforts on behalf of the child. However, most therapists who work with parents and also work with the parents' child will eventually encourage or discourage various parental actions. This occurs in matters of divorce or visitation, in living arrangements, sleeping and eating patterns, schedules, discipline, or in optimal classroom placements. For example, a therapist may suggest to a parent that a child needs to be referred to the school's committee on special education for assessment and possible remediation. Therapists recommend books to read, attitudes to take, techniques to adopt. Therapists also encourage parents to overcome their own lack of interest or involvement with childhood activities enough so that they can help the child find avenues for expression (athletic, social, artistic, etc.).

In doing so, therapists must judge the extent of their alliance with the parents. A strong alliance with the parent's wish to be a good parent outweighs the resentment that a parent may feel at being judged. There is a continuum of assumption of responsibility for advocacy. The more parents are invested in advocating on behalf of their child, the less the therapist needs to urge the parent into this role. Then the therapist's guidance is limited to decisions concerning which of several possibilities to advocate for. Here, responding to parents' clinical issues (fear of judgment, fear of assertiveness, fear of separation, attitudes toward authority) mingles with educating the parents concerning situations the parents have never come across before.

However, when parents do not act on their child's behalf, or when parents are anxious as they advocate on their children's behalf, the therapist may spend hours on the phone. This kind of case management is frustrating. The time is often not reimbursed, either because insurance does not cover such case management or because the therapist does not charge the parents for it. Therapists are often inclined to urge parents to make these advocacy calls to the schools, the foster care agencies, the court-appointed examiners, the educational consultants, the doctors, or the tutors. Yet some parents were never taken care of by their parents the way the therapist would now have them take care of their child. They do not conceive of this kind of advocacy. If they do, they do not know how to do it. If they know how to do it, they may be so envious of the child for getting what they never got that they deprive the child of that kind of support.

The therapist models advocacy, encourages the parents to take it over, and works through the feelings raised by the challenge to do so. But when the parent's transference to the therapist is that of a critical parent figure, and the parent's superego is dominated by similarly harsh internal objects, then therapeutic advocacy and suggestion are felt as dangerous attacks and are fended off. In the worst case, the resentment is redirected at the child or the spouse in the form of abuse. Or the parent is tempted to end the therapy, in self-protection. At such times, the therapist must refrain from advice and focus empathically on the parent's needs, not the child's. Once the parent feels supported and understood enough to work through unacknowledged paranoid projections, then the parent can again join in with the therapist to focus on the child's needs (Chethik 1989, Lieberman and Pawl 1984).

NEGOTIATING THE TUGS OF MULTIPLE RELATIONSHIPS: THE THERAPIST AS SHUTTLE DIPLOMAT

The child therapist who works actively with the parents as well as with the child can often find himself at the heart of conflicting anxieties and desires, the bearer of their mutual longings and fears. In these often complex relationships, it is imperative that the therapist, in order not to compromise his role as the child's individual therapist, keep two important priorities, derived from his role as the child's advocate, absolutely clear. First, the therapist is the child's person. As the child's advocate, his position in the relationships is not equidistant from all participants; of necessity he will have a closer involvement, understanding, and commitment to the child. His interventions will always be shaped by putting the child's interests first. Second, regardless of what contact the therapist may see fit to have with others, he will maintain a level of confidentiality regarding communications between himself and the child that is different from the confidentiality he may see fit to maintain in other relationships. These principles may seem obvious, but in the fray of a difficult case, they are not necessarily always observed. The child's trust in the privacy and confidentiality of the relationship must be earned and cannot be assumed, particularly when the therapist has contact with several important people in the child's life.

The therapist often functions like a shuttle diplomat between the child and others in the child's life. We have used the metaphor of the shuttle diplomat because it appears to capture some of the important features of the challenge inherent in this role. The therapist has a primary allegiance to the child, who, while not exactly a sovereign state, nevertheless can exercise a considerable degree of autonomy and independent decision-making power. But the therapist may also take on the task, similar to that of the diplomat, of bringing the interests and agendas of different participants into alignment.

The therapist, like the diplomat, has no independent power base, but only that given to him or her by others. In contrast to the role of a case manager or a field marshal, the therapist is not usually in a position to control events, assign specific responsibilities to others, and ensure that they complete them. Instead, the therapist's skills lie in the realm of clarification and persuasion, helping each person better understand the perspectives of the others. Through symbolic gestures, innuendo, tone of voice, the therapist allows each person to feel heard, understood, and respected, while helping them to move toward a more flexible, consensual position.

BETWEEN PARENTS AND CHILD: WHEN THE TREATMENT MODALITY IS INDIVIDUAL CHILD THERAPY

Parents who are unfamiliar with psychotherapy may find the relationship that the therapist attempts to establish with them and the child unnatural and frustrating. With other professionals from whom they may seek help for their child, be it the pediatrician, tutor, or educator, they are probably used to an arrangement in which they bring the child to the professional, who evaluates or works with their child, and then meets with the parents to tell them what they believe their child needs, what they have done, or what they plan to do. In this more typical arrangement, the parents defer to the expertise of the professional, give their child to this person for the services he can provide, and in turn expect a full accounting of what he has done. But in psychotherapy, the therapist expects the parents to become active participants in the process, hopes that they will examine themselves and their own role in their child's life, and will take active steps to alter or improve their participation. At the same time, the therapist will be sparing and careful in what he tells them regarding their child's concerns, and therefore the parents may feel thwarted and frustrated in their efforts to learn what the problem is. In child psychotherapy, in contrast to other more conventional relationships betwen parents and professionals who are providing services to their child, more is expected of them and less is given to them.

It is incumbent upon the therapist to help the parents understand the ways in which the therapeutic process differs from the more familiar types of professional relationships that parents may use as a model. It is equally important to help parents understand the rationale for such differences. The therapist's task is to be clear about the reasons for his own stance and what purposes it serves and to find ways to communicate that to the parents.

The therapist should make clear that he is, first and foremost, the child's therapist, even if he is meeting weekly with the parents. This means that the therapist will respect the child's confidentiality. Yet there is the need to communicate with parents. Thus a child may be told that the details of her sessions will be private, but the therapist may speak with the parent about general themes. An adolescent may be told that her parent will hear even less. A child or adolescent is usually told that confidentiality will not be kept if the therapist learns that the child is in danger, criminally involved, or decompensating. These compromises to confidentiality reflect the fundamental fact in child therapy that parents, at least under the best of circumstances, are partners in treatment (except in court-mandated psychotherapy). They retain their right to guide the treatment; they can also undermine it or cancel it. Younger children expect a parent to talk with teachers and doctors. Sometimes it is important to include children in decisions regarding what to tell parents, what not to, and what the agenda of parent therapy sessions should be. Also, some parents are engulfing and intrusive. It is just as critical to retain a sense of partnership with them by focusing on the child's needs for boundaries, the parent's need for involvement, and the conflicted feelings involved.

The therapist will also exercise judgment concerning the parents' confidentiality, and will reserve the right to inform his child patient of certain issues or information if he deems it appropriate. The parents cannot assume, therefore, that everything they say to the therapist will be held in strict confidence in relation to their child, and the therapist should make that clear.

Further, the therapist should articulate for the parents that he is the child's advocate. That is the therapist's role and responsibility. In meeting with the parents, and in attempting to aid them with difficulties in their own life, the therapist will view events and discuss them with regard to their impact on the child.

In some instances, the parents turn the child over to the therapist the way one might drop off one's car for repairs, expecting to pick the child up when the work is completed. The therapist's challenge then is to involve the parents in the treatment and to represent the child's interests and needs to them. In other instances, the parent may involve the child in treatment, but primarily as a vehicle for seeking solace, comfort, or attention for their own needs, dilemmas, and personal pain.

One 5-year-old boy lived with his mother, a single parent, and saw his father on an irregular basis. The boy, who was enuretic and encopretic, often felt agitated by the irregularity and unpredictability of contact with his father. In addition, his mother, who had paranoid tendencies, was embroiled in ongoing conflicts with work colleagues that preoccupied her and debilitated her.

Any contact with the mother usually involved a prolonged exchange about the many conflicts in which she was embroiled. At first, this was enormously frustrating, annoying, and anxiety producing for the therapist, who was very concerned about this boy's functioning and state of vulnerability. But eventually it became clear that no useful work could be done with the mother if the therapist did not first attend to her and her struggles.

In sessions with the mother, a considerable amount of time was taken up with her complaints about her former husband, and about her colleagues at work. Some of her grievances appeared to have validity, and, although she had her own individual therapist, some attention to these matters appeared to help her. These conversations seemed important in beginning to develop trust with the therapist. While attempting to be responsive to her, however, the therapist found that he frequently had to draw on the concept of role to remind her that his task was to help her see these issues in light of her son and their impact on him, and, specifically, to help her see how her way of responding to these issues and talking about them at home was very agitating to him. This task was a particularly challenging one, given his mother's readiness to see others as hostile and out to undermine her.

In individual sessions with her, the first several minutes always involved some discussion of the struggles in her own life, with the therapist either simply listening, asking a few clarifying questions, or offering an occasional thought. Following that exchange, the therapist would then shift the focus to her son, and would often preface his remarks by noting that, as her son's therapist, he was particularly interested in how things might be affecting her son (this is an example of what Chethik [1989] calls transference parenting). Most of the time, the mother accepted this shift, although often with some emotional distress or reluctance. In contrast, the boy's father was always ready to talk about his son and what he needed with apparent little resistance or hesitation. In spite of this willingness to talk, however, he consistently failed to follow through on anything discussed in the sessions, and by and large related to his son in a way that seemed to serve the father's own immediate need or convenience.

Overall the therapist's goal is to develop an active, ongoing relationship with parents who hopefully come to see themselves as an integral part of the treatment process, while at the same time respecting their child's right to privacy and need for an entirely separate, independent relationship with the therapist.

When the parent gives information to the therapist about the child, the therapist has to decide whether and how to use this information. It is often helpful for the therapist to introduce observations and reports from others in the child's life into the session, partly as a stimulus to explore the issues, partly as a way of letting the child know that such topics are appropriate and important for the therapy, and partly to prevent the therapeutic relationship from becoming one that is entirely separate and perhaps sealed off from the child's daily life, which can sometimes happen. At the same time, the therapist needs to protect the therapy from excessive and countertherapeutic intrusions by the parents or others. It would be a mistake for the therapist to become a conduit for channeling parental concerns and agendas into the child's sessions. It is not uncommon for the therapist to confront the dilemma in which the parent tells the child what he or she should discuss in the therapy, and similarly, tells the therapist what he or she should bring up. The therapist can address such a dilemma in several ways. Depending upon the age of the child, she can form something of a bond or an alliance with the child in considering the question of how to treat parental concerns and agendas. If the child actively objects to the introduction of any material other than what he brings in, the child may well have valid grounds for such a position.

Although one goal for the therapeutic relationship is to develop a sense of privacy, intimacy, and safety in which the child feels that he can say anything, at the beginning of most treatments, and often for a considerable period of time, the child is likely to share intimacies with a parent that he will not want to share with the therapist. Therefore, the child can easily feel betrayed and violated when parents report on conversations or events that have taken place with their child. This sense of violation can be particularly sharp when the child has chosen to use the therapy as a kind of play space in which he can leave daily concerns behind and explore imaginative realms. It is the therapist's task to try to understand the nature of such requests in terms of the parent–child relationship and the child's individual needs. The therapist must exercise discretion, ultimately, concerning what to bring up and when. With the parent, the therapist can empathize with the parents' wish to be part of the process and to help influence or shape the therapeutic process, while working with the parent to find more appropriate or effective means of doing so.

The child's sense of safety in the therapy will ultimately depend on several key factors. First, the child retains a significant degree of control over what is said and done in the sessions. Second, the child experiences the therapist making decisions, exercising limits, and shaping the therapy in a way that is directed toward her best interest, and is mindful of the child's need for protection. Third, the therapist and the child's parents have found some way in which to work with each other so that the child does not feel tugged between two poles or values or demands. These three factors may not always be in alignment, and at times the demands of one may pull against the other. For example, when the therapist finds it necessary to introduce material that the child has not brought up, and may be unwelcome to the child, the child is likely to feel a diminishment in her sense of control over the direction of the treatment. This threatened loss of control and feeling of momentary betrayal may be offset by the child's sense that the therapist and the parent are concerned about important matters that, although potentially painful to discuss, will help the child ultimately. The therapist's decision regarding what information to bring in, and when to bring it in, lies in the realm of the intuitive, artistic aspect of the work.

The therapist may also find it useful to bring information or requests from the individual sessions with their child to the parents. Sometimes this is initiated by the child and sometimes by the therapist. The child may raise certain issues that the therapist feels either warrant parental involvement or could benefit from parental clarification.

A boy complained that his two closest friends had been teasing him and excluding him from things. Their teasing had been adopted by others in his school class, and it appeared that he was becoming or had become the class scapegoat.

Although his mother was friends with the boys' mothers, he hadn't said anything to her because he feared that if she said something to them, it might jeopardize her relationship to her friends. The therapist felt that this problem went beyond the ability of the child to solve, and requested permission from him to bring it up with his mother. He consented, and they then met with his mother at the end of the individual session. The boy had been particularly concerned about the risk to his mother's friendship, as his parents had recently separated and his mother was devastated.

In her conversations with the other mothers, she found out that the boys were feeling quite upset at what they described as the loss of their old friend, who had recently become irritable, moody, and sad. This observation on their part then became something that the boy and his therapist were able to work on together. His sadness and irritability was part of his own response to the parental separation, which he had been very reluctant to discuss.

In another instance, a boy in therapy asked the therapist to speak with his dad about a particular way his dad disciplined him that he felt was too strict. The therapist voiced a general willingness to talk with his father about it, but then raised the possibility that the boy do it himself. He claimed to have spoken to his father without any apparent effect. In this particular instance, the therapist chose to talk directly with the father about his son's concerns, in light of his impression that the father had not been particularly responsive to his son in the past, often interpreting his children's complaints or requests as originating with their mother. In contrast, he had found the father to be pretty responsive to interventions by the therapist. In another instance, the therapist might well have decided to work on the issue with the boy, and find ways to help him speak more directly to his father. Having agreed to the boy's request, the therapist was surprised to learn in a subsequent session that, having had this conversation in session, the boy had gone on to speak with his father directly in a way that both father and son found satisfying.

Sometimes, the opportunity to say something out loud, to practice it, and to experience some support for one's position is all that is needed. In general, in the course of these exchanges, the more the child can feel that the therapist is willing to be his advocate and emissary if necessary, the more the two participants can become collaborators in a complex process, which includes a genuine exploration of what is within the child's own capacities. Ultimately this process increases what the child can do on his own.

When the therapist meets with parents, a frequent concern is how the parents are disciplining the child. The therapist may find he has to identify disciplinary needs or respond to questions regarding discipline. In some instances, these issues can put the therapist in a delicate position regarding his relationship to the child. The therapist may be aware of certain behaviors on the child's part that are potentially harmful to the child that warrant more aggressive parental intervention, or may simply require greater parental awareness. In these situations, the therapist faces the dilemma of drawing on information gleaned in the sessions in making suggestions to parents.

While the therapist does not have to directly reveal any confidential information, his interventions may be based on such information. This type of intervention can border on betrayal in the child's experience. The therapist may deal with this situation directly by telling the child what type of advice or suggestion he thinks is necessary for the parents. What approach to take will depend upon the age of the child, and the particular issues in the parent–child relationship. Where the therapist chooses not to say something explicitly, the child will sometimes implicitly acknowledge the therapist's influence, and perhaps indirectly indicate some gratitude for it. In other instances, the child may protest the "new approach" the parents are taking, without explicitly confronting the therapist for the therapist's part in it.

BETWEEN DIVORCED AND DIVORCING PARENTS

Because of the complex negotiations often involved, and the way in which the therapist can be drawn into assuming responsibilities and roles that are more properly those of the parents or even of the legal system, many therapists are reluctant to become involved in treatment cases with divorced parents. If the therapist is willing to treat a child in a divorced family, she should make clear from the outset that the therapist's role precludes taking any active part in any court-ordered evaluation or testifying in any matters related to custody. The therapist will also need to decide privately how much of a role she is willing to take and believes will be therapeutic, what the circumstances of the case call for, and what the parents seem to insist that the therapist do.

The parents of two boys, ages 9 and 11, refused to talk with each other, and believed that they could not usefully discuss any matters concerning the children. The children themselves inevitably became go-betweens in negotiating a range of issues. Both parents did agree that the boys could benefit from therapy, and both looked to the therapist to function both as the go-between and as the arbiter between them.

The therapist in this case agreed to accept this role, and, while it put an added burden on the therapist and seemed to legitimize a failure in the family system's capacity to care for the children, nevertheless it helped both parents to behave more reasonably and responsibly in their treatment of the boys. In another case, however, in which the parents would not or could not talk with each other in a useful way, the father closely evaluated any scrap of information that came to him from the therapy that might suggest that the therapist expressed views or opinions unfavorable to him. This level of conflict and close scrutiny threatened to undermine the whole therapeutic effort. In another instance, one parent in a session with the child's therapist informed her that she was planning on leaving her husband, who did not know of his wife's plans. In meeting with parents individually, the therapist should clarify that she will not necessarily treat what the parent says as confidential in relation to the other parent. Otherwise, the therapist might find herself in possession of secrets that could easily undermine the whole effort.

In those instances when the therapist does gain private information from one parent that is not intended to be conveyed to the other, she must evaluate how to respond to this information. The therapist can explain to the parent who conveyed the private information that having such knowledge can limit or restrict her ability to work effectively with both parents, and actively encourage the parent to find a way to talk about the information with the other parent. In a quite different situation, in which one parent harbored what appeared were highly provocative and apparently unfounded suspicions of child abuse on the part of the other parent, the therapist chose to keep these suspicions private and to work with the one parent on how to deal with them.

ENGAGING THE PARENTS IN TREATMENT

The presenting problems are a parent's ticket of admission into therapy. They explain what is wanted, how the therapist is viewed, and what is of concern to the parent. At the first appointment, the child's troublesome behavior or inexplicable mood may be a mystery waiting to be solved. The therapist is to become a partner with the parents and child in solving the mystery collaboratively. Over the course of this partnership, the therapist may be the first adult to break bad news to the parent concerning the extent of the child's difficulties, or to confront the parent's denial of the nature of the difficulties. Alternately, the therapist may be the first adult not to pathologize the child, but to view the child's problems as normative for his stage of development or for the trauma that he may have suffered. Tact, compassion, and timing are as necessary here as anywhere else in therapy.

In working with parents, there are valuable and memorable moments, perhaps short periods, of what feels like progress. During such periods, there is a successful examination of transferences to the child or to the therapist, or parents come to realize systemic influences on the child's behavior (for example, seeing how marital conflict is being expressed via arguments over the child). Mostly, however, sessions are taken up with longer periods of listening, support, parent education, and examination of parental conflict. Therapists working with parents should accept this as normal and respond to their own impatience as if to countertransference. The longer periods prepare the way for critical moments of insight concerning parent–child relationships (Pine 1985).

In first meetings with parents, the therapist wants to establish the parents' motivation for therapy as well as their sense of ownership of the therapy. A therapist should refer openly to prior information given or obtained in order to check it against the parents' knowledge. Nonetheless, the therapist–parent partnership must become the primary authority for the construction of a narrative of the child's life. Confusing, ignored, and contradictory areas of history should be explored

(Cooper and Witenberg 1983). Parents' ambivalence about coming for therapy should be addressed, as when school or court has applied pressure for the child to be in treatment, or when one parent is against therapy and the other parent is for it. In addition, the child's therapist should tell the parents that a central task will be to transform the child's therapy from something the parent initiates into something that the child will also find reason to participate in.

The frame of therapy must also be agreed upon, establishing the time and frequency of child and parent meetings, as well as the fee and the policy regarding payment for missed sessions. The therapist should urge regular attendance at scheduled meetings for child and parent, and should offer a responsiveness to phone calls. Phone work with parents is not only unavoidable but necessary in work with children. Early into the work with parents, a therapist should predict that it is likely that occasionally the parents and their child will resist coming to therapy, and that mixed feelings and attitudes about therapy and the therapist are to be expected. Parents should be asked not to react to those situations by dropping out of treatment, but to discuss them with the therapist as they arise. Indeed, parents may be the last to see progress that is evident at school, in the playground, and in therapy.

If managed care insurance is going to reimburse some of the cost of therapy, there should be clear agreements regarding insurance co-payments and seeking managed care authorizations. Policies should be explained for making insurance claims, for handling missed sessions, for handling final or temporary expiration of insurance authorizations, and so forth. Limits to confidentiality should be discussed from the start. These include the need to send insurance companies treatment reports, the companies' right to review treatment records, and the loss of confidentiality in the event of a judicial subpoena in a custody matter.

The therapist should review with the parent matters concerning the confidentiality of the child's therapy. Most child therapists agree to keep the details of the child's sessions confidential, but also state that they retain the discretion to share general themes and clinical impressions with the parents. Often a therapist will review with the child which details to tell the parents, and which to withhold. The therapist should tell child and parent that the parent must be informed in the event that the therapist learns that the child intends to carry out suicidal, homicidal, or criminal acts. Similarly, if the therapist is the first to realize that the child is deteriorating medically or psychiatrically, the parent must be informed. It is much better to persuade the child to tell the parent than for the therapist to do so, which should occur only as a last resort.

After hearing the presenting problems, the therapist should ask the parent what approaches or interventions the parent has used with the child, what advice others have given the parent, who has given that advice, what has worked and what has not worked, and how the parent feels about all the advice and effort. It is helpful to explore times when the parent has not been able to carry out or follow through on advice or plans for changing or coping with the child's behavior. Throughout, the therapist should empathize with the experience of parenting a troubling and troubled child. Parents need this support, and it also models an empathic approach for those parents who have trouble empathizing with their own child.

Most parents start therapy with some feeling toward a transference image of the therapist, including idealization, dependence, gratitude, and hope, or inadequacy, competition, resentment, envy, and fear. If the child had been in therapy before, the feelings involved in starting a new therapy are also influenced by the earlier treatments. Parents need compassion for these feelings, particularly the fear of being criticized or blamed and the concern that earlier mistakes will not be repeated. However, if the compassion is conveyed in a premature or perfunctory way, it becomes condescending. A therapist must find the right moment to acknowledge and support the parent at the start of therapy.

A therapist should also start to point parents toward their own experiences as children with their own parents (the child's grandparents), in order to help them empathize with the child (as well as with their own parents) in new ways. For example, parents who are overly intrusive or controlling toward the child must eventually look inward to their own experience as children, to see whether they are identifying with (or reacting against) unfortunate models of parenting. The individuality of the child should also be noted to the parents—the child is not doomed to repeat the parent's mistakes or those of someone else in the parent's life.

Therapy with parents often turns into marital therapy, once the parents agree that they are displacing marital issues into arguments over parenting.

A mother and father came to therapy expressing their concern over their 10-year-old daughter's poor frustration tolerance, crying before going to bed, and unpredictable temper tantrums over changes in plans, especially when the change prevented her from getting what she had expected. The daughter was said to be eager to see someone to help her control herself, since she had seen occupational therapists help her younger brother. The parents wanted short-term, goal-oriented therapy for their daughter, because time and money were short. They had been in parent education classes and had read popular self-help books on temperament and sleep problems, but with limited results. Father had had a lot of therapy and did not want to go back for more. Mother had not been in therapy but refused it, because it would feel like an admission that the problem was more hers than her husband's.

In this case, a treatment plan was set involving alternating weekly sessions with parents and with daughter. In individual therapy, the girl was engaging, spirited, and talkative about how quick she was to blow up but how much she didn't want to. These sessions were her first chance to try to solve her problems without being entangled in her parents' conflicts, and she was soon able to reduce (though not stop) her tantruming.

Mother was like her daughter in having a short temper. She was stricter than father and got angry more quickly when the children did not cooperate. Father would criticize her, complaining in front of the children that she was too critical, and complaining privately to her that she was not supportive enough of him. With these feelings, father also withdrew sexually and emotionally from her. But his verbal focus was on how her critical ways were harmful to the children. On the mother's side, maintaining an image of their daughter as a problem child allowed her to continue to criticize her husband as insufficiently tough with their daughter and as insufficiently supportive to her. Mother frequently used psychological explanations as attacks on father, who retaliated in kind. At first, the level of despair was high and both parents threatened divorce.

The progress in the parent sessions was to achieve a shared realization of how mother and father displaced their marital conflicts into arguments over their daughter. Until this point, this realization was only a weapon the mother used when she was criticizing the father. Therefore a major portion of the work was to recreate this insight as something useful rather than as a hostile act against the father.

The sequence was to recognize how difficult the daughter could be (supporting the mother), while acknowledging how delightful the daughter could be (supporting the father). The therapist could offer this support genuinely because he had experienced the daughter in both ways. The support temporarily polarized the parents, since it painted them as more absolute in their attitudes than they were. It also made them feel guilty for the absolute pictures of themselves that were being offered, leading to some resentment toward the therapist. This put them off balance. Then the therapist could restore the balance by acknowledging the other side of each of their attitudes: the mother's appreciation for her daughter and the father's impatience with her. Each was relieved to hear the other express a more compatible attitude, and there was a glimmer of what mutual support could feel like. Repetition and examination of this cycle opened a sense of hope, even as it made the marital conflict more salient than arguments over how to parent.

Here the therapist could function as container of projected, unacknowledged interpersonal configurations of parent–child interactions which each parent was reluctant to own and was projecting onto the spouse. By experiencing those configurations in sessions with the daughter, the therapist could genuinely recognize them and contain them as they arose in parent meetings. Since the therapist could contain these projections without needing to force them onto one or the other spouse, the parents' sense of urgency to stay polarized diminished and there could be openings to a fuller range of feeling concerning the daughter and each other.

In summary, we have employed the notion of the shuttle diplomat to suggest both the potential complexity of the therapist's role and its limitations. The therapist can move beyond the inner world of the child and play a role in external interrelationships, but largely as one who clarifies and shapes the dialogue and suggests possible directions.

15

The Therapist in the Child's
Larger World

A psychoanalytic field theory approach to child treatment, such as we have developed in this book, leads to a consideration of the interaction between the therapy and the various other professional interventions that may be occurring in the child's life. Children are or may be involved with teachers, tutors, social-service caseworkers, and various others in the community. We address the negotiations the child therapist may have with other professionals in which there is a potential for splitting and disruptive conflict, as well as for integration of various points of view in the interests of the child and family. We also develop more fully the concept of the therapist as mediator or negotiator in the external and internal worlds of the child. We see the therapist's integrative function with respect to diverse aspects of the child, as well as with respect to the various people who are involved with the child, as key to her therapeutic efficacy.

CLINICAL ILLUSTRATION: EFFORT AT INTER-THERAPIST COMMUNICATION

The following case raises various common issues regarding the question of a child's therapist communicating with a parent's therapist.

A male therapist was seeing an 8-year-old boy for individual treatment. He saw the mother briefly after each individual session. The parents were separated, and the father was resistant to meeting with the therapist. The therapist talked with him on the phone occasionally, and sometimes was able to convince him to come to the clinic in person. The mother was in individual treatment at the same clinic with a female therapist. It was the child therapist's impression that the mother saw the child therapist as her ally in her battles with her estranged husband. She used much of her time with him to complain about the child's father. Often there was a flirtatious quality to her interaction with him, and there was a sense that she easily felt rejected and abandoned when the child therapist questioned her point of view about the family situation or the child. The child therapist wanted to talk with the mother's individual therapist to let her know about his impressions of how the mother was interacting with him, and to check out his sense of the meaning of this interaction, but the mother's therapist did not want to talk with him. She felt it would compromise the integrity of the individual treatment.

In this case, the mother's individual therapist's concerns seem to flow from a model in which the mother is seen as an autonomous, "grown-up" person, in charge of her own treatment. The therapist may also regard the therapeutic dyad as autonomous in the sense that events within the dyad are sufficient for understanding the mother's psychic life. One can understand that the mother's therapist would feel that it is the mother's responsibility to bring in material for her individual treatment, that the mother's sense of privacy and confidentiality might be violated by communication between the two therapists, even if her permission were requested and granted. It also seems valid to be concerned that the mother's sense of agency and responsibility for bringing in relevant material might be compromised if the material comes in from outside the therapeutic dyad.

One might also be concerned that a therapist's impulse to communicate with another family member's therapist might arise from an overflow of anxiety originating within the dyad. For example, in the above case, anxiety between child therapist and mother may be manifest in the mother's flirtatiousness and the therapist's anxiety about this behavior. On one side, one could argue that this anxiety should be handled between child therapist and mother; on the other side, one could argue that the child therapist's agenda needs to be focused on the child, and the mother's relationship with the child. To discuss transference–countertransference phenomena between mother and child therapist might be thought to violate the boundaries of this treatment.

In favor of communication between child therapist and parent's individual therapist, one could argue that given the ubiquity of unconscious phenomena there is much to be gained by sharing perspectives among the various therapists involved. There is much that occurs within the therapeutic dyad that remains unformulated (Stern 1997); it is for this reason that supervision is nearly always illuminating. A third person's perspective, simply because it is different, is likely to reveal aspects of the patient's mental functioning, and of the dyadic interaction, that neither patient nor therapist are formulating or noticing. Further, if one adopts a familial model, communication among the various therapists can also be compared to the processes in a well-functioning family in which the parents work together for the benefit of the child.

It may seem infantilizing to compare an adult patient to a child in this sense, and we believe there is potential to underestimate the autonomous capacities of the patient, especially if the attitude of the therapist is relatively authoritarian. From our point of view, however, one way in which Western individualism is manifest in our therapeutic approaches is precisely in this belief that to be "grown up" means to be autonomous, not needing to be held by a network of supportive people, and so on. It seems to us, on the contrary, that even a fully capable and autonomous adult can benefit from such networks, that a person's autonomy is in fact made possible and enhanced by the presence of such networks. In work settings, for example, it is largely the function of an organization to provide a supportive network for its members. The autonomy of even a chief executive is not compromised by the presence of a network of supportive people around him or her. Similarly, we believe that a network of therapists can be valuable for a patient conceived of as ultimately responsible for her own treatment.

In summary, there are valid arguments for and against contact and communication between a child therapist and a parent's individual therapist. If one keeps in mind the various levels of the field in which one is operating as a child therapist, one has the best basis for assessing the potential costs and benefits of communicating or not communicating with a parent's therapist.

COORDINATING WITH OTHER PROFESSIONALS

It is typical for there to be a number of professional people working with the same child or family. There may be a child therapist, a family or couple therapist, adult therapist(s), psychopharmacologists, a learning specialist, one or more teachers, an occupational therapist, a school psychologist, school administrators, and so on. In such cases, it can be helpful for there to be communication and coordination among the various workers. In complicated cases, it is beneficial if one of the workers unofficially or officially takes on the role of case manager, talking to and gathering information from the different workers and holding the various pieces of the treatment in mind.

A problematic situation arises when different mental health professionals rigidly hold divergent treatment approaches and philosophies. When a nonpsychiatrist child therapist seeks out a psychopharmacologist for a medication consultation for a child patient, there are several potential pitfalls. The pharmacologist should be someone who respects the treatment approach of the child therapist, and should be comfortable occupying an auxiliary role in the overall treatment plan. Many psychiatrists are used to being the leader of the treatment team, and may also believe that the biological level is fundamental when it comes to mental illness. When there is a crisis in which hospitalization is required, the psychiatrist is also thrown into the central role when he is the only professional with admitting privileges and with the opportunity to continue with in-hospital treatment. Keeping such situations in mind, the child therapist is well-advised to seek out pharmacologists who are therapists themselves, or who respect the process of child psychotherapy, and then to cultivate a collaborative relationship with the other professional with frequent communication and consultation back and forth.

Collaboration in such a situation is a two-way street. Not only does the child therapist need to find a pharmacologist who respects the psychotherapy and the psychotherapist, but the psychotherapist must cultivate a respect for the pharmacologist's point of view. Such mutual respect can often not be taken for granted. The child therapist has chosen to do psychotherapy because she finds the psychological level of engagement the most meaningful. Biological psychiatry, to such a therapist, may seem reductionistic and mechanistic. The pharmacologist may see the child therapist's approach as inefficient and unrealistic in its deemphasis on biochemistry and genetic factors. The stage can easily be set for polarization and confrontation. The traditional hierarchy of hospitals, as mentioned above, may further complicate the situation.

In moving toward a collaborative working relationship in such situations, systemic thinking is indispensable. On one level, the system to which we refer is the child/family as a bio-psycho-social system, in which all the part-perspectives are relevant, whatever one's own personal values and preferences in terms of intervention. On another level, the system to which we refer is the child/family/professional workers system, which is prone to all the dysfunctional developments of any work group (Bion 1961). In the Kleinian tradition, growing out of work at the Tavistock clinic in England and the A. K. Rice Institute in the United States, there is a body of work that deals with the anxieties aroused in groups, and the defenses invoked at the group level to manage anxiety (see Menzies 1975 for an illustrative analysis of a nursing service in a hospital). When a child is having trouble, there are a multitude of potential anxieties. Starting with the parents, there may be anxieties about being inadequate as parents, and about their fantasied and actual destructiveness and aggression toward the child that may be thought, unconsciously, to have resulted in the child's impairment or dysfunction. There may be anxieties deriving from the parents' own personal histories of trauma or deprivation. There may be anxiety-laden identifications with the child, or with the parents' own parents. There may be anxiety about the child's aggression toward the parents. Therapists bring their own anxieties about being destructive and/or inadequate, leading to a need to feel successful therapeutically.

In the projective-introjective field that evolves around the therapeutic enterprise, the anxieties of the various people involved get bandied about (transferred from person to person as if contagious) and intensified. For example, in an effort not to feel guilty and inadequate themselves, parents may blame the therapist for a child's failure to improve. The therapist may end up feeling guilty and inadequate. An ability to step back and see the big picture is essential, if one wishes to avoid getting unreflectively sucked into the vortex of the group dynamics. As an extension of the last example, when a child therapist and a psychiatrist engage in a polarized struggle for control of a treatment, one can look at the struggle as representing an effort on the part of both professionals to externalize the sense of ineffectiveness that threatens both of them. The need to feel effective may inhere in both professionals as individuals, but it may be intensified as both professionals pick up the anxiety of the parents about their child's dysfunction, and their desperate need to see some improvement. Feeling this anxiety can be useful to the professionals if they can thereby get an experiential sense of the desperation felt by the parents. Such a productive use of one's experience depends on being able to "hold" (Slochower 1996) or "contain" (Bion 1967) the anxiety long enough to think about it. When defensive mechanisms such as externalization or projective identification are invoked unreflectively, the capacity to think is compromised and an impulsive, thoughtless group dynamic arises.

Some of these group dynamics, as well as a successful effort at thinking about the underlying anxieties, are illustrated in the following case.

> Dr. C was treating Michael, a 6-year-old boy with severe separation anxiety and phobias. His mother was an extremely anxious woman who frequently called the child therapist with worries about the school and other situations in the child's life. At the same time, she tended to bring him late to sessions or to cancel the sessions at the last minute. She often cancelled appointments set up to discuss worries that she had brought up with the child therapist over the phone. Her husband was emotionally distant and worked very long hours, traveling frequently for business. Michael's mother saw a psychiatrist, who prescribed a minor tranquilizer. The child therapist felt unsure that he could offer a supportive enough environment to

contain the anxiety of Michael's mother, so he called the mother's psychiatrist to talk about her needs for anxiety-containment, and about who might be best suited to perform this function for the mother. The psychiatrist said that he thought the mother was quite infantile and that she needed limit-setting more than an opportunity to spill over further with her anxieties.

In this case, perhaps it is useful to conceive of the various relationships, in the family as well as among the professionals, as organized in a common way. That is, one has an overwhelmed, anxious person, encountering a distant, unresponsive person. This pattern is self-perpetuating as the first person's anxiety, and the second person's withdrawal, reinforce each other. The relationship between Michael's father and mother is certainly organized this way. The child therapist gets drawn into the pattern as the mother turns to him for anxiety-containment. He, in turn, gets overwhelmed, and turns to the mother's psychiatrist, who tries to withdraw by setting limits.

The child therapist eventually tried to meet more frequently with the father, offering him support with the hope that he would be able to be more available to his wife. This approach met with some limited success. The child therapist, being in supervision, had a source of support that facilitated his being able to attain a degree of perspective on the way in which anxiety was being dysfunctionally managed in this system that involved both family and professionals.[1]

This case highlights how systemic dynamics, including individual psychodynamics, can be so powerful that they can envelop not only the family but the helping professionals who, by intervening, become part of the system themselves. In this case, Michael's therapist performed the function of a case manager. That function includes, most crucially, keeping an eye on these systemic dynamics, alerting the various participants to what is evolving, and formulating interventions to interrupt disruptive patterns. In contrast, when there are several therapists involved, each therapist's understanding of the child and family is based

---

1. One might speculate that Michael's mother's internal world is organized in a way similar to the pattern observed in the external system—that is, one might postulate a needy, anxious part of herself, in interaction with a judgmental, condemning part of herself that tends to get externalized.

primarily, if not solely, on what occurs in that therapist's office, and on the descriptions that family members provide of themselves and each other. A therapist's office constitutes a very specific context in which to reveal oneself, and the nature of the relationship with the particular therapist will influence the feelings and behaviors of the child and family. The case manager functions not only as a coordinator, but also as a repository for information about the child's and family's functioning in a variety of contexts, and for the various perspectives held on the child and family by a range of people (Ochroch 1983). This case also highlights the function of supervision in supporting the person who needs to contain such a high level of anxiety, as in this group of people.

COMMUNICATION AMONG THERAPISTS WHEN A PARENT IS IN INDIVIDUAL TREATMENT

Although our own approach is relational and systemic, we believe that there are times when it may be appropriate to limit one's involvement with parents to information gathering and occasional suggestions on parenting issues. One such occasion occurs when a parent is in a pre-existing individual treatment and the parent's therapist makes a referral of the child based on what she is hearing from the parent. Collateral meetings between a parent and child therapist may then result in a parent's becoming curious or concerned enough about herself to bring these concerns into her individual treatment. Nonetheless, in such cases, we believe that it can sometimes be helpful or even crucial that all therapists be in communication with each other to provide a coordinated and integrated approach to the various participants at the individual and family systemic levels. There are times when the failure of such communication can threaten to create therapeutic impasses. The decision to attempt such communication is a complex one, however. Considerations regarding boundaries and privacy must be weighed against the potential advantages.

BETWEEN THE FAMILY AND THE SCHOOL

In many instances, the therapist can be in a position to facilitate greater interest, attention, understanding, and willingness to help on the part of various school personnel. Sometimes such help can be essential for the child to overcome social and academic obstacles in her school experience. But the therapist's role can be difficult. School personnel may look to the therapist for definite answers that the therapist assuredly does not have, or school personnel may have questions pertaining to material that the therapist either believes must be kept confidential or is under great constraint to do so from the child.

The therapist may find it necessary to remind educators or other professionals of the restraints or limitations placed on him by virtue of the special role of the therapist in relation to the child. On the other hand, parents are sometimes very reluctant to allow any contact between the therapist and the school, and on occasion for good reason. This is something the therapist has to evaluate on an individual basis to decide if in his opinion such contact is likely to help the child and the treatment process or create unnecessary problems for the child.

In instances where the therapist thinks such contact is warranted, it may require extended reassurances and persuasion of the parent. Occasionally parents will resist such contact out of the belief that it is best for the therapist to come to know the child independently, uninfluenced by the opinions (often anticipated as bad) that others may have of their child. Here too the therapist faces the task of helping the parents see that he is not going to form an opinion solely on the basis of what others say, but that the therapist's work can only be enhanced by more knowledge and contact, including learning about what might well be erroneous views of their child. Once the parents develop a sense that the therapist is truly an independent voice and advocate for their child, then they will often relax their vigilance regarding such contact.

In the case of one particular child who had been in three different school systems over a short period of time, her mother wanted her to start off with a "clean slate" in the new system, and therefore did not want any contact between the therapist and the school. The therapist did manage to convince the parent that the child would bring her "old slate" into the new school setting, but unfortunately too late to avert a kind of trouble that developed between the child and other children that school personnel might have averted had they been given advance warning of the potential problems.

When the therapist talks to, or receives information from, learning specialists and, especially, teachers, she has the opportunity to see the child and family in far more complex, multifaceted ways, as in the following case.

A 10-year-old boy, Fred, was referred by his parents' couple therapist when the private school he attended suggested that he not return the next year. The parents felt that the school had scapegoated Fred, whose behavioral problems, in their view, were minor. The parents withheld permission from the child therapist to talk with the school, preferring that he develop his own impression of Fred before being exposed to the "biased" views of the school. Over the next few months the therapist met once weekly with Fred, as he began to attend a new school. Fred's behavior in sessions seemed quite disorganized. For several sessions play with puppets did not crystallize around any theme or coherent narrative. This would give way to competitive games, then lethargic inactivity. The therapist's attempts to talk about Fred's outside life were met with one-word responses or silence. The parents' descriptions of what Fred was like in school or at home were quite vague.

Eventually, the child therapist told the parents that, in order to help their child succeed in his new school, the therapist would need to be in touch with the teacher. He said that knowing where the problem spots were in school would help the therapist discuss them with Fred. The parents gave their permission, and the therapist got a much more clear and differentiated, nuanced picture of what was occurring in school. For example, the therapist learned that when Fred got frustrated because other children would not include him, or do what he wanted, he would stomp off in a rage and then sulk for an hour or more. The teacher's attempts to help Fred think of constructive ways to handle the situation were rejected angrily. These incidents occurred on at least a daily basis. The teacher also said that Fred had made friends with one boy, Eli, but that when Eli said one day that he and Fred were best friends, Fred had angrily denied that this was the case, and had begun to tease and reject Eli. The teacher commented that Fred seemed always to need somebody to tease.

The teacher appeared quite frustrated with Fred, feeling an urgent need for guidance from the therapist. The teacher mentioned that when kids were angry in her class, she encouraged them to fill out a "complaint form" that she would read and discuss with the child. Fred would reject complaint forms that he was in a rage. The therapist said he thought the complaint form was a wonderful idea, just the right thing for Fred if he could be encouraged to use it. He suggested that she talk to Fred in a calm moment, telling him that since he was too angry to fill out the complaint form in the heat of the angry moment, she would, from now on, offer him the form some time after an explosion, when he was beginning to recover. The teacher liked that idea. The therapist felt that the specific idea he had offered was less important for the teacher than the opportunity to share her frustration over Fred with another person who worked with him (the therapist felt similarly glad to have someone else to talk with about Fred). The therapist and teacher resolved to touch base regularly.

Prior to talking with the teacher, the therapist had informed Fred that he was going to do so. Fred had shrugged. After talking with the teacher, the therapist mentioned that he had done so. Fred was eager to hear what the teacher had said. The therapist mentioned that Fred seemed to get very angry and frustrated sometimes. Fred responded with a bitter denunciation of his teacher for scapegoating him, with details about ways in which he felt that she was noticing only what he did wrong, not what other kids did to provoke him. The therapist mentioned that Fred could write about his frustration in a complaint form, and Fred complained that the teacher never gave him one. The therapist responded that he had talked with the teacher about giving Fred a complaint form after Fred had calmed down a bit, and Fred said he thought that might be a good idea. In the next session, the therapist said he heard that Fred was having trouble with Eli. Fred complained that Eli tried to tell him what to do. It became clear that Fred experienced Eli's saying that they were best friends as Eli's trying to limit Fred's freedom. What if he didn't want to play with Eli? Eli always wanted to play games his way; he never listened to Fred. At this point, Fred said he did not like it that the therapist talked with his teacher. He began to sulk. When the therapist asked him to speak about what he felt, he muttered: "Private therapy."

There are many therapists who might agree with Fred that the boundaries of his "private therapy" had been broken as the therapist brought in information obtained from his teacher. Any therapist who believes that his job is to elicit and interpret the child's unconscious fantasy life is likely to view this use of collateral information as irrelevant at best, intrusive at worst. A therapist who emphasizes the importance of a supportive child–therapist relationship, or values the therapeutic space as an intersubjective, "potential" space (Winnicott 1971a), might also want to protect its boundaries, to help the child feel that the therapeutic space is safe and protected from the tumult taking place in the outside world.

This particular therapist was sympathetic to both these perspectives, but up to a point. He wanted to help the child succeed in his new school, and felt that it was an important part of his job to offer support to the teacher. He was also uncomfortable waiting for Fred to reveal the nature of his conflicts and anxieties in the sessions, especially since there seemed a real likelihood that Fred could have a demoralizing and unsuccessful experience in yet another school, and this was only a once-weekly treatment. The therapist also wondered about the extent to which Fred's claiming his right to a "private" therapy might also express his wish to avoid the anxiety associated with facing his difficulties in school in the presence of the therapist.

Most importantly, however, the interaction around the therapist's use of collateral information seemed to replicate some of the problematic interpersonal patterns that the therapist now knew existed in school as well. For example, Fred was feeling that the therapist was taking over control of the situation as he felt Eli did in school. If the therapist were to dig in and insist on bringing in material from the school, he would be joining in an enactment of this interpersonal pattern. It seemed important to point out to Fred that he was feeling that the therapist was trying to control him, and, further, to offer to seek out a collaborative solution to their impasse. In working out the following resolution, the therapist seemed to be seeking a balance among competing considerations all of which seemed valid, for instance, taking an interventionist approach about the child's school problems, and taking a more receptive stance with the child.

> In the next session, the therapist told Fred that he did not want to impose any way of working on Fred against his wishes. He wanted to respect Fred's wish for private therapy, but he also wanted to help Fred have a good experience in school. He suggested they find a compromise solution. Fred said he would tell the therapist when he had a problem in school. The therapist said that was a great idea, but that it would also help him to have the teacher's point of view. Perhaps he could talk with the teacher, but not bring up with Fred what the teacher had said unless Fred wanted to hear. Fred liked this idea. The problem seemed resolved (for the moment!).

Aside from illustrating the advantages of teacher–therapist collaboration, this vignette shows the way in which all such interventions get caught up in the transference–countertransference field. Attention to this field is always primary, in our view. The best-intentioned and planned-for interventions will founder in the absence of the therapist's ongoing efforts to become aware of continually evolving developments in the transference–countertransference domain.

Also demonstrated is the way in which the therapist might seek to strike a balance between a relatively more or relatively less interventionist treatment approach. Talking with the teacher allowed the therapist to intervene in the classroom life of his patient, but the transference complications of doing so led him to pull back, at least temporarily, from such efforts.

This vignette illustrates, as well, how communication and intervention with teachers and other school personnel most often takes place on the phone in relatively short conversations for economy of time and effort. Obviously, from a strictly clinical point of view, it would be better to have frequent meetings, face to face. The complexities of the teacher's task in dealing with a difficult child would ideally be addressed in depth and at length. School visits, in which the therapist could see the child first hand, talking with the teacher in the same visit, would have many advantages. Such visits are rarely practical. As is so often the case in child work, then, the therapist does her best under less than optimal circumstances.

In those cases in which a school visit is feasible, the therapist needs to inquire as to how the child feels about the therapist visiting his classroom. The child, especially younger children, may be quite enthusiastic (younger children often invite the therapist to visit them at home, as well). Older children may feel exposed, even humiliated, during such a visit, and they may object that a school visit is bound to expose the fact that they are in therapy. In such cases, a visit may be contraindicated. Even when a visit is indicated, it is advisable to discuss with the child in advance what will happen, why the therapist is visiting, how the therapist will be introduced, and so on. The child's input about these matters should be solicited.

BETWEEN THERAPIST AND CHILD WELFARE

When child abuse or neglect seems like a real possibility in the life of a child, child welfare personnel provide an essential service. They have investigative capabilities, power to remove a child from a damaging situation, and treatment resources that are not possessed by a child therapist or child therapy clinic. Many, if not most, child therapists cringe when they have to call in child welfare, however. There are several reasons. The child therapist calling in child welfare feels herself caught between concern and anxiety for the child's safety, and anxiety about being perceived by the parents as persecutory and punitive, perhaps to a point that destroys the treatment alliance. Some child therapists feel that their autonomy is infringed upon by state laws that require that child therapists report "suspicions" of child abuse or neglect, not only documented cases. The legal requirement, with threats of liability in case of noncompliance, can set up a polarized, adversarial relationship between therapist and child welfare officials. Feeling coerced, with his autonomy threatened, the therapist might take an oppositional position with respect to the reporting requirement. Therapist grandiosity might lead him to believe that he, alone, can manage the abuse or neglect potential in a family. Additionally, a therapist might well feel that he is risking his alliance with the patient, possibly destroying a valuable treatment, or that an overworked and poorly trained child welfare worker might do an inadequate investigation in an intrusive, insensitive way. These concerns are sometimes quite justified. Recent reports in the media have demonstrated how overburdened child welfare authorities are in many areas.

Nonetheless, there are several dangers involved in not reporting when there is real suspicion on the therapist's part. Child therapists and clinics, in fact, do not possess the capacity to do a thorough investigation of child abuse and neglect, and go far beyond a therapeutic function if they try to take on themselves the task of doing so. Child welfare authorities are the only people with the authority to go to court to make alternative living arrangements for children, and to require that parents enter treatment programs. These measures are sometimes necessary.

There are powerful transference–countertransference feelings in play when a therapist considers a child welfare report. The therapist who hesitates to call in child welfare, in "protecting" the treatment alliance, may be minimizing her own anger at a possibly abusive or neglectful parent, and avoiding the parents' rage at being confronted in this way by the therapist. Alternatively, a premature report could manifest an impulsive, rageful, or panicky reaction on the part of the therapist. More than any other clinical situation, cases of suspected abuse and neglect require consultation with colleagues and/or supervisors to manage and keep in perspective the feelings that get called into play. As in all clinical situations, there are transference–countertransference themes that tend to subsume both patient and therapist, shaping the meaning of actions taken by both participants. Thus, the therapist tends to feel caught between the Scylla of "abusing" the patient by calling in child welfare, and "neglecting" the patient by failing to do so. The patient may feel persecuted and abused by a child welfare report, but also taken seriously and protected. In the anxiety-laden, often chaotic days in the midst of which a child welfare report is considered or made, it is extremely difficult and important to recognize and sort out these feelings.

Once child welfare has entered the picture, there is a great potential for splitting and fragmentation between therapist and caseworker (and any other workers involved). The caseworker might become the "bad," that is, intrusive, punitive one, against whom the parent seeks an alliance with the therapist. The therapist may be tempted to join the parent in hatred or disdain for an insensitive or incompetent caseworker. Or, if the caseworker is more sympathetic to the parent, caseworker and parent may ally themselves against the therapist, seen as having overreacted. Or, caseworker and parent may join to scapegoat the child, seen as victimizing the parent. Or, therapist and parent may join to see the child as victimizer, while the caseworker takes a critical attitude toward the parent. Any of these patterns of splitting become self-perpetuating, as anyone whose feelings are unrecognized gets dug in to his or her position. These considerations once again highlight how coordination between the child therapist and other professionals, in this case the caseworker, is of the utmost importance.

This coordination can begin from the moment a child welfare report is filed. The therapist can make sure to ask the "hotline" worker to note that the therapist wants to be contacted by the caseworker before a home visit is made. Frequent contact thereafter, in which the therapist listens respectfully to the caseworker's point of view while offering her own, helps foster a collaborative attitude. When collaboration seems impossible, it may help to talk with the caseworker's supervisor. When parents are enraged with the caseworker, the therapist may be able to resonate with the parents' feelings without fueling them further, if the therapist has an independent relationship with the caseworker. The therapist is thus in a position to contain the various feelings and concerns that can otherwise get "split" up between the various people, creating antagonistic attitudes. Such an independent relationship with the caseworker also helps avoid an alliance between parent and caseworker against the therapist.

Following is a case example from Altman (1995) that illustrates a specific transference–countertransference constellation in which therapist, caseworker, and parent were all involved.

> Josephine was referred to a mental health clinic by a child abuse prevention program. She had hit her child on at least one occasion, leaving a bruise that had been noted by her son's school. The school made a report to the local child welfare agency, which referred her to a child abuse prevention program, the mission of which was to keep families together, to prevent placement of the children. One goal was to save money on foster care and other forms of residential placement. In order to accomplish this goal, child abuse prevention workers were available twenty-four hours a day to intervene in whatever way was necessary to prevent further child abuse.

Josephine had been raised by her mother as an only child. She did not know her father. Her mother had many boyfriends, with whom she was preoccupied, so that Josephine felt quite neglected. At age 14, Josephine become pregnant with her son. She and her mother got into severe conflict over her decision to have this baby, and Josephine ended up leaving home and going to live with the father of the baby. He became physically abusive to Josephine, and she left him at age 16, getting her own apartment with her son while being supported by an older man with whom she had entered a relationship.

Josephine missed several appointments when she first began treatment. As was required by the clinic's agreement with the child abuse prevention project, the therapist informed the worker, who began accompanying Josephine to her therapy appointments. After several such accompanied visits, Josephine began coming to appointments on her own. She came, at first, with her son. She used the time, however, almost exclusively to talk about her own life, about how she had no support from her mother, and about difficulties she was having with her boyfriend, the older man, who seemed to have quite a bit of money. She talked of feeling enraged with her son when he demanded attention at times when she felt unsupported by her mother and boyfriend. She had abused her son on an occasion when her boyfriend had not called her for a few days. Josephine missed about half of our sessions, but always responded to a phone call. Her therapist felt no need to involve the child abuse prevention worker again. After a while, she stopped bringing her son. She was able to discipline him without physical means, and she seemed to be moving forward in her life. She had gotten a job and felt quite proud of herself.

After seeing Josephine for about a year, having decided to leave the clinic and go into full-time private practice, the therapist was in the anguished position of having to tell her that he would be leaving her and their work. He told Josephine about his departure in a session two months before he was planning to leave. She said she understood; she thought that he was moving ahead in his life, as she was in hers. Josephine, however, did not show up for her next several sessions, and she did not respond to the therapist's phone calls. Eventually, it seemed that he would not even have the opportunity to say good-bye to her. At this point the therapist decided to inform the child abuse prevention worker that he was leaving and that Josephine had missed her last few therapy appointments. He asked the worker to encourage Josephine to come to the clinic to say good-bye and to inform her of arrangements to be transferred to another therapist.

On his last day of seeing patients in the clinic, Josephine arrived, accompanied by the child abuse prevention worker and her son. Her son had a large bruise on the side of his face. Before seeing Josephine, the therapist asked the worker if she had reported this new incident of abuse. She said no, that she saw no need to report it, since Josephine had generally been doing so well. He felt very uneasy, however, since he was required by law to report the incident if it had not already been reported. The child abuse prevention worker refused to report it, and so in his last session with Josephine the therapist had to tell her that he was going to report the bruise on her son's face. She was furious with him and said that she had just gotten her life together and that this incident would set her back. She would have home visits again, people looking over her shoulder, and perhaps she would even lose her son. The therapist tried to talk about the recurrence of her abusive behavior toward her son in terms of the impact on her of his abandoning her by leaving the clinic. Josephine sat sullen, not speaking. In this way, they said good-bye.

In retrospect, the therapist believed that Josephine saw the child abuse prevention worker and him as a team, as an attentive, caring mother, preoccupied with her and protective of her. Her son represented both his father, who had abused Josephine, and her own needy self, in relation to which she took a violently repressive attitude. In relation to her son, she enacted her identification with her own abusers. At first, Josephine thrived with the attention the therapy team was paying her. When the therapist told her he would be terminating the treatment, she reacted at first by mobilizing an independent, self-reliant, non-needy side of herself. Staying away from therapy for weeks thereafter both expressed and defended against the arousal of rage against the therapist as an abandoning object. In this context, when he pressed Josephine to come for a final session and called in the child abuse prevention worker, he became a persecutory object. The alternative, which seemed even less desirable, was to leave without processing the termination with Josephine at all. Despite his knowledge that he would be perceived as intrusive and persecutory, he was stunned to see the bruise on her son's face—a concrete sign of her rage at him and her own deprived, abandoned self. The therapist reported that he felt the pain more acutely, in some ways, than he would have if his own face had been punched. It was as if Josephine were showing him what she felt he was doing to her in leaving her. The child abuse prevention worker, knowing that she had been drawn into the force field between Josephine and the therapist, refused to be drawn in further by calling the child welfare authorities. She may have had other reasons for not wanting to call: further child abuse in one of her families might have seemed like evidence of a failure on her part to her superiors. A final consideration was that, by hitting her son, Josephine may have been trying to mobilize further care from the child abuse prevention worker, who had largely withdrawn from the case. [pp. 24–26]

When the family has gotten involved with child protective services or other similar agencies, the therapist may be experienced as simply another authority who is a potential threat to the integrity of the family unit. Under such circumstances the therapist may have to work very hard to establish any sense of separateness and any sense of trust. Within limits, the therapist's task may be to draw a line of privacy around the family and the therapist or the therapeutic relationship.

The children in a particular family had been put in foster care for several months, following several reports of child abuse. It appeared that the allegations of abuse were inaccurate, and that the intervention of removing the children from the family had a damaging effect on the children and on the relationship between the parents and the children. At the time of the referral, the parents were involved in two legal actions: first, to regain full custody of their children, and second, to sue the municipal authorities for the damages caused by their intervention. The parents' motivation for seeking therapy was complex, to say the least. The parents and children were both tired of being investigated and probed by professionals. They also had a clear stake in getting a clean bill of health from the clinicians. Thus they were seeing a therapist from whom they wanted validation, but whom they also did not trust. To complicate the picture further, in the therapist's view, the parents, while perhaps not being sufficiently neglectful to warrant the removal of the children, nevertheless were often lax and inattentive in their parenting. Thus a clinical intervention, to be thorough and effective, required that the therapist confront these issues with the parents, including a pattern of excessive drinking.

The therapist strove to address the reality of the parents' mixed motivations for seeking therapy, including their understandable mistrust, while at the same time identifying as one of the treatment goals re-establishing a boundary of privacy around the family. The therapist, while sharing some common responsibilities with the protective services workers, also separated himself from them as advocate and protector of the family's privacy.

Once the therapist chooses to move beyond the more clearly defined and potentially limited role of therapist to the child only, and is willing to accept responsibility for intervening in the larger systems of which the child is a part, the task becomes exponentially more complex, and there are no consistent and certain guidelines about how and when to limit one's role. These are largely individual, case-by-case decisions dictated by questions of not only what will be therapeutic for the child, but also what is comfortably within the resources of the therapist to do. It is crucial that the therapist not overestimate his ability to effect complex systems, or the personal time and energy needed to do so. What a therapist might contemplate doing in the context of a clinic or a day treatment setting, for example, would be quite different from what that same therapist could realistically take on as a private practitioner.

Before concluding this section on child abuse and neglect, and the interface with child welfare workers, it should be mentioned that reports to child welfare authorities are very rarely made on middle-class-and-up families. This fact is independent of what appears to be a higher incidence of child abuse in lower socioeconomic-status families (Barnett et al. 1993, Barth 1998, Wilson and Saft 1993). We are confronted here with an interaction between social class and countertransference that results in lower-class people being given more severe diagnoses, and more restrictive treatments (Hollingshead and Redlich 1958), as well as more frequently being seen as abusive and neglectful of their children. As has been pointed out (Fernando 1995), many mental health professionals are as biased against lower-class and racially/ethnically non-mainstream people as anyone else in our society. The therapist may be more inclined to disbelief that a middle-class parent is abusing his child, or may be more likely to develop a dissociative response to evidence of abuse, than would be the case with a lower-class parent. There may also well be a greater readiness to turn a lower-class parent over to the public authorities (as there is a greater readiness to send a lower-class person to jail) than there is in the case of a middle-class parent. Given these considerations, one should not dismiss as purely defensive the sense of persecution experienced by a parent of lower socioeconomic status who is being reported to child welfare.

MONEY AND MANAGED CARE

As in the case of child welfare, managed care has taken a legitimate concern (cost control and cost effectiveness) and created a polarized, adversarial relationship with therapists by setting up a bureaucracy with a one-dimensional mission, to save money. The situation is made worse, however, because for-profit managed-care companies have a serious conflict of interest. On one hand, they are responsible to patients to provide medical and mental health care. On the other hand, they are responsible for delivering the highest possible returns to their shareholders. Thus, in the position of rationing health care, managed-care personnel have a significant interest in denying approval for care whenever possible, without unduly alienating their clients or exposing themselves to legal liability.

Therapists, faced with this situation, may adopt an ideology such as a belief in short-term treatment approaches that promotes a rapprochement with managed care. Otherwise, they may find themselves in an extended war of attrition with managed-care companies, filling out forms and arguing with clerks on the phone trying to get more sessions for their patients as long as they have the patience to do so. The situation is not dissimilar to that which occurs in mental health clinics, in which one group of people, the administrators, think only about documentation and cost-control, while another group, the clinicians, think only about non-administrative treatment issues (Altman 1995). The stage is set for conflict and polarization as one group tries to extract more money from the treatment process while saving on costs, while the other protests the infringements on their autonomy as therapists. In private practice, when the patient is solely responsible for the fee, the therapist must integrate money issues with the rest of the treatment. Money becomes a central issue in the transference/countertransference. When managed care enters the scene, the managed-care company takes over the function of watching the money. As the patient disowns this function, and the therapist is forced into a helpless, adversarial position, the transference–countertransference field is powerfully shaped while the room for therapeutic action around these issues is restricted.

Thirteen-year-old John was referred to Dr. B because of severe anxiety around social contacts, which restricted his development of peer relationships and his ability to engage in after-school activities. He also had episodic severe tantrums at home, crying, screaming, and throwing things. These incidents usually began with an escalating power struggle over doing homework or chores. The incidents often ended with mother saying she could not take the stress of John's tantrums. On more than one occasion, she had said that her health would suffer if she did not remove herself from John and go to sleep. John's father would be left to calm John down, to the point where he could go to sleep. John's father, when he felt overwhelmed, had once said that John was going to give him a heart attack.

Dr. B began meeting with John and his parents to discuss the incidents. In the office, everybody could talk calmly about his or her feelings and listen to each other. For example, at one point John said to Dr. B, "You know how it is when you just have to cry?" John seemed to be saying that there were times when he felt an almost physical need to cry, out of any particular emotionally charged context. He said that he might provoke a confrontation with his parents at such times to stimulate a catharsis. In a subsequent session, John's mother, who had previously been very angry at what seemed like willfully provocative behavior, said that she had been very moved to hear John describe his experience in this way. She said she had never felt the kind of physical and emotional tension that John described, and that she had begun to understand him in a new way. Further, Dr. B suggested to the parents that it must make John feel very anxious and guilty when his parents suggested that they might not survive having to deal with him. Perhaps at times he was driven to find out just how destructive he actually was, by going one step further with his tantrums. The therapist suggested that the parents do whatever they could think of, short of physical force, to get John into his room when he was having a tantrum, telling him that he could only come out when he could talk about what was bothering him.

Despite these very productive family sessions, John continued to have tantrums, though less frequently. He also continued to resist going out with peers after school or enrolling in after-school activities. Dr. B suggested that, to the extent that there was a depressive condition, medication might help John be less irritable and agitated at times, and make him less fearful of social situations. The parents were hesitant, but willing to have a psychiatric consultation.

By this time, the ten sessions initially authorized by the family's managed-care company had been used. Dr. B applied for ten more sessions; the company responded that since the symptoms were persisting, a consultation for medication was indicated. Dr. B told the benefits manager with whom he spoke that the psychiatric consultation was being arranged, but that he recommended continued family sessions even if the medication were effective. He said that the resistance to social activities was quite entrenched and unlikely to respond to medication, and that the family needed help changing their patterns of interaction even if John's behavior changed. The managed-care company eventually allocated three more family sessions, following which they withdrew their support of the psychotherapy.

In the last of the three family sessions allowed by the managed-care company, the father expressed a cynical acceptance of the cut-off of funding: "The bottom line is shareholder value," that is, the managed-care company was putting profits first. Dr. B, who had been quite furious at the managed-care company, nodded assent. But then John's mother asked whether Dr. B would continue to see the family at a reduced fee, and Dr. B suddenly realized that he was resisting putting his own financial self-interest on a lower priority. As he contemplated asking the family how much they were prepared to pay, he realized that financial self-interest as a driving force was not at all restricted solely to the managed-care company. Dr. B then thought that his anger at the managed-care company had partly to do with the power they had simply to stop paying. Dr. B felt he could not act unconflictedly; he wanted to continue the treatment, he felt a responsibility to do so, yet he did not want to work for the lower fee the family was suggesting. The family also wanted to continue the treatment, but they did not want to pay the therapist's full fee out of pocket. Finally, Dr. B said something like: "You know, we are all very angry at the insurance company, but as we begin to talk about how we can continue I realize that none of us is immune to wanting to put our own bottom line first."

The father asked Dr. B what he meant. Dr. B said, "As we begin to discuss a specific fee at which we'll all feel more or less comfortable continuing, we're all going to be juggling various considerations, and one of them is going to be our own financial self-interest." John's mother turned to her husband and said, "Why don't we just pay Dr. B's fee and see how it goes." Dr. B was tempted at that moment to inquire into how the mother had come to give up arguing for her own interest, but knowing that he sometimes gave in too easily himself, he considered desisting and saying nothing. John's father assented somewhat grudgingly, with the proviso that they would talk about the matter again if the family felt too pressured. But then Dr. B said: "I have no problem with accepting my full fee, of course, and perhaps I will eventually ask you to pay it. But I'm curious about how you (John's mother) came to decide to offer to pay my full fee at that moment. I was wondering if you might have been worried about the survivability of our relationship if you did not give in then, just as John might worry about how much harm you, or the relationship, might suffer when he makes a fuss."

This case illustrates how the advocacy or abandonment of self-interest, greed, reaction formations against greed, and so on, all get activated when fees are discussed in psychotherapy. These are far from peripheral issues in a therapy. In this particular case, Dr. B found a way to suggest a link between the financial negotiations and the issues that had been discussed between John and his family.

Fee-setting raises many complex issues for the child therapist. Some therapists simply state their fee (in the initial phone call, or in the first visit), and let the parents go elsewhere if the fee is too high. This policy comes easily when one has a full practice and a steady stream of referrals. Most often, the therapist would like to get her highest fee, but would not forego a somewhat lowered fee. Some therapists state a fee range; if the parents ask for a fee lower than the therapist's highest or standard fee, such therapists often ask for details about the family's financial situation to justify the lowered fee. Some therapists charge more for child patients than for adult patients because children often are away at camp for two or more months in the summer, and because of the extra time spent on the phone with teachers and other professionals. Other therapists charge for the time spent on such calls. There is also a range of policies on cancellations, from charging for all appointments except when the therapist can schedule another patient during the same hour, to not charging when a certain amount of notice is given. When the fee is negotiated, and policies about cancellations stated, there is often quite a bit of awkwardness and discomfort. Therapists, generally speaking, like to see themselves as helpers rather than as self-interested entrepreneurs. The fact is that we are both, and fee-setting along with other financial arrangements requires us to be clear about that fact, first and foremost in our own minds. Setting a relatively low fee may allow one to feel generous, not greedy, for the moment. Later, if the therapist feels resentful about the low fee, no one benefits. If the fee is set too high, the family's resentment may also create complications. There are no clear guidelines about what is the right fee, and the therapist must struggle with a wide range of feelings in setting and implementing a fee policy.

16

Therapeutic Action

RELATIONAL VIEW OF DEVELOPMENT

Our relational point of view has led us to rethink our notions of the developmental process, the nature of psychopathology, the role of parent work in the treatment of children, the larger question of "Who is the patient?" and, finally, the question of therapeutic action. In this concluding chapter, we sum up the implications of our perspective in these key areas. Consider first the concept of development. Thinking relationally, child development must be seen in an interpersonal and sociocultural context. These contexts, or levels of analysis, are all interrelated. For example, following Erikson, we would argue that theories of development reflect the nature of the culture of which they form an important part. An individualistic culture produces theories of development that take the individual child as the unit of analysis. We speak of *child* development. Independent, or individual, status is both an assumption of the model, and its privileged goal, its definition of maturity (Mahler et al. 1975). To the extent that a model of development is biased in a one-person direction, it tends to highlight, to emphasize, those aspects of development that lead from dependence to independence. From our point of view, such a theory of development is not wrong, only biased in its own way, as all theories must be biased in one way or another so as to bring to light a set of phenomena. By point of cultural contrast, the communal Japanese culture tends to see children as developing from an isolated state to a more socially integrated one. Even within our own culture, we have the contrasting view of the child as initially self-centered and selfish, needing to be socialized. Nonetheless, socialization is thought to be internalized, carried within in the form of the superego of an autonomous person.

As relationalists, our effort is to emphasize the connections between people without losing sight of the individual. Thus, the developmental model we have offered includes the notion of "parent development" to supplement "child development." Without losing sight of the way children move from relatively dependent to relatively independent states, we would add that this move can also be seen as a move from one form of relatedness between parents and children to another form of relatedness. We would emphasize that the relatively independent child or adolescent is not necessarily, by virtue of his independence, less involved with his family. Many parents of adolescents have had to learn that the American adolescent who turns up her nose at family activities is not only creating an intense form of relationship with her family, but still needs her family, albeit in a possibly new and different way. At that point she may, in fact, need her parents to try to find a way to support her in her efforts to let go. This commonplace example illustrates the ambiguity of dependence and independence—how you can't really have one without the other—and how mutually influential the parents and daughter are upon one another. The daughter's efforts to push away her parents may stimulate her parents to try to hold on to her, but their efforts to hold on to her may stimulate her to push away. In one way the daughter needs her parents less, but in another way she needs them more, specifically to accept her new level of autonomy. We aim to take account of these interactive processes in our model of the therapeutic process and in our therapeutic work.

Putting developmental theory in a cultural context leads us to move away from linear views of development with absolute criteria of maturity. Knowing that criteria of maturity are culturally specific does not mean that we can avoid making value judgments on that basis, but we can be aware that our value judgments are culturally specific and thus revisable. Since linear developmental models (for example, one that posits a linear move from dependence to independence) entail one-dimensional value judgments, we prefer nonlinear models (such as the Kleinian model built around positions rather than stages) that allow for more flexible notions of maturity. Our effort is to retain a notion of sequential development without ignoring context, without devaluing earlier stages, and without assuming that they must be given up in favor of privileged later stages.

THE NATURE OF PSYCHOPATHOLOGY

New notions of development and maturity necessitate rethinking our conceptions of psychopathology and health. Linear conceptions of development make it easy to know what is sick and what is healthy, since these concepts can map simply onto the continuum from the primitive to the mature, which tends to coincide with a continuum from the maladaptive to the adaptive in terms of functionality. Nonlinear schemas of development require more complex notions of maturity. Flexible access to different levels of functioning recommends itself as one new criterion of maturity or health for individuals seen as developing in nonlinear fashion. From this point of view, rigidity may be seen as an essence of pathology. In terms of Kleinian theory, one might speak in this connection of having access to both paranoid-schizoid and depressive position modes.

The shift from a one-person to a two-person mode further transforms how we define pathology and health. One-person models, like the medical model, tend to speak of pathology as residing in the individual, which then affects the organism's ability to function in, or adapt to, the environment. From a two-person perspective, one would speak of pathology as residing in the interaction between the organism and the environment, not as residing solely within the organism. A good example here is the way the significance of child temperament has come to be thought of in terms of the "goodness of fit" (Thomas and Chess 1977) between the child and the caretaker. That is, a highly reactive child may fit well with one parent, who sees the child as lively and animated. Another parent may feel overstimulated or intruded upon by the same child. This is not to say that, at the extreme, some children's temperaments are not inherently more difficult or easy than others'; even in these cases, however, the interaction with the caretaker's (more accurately, caretakers') temperament and adaptability is crucial in terms of the interpersonal outcome.

IMPLICATIONS OF OUR RELATIONAL POINT OF VIEW FOR THERAPEUTIC ACTION

Finally, we turn to the issue of therapeutic action. What makes for change in psychoanalytically informed child treatment, as we conceive it? In classical child work as described by Kleinians and Freudians, therapeutic change resulted essentially from interpretation that led to increased insight into, and thus ego control over, the workings of the unconscious. Additionally, the Freudian child analyst, in work preparatory to interpretation, would focus on developing enhanced ego strength in the form of more effective, less debilitating defense mechanisms and better regulation of anxiety. These ego-building measures, of course, would lead to therapeutic change in their own right. In contrast, in the work we describe, interventions take place between therapist and child, therapist and family, therapist and school, and so on. The potential sources of therapeutic action in this work are thus multiple and diverse, extending beyond changes in the mental functioning of the child as an isolated individual. (In considering multiple "ports of entry" into a problem, we follow Stern 1995.)

Considering the interaction between therapist and child for the moment, the child might benefit from:

1. enhanced self-understanding developed in discussion with the therapist
2. enhanced capacity to use play for symbolic processing of affectively charged interpersonal experience (Frankel 1998b)
3. enhanced self-regulatory capacities as a result of becoming better able to use play symbolically, which may also be enhanced with pharmacological interventions
4. enhanced personality integration as a result of becoming able

to reclaim previously disowned and dissociated feelings, self-representations, and representations of other people (Bromberg 1999, Caspary 1993).

5. enhanced capacity for curiosity about self and others as a result of participation in a therapeutic inquiry
6. broadened repertoire of ways to express affect and to interact with other people, leading to symptomatic improvement
7. enhanced self-esteem as a result of the therapist's nonjudgmental attitude.

Family interventions can benefit the child in the following ways:

1. Changes in family dynamics, or systemic patterning, can remove the child from a symptomatic role.
2. Parents can be helped to attune to, or empathize with, their child's affective states. Strategies can be developed to minimize the destructive effects of temperamental mismatches and misattunements based on parental projections and misunderstandings of the child's affective states. Strategies can be developed to interrupt vicious circles, power struggles, and so on.
3. Parents can be helped to gain perspective on projections onto the child that result from unprocessed trauma or unmourned losses in their own lives.

With respect to interventions in the school and community:

1. The child can obtain needed remedial services in the school and outside the school, from learning specialists, speech and language specialists, occupational therapists, and so on. As remedial measures begin to give the child a more defined sense of his difficulty, he may be less likely to feel that something is wrong with him in a global sense. He may gain hope that his difficulty is limited and reversible, rather than constituting a profound and pervasive incompetence.
2. Teachers can develop an enhanced understanding of the child. In collaboration with the therapist, they can develop approaches to help the child learn and develop social relations in the classroom.

3. The family can obtain needed support services such as drug and alcohol services, parenting education, income support, or health care services.
4. The family can be helped to select after-school activities (sports, the arts, etc.) that can advance the development of the child and enhance the child's self-esteem.

This list, necessarily incomplete, gives an idea of how the multifaceted interventions we are recommending can benefit the child and family. In an effort to find some common threads, to make explicit what guides our therapeutic efforts, we will outline some underlying principles of what helps children in therapy. First of all, parental mobilization of effort and resources to help the child is, itself, a powerfully therapeutic act. Seeking therapy for a child can be a major statement to the child that his parents care about him and are sensitive to his pain. Of course, parents sometimes seek therapy for a child for less laudable reasons, with a punitive intent or to wash their own hands of a child's problems. Even in cases where such negative motivation is not present or is only minimally present, children may experience being brought to a therapist as a punishment or as evidence of failure. Shame, of course, is always a factor for both parents and child when there is a need to seek professional help. The child's sense of pride may mitigate against expressing appreciation for parental concern, but we believe that in many, if not most, cases children tacitly appreciate the family concern for their well-being. The therapist can be the focus for a concerted effort on behalf of the child, involving parents, other family members, and school personnel. These efforts can inspire a renewed sense of hope and engagement in the people who deal with the child. In our experience, this factor alone can often contribute to symptomatic improvement, aside from the specific interventions made.

NEGOTIATION: TOWARD MUTUAL UNDERSTANDING AND PSYCHIC INTEGRATION

Our relational perspective on therapeutic action focuses on the interactions between therapist and patient, therapist and family, and therapist and the larger environment as the places where change takes place. Within these interactions, we use the language of several perspectives to describe the process of negotiating different points of view among the various participants in the therapeutic effort.

For example, we use the perspective of lifespan developmental psychology in order to understand parenthood as a period of development in its own right. This perspective allows us to examine what children mean to parents, as well as the origins of a parent's concern, identity, and sense of responsibility as a parent. Our application of Stern's (1995) work on the motherhood constellation has been particularly relevant here. This perspective provides the context for understanding why parents engage a stranger, the therapist, as an employee to help them achieve certain goals that are passionately important to them as parents. It also clarifies the conflicts and resonance between the parents' goals for the therapy, and those of the therapist and the child.

Then we use neo-Kleinian language and concepts to examine how therapy can heal intrapsychic and interpersonal splits. We believe that the process of negotiating different points of view between and among the various participants in the therapeutic effort contributes to healing these splits. In Bromberg's (1999) language, such negotiation contributes to a capacity to "stand in the spaces" among various self-states and thus transcend dissociative splits in the personality and, by extension, in the family. Ultimately, then, psychic and interpersonal integration is at the heart of our concept of what constitutes therapeutic change. This formulation implies that psychopathology, or difficulties in living, result when an individual disowns in a rigid way some of his or her psychic states and feelings. Such disowning results in alienation from parts of oneself. It also results in interpersonal difficulties, as psychic states and feelings that one rejects become attributed to others, who then become objects of rejection, fear, or contempt. We do not mean to exclude from our definition of psychic "health" states of being deeply and passionately involved in one or another feeling or state of mind to the exclusion of others. Rather, we are describing the capacity, over time, to recognize and experience the full range of such feelings and psychic states. We also do not mean to imply that all such feelings necessarily lead to action. One may choose not to act out destructive rage, for example, while being fully aware of destructiveness as a feeling, or state of mind, in oneself.

To see how psychic integration is fostered in practice, consider first the relationship between therapist and child. Caspary (1993) has shown how such psychic healing processes can occur via symbolic play. In Caspary's model of the therapeutic process, the various characters in a play narrative represent various aspects of the patient's psyche. The therapist is often assigned a role that is disowned by the child. The therapist's job is to own that which the child disowns, to develop an understanding of the character he (the therapist) is "containing" (the language of Bion 1967), and to express that understanding to the child in words. This process enables the child to re-own a dissociated self-state; ultimately he may be able to take on the role that had been previously assigned to the therapist, signaling that psychic integration has occurred.

Caspary gives an example of a boy who plays cops and robbers with his therapist. The role of the robber is assigned to the therapist, while the boy takes on the role of punitive cop. The therapist thinks aloud about what motivates a robber, develops an understanding of the robber's feelings; eventually the cop's treatment of the robber becomes less harsh. Ultimately, therapist and patient exchange roles. In this treatment, the robber might be thought to represent a greedy, ruthless part of the boy, while the cop represents a harsh superego attitude toward the child's greedy self-states. The therapist, in containing the robber, must connect with his own greedy and ruthless self-states enough to develop an in-depth understanding of the role. His out-loud musings about the robber bring the child in on the process of accepting and tolerating greedy, ruthless feelings, without necessarily acting them out in destructive form. The child identifies with the therapist's more accepting attitude toward these feelings, as reflected in the cop's less punitive treatment of the robber. The dissociation of greed within the child has begun to break down, ultimately to the point where the child is able to go back and forth ("stand in the spaces between") cop and robber.

This sort of negotiation between different perspectives can also occur in the nonplay relationship between therapist and patient. Altman (1997) has recounted a treatment in which a 7-year-old boy wanted to play basketball in the sessions. At first, the therapist wonders if there is any therapeutic benefit to be gained from playing basketball. Eventually, through remembering and reconnecting with his own boyhood love of sports, he finds a way to view the basketball play as a forum for the expression and negotiation of hero worship, grandiose fantasies, and oedipal competition. Aside from the symbolic elements of the basketball play, we believe that the therapist's effort to transcend his initial difficulty accepting the basketball play has therapeutic benefit in itself. As the therapist works to find a way to feel good about playing basketball with his patient, he provides an experience of interpersonal and intrapsychic negotiation and integration within their relationship. The therapist's willingness to do so expresses his caring for his patient, as well as his ability to "stand in the spaces" between their points of view when they (initially, at least) diverge. The therapist may at times ask the child to accommodate to the therapist's point of view as well. For example, the therapist may eventually feel that the therapy has begun to revolve too much around the basketball play, that it has become repetitive and stereotyped. He may then ask the child to add a period of talking or some other form of play to a portion of the session. Negotiating this change provides a forum for trying to work out differences, sometimes power struggles, in their "real" relationship. In this sense, differences between therapist and child patient, leading to occasions when the patient experiences the therapist as an obstacle, constitute therapeutic opportunities.

Thus in our approach, play can be negotiated flexibly, at times between the child and the therapist and at other times between the various self-states of the child.

A 9-year-old boy whose divorced parents fought constantly was anxious and encopretic. He was so immersed in fantasy that he spent most of his time in the classroom looking out the window. He knew that his fantasy was not real but he engaged in it for hours on end. In therapy he would walk in silently, reading waiting-room literature on stress. Then he would show the therapist imaginary videos of fantasies he had constructed, inserting them into and ejecting them from imaginary video cassette recorders. He would enact the action from these fantasies, pacing about, throwing himself down onto the couch, or twirling on the footstool. A typical, frenetic sequence involved detailed re-enactments of images of chase, attack, and capture, with frequent shifts in character. One evil character was in love with his "hiney," admiring it, showing it off, wanting to marry it. Abruptly the boy "ejected the cassette," and prepared to insert the next scene.

At that point, the therapist, feeling nearly overwhelmed by the primitive and chaotic nature of the material, was struggling to contain the fragmented nature of the boy's experience. The boy, projecting it, was calmly in charge as the video director. Negotiating the play interpersonally, the therapist stopped the boy from going on to the next scene. He explained his response to the video, how overwhelming, fragmented, and ominous it seemed. He insisted that the boy consider its relation at least to his problem with soiling, given the character who was so enthralled with his backside, before going on to the next scene. Then the boy "ejected" the second imaginary video. He sat down, and said that he thought that that character indeed had something to do with his problem with soiling. He said that he felt attached to the feces ("it makes me feel different, alive") as something valuable when he felt stressed by his parents' fighting and threats.

By now the boy had taken back into himself the experience of chaos and devaluation. For the time being, he could consider it verbally and more calmly, negotiating with it intrapsychically rather than needing to expel it onto the therapist.

RELATIONAL CHILD THERAPY: TECHNICAL AND PRAGMATIC ISSUES

Our views about therapeutic action raise several technical and pragmatic issues for child therapists: (1) whether our therapeutic focus should be on the child or the family; (2) the relative importance of play and negotiation in child therapy; (3) what is play, and what play is therapeutically useful; (4) the relationship of healing experiences in "ordinary life" to those that are part of psychotherapy; and (5) the role of medication in work with children.

Issue 1: Who Is the Patient? How Do We Blend Work with the Parents and Work with the Child?

How does our two-person approach translate into concrete treatment-planning decisions? Specifically, which treatment do we consider primary, individual or family? We think both individually and systemically about every child's therapy, but how do we balance these often competing viewpoints? Are we biased in either direction? Should we think of the child primarily as an individual with largely internalized motives who is also influenced by the systems in which she lives, or as a creature of her systems, with intra-individual influences seen and treated as epiphenomena of these systems?

To an extent, this set of questions appears academic and based on an unnecessary theoretical dichotomy. There are those in the field who take the position that the family level of intervention is always preferable. The traditional psychoanalytic approach has assumed the opposite stance. We do not hold to either position. The dichotomy is not only unnecessary but faulty. A child struggles at once with her internal life and with her family system. Even when we enter the child's world as her individual therapist, we still also must think systemically. But as a practical matter, choices must be made.

Our approach in any particular case is mainly determined by the answers to two sets of questions. The first involves diagnostic considerations: Where is the problem? What are the specific causes of a given child's difficulties? The second set of questions is more pragmatic: Where is the therapeutic leverage within the family system? What are the characteristics of child and family that suggest one approach or another? And, related to this, what are the particular stylistic and personal abilities of the therapist? Where is she personally most likely to get therapeutic traction?

In thinking about how the diagnosis bears on the plan for treatment, one basic question is helpful to consider. With children we see as mainly reacting to environmental stresses, should we address ourselves exclusively or primarily to the system? The answer depends, first, on the extent to which the disturbing situation has become an internal, self-sustaining problem for the child. If this has not happened, we probably should focus our therapeutic attention on the system.

But often, children symbolically transform the events of their lives and incorporate the trauma into an inner fantasy life and altered internal representational models that perpetuate the situation and the experience of trauma. A child may even keep the experience of trauma going for a long time after the situation changes. He may do this for various reasons, all ways of coping with the trauma. For instance, what was once a trauma that a child endured passively has become an interaction that he may try to master by actively provoking its repetition because he may be unable to endure the sense of helplessness or humiliation that victimization entails. Or he may internalize and identify with aspects of those people who have caused the situation, due to love or fear of these people. In these cases, even though we see inner symbolism and fantasy as secondary to external events, nevertheless the child's inner life has become a force to be reckoned with. The aspect of the child's continuing difficulties that reflects a stable, internalized organization is often best reckoned with, we believe, through individual therapy.

Children suffering through their parents' divorce are often an example of an external problem that becomes an internal one. They are certainly victims. They are reacting to a traumatic situation caused by others. Yet during an acrimonious divorce, they may side actively with one parent against another. This may result from their independent sense of what is right, but it can also be due to an identification out of fear of a custodial parent who has considerable power over them. In fact, many children who have suffered this or other kinds of trauma keep their traumatic reactions even long after the trauma has stopped being a threat. The child's sense of safety, and of the benevolence and protective power of caregivers, has been damaged, and identifications with those perceived as powerful and dangerous, or as hurt and victimized, may remain in their place. In such a situation, a therapist clearly must address the child's internal world, not just the circumstances that started the problems.

This brings us to the second, more pragmatic set of questions whose answer bears on our treatment plans. Even in situations where a child's difficulties are clearly a response to pressures from the parents, the parents may not be physically available or emotionally able to participate in the treatment. The therapist therefore needs to make a judgment about where therapeutic leverage lies, regardless of her understanding of the causes of the child's problems. In our experience, important work can be done even when parents do not become involved in the treatment or change, if the environmental situation is not too dire. The child may change in ways that push the parents to respond in a manner that supports the child's new ways of being. The child may also change in ways that do not challenge the parent's requirements of the child. These changes may reflect the establishment of new self–other configurations arising out of interactions with the therapist—altered or additional internal representational models, in the language of attachment theory.

In an ideal situation where both parents and child are available and eager to participate in treatment, and where time and money are not an issue, should we not address the problem at both a systemic and an individual level? Often we should. But there are times when we may judge (as a structural family therapist might) that only the parents should be engaged in direct therapeutic work, as a statement that they need to take greater responsibility or authority in their families or must function more as a team. We may also make a point of involving the parents when we want to communicate to the child that we do not see the problem as his alone. Some preadolescents, for instance, may consent to see a therapist only if it is clear to them that the therapist does not endorse the parents' view that the child is the source of all the difficulties; and such reassurance may become real for the child only when the therapist includes the parents in the treatment. Conversely, as children move into preadolescence, when concerns about separation and privacy come more into the foreground, work with the family may undermine the child's trust that the therapist will keep his confidences or see things from his point of view.

Sometimes a child's parents are insightful about the child's difficulties and their own role in them. The parents may even be in their own therapy, where they explore their relationships with their children. Does the child therapist need to get involved with the parents in this case? We believe the answer is a qualified yes. Qualified, because the therapist may not need to work with such parents in as educative a way, or perhaps in as intensive a way, as she would with other parents. Yes, because the therapist will still have an important and useful, if incomplete, point of view about the child and the family situation based upon her work with the child. These ideas may be important for the parents to hear. There will also be times when it is important for the child to have his parents participate in the therapy, so he knows they are aware and involved with certain things that the child has focused on in his therapy.

One example in which this type of family involvement arose naturally in the evolution of what was primarily an individual treatment came in working with a 7-year-old boy who always felt he had to be well behaved and agreeable, especially now that his parents were under stress due to the birth of a new child. In individual sessions, he gradually came to understand how angry he was about his baby sister. We decided to invite his parents to join us. We discussed at length how we would present his concerns to them, and we came up with a detailed agenda for the meeting. The next week, when his parents came in, this boy simply went to the toy cabinet, picked up a baby doll, pulled off its head, smashed the doll against the wall, and smiled at his parents. They got the message that he needed them to get.

Even in the case (possible only in the abstract, not in the real world) where we were to understand a child's difficulties as purely internal and not reflecting family dynamics—as a response to a trauma outside the family, for instance—would we want to be only individual therapists to a child? Probably not, for two reasons. First, in many cases, parents may function more effectively as therapeutic agents than a therapist can. Whether this is so depends on the specifics of the relationship between parent and child—the degree of trust, of openness, and the attitudes of parent and child toward the boundaries between them. In some situations, we may intervene most effectively as consultants to a parent about how to help a child through her difficulties. Freud (1909) was the first to use a parent as a child's therapist in his case of Little Hans.

The other reason that eliminating parents from the therapeutic equation is probably not a good idea is that children's ways of coping with trauma have taken shape in the context of family identifications and relationships. At the least, we need to get to know the parents in order to learn how the family perceives and copes with such events as have befallen their child, and how they encourage their child to cope. And as we understand how the family style of coping affects the child's ability to work through traumatic events, we are likely to have some ideas that will be useful to the parents about how they may enhance their repertoire of ways of engaging and helping their child through her current difficulties.

A final reason that therapists must work with all parents in some fashion is that "resistances" (the traditional, judgmental word used to describe a patient's reluctance to cooperate in treatment) by parents are inevitable in all child treatments. It may be more accurate to say that friction between parents and therapist is inevitable. While the traditional view of resistance assumes that the therapist's ideas about the patient and the treatment are objective and correct and that the patient's (or parent's) reluctance to cooperate is irrational, this view is not supportable given current understandings of the inevitability of personal and cultural influences on the perceptions and formulations of every therapist. In this light, a parent's "resistance" may be based on differing values about or perceptions of the child's difficulties. And beyond the assumption that the therapist is fully rational and the parent who disagrees is not, it would be arrogant to dismiss a parent's point of view about her child, given that she has far more motivation and opportunity to observe and think about her child's difficulties than does the therapist. Misunderstandings between therapist and parents are unavoidable, even if only as a result of parents not knowing what is happening in the treatment. It would be unwise, both strategically and because of the importance of learning what the parent sees and thinks about the child, to exclude her. The therapist must establish a relationship with the parents in which their perceptions of and hesitations about therapy can be explored and addressed. Such a relationship must have a sufficient intensity and openness.

In summary, we are not family therapists with little use for individual therapy. The child's internal world, while shaped by outer events, becomes its own resilient and resistant influence on the interpersonal systems of which the child is a part. Nor are we simply individual therapists. We favor work with family and with child when possible, in formats that make clinical sense in each particular case, and when there is no specific clinical reason not to do so.

Issue 2: The Roles of Play and Negotiation in Therapeutic Action

This discussion raises several questions. Which do we believe is therapeutic, self-expression or confronting reality? What is the balance between the therapeutic value of self-expression and the value of coming to terms with personal and interpersonal realities one would rather avoid? In child (and adult) therapy, these two concepts are embodied, though roughly, in the processes of play and negotiation as aspects of therapeutic action (Frankel 1998b). We say roughly, because we see interpersonal and intrapsychic processes as inextricable; therefore, both are present in play and in negotiation.

Play is a process of self-expression. As self-expression, play involves the symbolic representation and creative manipulation of one's experiential world. It allows a child to gain some distance from a reality that is overwhelming, threatening, or upsetting, and to come to terms with it with a greater feeling of safety, at one's own pace and in one's own way. It facilitates familiarity, acceptance, and increased perspective on disavowed aspects of one's experience of oneself. As such, we see play as inherently therapeutic, even without interpretive intervention.

Playing with (or in the presence of) the therapist is also a vehicle for an interpersonal relationship. The therapist's attention, respect, and responsiveness to the child's play provides the safe, protective space for the child that is necessary for play (Bruner 1972b). This "holding environment" (Winnicott 1960, 1963) itself may constitute a benign, corrective kind of relationship, and also amounts to a recognition of those disavowed, problematic aspects of herself that the child represents in her play, thus helping the child to accept and own those parts of herself (Frankel 1998b).

Negotiation is also both an interpersonal and an intrapersonal process (Pizer 1998). On an interpersonal level, the child pursues her wishes and interests in a relationship with another person, the therapist, who is flexible and responsive but who also has his own interests and requirements. The therapist's interests include having a presence and a value in the relationship with the child, and also getting to know the child more fully. The child's anxieties may lead her to oppose either of these interests of the therapist. Through the process of negotiation, the child and therapist move closer to a relationship characterized by mutual recognition, rather than domination and compliance.

The most overt form of interpersonal negotiation in child therapy occurs when the child pushes the therapist's established limits and the therapist insists on enforcing them. Subtler forms happen when the child withdraws from or avoids the therapist. The therapist's interests in getting to know the child and in being a presence in the relationship with the child are thwarted. The therapist must assert these interests in a manner that does not push the child away. Children (and adults) often confront the therapist with behavioral tests designed to disconfirm beliefs about themselves and other people that lie behind their problematic behavior (Weiss, Sampson et al. 1986). If the therapist passes the tests, children's internalized models of self–other relationships may be renegotiated (Lachmann and Beebe 1996). Negotiation with the therapist is most productive within a context of play. When play is not possible, negotiation may help create the kind of relationship where the child is more able to play.

Paradoxically, the therapist's asserting his own feelings and requirements by setting limits is often just the kind of negotiating strategy that helps a child become able to play more freely.

> A very active and reactive 10-year-old boy would typically work himself into an excited and overstimulated state during his play in sessions. When it came time to end a therapy session, he would throw toys around the room and refuse to help clean up. The therapist ended up feeling angry and distant from him. Only when the therapist restricted the playtime in subsequent sessions as a consequence of his defiance did this boy's excitement become more manageable for him, and his play calmer, more focused, and more genuinely playful rather than impulsive and driven.

Children also negotiate with themselves, or more accurately, they negotiate between different experiences of self. Some aspects of self are more comfortable and some less, although this is influenced by the person with whom the child is playing, to some extent. Playing can provide a conducive environment for usually disavowed experiences of self to have more of a voice; as such, play is a kind of negotiation with oneself. The therapist also inevitably actively mediates the child's negotiations with herself. For instance, child therapists often take on the play-roles of disavowed aspects of the child's self, easing the child's difficult task of facing these repudiated parts of self (see Caspary 1993). Ideally, the therapist will respond to problematic aspects of the child's self that are beginning to be expressed so that they may find more of a place in the child's comfortable ways of being. But because each therapist responds to, recognizes, and identifies with certain aspects of the child more than others, based upon the therapist's own personality, play in therapy is also always a negotiation with the therapist.

We believe that interpersonal processes involved in therapeutic action have historically been slighted by psychoanalysis in favor of intrapsychic processes. We seek to bring greater attention to the interpersonal processes involved in child therapy not only because they have been neglected, but because child therapists often feel they are not really doing therapy when they are struggling with a child around limits or when they are simply sitting with a child who is playing. Both can be essential therapeutic activities. We see both interpersonal and intrapersonal processes as crucial in therapeutic action.

Issue 3: What Is Play, and What Play Is Therapeutically Useful?

We now move to a related, even more basic question whose answer is important to every practicing child therapist: What is play? Play is a more elusive concept than it appears to be at first glance. Ethological, anthropological, and experimental—psychological researchers have difficulty defining play (Bekoff and Byers 1998, Fagen 1981). It seems to have no immediate functional or adaptive benefit and no immediate objective. While it is sometimes seen as practice for future tasks, the behavior sequences that characterize play would often not be very effective at the serious life tasks that they seem related to. For instance, play-fighting behaviors would be very ineffective if used in real combat. One thing that seems clear is that play is intrinsically rewarding. The activity of playing itself, not some subsequent reward, is what is pleasurable; more specifically, the "joy in being the cause" (Groos 1896, cited in Piaget 1951, p. 151), in making things happen, brings pleasure.

Play requires freedom from threat, pressure, or worry about consequences (Lorenz 1971), and it "does not count"—it cannot have serious consequences and still remain play. This freedom is required so that someone may test limits, try new solutions, experiment with new combinations of behavior and new ways of doing things, without risk of dire results. This atmosphere fosters the freedom, innovation, creativity, and openness to new ideas that is precisely how a patient in therapy needs to approach his problems if he is to let go of old patterns and risk new experience. Social play also involves a different kind of openness: a receptiveness not just to one's own new ideas but also to the other person's feelings and ideas, and pleasure in the interplay between one's own and the other person's spontaneity and creativity (see Frankel 1998b, Winnicott 1971a).

Given these ideas about play, is all that passes for play in therapy really play? What about agitated, instinctually charged play? Winnicott (1971a) explicitly distinguished masturbatory activity from play. From an intersubjective standpoint, we can also say that both sadistic and mean behavior, and masochistic and provocative behavior, lack the simultaneous appreciation of self and other as creative agents, the mutual responsiveness, that is at the heart of truly creative social play. Instead, one person is treated as an object, implying an underlying sense of threat and resulting in rigidification and constriction, not the full freedom that facilitates play.

What about repetitive scenarios that seem never to evolve toward new solutions or greater freedom? What about the constricting, rule-bound play of board games? Often, play in child therapy has a sense of evolution, a sense that something is being worked through, even if it is not clear what this is. But sometimes this sense of evolution is lacking, whether the constriction seems self-imposed by rigidly repeating a scenario and not letting it develop, or by choosing an activity, like a board game, that has inherent limitations on creativity. In both cases, we need to ask whether productive play is occurring.

In the first situation, that of rigid, repetitive play, the activity seems defensive and anxiety-driven, rather than playful. A therapist in that situation may need to intervene in such a way as to help the child feel safer in order for the child to become more able to play. Alternately, the therapist might wait and see if this will happen simply as a function of the greater familiarity that comes with the passage of time.

Board games, despite their highly rule-bound nature, do offer opportunities to experiment with, negotiate, and manipulate rules, and with the experiences of winning and losing, they offer the chance to experiment with competing. While this is not the free-form play that can occur in therapy, the safety offered by the structure of games may be necessary for some children at some points in their treatment and does provide opportunities for experiment and play. Further, board games can sometimes be springboards for freer forms of play, as game pieces become personified and as new self-states and feelings emerge during the game. A game of chess with one young girl ended with patient and therapist jumping up and down on the plastic pieces until all were shattered.

Issue 4: The Healing Roles of "Ordinary Life" and Psychotherapy

What about the healing value of factors outside the formal therapy process? All child therapists, but especially relational therapists who appreciate the healing value of many factors within the child and in the various systems of which the child is a part, must think about the question: To what extent do the events of "ordinary life," rather than psychotherapy, constitute the real treatment?

As with some of the other issues discussed in this chapter, this question is something of a straw man. Each case must be decided on its own particulars. Some children require longer-term treatment, while others need relatively little intervention before life can begin to take over as the therapy. Other children may get past particular difficulties without any direct therapeutic help at all; if this can happen, it may be the best approach, especially if it gives a child confidence in her own inner resources. Seeing a therapist may also play into developmentally related or peer group-based anxieties about being weak or dependent, especially in early adolescents, suggesting caution at times in recommending therapy when it can be avoided.

The question of life versus therapy is not an either–or question: Children learn from both life and psychotherapy; if this yields the best results for a child, why choose? There are also situations when psychotherapy may be necessary in order for someone to begin to learn from her own life experience. Psychotherapy is designed to help people develop their ability to respond to the learning and healing experiences that life offers.

In general, we see children's difficulties as more reactive to their environments, and their personalities as more responsive to favorable changes in their environments, as compared with adults. When a child proves to be responsive in this way and a family is relatively flexible and thoughtful, psychotherapy can work fairly quickly. Also, sometimes a key intervention can make a big difference for a child and (especially when there is a benign family environment) help him find resources within himself to deal more effectively with a stalemate in his life.

To return to an example cited in Chapter 7: A boy had a long history of obsessive thoughts and compulsions, and a feeling that he needed to be excessively good. He came to his session one day saying that his father had told him to talk about a particular behavior that concerned the father. The therapist asked whether the boy wanted to talk about that, which was a surprising question for the boy. This led to the discovery that the boy had a constant sense that his father was sitting on his shoulder, looking into his mind. The boy felt he had no right to feel he owned the contents of his mind, that he could think what he wanted and keep his thoughts private if he chose. The therapist's questioning these assumptions was striking to the boy. The idea that the boy owned his own mind, and the therapist's sponsorship of his being able to think and feel what he wanted regardless of what others wanted him to think or feel, and of his being able to keep the contents of his mind as separate from other people as he wished, seemed crucial in the resolution of his obsessive and compulsive symptoms, including a lifting of his personality constriction, which followed shortly after these sessions.

Sometimes, certain life events must take place before a child or parent will accept therapy, or before someone feels sufficiently motivated to become really involved in it. As examples, a child may need to have serious behavior problems in school before a parent will agree to bring him to therapy, or a child or young adolescent may need some indication that their parents genuinely approve of therapy or accept some responsibility for problems in the parent–child relationship, in order for a child to let herself become more emotionally involved in the treatment.

Issue 5: The Question of Medication in Child Therapy

We see psychopathology as the product of the interaction between environmental and biological influences. This forces us to ask: How do we see the role of medication in child treatment?

Because we understand children's difficulties as always being shaped and to some extent maintained by their interpersonal environment (in interaction with temperament or other biological factors; see Chapter 6 on our assumptions about psychopathology), and also because children's difficulties always involve their sense of who they are, who other people are, and what they expect in their interactions with other people, we believe that it is never appropriate to treat a child with medication alone without psychotherapy. Medication is not a substitute for psychotherapy.[1] The discussion that follows is about the value of medication in the context of psychotherapy.

There is something to be said for both pro and con biases on medication in conjunction with psychotherapy. On the pro side, highly anxious or depressed children, and of course severely disturbed children, may be relieved of suffering in the relatively short run with medication. For example, a boy with longstanding encopresis and separation anxiety was substantially helped when he started to take Paxil, a selective serotonin-reuptake inhibitor (SSRI), in conjunction with psychotherapy. Medication may also help children become more responsive to whatever positive experiences are offered by life, with a consequent benign feedback loop between how others respond to the child and the child's sense of himself. A child who can be helped by medication to pay attention in school and with friends,[2] or to be part of the social group with other children, will not only be in less conflict with his environment but will also learn more of what he needs to succeed and be happy in these settings.

On the other side of the issue, there are important learning experiences that will be bypassed when medication is used in place of psychotherapy, and that are likely to be bypassed when psychotherapy is used or perceived as a secondary support and not a primary treatment approach. Medication is seen to have such magical power in our culture—see the literature on the effectiveness of placebos, for instance (Hart 1999)—that it may be hard not to see medication as the more potent treatment when it is used, regardless of the facts. These percep-

---

1. Many psychiatric medications that are used with children have only been tested on adults, not on children, raising additional questions of efficacy and safety.

2. Stimulant medication used to treat attention deficits is something of a special case. There are alternative treatments involving biofeedback. A small body of research supports the comparable effectiveness of these treatments as opposed to medication (Rossiter and LaVague 1995), but the treatments are relatively new.

tions are actively fostered by the marketing done by drug companies that manufacture these tremendously profitable medications.

One important learning experience we have discussed in the chapters on psychopathology that may be missed when medication is seen as the primary treatment is being able to see clearly what is happening around oneself—to demystify experience. We have discussed how psychopathology often reflects a child's collusion with the family's unconscious efforts to confuse the child about the motives of those around her. The process of therapy, both individual and with the family, provides many opportunities to clarify what is happening that the child (until then) has learned not to notice, and to awaken the child's dormant skills at perceiving others' motives. Some degree of struggle and discomfort—we are not recommending prolonging real suffering—may be necessary for the child to be motivated to focus on the interpersonal dynamics around her. Other learning experiences may also be minimized when psychotherapy is bypassed. These include learning how one's own states of mind are responsive to moment-to-moment interactions with other people and in turn influence others, anticipating one's own responses, and coping with one's own moods and feelings.

In a more general sense, not using medication and discovering the sense in what she is doing allow a child to learn that her thoughts, emotions, and behavior have meaning, both personally and interpersonally, and that they are not simply epiphenomena of genes or "chemical imbalances." Along with this, the child can also learn what she has been saying, through her symptoms, to her family and to other important people in her life. She gains a sense of agency and experiences herself as active, purposeful, socially potent, and effective.

Finally, a child in psychotherapy learns new ways to cope with personal difficulties—by thinking about them, by being honest with herself, by playing, by expressing herself, by allowing herself access to a wider range of feelings, by paying more attention to other people, and so on. These ways of coping usually not only enrich her experience of herself but also enrich her ways of interacting with other people, and so are likely to lead to more satisfying interpersonal relationships. This increased flexibility may also serve to prevent future difficulties that can arise from a more rigid coping style.

In certain cases—a child mourning a loss or coming to terms with a trauma—we tend to be reluctant about the use of medication to "normalize" mood. In cases of loss or trauma, it is crucial that the child gradually become able to face what has happened to him. We believe it is by far preferable—if the child's suffering would not be too great—that the child be helped to do this with the aid of the concern and support of those around him rather than with medication, although in extreme cases, medication may make it more possible to face traumatic experiences. Our concern is that in many other cases, medication may make it easier for a child to try to cope by forgetting these experiences rather than by coming to terms with them, a process that often leads to acting out these traumatic experiences. In these cases, a bearable level of current suffering seems a smaller evil than the long-term consequences (discussed in the chapter on psychopathology) of unmourned loss or unresolved trauma. There is an increasing appreciation for the extent to which most psychopathology reflects unmourned loss (Bowlby 1980) or unresolved trauma (Lyons-Ruth and Jacobvitz 1999), in which case the criteria for using medication in a broad range of cases should become more stringent.

In summary, we see great value in not using medication, yet we support its use, in many cases, when a child's suffering or social maladaptation are too great.

THE TECHNIQUE OF CHILD THERAPY IN A NONPRESCRIPTIVE, MULTIDIMENSIONAL THEORETICAL WORLD

It should be clear from what has been said so far that no general technical principles can guide the therapist's behavior across various therapeutic situations. The therapist, from our point of view, is not a technician carrying out a standardized procedure. Rather, the therapist is a unique human being engaged in a personal interaction with another unique human being. The therapist's job is to use this unique interaction to expand the patient's psychic and behavioral repertoire. Often, in a particular clinical situation, the therapist will feel that there are competing, possibly incompatible, values in play and courses of action open to pursue. Consider, for example, a situation in which a therapist must decide how to use a piece of information provided by a parent about a child—such as some way in which the child has misbehaved at home or school. The therapist may feel pulled between the desire to respect the child's privacy and autonomy by not bringing in material from outside, the desire to bring an aspect of the child's life into the domain of the therapy by sharing the information with the child, and the desire not to hide from the child that the therapist knows about the misbehavior. Can there be an a priori answer to the question of what the therapist should do? Much depends on the therapist's sense of values and assessment of the child's psychic situation. Is the child denying too much of his distress as it occurs out in the world? Is he ready to be confronted with some of his provocative behavior? Would he bring in some of this material on his own if the therapist is patient? Is the therapist being impatient in his desire to bring in the information from the parents, or would the therapist be too cautious or timid in not bringing it up? Is the therapist overestimating or underestimating the child's resources in dealing with this anxiety-laden material? None of these questions can be answered definitively in advance. The therapist's interventions are often the outcome of a complex process of negotiating and making choices in the face of diverse considerations.

Often an intervention is a probe, an experiment. The child's response yields information about the child's mind in the context of that moment, as well as about the therapist. For example, the therapist says he has heard from the parent that the child got into a fight in school. The child may tell the therapist to shut up, or shut down with an obvious sense of shame, or ignore the therapist's comment, or come forth with some self-reflective comments or communicate some important feelings. In the case of silence, was it oppositional or shame-ridden? In the case of a cooperative response, was it anxiously compliant or more authentically reflective? The meaning assigned by the therapist to the patient's response guides his further interventions, but there is no need to come up with definitive answers to such questions in the interest of "knowing what to do." Rather, the ongoing meaning-making activity of patient and therapist together in a context of uncertainty forms the heart of the therapeutic process, fostering the child's flexibility and self-reflectiveness. Misattunements, when patient and therapist are aware of them together, can provide the occasion for reparative activities that foster resiliency. Negotiation between child and therapist, and among various feelings, values, and psychic states, fosters integration as opposed to splitting and dissociation. The absence of clear technical principles opens the door to a rich and growth-promoting therapeutic process.

Turning our attention to the broader interpersonal field, the therapist can serve an integrating, containing function with respect to diverse and conflicting perspectives about the child held by different people in the child's life. Keeping in mind the perspectives, concerns, and anxieties held by mother, father, and teacher, for example, the therapist can contain and integrate the various feelings within the countertransference. The therapist is then in a position to help these people take account of the points of view of the others, thus helping them to "stand in the spaces" between the various sides of the child. Thereby, splitting and conflict can be avoided or defused in the child's environment.

Consider a child whose mother is strongly reactive, with her own anxiety to his separation anxiety, leading to an enmeshed relationship between the two. The father, meanwhile, feels that the mother is spoiling the child, coddling him too much, encouraging his dependence. The father advocates a "tough love" approach. Therapists, trained as they are to listen respectfully to everybody, are oriented to trying to find a way to integrate these two points of view. A therapist might take a larger perspective in which the mother and father are seen as caught up in a polarized vicious circle, with the mother's protectiveness and the father's toughness stimulating each other. The more the mother protects the child, the more the father asserts the child's need to grow up, while the more the father advocates a tough approach to the child, the more the mother feels the need to protect him.

It may happen that the therapist not only sees but feels the father's point of view, if the mother cancels an appointment at the last minute because the child doesn't want to leave home. Or, the therapist may feel the mother's point of view if the father is taking an exceedingly intolerant position about the child's dependence in a session. Now, the therapist is challenged with integrating the parents' perspectives not only cognitively, but emotionally as well. Can the therapist find a way to process his anger, anxiety, and other feelings toward the mother and father in a productive way? Can the therapist find a way to talk with the mother about how it felt when her child refused to leave home to come to the session and the various options the mother had at that point? Does the therapist charge for the session or try to reschedule it, and how do therapist and parents feel about these arrangements? Can the therapist talk with the father about the reactions stimulated in him by the child's dependence, perhaps in the context of his own childhood and the way his parents dealt with his dependence? Dealing with these situations is always a struggle and a balancing act; perhaps what is important is not that the therapist succeed in any definite way, but the fact that the therapist is trying.

If child and parents are to take something of value from their experience with the therapist, it may very well be a sense of how to work toward containing and integrating various states of mind such as we are describing. In the case under discussion, if the therapist can find a way to "hold" the feelings of both mother and father as well as his own, he is in a good position to help the child with his clinginess, dependence, wishes for autonomy, anxiety about autonomy and dependence, and so on. The parents may be helped to help the child in this way, as well. The therapist thus offers herself as a sort of depository for affects and states of mind, but not an initially empty or passive depository. Rather, the therapist's own character and psychological make-up are part and parcel of how the therapist experiences the child, family, and others; the therapist's personality also determines the nature of the struggle the therapist must engage in, to be able to recognize and identify with the feelings and mental states of each person.

In classical psychoanalysis, the analyst's job was to analyze, pure and simple. Nonanalytic interventions were to be avoided, if at all possible. The analyst's primary purpose was not to be helpful (often framed as "supportive" in the analytic literature) in any direct or simple way. In fact, actions that might relieve the patient's anxiety, for example, tended to be seen as bolstering the defenses and thus at cross purposes with making the unconscious conscious. At best, such anxiety-relieving interventions might be seen as ego building, in the case of an "ego-deficient" patient, and thus preparatory to "true" analytic, that is, interpretive, work. The distinction between "therapy" and "analysis" often turned on this distinction between work that aimed to help, and work that aimed to enhance awareness.

If the analyst's primary concern was to analyze, not to help directly, the question arose as to how therapeutic change occurred; how were people helped, in the end, by a procedure that did not set out to help? The classical analytic answer was that the ego was in a stronger and more autonomous position when the unconscious was made conscious. The person was in a better position to take conscious control of his life, rather than be driven by forces out of his awareness. Our effort has been to develop a model that is basically analytic, yet one within which the therapist is free to undertake directly helpful actions. We do not counterpose helpful or supportive action to awareness-enhancing interpretive work. Within a classical framework, Pine (1985) was among the first to propose that interpretation could take place within a context of support as well as within the usual context of abstinence (in which the analyst took care to withhold any action that might be gratifying to the patient). Thus, Pine began to break down the traditional opposition between analysis and therapy. The distinction between support and abstinence was critical in a theoretical framework within which support implied participation, thus a departure from the analytic role. For us, as interpersonally oriented analytic clinicians, seeing the analyst as inevitably a participant in one way or another, the distinction between support and abstinence is less salient.

So we aim to be helpful, and we aim to foster an analytic process. We try to be helpful in ways that also foster an analytic process. Let us conclude, then, with an effort to be explicit about our notion of what constitutes an analytic process. On one level, we view an analytic process as one that aims to enhance awareness of the meaning-making processes occurring in the participants, especially as relates to the interaction among them. This definition of the analytic process is quite consistent with classical formulations. On another level, and not consistent with a classical model, we view an analytic process as one that promotes psychic integration in the child and in the various individuals involved in the child's psychological world, as discussed above.

We aim to promote psychic integration, in terms of "standing in the spaces," as discussed above, in our work with individual children and adolescents, and in the work we do with the parents, teachers, siblings, and others in their family and community networks. This task requires the analyst to identify with a number of different people, some of whom are quite at odds with one another, and to do considerable "working through in the countertransference" (Pick 1988) in the service of containing and integrating the various feelings and anxieties in play. The analyst often experiences this process as psychologically challenging, distressing, and ultimately, growth promoting. She will likely be called on to do considerable soul searching and self-analysis. This personal struggle, as we have described it throughout this book, is also at the core of the therapeutic action of the work we do; the therapist's struggle to find a place for each person in the child's life, and for each feeling in the child's mental life, represents the therapist's personal engagement with the people she works with. Without this sort of personal engagement, any technical intervention, no matter how sophisticated and theoretically informed, will fail to touch people profoundly. When such engagement is present, appropriate technique tends to fall into place quite intuitively.

Postscript on Endings[1]

In an ideal world, the ending of a child therapy would be like the experience of finishing the writing of a book. One would have covered most of the ground one intended to cover, one would have achieved a sense of completeness. In real life, the experiences, both of terminating a treatment and of finishing a book, are quite different. In the case of writing a book, one keeps wondering what is missing, what could have been written about differently, more intelligently, more clearly. Mitchell (1993) noted how, as time passes, even in the course of writ-

---

1. The traditional psychoanalytic word for the ending of an analysis is "termination." We prefer the word "ending." Perhaps because of the association with Arnold Schwartzenegger's film "The Terminator," this word sounds too final and too impersonal. As will be clear in the discussion that follows, our concept of "ending" is quite different from the classical "termination" in that we do not envision a completely analyzed person emerging from the treatment, nor do we conceive of a universal developmental process that we aim to have our patients resume as a criterion for the ending of treatment.

ing a book but certainly after finishing the book, one's views keep evolving and one finds oneself disagreeing with something one wrote earlier, or finding it limited in some way. If an author kept going back to revise sections of the manuscript that no longer quite fit with the author's evolving views, the book would never be finished. So completing a book always entails tolerating a sense of imperfection and dissatisfaction.

So it is with any therapy or analysis, but especially those with a child. One of the liabilities of classical psychoanalysis was that it gave too idealized a picture of termination, too definite an idea of the product: an analyzed person. The unconscious was to be made conscious (an impossibility on the face of it: Was the analyzed person to be left without an unconscious?) or where id was, there ego was to be (leading Lacan to his provocative counterproposal that where ego was, there id was to be). When enough "working through" was accomplished, new structures would be in place, and the analysis was complete. As Mitchell (1993) has pointed out, this view of termination suggests that the fully analyzed person has stopped changing, his psyche having been rendered whole. An alternative view of when an adult analysis is ready to end might emphasize process, a habit of self-reflection that the patient has adopted so that self-analysis can continue after ending. Given a two-person view of the analytic situation, however, one would expect that the ground that is covered in an analysis would depend on the particularities of the patient and analyst and the interaction between them. It is not simply a question of blind spots and limitations of the analytic couple, but of what particular "clearing" will be made in the vast forest of the unconscious by these two people. Different issues will become salient for a given patient with a different analyst, or with the same analyst at a different point in each of their lives. And so the question of when to end an analysis becomes one that must be answered by these two particular people in terms of the logic of the process that has developed between them. An analysis might go on forever, just as the writing of a book could go on forever. From this point of view, ending depends more on acceptance of imperfection and limitation than on striving for or awaiting an ideal outcome.

In the child analytic literature on termination, the emphasis has been on the resumption of a stalled or derailed developmental process. This criterion for termination depends on an idealized notion of child development, one that we have eschewed, or at least revised and complicated, in this book. We do not believe that there is any singular developmental pathway that all children ideally should progress along, especially when it is a question of social–emotional development. Our notion of development is contextual and relational in any case, so that it becomes inconceivable to consider a child's development in isolation from the interpersonal environment. Nonetheless, in considering when a treatment is ready to end, we do consider in a more individualized way when a particular child's development seems to be back on track. For example, we might ask questions such as: Is the child taking more satisfaction from peer relationships? Is she interested in learning in and out of school? In and outside the therapy, is the child able to play and be playful? Is the child able to relax, act spontaneously, and enjoy life, at least some of the time? Is the child less guilt-ridden, inhibited, anxious, or depressed? Does the child have a better feeling about herself? We make some of these judgments based on what we hear from parents and teachers, but we also rely on developments within the therapeutic interaction. We hope that by the time the therapy ends, the child will have engaged in a relatively free process of communication with the therapist, via play and via verbal communication. Often the play process has a intrinsic dynamic that defines its state of development: for example, Frankel (1998b) describes a process of increasing symbolization in fantasy play, while Caspary (1993) describes a process of progressive re-owning of disavowed psychic content.

We do hope that we will be able to engage the child and family in an ending *process*, that is, that everyone involved will be thoughtful about the decision to end the treatment in the light of their goals and the progress achieved. Additionally, we hope that all concerned will be open to the *experience* of saying good-bye, with all the sadness, regret, relief, disappointment, pride, and other feelings that may be entailed.

Often enough, however, we do not get the kind of ending we hope for. Therapy, like life itself, does not always come to an orderly ending. Sometimes therapies end arbitrarily, tied to external events: a child may go to boarding school, or an adolescent may graduate and go away to college, or the family may move (in such cases, it is often useful to make a referral to a new therapist). Parents' ideas about when therapy should end may have little to do with the logic of the particular process that has developed between child and therapist. While some parents may have the inclination and resources to let the child therapy take its course, other parents may simply be looking for life to become easier or more rewarding at home, or they may be looking for the school to stop complaining about their child. Symptom relief may be enough for them, while the therapist may have her eye on other, less obvious, changes. Some parents may be eager for the child therapy to end because they feel excluded from the therapist's relationship with the child, while other parents may be glad to share responsibility for their child with the therapist, so that they may even resist an ending that makes sense to the therapist and child. Or there may be financial considerations (as is often the case with adult patients as well), or considerations having to do with the pros and cons of using the time spent in therapy on other activities that have social, emotional, or intellectual value to the child, and so on. Periodic reviews with the parents of goals achieved and goals unmet from the points of view of therapist and each parent may help clarify where there are differences in goals and perceptions of progress, and allow for some degree of meeting of the minds. At the least, discussion of such differences may help prevent sudden and unexpected terminations that catch therapist and child off-guard. But the bottom line here is that, in the real world, endings do not fit any idealized pattern, and therapists are well advised to cultivate flexibility. As Phillips (1993) points out, one never knows what elements in any particular day will turn out to stimulate a dream that night. Similarly, as analysts and therapists we can never know what elements in any particular treatment will turn out to be meaningful and valuable to the child and the family, as life goes on. Therapists should keep in mind that children may often return to therapy, with the same therapist or a different one, at a new life stage or when a new challenge arises. In the most general terms, in the complex flow of the life of a child and a family, there are times when the balance of forces makes child therapy seem like a good idea, while a few months or years later a dance or karate class may seem a better way to use the time. Therapists who are able to go with the flow, without sacrificing their own values and opinions about what is best for the child, will be best positioned to take advantage of the opportunities for growth and change at those moments when the family seeks outside help.

References

Aber, J. L., and Slade, A. (1986). *The internal experience of parenting toddlers: toward an analysis of individual and developmental differences.* Unpublished paper presented at the International Conference of Infant Studies, Los Angeles, CA, April 10.

Abraham, N., and Torok, M. (1994). *The Shell and the Kernel*, ed. and trans. N. T. Rand. Chicago, IL: University of Chicago Press.

Achenbach, T. M., and Edelbrock, C. S. (1978). The classification of child psychopathology: a review and analysis of empirical efforts. *Psychological Bulletin* 85: 1275–1301.

Adam, K. S., Keller, A. E. S., and West, M. (1995). Attachment organization and vulnerability to loss, separation, and abuse in disturbed adolescents. In *Attachment Theory: Social, Developmental, and Clinical Perspectives*, pp. 309–341. Hillsdale, NJ: Analytic Press.

Ainsworth, M. D. S., Blehar, M. C., Waters, E., and Wall, S. (1978). *Patterns of Attachment: A Psychological Study of the Strange Situation.* Hillsdale, NJ: Erlbaum.

Ainsworth, M. D. S., and Bowlby, J. (1991). An ethological approach to personality development. *American Psychologist* 46: 331–341.

Altman, N. (1992). Relational perspectives on child psychoanalytic psychotherapy. In *Relational Perspectives in Psychoanalysis, ed.* N. J. Skolnick and S. C. Warshaw, pp. 175–194. Hillsdale, NJ: Analytic Press.

——— (1995). *The Analyst in the Inner City: Race, Class, and Culture through a Psychoanalytic Lens.* Hillsdale, NJ: Analytic Press.

——— (1997). The case of Ronald: oedipal issues in the treatment of a seven-year-old boy. *Psychoanalytic Dialogues* 7: 725–740.

Alvarez, A. (1992). *Live Company.* London and New York: Routledge & Kegan Paul.

American Psychiatric Association. (1994). *Diagnostic and Statistical Manual of Mental Disorders—Fourth Edition (DSM-IV).* Washington, DC.

Anthony, E. J. (1970a). The reactions of parents to adolescents and to their behavior. In *Parenthood: Its Psychology and Psychopathology,* ed. E. J. Anthony and T. Benedek, pp. 307–324. Boston: Little Brown.

——— (1970b). The reactions of parents to the oedipal child. In *Parenthood: Its Psychology and Psychopathology,* ed. E. J. Anthony and T. Benedek, pp. 275–288. Boston: Little Brown.

Anthony, E. J., and Benedek, T., eds. (1970). *Parenthood: Its Psychology and Psychopathology.* Boston: Little Brown.

Aries, P. (1962). *Centuries of Childhood: A Social History of Family Life.* New York: Knopf.

Arnold, L. E. (1978). *Helping Parents Help Their Children.* New York: Brunner/Mazel.

Aron, L. (1993). Working toward operational thought: Piagetian theory and psychoanalytic method. *Contemporary Psychoanalysis* 29: 289–313.

——— (1995). The internalized primal scene. *Psychoanalytic Dialogues* 5: 195–238.

——— (1996). *A Meeting of Minds: Mutuality in Psychoanalysis.* Hillsdale, NJ: Analytic Press.

Attwood, T. (1998). *Asperger's Syndrome: A Guide for Parents and Professionals.* Philadelphia, PA: Jessica Kingsley.

Axline, V. (1969). *Play Therapy.* New York: Ballantine.

Ayres, A. J., and Robbins, J. (1991). *Sensory Integration and the Child.* Los Angeles: Western Psychological Services.

Bachelard, G. (1994). *On Poetic Imagination and Reverie.* Dallas, TX: Spring.

Barnett, D. W., Manley, J. T., and Cicchetti, D. (1993). Defining child maltreatment. In *Child Abuse, Child Development, and Sound Policy: Advances in Applied Developmental Psychology, Vol. 8.,* ed. D. Cicchetti and S. L. Toth. Norwood, NJ: Ablex.

Barth, R. P. (1998). Abusive and neglectful parents and the care of their children. In *All Our Families: New Policies for a New Century,* ed. M. A. Mason and A. Skolnick. New York: Oxford University Press.

Bateson, G. (1955). A theory of play and fantasy. In *Play: Its Role in Development and Evolution,* ed. J. S. Bruner, A. Jolly, and K. Sylva. New York: Basic Books, 1976.

Bateson, G., Jackson, D. D., Haley, J., and Weakland, J. (1956). Toward a theory of schizophrenia. *Behavioral Science* 1: 251–264.

Beebe, B. and Lachmann, F. (1988). The contribution of mother–infant mutual influence to the origins of self- and object-representations. *Psychoanalytic Psychology* 5: 305–337.

———— (1992). The contributions of mother–infant mutual influence to the origins of self- and object-representations. In *Relational Perspectives in Psychoanalysis,* ed. N. J. Skolnock and S. C. Warshaw, pp. 83–118. Hillsdale, NJ: Analytic Press.

———— (1994). Representation and internalization in infancy: three principles of salience. *Psychoanalytic Psychology* 11: 127–165.

———— (1997). Mother–infant interaction structures and presymbolic self- and object-representations. *Psychoanalytic Dialogues* 7: 133–182.

Bekoff, M., and Byers, J. A. (1998). Introduction. In *Animal Play: Evolutionary, Comparative, and Ecological Perspectives,* pp. xiii–xvi. Cambridge: Cambridge University Press.

Benedek, T. (1959). Parenthood as a developmental phase: a contribution to libido theory. *Journal of the American Psychoanalytic Association* 7: 389–417.

———— (1970). Parenthood during the life cycle. In *Parenthood: Its Psychology and Psychopathology,* ed. E. J. Anthony and T. Benedek, pp. 185–206. Boston: Little Brown.

Benjamin, J. (1988). *The Bonds of Love.* New York: Pantheon.

———— (1990). Recognition and destruction: an outline of inter-subjectivity. *Psychoanalytic Psychology* 7 (supplement): 33–47.

———— (1991). Father and daughter: identification with difference—a contribution to gender heterodoxy. *Psychoanalytic Dialogues* 1(3): 277–299.

———— (1995). *Like Subjects, Love Objects.* New Haven, CT: Yale University Press.

———— (1998). *The Shadow of the Other: Intersubjectivity and Gender in Psychoanalysis.* New York and London: Routledge & Kegan Paul.

Bergmann, A. (1993). Parents participating in their children's therapy. *Newsletter*, Section 2 (Childhood and Adolescence), Div. 39 (Psychoanalysis), vol. 1, pp. 17–20. Washington, DC: American Psychological Association.

Bergmann, M., and Jucovy, M. (1982). *Generations of the Holocaust.* New York: Basic Books.

Bion, W. R. (1959). Attacks on linking. In *Melanie Klein Today, Vol. 1*, ed. E. Bott-Spillius. London: Routledge & Kegan Paul, 1988.

———— (1961). *Experiences in Groups.* London: Routledge.

———— (1962). A theory of thinking. *International Journal of Psycho-Analysis* 43: 306–310.

———— (1967). Notes on memory and desire. In *Melanie Klein Today: Developments in Theory and Practice Vol. 2: Mainly Practice.* London: Routledge & Kegan Paul, 1988.

Birch, M. (1993). Who's holding the environment? Issues of parents of traumatized children. *Newsletter*, Section 2 (Childhood and Adolescence), Div. 39 (Psychoanalysis), vol. 2, pp. 14–16, 20. Washington, DC: American Psychological Association.

Blatt, S. J., and Blass, R. B. (1990). Attachment and separateness: a dialectic model of the products and processes of development throughout the life cycle. *Psychoanalytic Study of the Child* 45: 107–127. New Haven, CT: Yale University Press.

Bollas, C. (1987). Expressive uses of the countertransference. In *The Shadow of the Object.* New York: Columbia University Press.

Bornstein, B. (1951). On latency. *Psychoanalytic Study of the Child* 6: 279–285. New York: International Universities Press.

———— (1953). Fragment of an analysis of an obsessional child. *Psychoanalytic Study of the Child* 8: 313–332. New York: International Universities Press.

Bowlby, J. (1969). *Attachment and Loss: Vol. 1, Attachment*. New York: Basic Books.

——— (1973). *Attachment and Loss: Vol. 2, Separation: Anxiety and Anger*. New York: Basic Books.

——— (1980). *Attachment and Loss: Vol. 3, Loss: Sadness and Depression*. New York: Basic Books.

Brazelton, T. B., Kozlowski, B., and Main, M. (1974). The origins of reciprocity. In *The Effect of the Infant on Its Caregiver*, ed. M. Lewis and L. Rosenblum, pp. 49–76. New York: Wiley-Interscience.

Bretherton, I. (1995). The origins of attachment theory. In *Attachment Theory: Social, Developmental and Clinical Perspectives*, ed. S. Goldberg, R. Muir, and J. Kerr, pp. 45–84. Hillsdale, NJ: Analytic Press.

Breuer, J., and Freud, S. (1893–1895). Fraulein Anna O. *Standard Edition* 2: 21–47.

Brinich, P. (1984). Aggression in early childhood: joint treatment of children and parents. *Psychoanalytic Study of the Child*, 39: 493–508.

Bromberg, P. M. (1994). "Speak! That I may see you": some reflections on dissociation, reality and psychoanalytic listening. *Psychoanalytic Dialogues*, 4: 517–547.

——— (1996). Standing in the spaces: the multiplicity of self and the psychoanalytic relationship. *Contemporary Psychoanalysis* 32: 509–535.

——— (1998). *Standing in the Spaces*. Hillsdale, NJ: Analytic Press.

Bruner, J. S. (1972a). Introduction. In *Play: Its Role in Development and Evolution*, ed. J. S. Bruner, A. Jolly, and K. Sylva, pp. 13–24. New York: Basic Books, 1976.

——— (1972b). Nature and uses of immaturity. In *Play: Its Role in Development and Evolution*, ed. J. S. Bruner, A. Jolly, and K. Sylva, pp. 28–65. New York: Basic Books, 1976.

Burlingham, D. (1951). Present trends in handling the mother–child relationship during the therapeutic process. *Psychoanalytic Study of the Child* 6: 31–37.

Bush, D. (1960). *The Portable Milton*. New York: Viking.

Casement, P. (1985). *Learning from the Patient*. New York: Guilford.

Caspary, A. (1993). Aspects of the therapeutic action of child analytic treatment. *Psychoanalytic Psychology* 10: 207–220.

Cassidy, J., Kirsh, S. J., Scolton, K. L., and Parke, R. D. (1996). Attachment and representations of peer relationships. *Developmental Psychology* 32: 892–904.

Cavell, M. (1993). *The Psychoanalytic Mind.* Cambridge, MA: Harvard University Press.

Chazan, S. (1995). *The Simultaneous Treatment of Parent and Child.* New York: Basic Books.

Chess, S. (1980). Temperament and children at risk. In *The Child In His Family,* ed. E. J. Anthony and C. Koupernik, pp. 121–130. New York: John Wiley.

Chethik, M. (1989). *Techniques of Child Therapy: Psychodynamic Strategies.* New York: Guilford.

Chodorow, N. (1994). *Femininities, Masculinities, Sexualities.* Lexington: University of Kentucky Press.

Coates, S. (1997). Is it time to jettison the concept of developmental lines? Commentary on de Marneffe's paper "Bodies and Words." *Gender and Psychoanalysis* 2: 35–54.

Cohen, R. S., and Weissman, S. H. (1984). The parenting alliance. In *Parenthood: A Psychodynamic Perspective,* ed. R. S. Cohen, B. J. Cohler, and S. H. Weissman, pp. 33–49. New York: Guilford.

Colarusso, C. A. (1990). The third individuation: the effect of biological parenthood on separation-individuation processes in adulthood. *Psychoanalytic Study of the Child* 45: 179–194.

Collins, W. A., ed. (1984). *Development During Middle Childhood: The Years from Six to Twelve.* Washington, DC: National Academy Press.

Constantine, L., and Martinson, F. (1981). *Children and Sex: New Findings, New Perspectives.* Boston: Little, Brown.

Cooper, A., and Witenberg, E. (1983). The stimulation of curiosity in the supervisory process. *Contemporary Psychoanalysis* 19: 248–264.

Crittenden, P. McK. (1995). Attachment and psychopathology. In *Attachment Theory: Social, Developmental, and Clinical Perspectives,* ed. S. Goldberg, R. Muir, and J. Kerr, pp. 367–406. Hillsdale, NJ: Analytic Press.

Davies, J. M., and Frawley, M. G. (1994). *Treating the Adult Survivor of Childhood Sexual Abuse: A Psychoanalytic Perspective.* New York: Basic Books.

de Marneffe, D. (1997). Bodies and words: a study of young children's genital and gender knowledge. *Gender and Psychoanalysis* 2(1): 3–33.

Demos, E. V. (1992). The early organization of the psyche. In *Interface of Psychoanalysis and Psychology*, ed. J. W. Barron, M. N. Eagle, and D. Wolitzky, pp. 200–232. Washington, D C: American Psychological Association.

———— (1999). The search for psychological models: commentary on papers by Stephen Seligman and by Robin C. Silverman and Alicia F. Lieberman, *Psychoanalytic Dialogues* 9: 219–227.

Donnellan, G. (1989). Borderline children and the dilemma of therapeutic efficacy. *Contemporary Psychoanalysis* 25: 393–411.

Dreger, A. (1998). When medicine goes too far in the pursuit of normality. *New York Times*, July 28, p. F4.

Eagle, M. (1995). The developmental perspectives of attachment and psychoanalytic theory. In *Attachment Theory: Social, Developmental, and Clinical Perspectives*, ed. S. Goldberg, R. Muir, and J. Kerr, pp. 123–150. Hillsdale, NJ: Analytic Press.

Ehrenberg, D. B. (1992). *The Intimate Edge*. New York: Norton.

Ekstein, R. (1966). *Children of Time and Space, of Action and Impulse*. New York: Appleton-Century-Crofts.

Elkisch, P. (1953). Simultaneous treatment of a child and his mother. *American Journal of Psychotherapy* 7: 105–121.

Elmhirst, S. I. (1988). The Kleinian setting for child analysis. *International Review of Psycho-Analysis* 15: 5–12.

Emde, R. (1981). The prerepresentational self and its affective core. *Psychoanalytic Study of the Child* 36: 165–192.

Epstein, L., and Feiner, A. H. (1983). *Countertransference: The Therapist's Contribution to the Therapeutic Situation*. New York: Jason Aronson.

Epstein, S. (1979). The stability of behavior: I. On predicting most of the people much of the time. *Journal of Personality and Social Psychology* 37: 1097–1126.

Erikson, E. H. (1950). *Childhood and Society*. New York: Norton, 1963.

———— (1956). The concept of ego identity, *Journal of the American Psychoanalytic Association* 4: 56–121.

———— (1959). *Identity and the Life Cycle*. New York: Norton.

Erlanger, S. (1999). Serbian protesters install their own government. *New York Times*, September 25.

Fagen, R. (1981). *Animal Play Behavior*. Oxford: Oxford University Press.

Fairbairn, W. R. D. (1943). The repression and the return of bad objects. In *Psychoanalytic Studies of the Personality*, pp. 59–81. London and Boston: Routledge & Kegan Paul, 1952.

——— (1944/1952). Endopsychic structure considered in terms of object relationships. In *Psychoanalytic Studies of the Personality*, pp. 82–136. London and Boston: Routledge & Kegan Paul.

——— (1952). *Psychoanalytic Studies of the Personality: The Object Relation Theory of Personality*. London and Boston: Routledge & Kegan Paul.

Fast, I. (1990). Aspects of early gender development: toward a reformulation. *Psychoanalytic Psychology* 7 (Supplement): 105–117.

Feinaur, L., Mitchell, J., Harper, J., and Dane, S. (1996). The impact of hardiness and severity of childhood sexual abuse of adult adjustment. *American Journal of Family Therapy* 24: 206–214.

Feldman, S. S., and Elliott, G. R. (1990). *At the Threshold: The Developing Adolescent*. Cambridge, MA: Harvard University Press.

Ferenczi, S. (1913). Stages in the development of the sense of reality. In *First Contributions to Psycho-Analysis*, pp. 213–239 (originally published in 1916). London: Hogarth, 1952.

——— (1930–1932). Notes and fragments. In *Final Contributions to the Problems and Methods of Psychoanalysis*, pp. 219–279. London: Hogarth, 1955.

——— (1932). *The Clinical Diary of Sandor Ferenczi*, ed. J. Dupont, trans. M. Balint and N. Z. Jackson. Cambridge, MA: Harvard University Press, 1988.

——— (1933). Confusion of tongues between adults and the child. In *Final Contributions to the Problems and Methods of Psycho-analysis*, pp. 156–167. London: Hogarth, 1955.

Fernando, S. (1995). *Mental Health in a Multi-Ethnic Society*. London and New York: Routledge & Kegan Paul.

First, E. (1994). The leaving game, or I'll play you and you play me: the emergence of dramatic role play in 2-year-olds. In *Children at Play: Clinical and Developmental Approaches to Meaning and Representation*, ed. A. Slade and D. W. Wolf, pp. 111–132. New York: Oxford University Press.

Fischer, K., and Bullock, D. (1984). Cognitive development in school-age children. In *Development during Middle Childhood: The Years from Six to Twelve*, ed. W. A. Collins. Washington, DC: National Academy Press.

Fish-Murray, C. C., Koby, E. V., and van der Kolk, B. A. (1987). Evolving ideas: the effect of abuse on children's thought. In *Psychological Trauma*, ed. B. A. van der Kolk, pp. 89–110. Washington, DC: American Psychiatric Press.

Fonagy, P., Steele, M., Steele, H., et al. (1995). Attachment, the reflective self, and borderline states: the predictive specificity of the adult attachment interview and pathological emotional development. In *Attachment Theory: Social, Developmental, and Clinical Perspectives*, ed. S. Goldberg, R. Muir, and J. Kerr. Hillsdale, NJ: Analytic Press.

Foucault, M. (1980). *The History of Sexuality, Volume 1*. New York: Vintage.

Fouts, R. (1997). *Next of Kin: My Conversations with Chimpanzees*. New York: Avon.

Fraiberg, S., Adelson, E., and Shapiro, V. (1975). Ghosts in the nursery: a psychoanalytic approach to the problems of impaired infant–mother relationships. *Journal of the American Academy of Child Psychiatry* 14: 387–421.

Frankel, J. B. (1998a). Ferenczi's trauma theory. *American Journal of Psychoanalysis* 58: 41–61.

——— (1998b). The play's the thing: how the essential processes of therapy are seen most clearly in child therapy. *Psychoanalytic Dialogues* 8: 149–182.

Freedman, N. (1985). The concept of transformation in psychoanalysis. *Psychoanalytic Psychology* 2: 317–339.

Freud, A. (1927 [1926]). Four lectures on child analysis. In *The Writings of Anna Freud, Volume 1, Introduction to Psychoanalysis*. New York: International Universities Press, 1974.

——— (1936). *The Writings of Anna Freud, Volume 2: The Ego and the Mechanisms of Defence*. New York: International Universities Press, 1966.

——— (1946). *The Psychoanalytic Treatment of Children*. New York: International Universities Press.

—— (1965). Normality and pathology in childhood: assessments of development. In *The Writings of Anna Freud, Volume 6.* New York: International Universities Press.

—— (1966). *The Ego and the Mechanisms of Defence.* New York: International Universities Press.

Freud, S. (1905). Three essays on the theory of sexuality. *Standard Edition* 7: 125–245.

—— (1909). Analysis of a phobia in a five-year-old. *Standard Edition* 10: 3–149.

—— (1912). The dynamics of transference. *Standard Edition* 12: 99–108.

—— (1914). On narcissism: an introduction. *Standard Edition* 14: 73–102.

—— (1916). Some character types met with in psychoanalytic work. *Standard Edition* 14: 311–333.

—— (1917). Mourning and melancholia. *Standard Edition* 14: 243–258.

—— (1923). *The Ego and the Id. Standard Edition* 19: 3–66.

—— (1926). *Inhibitions, Symptoms and Anxiety. Standard Edition* 20: 87–172.

—— (1933). *New Introductory Lectures on Psycho-Analysis:* Femininity. *Standard Edition* 22: 112–135.

Fromm, E. (1941). *Escape from Freedom.* New York: Holt, Rinehart, & Winston.

—— (1947). *Man for Himself: An Inquiry into the Psychology of Ethics.* New York: Holt, Rinehart, & Winston.

—— (1980). *Greatness and Limitations of Freud's Thought.* New York: Harper & Row.

—— (1982). *The Forgotten Language.* New York: Grove.

Furman, E. (1957). Treatment of under-fives by way of their parents. *Psychoanalytic Study of the Child* 12: 250–262. New York: International Universities Press.

—— (1969). Treatment via the mother. In *The Therapeutic Nursery School,* ed. R. A. Furman and A. Katan, pp. 64–98. New York: International Universities Press.

Gardner, R. (1971). *Therapeutic Communication with Children: The Mutual Storytelling Technique.* Northvale, NJ: Jason Aronson, 1986.

———— (1976a). Advising separating parents. In *Psychotherapy with Children of Divorce*, pp. 3–37. New York: Jason Aronson.

———— (1976b). Advising parents subsequent to the separation and divorce. In *Psychotherapy with Children of Divorce*, pp. 329–363. New York: Jason Aronson.

Garmezy, N. (1991). Stress, competence, and development: continuities in the study of schizophrenic adults, children vulnerable to psychopathology, and the search for stress-resistant children. *American Journal of Orthopsychiatry* 57: 159–174.

Ge, X., Conger, R. D., Cadoret, R. J., et al. (1996). The developmental interface between nature and nurture: a mutual influence model of child antisocial behavior and parent behaviors. *Developmental Psychology* 32: 574–589.

Ge, X., Lorenz, F. O., Conger, R. D., et al. (1994). Trajectories of stressful life events and depressive symptoms during adolescence. *Developmental Psychology* 30: 467–483.

Gensler, D. (1994). Soliciting dreams in child psychotherapy: the influence of the therapist's interest. *Contemporary Psychoanalysis* 30(2): 367–383.

Gill, M. M. (1982). *Analysis of Transference, Volume 1*. New York: International Universities Press.

———— (1994). *Psychoanalysis in Transition*. Hillsdale, NJ: Analytic Press.

Gilligan, C. (1982). *In a Different Voice: Psychological Theory and Women's Development*. Cambridge, MA: Harvard University Press.

Glenn, J., Sabot, L., and Bernstein, I. (1978). The role of the parent in child analysis. In *Child Analysis and Therapy*, ed. J. Glenn, pp. 393–426. New York: Jason Aronson.

Goldberg, S. (1995). Introduction. In *Attachment Theory: Social, Developmental, and Clinical Perspectives*, ed. S. Goldberg, R. Muir, and J. Kerr, pp. 1–15. Hillsdale, NJ: Analytic Press.

Grand, S. (1997). The paradox of innocence: dissociative "adhesive" states in perpetrators of incest. *Psychoanalytic Dialogues* 7: 465–490.

Greenberg, J. R. (1986). Theoretical models and the analyst's neutrality. *Contemporary Psychoanalysis* 22: 87–106.

———— (1991). *Oedipus and Beyond: A Clinical Theory*. Cambridge, MA: Harvard University Press.

Greenberg, J., and Mitchell, S. (1983). *Object Relations in Psychoanalytic Theory*. Cambridge, MA: Harvard University Press.

Greenspan, S. I. (1992). *Infancy and Early Childhood: The Practice of Clinical Assessment and Intervention with Emotional and Developmental Challenges.* Madison, CT: International Universities Press.

Guntrip, H. (1969). *Schizoid Phenomena, Object Relations, and the Self.* New York: International Universities Press.

Haley, J., and Hoffman, L. (1967). *Techniques of Family Therapy.* New York: Basic Books.

Harris, A. (1996). The conceptual power of multiplicity. *Contemporary Psychoanalysis* 32: 537–552.

——— (1999). Gender as a soft assembly: tomboys' stories. *Studies in Gender and Sexuality* 1: 223–250.

Harris, J. (1998). *The Nurture Assumption: Why Children Turn Out the Way They Do.* New York: Free Press.

Hart, C. (1999). The mysterious placebo effect. *Modern Drug Discovery* 2: 30–40.

Hartmann, T. (1997). *Attention Deficit Disorder: A Different Perception (A Hunter in a Farmer's World).* Grass Valley, CA: Underwood.

Henry, B., Caspi, A., Moffitt, T. E., and Silva, P. A. (1996). Temperamental and familial predictors of violent and nonviolent criminal convictions: age 3 to age 18. *Developmental Psychology* 32, 614–623.

Herman, J. L. (1992). *Trauma and Recovery.* New York: Basic Books.

Herman, J. L., and van der Kolk, B. A. (1987). Traumatic antecedents of borderline personality disorder. In *Psychological Trauma*, ed. B. A. van der Kolk, pp. 111–126. Washington, DC: American Psychiatric Press.

Hofer, M. A. (1995). Hidden regulators: implications for a new understanding of attachment, separation, and loss. In *Attachment Theory: Social Developmental and Clinical Perspectives*, ed. S. Goldberg, R. Muir, and J. Kerr, pp. 203–230. Hillsdale, NJ: Analytic Press.

Hoffman, I. Z. (1998). *Ritual and Spontaneity in Psychoanalysis.* Hillsdale, NJ: Analytic Press.

Hoffman, M. B. (1984). The parents' experience with the child's therapist. In *Parenthood: A Psychodynamic Perspective*, ed. R. S. Cohen, B. J. Cohler, and S. H. Weissman, pp. 164–172. New York: Guilford.

Hollingshead, A. B., and Redlich, F. C. (1958). *Social Class and Mental Illness.* New York: Wiley.

Hug-Hellmuth, H. (1921). On the technique of child psychoanalysis. *International Journal of Psycho-Analysis* 2: 287–305.

Huizinga, J. (1955). *Homo Ludens: A Study of the Play Element in Culture*. Boston: Beacon.

Inhelder, B., and Piaget, J. (1964). *The Early Growth of Logic in the Child*. New York: Harper & Row.

Jacobs, T. (1991). *The Use of the Self*. Madison, CT: International Universities Press.

Jessner, L., Weigert, E., and Foy, J. L. (1970). The development of parental attitudes during pregnancy. In *Parenthood: Its Psychology and Psychopathology*, ed. E. J. Anthony and T. Benedek, pp. 209–244. Boston: Little Brown.

Joseph, B. (1985). Transference: the total situation. *International Journal of Psycho-Analysis* 66: 447–454.

——— (1987). Projective identification—some clinical aspects. (And) Discussion of Joseph's paper. In *Projection, Identification, and Projective Identification*, ed. J. Sandler. New York: International Universities Press.

——— (1989). *Psychic Equilibrium and Psychic Change*. New York: Tavistock.

Kagan, J. (1984). *The Nature of the Child*. New York: Basic Books.

——— (1994). *Galen's Prophesy: Temperament in Human Nature*. New York: Basic Books.

Katz, L. F., and Gottman, J. M. (1993). Patterns of marital conflict predict children's internalizing and externalizing behaviors. *Developmental Psychology* 29: 940–950.

Kernberg, O. (1985). *Borderline Conditions and Pathological Narcissism*. New York: Jason Aronson.

Kestenberg, J. (1970). The effect on parents of the child's transition into and out of latency. In *Parenthood: Its Psychology and Psychopathology*, ed. E. J. Anthony and T. Benedek. New York: Jason Aronson.

Klein, M. (1932). *The Psycho-Analysis of Children*. New York: Free Press, 1975.

——— (1946). Notes on some schizoid mechanisms. In *Envy and Gratitude and Other Works 1946–1963*. London: Hogarth, 1980.

——— (1955). The psycho-analytic play technique: its history and significance. In *New Directions in Psycho-Analysis*, ed. M. Klein, D. Heimann, and R. Money-Kyrle. New York: Basic Books.

——— (1959). Our adult world and its roots in infancy. In *Envy and Gratitude and Other Works 1946–1963*. London: Hogarth, 1980.

———— (1961). *Narrative of a Child Analysis*. London: Hogarth.

———— (1975). *Love, Guilt, and Reparation and Other Works: 1921–1945*. New York: Delta.

———— (1976). Some theoretical conclusions regarding the emotional life of the infant. In *Envy and Gratitude and Other Works 1946–1963*. London: Hogarth.

Knell, S. (1997). *Cognitive-Behavioral Play Therapy*. Northvale, NJ: Jason Aronson.

Kohlberg, L. (1969). Stage and sequence: the cognitive developmental approach to socialization. In *Handbook of Socialization Theory and Research*, ed. E. A. Gossin. Chicago: Rand McNally.

Kohut, H. (1971). *The Analysis of the Self*. New York: International Universities Press.

Krimendahl, E. (1998). Metaphor in child psychoanalysis: not simply a means to an end. *Contemporary Psychoanalysis* 34(1): 49–66.

Kris, A. O. (1981). On giving advice to parents in analysis. *Psychoanalytic Study of the Child* 36: 151–162. New Haven, CT: Yale University Press.

Krugman, S. (1987). Trauma in the family: perspectives on the intergenerational transmission of violence. In *Psychological Trauma*, ed. B. van der Kolk, pp. 127–151. Washington, DC: American Psychiatric Press.

Lachmann, F., and Beebe, B. (1996). Three principles of salience in the organization of the patient–analyst interaction. *Psychoanalytic Psychology* 13: 1–22.

Lakoff, G., and Johnson, M. (1980). *Metaphors We Live By*. Chicago: University of Chicago Press.

Langer, S. (1967). *Mind: An Essay on Human Feeling*. Baltimore, MD: Johns Hopkins Press.

Levenson, E. A. (1972). *The Fallacy of Understanding*. New York: Basic Books.

———— (1983). *The Ambiguity of Change*. New York: Basic Books.

———— (1992). Harry Stack Sullivan. *Contemporary Psychoanalysis* 28: 450–466.

Lewis, O., and O'Brien, J. (1991). Clinical use of dreams with latency-age children. *American Journal of Psychotherapy* 45: 527–543.

Lieberman, A. F. (1992). Infant–parent psychotherapy with toddlers. *Development and Psychopathology* 4: 559–574.

Lieberman, A., and Pawl, J. (1984). Searching for the best interests of the child: intervention with an abusive mother and her toddler. *Psychoanalytic Study of the Child* 39: 527–548. New Haven, CT: Yale University Press.

Loewald, E. (1987). Therapeutic play in space and time. *Psychoanalytic Study of the Child* 42: 173–192. New Haven: Yale University Press.

Lorenz, K. (1971). Psychology and phylogeny. In *Play: Its Role in Development and Evolution*, ed. J. S. Bruner, A. Jolly, and K. Sylva, pp. 84–95. New York: Basic Books, 1976.

Lyons-Ruth, K., Bronfman, E., and Atwood, G. (2000). A relational diathesis model of hostile-helpless states of mind: expressions in mother–infant interaction. In *Attachment Disorganization*, ed. J. Solomon and C. George. New York: Guilford.

Lyons-Ruth, K., and Jacobvitz, D. (1999). Attachment disorganization: unresolved loss, relational violence, and lapses in behavioral and attentional strategies. In *Handbook of Attachment: Theory, Research, and Clinical Implications*, ed. J. Cassidy and P. Shaver, pp. 520–554. New York: Guilford.

Maddi, S., and Kobasa, S. (1991). The development of hardiness. In *Stress and Coping: An Anthology* (3rd ed.), ed. A. Monat and R. S. Lazarus, pp. 245–257. New York: Columbia University Press.

Mahler, M. S., Pine, F., and Bergman, A. (1970). The mother's reaction to her toddler's drive for individuation. In *Parenthood: Its Psychology and Psychopathology*, ed. E. J. Anthony and T. Benedek, pp. 257–274. Boston: Little Brown.

——— (1975). *The Psychological Birth of the Human Infant*. New York: Basic Books.

Main, M. (1995). Recent studies in attachment: overview, with selected implications for clinical work. In *Attachment Theory: Social, Developmental and Clinical Perspectives*, ed. S. Goldberg, R. Muir, and J. Kerr, pp. 407–474. Hillsdale, NJ: Analytic Press.

Main, M., and Hesse, E. (1990). Parents' unresolved traumatic experiences are related to infant disorganized attachment status: is frightened and/or frightening parental behavior the linking mechanism? In *Attachment in the Preschool Years: Theory, Research and Intervention*, ed. M. Greenberg, D. Cicchetti, and E. M. Cummings, pp. 161–184. Chicago: University of Chicago Press.

Main, M., Kaplan, N., and Cassidy, J. (1985). Security in infancy, childhood and adulthood: a move to the level of representation. In *Growing Points of Attachment Theory and Research* (*Monographs of the Society for Research in Child Development, Volume 50*), ed. I. Bretherton and E. Waters, pp. 66–104.

Markus, H., and Nurius, P. (1984). Self understanding and self regulation in middle childhood. In *Development During Middle Childhood: The Years from Six to Twelve*, ed. W. A. Collins, pp. 213–221. Washington, DC: National Academy Press.

McDougall, J. (1978). *Plea for a Measure of Abnormality*. New York: Brunner Mazel.

Menzies, I. E. P. (1975). A case study of the functioning of social systems as a defense against anxiety. In *Group Relations Reader, Volume 1*, ed. A. D. Colman and W. H. Bexton. Jupiter, FL: A. K. Rice Institute.

Miller, A. (1981). *The Drama of the Gifted Child*. New York: Basic Books.

Minuchin, S. (1974). *Families and Family Therapy*. Cambridge, MA: Harvard University Press.

Mishne, J. (1992). The grieving child: manifest and hidden losses in childhood and adolescence. *Child and Adolescent Social Work Journal* 9: 471–490.

Mitchell, S. A. (1988). *Relational Concepts in Psychoanalysis*, Cambridge, MA: Harvard University Press.

——— (1993). *Hope and Dread in Psychoanalysis*. New York: Basic Books.

——— (1997). *Influence and Autonomy*. Hillsdale, NJ: Analytic Press.

Moustakas, C. (1997). *Children in Play Therapy*. Northvale, NJ: Jason Aronson.

Neiman, L. (1987). A critical review of the resiliency literature and its relevance to homeless children. *Children's Environments Quarterly* 5: 17–25.

Neubauer, P., and Neubauer, A. (1990). *Nature's Thumbprint: The New Genetics of Personality*. New York: Addison-Wesley.

Ochroch, R. (1983). *Minimal Brain Dysfunction in Children: A Clinical Approach*. New York: Human Sciences Press.

Ogden, T. H. (1979). On projective identification. *International Journal of Psycho-Analysis* 60: 357–373.

——— (1982). *Projective Identification and Psychotherapeutic Technique*. New York: Jason Aronson.

———— (1985). The mother, the infant, and the matrix: interpretations of the work of Donald Winnicott. *Contemporary Psychoanalysis* 21: 346–371.

———— (1986). *The Matrix of the Mind*. Northvale, NJ: Jason Aronson.

Olden, C. (1953). On adult empathy with children. *Psychoanalytic Study of the Child* 8: 111–126. New York: International Universities Press.

Ornstein, A. (1976). Making contact with the inner world of the child: toward a theory of psychoanalytic psychotherapy with children. *Comprehensive Psychiatry* 17: 3–36.

Pantone, P. J. (1995). Preadolescence and adolescence. In *Handbook of Interpersonal Psychoanalysis*, ed. M. Lionells, J. Fiscalini, C. H. Mann, and D. B. Stern, pp. 277–291. New York: Analytic Press.

———— (2000). Treating the parental relationship as the identified patient in child psychotherapy. *Journal of Infant, Child, and Adolescent Psychotherapy* 1: 19–38.

Paul, N. L. (1970). Parental empathy. In *Parenthood: Its Psychology and Psychopathology*, ed. E. J. Anthony and T. Benedek, pp. 337–352. Boston: Little Brown.

Pedlow, R., Sanson, A., Prior, M., and Oberklaid, F. (1993). Stability of maternally reported temperament from infancy to 8 years. *Developmental Psychology* 29: 998–1007.

Phillips, A. (1993). *On Kissing, Tickling, and Being Bored*. Cambridge, MA: Harvard University Press.

Piaget, J. (1932). *The Moral Judgment of the Child*. London: Kegan Paul.

———— (1937). *The Construction of Reality in the Child*. New York: Basic Books, 1954.

———— (1951). *Play, Dreams and Imitation in Childhood*. New York: Norton.

Pick, I. B. (1988). Working through in the countertransference. In *Melanie Klein Today*, ed. E. Bott-Spillius. London: Routledge.

Pine, F. (1985). *Developmental Theory and Clinical Process*. New Haven, CT: Yale University Press.

———— (1990). Infant research, the symbiotic phase and clinical work: a case study of a concept. In *Drive, Ego, Object and Self*. New York: Basic Books.

Pizer, S. A. (1998). *Building Bridges: The Negotiation of Paradox in Psychoanalysis*. Hillsdale, NJ: Analytic Press.

Plomin, R. (1986). Behavioral genetic methods. *Journal of Personality* 54: 226–261.

Racker, H. (1968). *Transference and Countertransference*. New York: International Universities Press.

Rak, C., and Patterson, L. (1996). Promoting resilience in at-risk children. *Journal of Counseling and Development* 74: 369–373.

Rapaport, D. (1967). *Collected Papers*, ed. M. Gill. New York: Basic Books.

Roiphe, H., and Galenson, E. (1981). *Infantile Origins of Sexual Identity*. New York: International Universities Press.

Rossiter, T., and LaVague, T. J. (1995). A comparison of EEG biofeedback and psychostimulants in treating attention deficit hyperactivities disorders. *Journal of Neurotherapy* 1: 48–59.

Rubins, Jack. (1978). *Karen Horney: Gentle Rebel of Psychoanalysis*. New York: Dial.

Rutter, M. (1987). Psychosocial resilience and protective mechanisms. *American Journal of Orthopsychiatry* 57: 316–331.

Sandler, J., Kennedy, H., and Tyson, R. L. (1980). *The Technique of Child Analysis: Discussions with Anna Freud*. Cambridge, MA: Harvard University Press.

Sandler, J., and Rosenblatt, B. (1962). The concept of the representational world. *Psychoanalytic Study of the Child* 17: 128–145. New York: International Universities Press.

Sanville, J. (1991). *The Playground of Psychoanalytic Therapy*. Hillsdale, NJ: Analytic Press.

Sarnoff, C. (1976). *Latency*. New York: Jason Aronson.

Schaefer, C., and Millman, H. (1977). *Therapies for Children*. San Francisco: Jossey-Bass.

Schafer, R. (1992). *Retelling a Life*. New York: Basic Books.

Schwartz, D. (1984). Psychoanalytic developmental perspectives on parenthood. In *Parenthood: A Psychodynamic Perspective*, ed. R. S. Cohen, B. J. Cohler, and S. H. Weissman, pp. 356–372. New York: Guilford.

Schweder, R. A. (1991). *Thinking Through Cultures*. Cambridge, MA: Harvard University Press.

Searles, H. (1979). The dedicated physician. In *Countertransference*. New York: International Universities Press.

Segal, H. (1964). *Introduction to the Work of Melanie Klein*. New York: Basic Books.

Seifer, R., Schiller, M., Sameroff, A. J., et al. (1996). Attachment, maternal sensitivity, and infant temperament during the first year of life. *Developmental Psychology* 32: 12–25.

Seligman, S. (1999). Integrating Kleinian theory and intersubjective infant research: observing projective identification. *Psychoanalytic Dialogues* 9: 129–159.

Sennett, R., and Cobb, J. (1972). *The Hidden Injuries of Class*. New York: Basic Books.

Shafran, R. B. (1995). Infancy. In *Handbook of Interpersonal Psychoanalysis*, ed. M. Lionells, J. Fiscalini, C. H. Mann, and D. B. Stern, pp. 235–252. Hillsdale, NJ: Analytic Press.

Shanok, R. S. (1990). Parenthood: a process marking identity and intimacy capacities: theoretical discussion and a case report. *Zero to Three* 11(2): 1–9, 11–12.

Shapiro, E. (1977). The borderline ego and the working alliance: indications for family and individual treatment in adolescence. *International Journal of Psycho-Analysis* 58: 77–87.

Shapiro, T., and Perry, R. (1976). Latency revisited: the age 7 plus or minus 1. *Psychoanalytic Study of the Child* 31: 79–105. New Haven, CT: Yale University Press.

Sillitoe, A. (1959). *Loneliness of the Long-Distance Runner*. New York: Knopf.

Silverman, M. (1981). Cognitive development and female psychology. *Journal of the American Psychoanalytic Association* 29: 581–605.

Silverman, R. C., and Lieberman, A. F. (1999). Negative maternal attributions, projective identification and the intergenerational transmission of violent relational patterns. *Psychoanalytic Dialogues* 9: 161–186.

Simpson, E. L. (1974). Moral development research: a case of scientific cultural bias. *Human Development* 17: 81–106.

Singer, E. (1965). *Key Concepts in Psychotherapy*. New York: Random House.

Slade, A. (1994). Making meaning and making believe: their role in the clinical process. In *Children at Play: Clinical and Developmental Approaches to Meaning and Representations*, ed. A. Slade and D. W. Wolf, pp. 81–107. New York: Oxford University Press.

Slochower, J. A. (1996). *Holding and Psychoanalysis*. Hillsdale, NJ: Analytic Press.

Smith, J., and Prior, M. (1995). Temperament and stress resilience in school-age children: a within-families study. *Journal of the American Academy of Child and Adolescent Psychiatry* 34: 168–179.

Spiegel, S. (1989). *An Interpersonal Approach to Child Therapy.* New York: Columbia University Press.

Spitz, R. (1946). Anaclitic depression. *Psychoanalytic Study of the Child* 2: 313–342.

Sroufe, A. (1995). *Emotional Development: The Organization of Emotional Life in the Early Years.* New York: Cambridge University Press, p. 39.

Stern, Daniel. (1985). *The Interpersonal World of the Infant: A View from Psychoanalysis and Developmental Psychology.* New York: Basic Books.

———— (1995). *The Motherhood Constellation: A Unified View of Parent–Infant Psychotherapy.* New York: Basic Books.

Stern, Donnell. (1997). *Unformulated Experience: From Dissociation to Imagination.* Hillsdale, NJ: Analytic Press.

Stolorow, R. D., and Atwood, G. E. (1992). *Contexts of Being: The Intersubjective Foundations of Psychological Life.* Hillsdale, NJ: Analytic Press.

Sullivan, H. S. (1953). *The Interpersonal Theory of Psychiatry.* New York: Norton.

Suomi, S. J. (1995). Influence of attachment theory on ethological studies of biobehavioral development in nonhuman primates. In *Attachment Theory: Social, Developmental and Clinical Perspectives,* ed. S. Goldberg, R. Muir, and J. Kerr, pp. 185–202. Hillsdale, NJ: Analytic Press.

Sutton-Smith, B. (1995). *Ambiguity of Play.* Cambridge, MA: Harvard University Press.

Thelen, E., and Smith, L. (1994). *A Dynamic Systems Approach to the Development of Cognition and Action.* Cambridge, MA: MIT Press.

Thomas, A., and Chess, S. (1977). *Temperament and Development.* New York: Brunner/Mazel.

Thomas, A., Chess, S., Birch, H. G., et al. (1963). *Behavioral Individuality in Early Childhood.* New York: New York University Press.

Trad, P. S. (1992). *Interactions with Infants and Parents: The Theory and Practice of Previewing.* New York: Wiley.

van der Kolk, B. A., and Greenberg, M. S. (1987). The psychobiology of the trauma response: hyperarousal, constriction, and addiction to traumatic reexposure. In *Psychological Trauma*, ed. B. A. van der Kolk, pp. 68–87. Washington, DC: American Psychiatric Press.

Vygotsky, L. S. (1962). *Thought and Language*. Cambridge, MA: MIT Press.

Wachtel, E. (1994). *Treating Troubled Children and Their Families*. New York: Guilford.

Walsh, F. (1996). The concept of family resilience: crisis and challenge. *Family Process* 35: 261–281.

Warshaw, S. C. (1992). Mutative factors in child psychoanalysis: a comparison of diverse relational perspectives. In *Relational Perspectives in Psychoanalysis*, ed. N. J. Skolnick and S. C. Warshaw, pp. 147–173. Hillsdale, NJ: Analytic Press.

Weisner, T. S. (1984). Ecocultural niches of middle childhood. In *Development during Middle Childhood: The Years from Six to Twelve*, ed. W. Andrew Collins. Washington, DC: National Academy Press.

Weiss, J., Sampson, H., and the Mount Zion Psychotherapy Research Group. (1986). *The Psychoanalytic Process*. New York: Guilford.

Whitaker, C. A., and Bumberry, W. M. (1988). *Dancing with the Family: A Symbolic/Experiential Approach*. New York: Brunner/Mazel.

Wilson, M. N., and Saft, E. W. (1993). Child maltreatment in the African-American community. In *Child Abuse, Child Development, and Sound Policy: Advances in Applied Developmental Psychology*, Vol. 8, ed. D. Cicchetti and S. L. Toth. Norwood, NJ: Ablex.

Winnicott, D. W. (1945). Primitive emotional development. In *Through Paediatrics to Psycho-Analysis*, pp. 45–56. London: Tavistock, 1958.

———— (1948). Reparation in respect of mother's organized defence against depression. In *Through Paediatrics to Psycho-Analysis*, pp. 91–96. New York: Basic Books, 1975.

———— (1956). Primary maternal preoccupation. In *Through Paediatrics to Psycho-Analysis*, pp. 300–305. New York: Basic Books, 1975.

———— (1958a). The capacity to be alone. In *The Maturational Processes and the Facilitating Environment*, pp. 29–36. New York: International Universities Press, 1971.

———— (1958b). *Collected Papers*. New York: Basic Books.

———— (1958c). Child analysis in the latency period. In *The Maturational Processes and the Facilitating Environment*, pp. 115–123. New York: International Universities Press.

—— (1960). The theory of the parent–infant relationship. *International Journal of Psycho-Analysis* 41: 585–595. Also in D. W. Winnicott, *The Maturational Processes and the Facilitating Environment*, pp. 230–241. New York: International Universities Press.

—— (1960/1965). Ego distortion in terms of true and false self. In *The Maturational Processes and the Facilitating Environment*. New York: International Universities Press.

——(1963). From dependence toward independence in the development of the individual. In *The Maturational Process and the Facilitating Environment*. New York: International Universities Press, 1965.

—— (1969). The use of an object and relating through identifications. In *Playing and Reality*, pp. 86–94. London: Tavistock, 1971.

—— (1971a). *Playing and Reality*. New York: Basic Books.

—— (1971b). *Therapeutic Consultations in Child Psychiatry*. New York: Basic Books.

—— (1974). The fear of breakdown. *International Review of Psychoanalysis* 1: 103–107.

—— (1975). Transitional objects and transitional phenomena. In *Through Paediatrics to Psycho-Analysis*. New York: Basic Books.

—— (1977). *The Piggle: An Account of the Psychoanalytic Treatment of a Little Girl*. Madison, CT: International Universities Press.

Worden, J. W. (1996). *Children and Grief: When a Parent Dies*. New York: Guilford.

Index

separation anxiety, 34, 165–166, 170
separation reaction, 34–36
separation-individuation, 37–39, 47, 49–50
sexism, 88–88
sexuality, 7–8, 20–21, 64, 73, 88
shame, 21–22, 139
Shanok, R. S., 73
siblings, 74
  in assessment process, 154–156, 160, 173
Sillitoe, A., 143–144
Silverman, R. C., 84, 221–222
Smith, J., 109
social relatedness, 118–120
socialization, 63–64, 69, 74–75, 192
sociocultural environment, 58
socioeconomic factors, 99–102, 330–331
"Some Character Types Met with in Psychoanalytic Work" (Freud), 139
space, treatment, 203–204, 235, 241–244, 276
Spiegel, S., 256
Spitz, R., 33
splitting, 96–97, 325–326, 343
  and family projections, 12–13, 84
  integrating perspectives of child, 12, 362–363
  in paranoid-schizoid position, 23–24, 89
Sroufe, A., 55
Stern, D., 13–14, 38–43, 80, 343
stimulation, 78, 107

stimulus barrier, 37–38
stories, child's, 281
Strange Situation protocol, 34–35
stress, 68
subjectivity, 126. *See also* intersubjectivity
sublimation, 66, 71
Sullivan, H. S., 7, 83, 150
  on anxiety, 120, 137
  developmental theories of, 30–32, 60–65, 110
  interpersonal theories of, 55, 141, 142
  on self-system, 125, 145
superego, 45–46, 71
Sutton-Smith, B., 190–191, 193, 195–197
symbiotic phase, 38
symbolism, 190, 207–208
symptoms, 308
  child characterized by, 138, 157–159
  and diagnosis, 127–130, 148–150
  and termination, 369–370
systems theory, 284, 306, 347–349
  on family dynamics, 13–15, 315–318

"Talking, Feeling, Doing" game (Gardner), 233
teachers, 154. *See also* schools
temperament. *See also* personality
  and goodness of fit, 339–340
  individual differences in, 56–58
  and psychopathology, 106, 108–109